Elizabeth I and the 'Sovereign Arts':
Essays in Literature, History,
and Culture

Medieval and Renaissance
Texts and Studies
Volume 407

Elizabeth I and the 'Sovereign Arts':
Essays in Literature, History, and Culture

edited by
Donald Stump, Linda Shenk,
and Carole Levin

ACMRS
(Arizona Center for Medieval and Renaissance Studies)
Tempe, Arizona
2011

Published by ACMRS (Arizona Center for Medieval and Renaissance Studies), Tempe, Arizona.
© 2011 Arizona Board of Regents for Arizona State University.
All Rights Reserved.

Library of Congress Cataloging-in-Publication Data

Elizabeth I and the 'sovereign arts' : essays in literature, history, and culture / edited by Donald Stump, Linda Shenk, and Carole Levin.
    p. cm. -- (Medieval and renaissance texts and studies ; v. 407)
  Includes bibliographical references.
  ISBN 978-0-86698-455-3 (acid-free paper)
  1. Elizabeth I, Queen of England, 1533-1603--In literature. 2. Great Britain--History--Elizabeth, 1558-1603--Historiography. I. Stump, Donald V., 1946- II. Shenk, Linda. III. Levin, Carole, 1948-
  PR428.E43E45 2011
  820.9'351--dc23

                                                                          2011045537

∞
This book is made to last. It is set in Adobe Caslon Pro,
smyth-sewn and printed on acid-free paper to library specifications.
Printed in the United States of America

*In memory of my father, Robert Byron Stump,
who loved history and fine writing* — DS

For my family — LS

*For Rick and Casey, dear old friends,
and Cassie and Mark, dear new ones* — CL

Table of Contents

Acknowledgments — ix

List of Contributors — xi

Introduction — xv

Elizabeth and Expectations of Family

"Maternal Memory: Elizabeth Tudor's Anne Boleyn" — 1
  Mary Hill Cole

"Elizabeth Tudor: Maidenhood in Crisis" — 15
  Janel Mueller with Carole Levin and Linda Shenk

"The Two Virgin Queens" — 29
  Sarah L. Duncan

"Elizabeth I and Mary Stewart: Two British Queens Regnant" — 53
  Retha Warnicke

"Grave Histories: Women's Bodies Writing Elizabethan History" — 69
  Catherine Howey Stearn

"All the Queen's Children: Elizabeth I and the Meanings of Motherhood" — 85
  Carole Levin

Queen of Words

"Elizabeth Tudor: Poet" — 105
  Ilona Bell

"Queen Elizabeth to Her Subjects: The Tilbury and Golden Speeches" — 125
  Steven W. May

Mistress of Court and State

"Elizabeth, Burghley, and the Pragmatics of Rule: Managing Elizabethan England" 143
Norman Jones

"Elizabeth and Her Favorites: The Case of Sir Walter Ralegh" 157
Susan Doran

"Elizabeth I and Court Display" 175
Debra Barrett-Graves

"Elizabeth I and the Heraldry of the Face" 189
Anna Riehl Bertolet

Worldly Monarch and Divine Governor

"Elizabeth I and State Terror in Sixteenth-Century Ireland" 201
Vincent P. Carey

"Elizabeth Through Venetian Eyes" 217
John Watkins

"Advising the Queen: Good Governance in Elizabeth's Entry Pageants into London, Bristol, and Norwich" 233
Tim Moylan

"'Give ear, O princes': Deborah, Elizabeth, and the Right Word" 251
Michele Osherow

"Elizabeth I's Divine Wisdom: St. Paul, Conformity, and John Lyly's *Endymion*" 261
Linda Shenk

"Abandoning the Old Testament: Protestant Dissent and the Shift in Court Paradigms for Elizabeth" 281
Donald Stump

Bibliography 301

Index 329

Acknowledgments

We would like to thank the South-Central Renaissance Conference, the organization with which the Queen Elizabeth I Society has met since its inception. The essays in this book were all presented there over the last decade, and several were first printed in its journal, *Explorations in Renaissance Culture*. Special thanks to Tita French Baumlin, whose fine editorial skills were so valuable in preparing those pieces for publication.

We are also grateful to Roy Rukkila of Medieval and Renaissance Texts and Studies and to his readers, who gave us helpful criticism to make this a better book. We are most grateful to Iowa State University for its financial support. We are also deeply grateful to Laura Damuth, the director of the University of Nebraska undergraduate research program, UCARE. Carole wishes to acknowledge the help of her UCARE students, Jo Crowl, Jennifer Hewitt, and Rhianna Needham.

The editors also acknowledge the great pleasure that they had in working together on this project.

List of Contributors

Debra Barrett-Graves, Professor of English at California State University, East Bay, has published articles on the iconography of service in Shakespeare's plays. Carole Levin, Jo Eldridge Carney, and Barrett-Graves were among the authors of *Extraordinary Women of the Medieval and Renaissance World* (2000) and *Elizabeth I: Always Her Own Free Woman* (2003). Barrett-Graves received the Robert A. Miller Memorial Award for her article on "Edmund Spenser's Use of the Poison-Tipped Tongue in *The Faerie Queene*," which appeared in *The Critic* (2005–2006). Barrett-Graves is currently working on articles for *A Biographical Encyclopedia of Early Modern Englishwomen: Exemplary Lives and Memorable Acts, 1500–1650*.

Ilona Bell, Clarke Professor of English at Williams College, is the author of *Elizabeth I: the Voice of a Monarch* (2010) and *Elizabethan Women and the Poetry of Courtship* (1998), as well as numerous essays on English Renaissance poetry and early modern women. The editor of Penguin's *John Donne: Selected Poems* (2006) and *John Donne: Complete Poems*, she is currently writing about and editing the manuscript and printed versions of Mary Wroth's *Pamphilia to Amphilanthus*.

Anna Riehl Bertolet received her Ph.D. from the University of Illinois at Chicago and is Assistant Professor of Literature at Auburn University. She is the author of *The Face of Queenship: Early Modern Representations of Elizabeth I* (Palgrave, 2010) and co-editor of *Tudor Court Culture* (Susquehanna University Press, 2010). Her articles on John Donne, George Chapman, and Elizabeth I have appeared in *English Literary Renaissance* and various essay collections. Her research has received support from the American Association of University Women, University of Illinois at Chicago, Auburn University, and the English-Speaking Union.

Vincent P. Carey teaches early modern European history at the State University of New York at Plattsburgh in Upstate New York. When not teaching and writing, he helps raise his four children: Úna, Rory, Niamh and Róisín.

Mary Hill Cole is Professor of History at Mary Baldwin College, where she teaches Tudor-Stuart history to undergraduates and to graduate students in the Shakespeare in Performance M.Litt./M.F.A program. Her publications on Elizabethan progresses include *The Portable Queen: Elizabeth I and the Politics of Ceremony* (1999), and chapters in Jayne Elisabeth Archer, Elizabeth Goldring, Sarah Knight, eds., *The Progresses, Pageants, and Entertainments of Queen Elizabeth I* (2007); Donald Stump and Susan M. Felch, eds., *Elizabeth I and Her Age* (2009); Carole Levin, Jo Eldridge Carney and Debra Barrett-Graves, eds., *Elizabeth I: 'Always Her Own Free Woman'*(2003), and Doug Rutledge, ed., *Ceremony and Text in the Renaissance* (1996).

Susan Doran is a Senior Research Fellow at Jesus College, University of Oxford, and Director of Studies at Regent's Park College, University of Oxford. She has written books, essays, and articles on all the Tudors, but Elizabeth I is her special area of interest. At present she is co-editing with Paulina Kewes a collection of essays on the late Elizabethan Succession question and working on a study of the political and personal relationships between Elizabeth and her courtiers.

Sarah L. Duncan, Assistant Professor of History at Spring Hill College, Mobile, Alabama, received her Ph.D. from Yale University. Her articles have appeared in the journal *Explorations in Renaissance Culture*, and in the collection *Queens and Power in Medieval and Early Modern England*. She is currently working on a book manuscript titled *England's First Queen: Gender, Power, and Ceremony in the Reign of Mary I*.

Norman Jones is Professor and Chair of History and Director of General Education at Utah State University. He took his Ph.D. at Cambridge University in 1978. He has held visiting fellowships at Harvard University, the Huntington Library, the Folger Library, the University of Geneva, and Oxford University. His books include: *Faith by Statute: Parliament and the Settlement of Religion, 1559* (1982), *God and the Moneylenders: Usury and Law in Early Modern England* (1989), *The Birth of the Elizabethan Age: England in the 1560s* (1993), *The English Reformation: Religion and Cultural Adaptation* (2002), *and The Elizabethan World*, edited with Susan Doran (2011). In the academic year 2008–2009, he was the Visiting Senior Research Fellow at Jesus College, Oxford.

Carole Levin is Willa Cather Professor of History and Director of the Medieval and Renaissance Studies Program at the University of Nebraska. She and Donald Stump co-founded the Queen Elizabeth I Society. She has published a number of books, including *The Heart and Stomach of a King: Elizabeth I and the Politics of Sex and Power* (1994), *The Reign of Elizabeth I* (2002), *Dreaming the English Renaissance: Politics and Desire in Court and Culture* (2008), and (co-authored John Watkins) *Shakespeare's Foreign Worlds* (2009).

Steven W. May is adjunct Professor of English at Emory University, Atlanta, and Senior Research Fellow in the School of English at Sheffield University. His books include *The Elizabethan Courtier Poets* (1991), an edition of *Queen Elizabeth I: Selected Works* (2004), and *Elizabethan Poetry: A Bibliography and First-Line Index of English Verse, 1559–1603* (2004). His research interests center on English Renaissance manuscript culture, the Tudor court, and editing early modern documents.

Tim Moylan completed his Ph.D. at St. Louis University in 2009. During his doctoral studies, he received the Lucien Fournier Award for Excellence in Teaching and the Walter J. Ong Award for exceptional scholarly achievement. His article "Sound and Silence: Interpretive Pause in Milton's *Paradise Regained*" was published in *Uncircumscribed Mind: Reading Milton Deeply*, ed. Kristin A. Pruitt and Charles W. Durham (2008). He currently teaches writing, speech communications, and literature as well as directs the theatre program at the St. Louis College of Pharmacy.

Janel Mueller is the William Rainey Harper Distinguished Service Professor Emerita in the Department of English at the University of Chicago. Besides authoring several critical essays on Elizabeth, she has co-edited a series of volumes for the University of Chicago Press: *Elizabeth I: Collected Works* (2000), *Elizabeth I: Autograph Compositions and Foreign Language Originals* (2003), *Elizabeth I: Translations, 1544–89* and *Elizabeth I: Translations, 1592–1598* (both 2009).

Michele Osherow is Associate Professor of English and Affiliate Associate Professor of Judaic Studies at University of Maryland, Baltimore County. Her book *Biblical Women's Voices in Early Modern England* was released from Ashgate in 2009. Her publications primarily attend to the Bible and early modern literature; current research addresses biblical resonances in post-Holocaust Jewish American texts. In addition, Osherow serves as resident dramaturg at the Folger Theatre in Washington, D.C. and is co-writing a book with theatre director Aaron Posner on *Staging Shakespeare at the Folger*.

Linda Shenk is Associate Professor of English at Iowa State University, where she teaches early modern drama and poetry. She is currently working on a book project that examines the intersections between early modern drama and diplomatic culture. Her recent book *Learned Queen: The Image of Elizabeth I in Politics and Poetry* (2010) explores ways in which Elizabeth I's image as educated was the queen's most powerful persona abroad—an image so effective that it prompted many of her most geo-politically ambitious courtiers to praise her learning in their poetry when seeking her intervention in the international arena.

Catherine Howey Stearn is Assistant Professor of History at Eastern Kentucky University. She received her Ph.D. from Rutgers, the State University of New Jersey, and her M.A. from the Courtauld Institute of Art, where she studied dress history. Her research, which utilizes non-traditional sources such as dress and portraiture in conjunction with more traditional historical records, focuses on how Elizabethan female courtiers shaped Queen Elizabeth I's reign, most especially in the ways in which they helped Elizabeth craft her public personae and make connections to her subjects outside the court.

Donald Stump is Professor of English at Saint Louis University. With Carole Levin, he founded the Queen Elizabeth I Society and served as its first president. With friends, he edited *Elizabeth I and Her Age: Authoritative Texts and Criticism*, (2009); *Images of Elizabeth I* (special issue, *Explorations in Renaissance Culture*, 2004); *Sir Philip Sidney: An Annotated Bibliography of Texts and Criticism (1554–1984)* (1994); and *'Hamartia': The Concept of Error in the Western Tradition* (1983). He edits the *Sidney World Bibliography* and *Spenser World Bibliography* and is writing a book on Spenser and Elizabeth.

Retha M. Warnicke is Professor of History at Arizona State University. Her publications include *The Rise and Fall of Anne Boleyn: Family Politics at the Court of Henry VIII* (Cambridge University Press, 1989), *The Marrying of Anne of Cleves: Royal Protocol in Tudor England* (Cambridge University Press, 2000), and *Mary Queen of Scots* (Routledge, 2006).

John Watkins is Distinguished McKnight University Professor of English and Italian Studies at the University of Minnesota. He is the author of *The Specter of Dido: Spenser and Virgilian Epic* (1995), *Representing Elizabeth in Stuart England: Literature, History, Sovereignty* (2002), and with Carol Levin, *Shakespeare's Foreign Worlds: National and Transnational Identities in the Elizabethan Age* (2009). He is currently writing a book on medieval and early modern marriage diplomacy.

Introduction

In looking back on the reign of Elizabeth I in 1608, Sir Francis Bacon remarked on the queen's political craft. With her reign still fresh in his memory, he extolled Elizabeth for her wisdom, the consistency of her approach to religious issues, and her use of courtship as a political device. He then offered a revealing anecdote. "I cannot forget one passage," he wrote,

> when letters were written to her ambassadors in France to deliver some private message to the queen mother then of Valois [Catherine de Medici], wherein her secretary, as it were, to curry favor had inserted this clause: that the ambassador should say they two were two such queens so versed in sovereign arts and seen in politic affairs as no kings nor men in the world went beyond them. She misliked the association and commanded it to be blotted out, saying the arts she had learned were of a better stamp and the principles of a far higher nature whereby she ruled her people.[1]

In his comments on the "sovereign arts," the unnamed secretary was, of course, seeking to establish goodwill by honoring both Elizabeth and Catherine for their ability to use calculated strategy—a flattering reversal of the misogynistic stereotype that women in power could not be expected to rule rationally. However helpful politically the statement might have been, though, Elizabeth demanded that it be taken out. In the arts of rule, she would allow no comparison with Catherine, who was regarded by the English as the instigator of much that was villainous at the French court, including the 1572 Saint Bartholomew's Day Massacre.

The questions of royal authority and womanly virtue at play in Bacon's anecdote provide an appropriate window into the delicate and complicated exercise of the "sovereign arts" that Elizabeth negotiated with her subjects. Her way of ruling had to be of a "better stamp" than that of her French, Catholic rival. Her government had to be based on higher principles—no mean feat in an age of international subterfuge, invasion, and assassination carried out in the name of godliness and religion. In seeking to preserve her reputation as a good woman and a just ruler, Elizabeth was dependent on the energetic loyalty and integrity

---

[1] *The Felicity of Queen Elizabeth And Her Times* (London: George Latham, 1651), 40–41 (punctuation modernized). Bacon's reflections were first published in Latin in 1608.

of those who enacted her will — a dependency made all the greater because as a woman, and an unmarried one at that, she had to demonstrate her fitness for rule every day. Neither in her personal ethics nor in her manner of governing could she be like her father. To borrow the terms of her early supporter and counselor, John Aylmer, she could not be an absolutist "mere monarche" but must be a "mixte ruler," one who governed with the earned support and guidance of her principal subjects and advisors.[2]

In recent years, a good deal of scholarly research has been devoted to the extent to which these subordinates pursued agendas that were, at least in part, their own rather than those of their monarch. In an approach that Patrick Collinson has described as "less Queen-fixated" than that of earlier generations, scholars such as Simon Adams, Stephen Alford, Susan Doran, John Guy, Anne McLaren, and Collinson himself have expanded our understanding of the intricacies of Elizabethan ruling hierarchies.[3] The result has been a greater appreciation for the networks of political influence — conciliar, diplomatic, aristocratic, and popular — that often guided, and sometimes constrained, the queen. As Norman Jones remarks in this volume in his article "Elizabeth, Burghley, and the Pragmatics of Rule," "In this world of multiple, overlapping, formal, informal, and confusing governmental structures, it was difficult for a monarch to be effectively imperious."[4] From scholarly investigations of such multiple hierarchical structures, a surprisingly dynamic and complex model of the Elizabethan polity has emerged.

This model has, in turn, done much to reinvigorate studies of Elizabeth herself. It has led scholars to investigate sites of reciprocal influence outside the privy and presence chambers and the foreign courts where earlier historians focused so much of their attention. New studies have, for example, extended our knowledge of the female attendants who served in her withdrawing chamber, where for periods in every day they were her sole companions and confidants. Fuller attention

---

[2] *An Harborowe for Faithfull and Trewe Subjects* (London, 1559), H4r.

[3] Collinson makes this observation in "Pulling the Strings: Religion and Politics in the Progress of 1578," in *The Progresses, Pageants, and Entertainments of Queen Elizabeth I*, ed. Jayne Elisabeth Archer, Elizabeth Goldring, and Sarah Knight (Oxford: Oxford University Press, 2007), 122–41, here 124. Other crucial studies that include a focus on the network of Elizabeth's advisors include Simon Adams, *Leicester and the Court: Essays on Elizabethan Politics* (Manchester: Manchester University Press, 2002); Stephen Alford, *The Early Elizabethan Polity: William Cecil and the British Succession Crisis, 1558–1569* (Cambridge: Cambridge University Press, 1998); Patrick Collinson, "The Monarchical Republic of Queen Elizabeth I," *Bulletin of the John Rylands University Library of Manchester* 69 (1986–1987): 394–424; Susan Doran, *Monarchy and Matrimony: The Courtships of Elizabeth I* (London: Routledge, 1996); and A. N. McLaren, *Political Culture in the Reign of Elizabeth I: Queen and Commonwealth 1558–1585* (Cambridge: Cambridge University Press, 1999).

[4] See his paper in this volume, 143–56, here 147.

has also been paid to her relations with members of her own extended family and to local hierarchies in the rural counties, the small towns, and the principal cities of the realm, particularly London, where artists, writers, entertainers, lawyers, minor magistrates, popular clergymen, foreign refugees, spies, rumor-mongers, and merchant adventurers helped to shape the material, economic, intellectual, and spiritual conditions in which Elizabeth ruled. All had effects, however distant and attenuated, on what she saw was necessary to say and do in order to successfully pursue her own interests and those of her kingdom.

The essays in this collection illustrate the value of exploring such broad fields of investigation. In doing so, they also, of necessity, bring together a variety of disciplines and of methods of inquiry. To do justice to a woman of Elizabeth's complex interests, personal relationships, and achievements — a figure who was arguably the greatest Western queen of the modern period — requires a great deal of scholarly collaboration, and it was to facilitate such collaboration that, in the year 2000, the Queen Elizabeth I Society was founded.

All the papers in the present collection were originally delivered at the annual meetings of the Society. A number were first printed in a special issue on the queen published by the journal *Explorations in Renaissance Culture*, to the editor of which, Francis Malpezzi, we are grateful for the rights to reprint them. They include all but one of the keynote addresses delivered by senior scholars in the period 2003–2007 as well as work by younger contributors who have, each year, received the Society's Strickland Prize for the best paper in an open session. This award, which is named for the nineteenth-century historian Agnes Strickland who was instrumental in recovering archival materials on Elizabeth I and other British queens, has (in the period covered by this volume) been received by Sarah L. Duncan, Catherine L. Howey, Anna Riehl, Tim Moylan, and Michele Osherow.

Although the papers were not solicited by theme or topic, and so are various in the subjects and questions that they raise, they all in one way or another explore Elizabeth's arts of ruling and, more specifically, ruling in circumstances where her authority and her positions had to be hard won. The results of such investigation lean heavily against the popular, romanticized image of the queen as a woman governed more by her heart than by education, long practice, and sheer determination. They also lend little support to images of her as a woman fully and centrally in command of the government in ways that we, living in modern nation-states, might be inclined to expect. The Elizabeth of these essays is a self-conscious discursive agent whose letters, speeches, and poetry reveal a facility in persuasive rhetoric that more than matched her responsibilities to her family, her court, her country, and the world. She is also a vulnerable figure, forced into constant renegotiations to maintain and extend her authority as she thought necessary.

The first section of the collection begins with the intimate, domestic world of the queen's family. It explores her early years, her later, troublesome relations with Mary Tudor and Mary Stuart, and her appropriation of the language of marriage and family to support her royal authority. The section also considers rumors that she gave birth to children that she subsequently concealed or murdered to hide her shame. The second section investigates Elizabeth's skills in writing poetry and speaking, suggesting not only her artful use of words but also some of the difficulties that Elizabethan readers and modern editors faced in attempting to recover and interpret them. The third takes up Elizabeth's arts in governing her court and the nation, and the fourth the difficulties involved in negotiating her roles as worldly monarch and divinely ordained ruler.

Though many imagine Elizabeth as a rather solitary figure with no family, she had, of course, a father, a mother, and two half-siblings who remained important to her throughout her life. She also had a number of cousins as well as a series of step-mothers and even a step-step-father, Thomas Seymour. The issue of the succession and her circuitous path to the throne made her family relationships difficult. During the reigns of her brother Edward and her sister Mary, her life was repeatedly in danger, and even after she herself came to the throne, she feared the potential claims of her cousins Catherine Grey and Mary Stewart, who put her skills and her authority as a ruler to the test beginning in the earliest years of her reign. Although she honored her Tudor forebears, as Mary Hill Cole tellingly puts it, she "found dead Tudors easier to embrace than live ones." In the essay "Maternal Memory: Elizabeth Tudor's Anne Boleyn," Cole argues that, although Elizabeth was discreet when speaking publicly about her mother because she wished to avoid tarnishing her father's image, she honored her mother's memory and treated relatives on the Boleyn side well. Revealing in this regard is a ring that Elizabeth owned, which opened like a locket to reveal two portraits: one of herself and the other of her mother.

In "Elizabeth Tudor: Maidenhood in Crisis," Janel Mueller explores what Elizabeth learned during the crisis that Thomas Seymour set in motion during the reign of her brother Edward. Analyzing Elizabeth's letters from the fall of 1548 through the early months of 1549, Mueller examines Seymour's scandalous attentions to the princess, then a girl of just fifteen. The letters reveal a change in Elizabeth's tone as she comes to a more assured, independent sense of self — a transformation also evident in Elizabeth's responses during the interrogation that followed. Mueller suggests that the scandal shaped Elizabeth's maturation and her later decision to rule alone, as a maiden queen.

Elizabeth's experiences under her sister Mary were similarly important for her developing sense of self and her response to challenges to her authority. In the essay "The Two Virgin Queens," Sarah Duncan explores ways in which she learned from her sister's self-presentation as a queen prior to her marriage with Philip of Spain. For Mary, as for her, the image of a royal virgin was more advantageous than that of a royal wife. In 1553 and early 1554, fully three and a half decades before Elizabeth's famous Tilbury speech, Mary employed the concept of the monarch's two bodies to establish her authority. Not only was she, in her natural body, a woman and a queen but also, in her political headship of the body of the state, every inch a king.

In the essay "Elizabeth I and Mary Stewart: Two British Queens Regnant," Retha Warnicke takes a similarly fresh approach to the comparison of Elizabeth with her famous cousin Mary Stewart. Depictions of Elizabeth as controlled, masculine, and rational in contrast to Mary, seen as impulsive, feminine, and governed by passion, are, according to Warnicke, too simple. They fail to take into account the complex characters of both queens, the pressures they were under, and the ways in which each represented different influences within Renaissance culture.

Mary Stewart was not the only cousin of Elizabeth to be put forward as her proper successor and rival. Another was Catherine Grey, younger sister to Jane, the "nine days' queen," who had been executed in Mary's reign. In 1560, Catherine secretly married Edward Seymour, earl of Hertford, and they subsequently had two sons. Because the clergyman who had performed the ceremony could not be found and the couple could not, therefore, prove that they had been lawfully married, Elizabeth had them held, first in the Tower of London and later under house arrest, until Catherine's early death in 1568. In the essay "Grave Histories: Women's Bodies Writing Elizabethan History," Catherine Howey Stearne uses the marble effigies at the Seymour tomb in Salisbury Cathedral to present an alternate reading of this history, arguing that we should not see the queen simply as an isolated woman surrounded by men but as one of a number of powerful women at court—some, like Catherine, potential threats to her power and others seeking to protect her. Howey's analysis of the conflict between the queen and Seymour leads to an examination of the tomb of another such lady, Helena, marchioness of Northampton, who served as Elizabeth's chief mourner, and to an examination of the tomb-building program at Westminster Abbey by James I.

Among the reasons that Catherine Grey posed such a threat was that Elizabeth refused to marry and produce a child of her own. To counter the anxiety that this refusal produced, the queen appropriated the language of marriage and childbearing, describing herself as a mother to her people. In "All the Queen's Children: Elizabeth I and the Meanings of Motherhood," Carole Levin places this effort within the context of scurrilous rumors of a more direct form of maternity, one supposedly involving secret affairs and bastard children. Such rumors suggest a contemporary tendency to discount the possibility that ruling women could retain both their independence and their honor, a doubt that is still evident in representations of the queen in our own day. Some manifestations of popular culture, such as romance novels and the writings of those ensnarled in the Shakespeare authorship controversy, also present Elizabeth as a secret mother.

The next two essays in the collection show Elizabeth's skill in crafting words to consolidate her position, both when she was most vulnerable and when she was at the height of her power. In "Elizabeth Tudor: Poet," Ilona Bell points out that, though Elizabeth did not publish her verses, she did not create them for herself alone. They were written to be circulated in manuscript, recited, or placed strategically where they would be seen by someone known to the queen. Bell begins her analysis with poems that Elizabeth wrote while a prisoner at Woodstock in the mid-1550s, then turns to lyrics composed while she was queen, concluding that she saw poetry throughout her adulthood as a means of action, shaping it to have an impact, either on her immediate situation or on a particular private audience.

Though the texts of Elizabeth's poems present an array of editorial difficulties, those of her speeches are even more doubtful simply because, in the days before a widely accepted system of shorthand, they were almost impossible to transcribe as they were delivered, and subsequent versions put out by the government were often rewritten and "improved." Her reading subjects had as much difficulty gaining an accurate sense of her as a commanding public figure as she had in conveying her character and will unmediated by the efforts of others. In the essay "Queen Elizabeth to Her Subjects: The Tilbury and Golden Speeches," Steven May details the difficulties in determining what was actually said, noting wide variations in the texts even of these two much-celebrated speeches. Sorting out internal and external clues, he nonetheless finds grounds to determine which of the competing versions has the greatest likelihood of authenticity.

From Elizabeth's use of words, the collection next turns to her style of governance. In "Elizabeth, Burghley, and the Pragmatics of Rule: Managing Elizabethan England," Norman Jones examines Elizabeth's response to limitations imposed not only by her gender but also by the various interlocking systems of authority on which the English government of her day was based. According to Jones, subjects deferred to Elizabeth out of respect for law, deference to hierarchy, greed, and fear of disgrace or dishonor. Using her relations with William Cecil and various churchmen of the day as examples of Elizabeth's indirect management style, Jones demonstrates that the queen exerted her authority by utilizing a loosely organized social network and by surrounding herself with men whom she could trust to use their intelligence and power in her service.

As Elizabeth's close counselor, William Cecil, Lord Burghley was concerned about her relationship with courtiers who were perceived as "favorites," men who because of their attractiveness and powers of flattery were in a position to captivate a monarch. In 1572, while assuring Elizabeth that he knew she needed no such warning, Burghley presented her with a "memorial" on the subject. As Susan Doran demonstrates in the essay "Elizabeth and Her Favorites: The Case of Sir Walter Ralegh," his fear is frequently echoed in other texts and plays of the period, particularly in the 1580s and early 1590s, when Ralegh was in his ascendancy. Contrary to assumptions that still persist in scholarship on the famous courtier, however, Doran argues that Ralegh never actually controlled the queen, who worked hard to keep many channels of information open and never allowed any favorite to dominate her.

Along with her employment of able men in government service, Elizabeth also exerted and reinforced her authority by less direct means. As Debra Barrett-Graves argues in her essay "Elizabeth I and Court Display," tournament pageantry was staged both to impress foreign ambassadors and to display royal magnificence to citizens in various ranks of English society. Such formalized military exercises, so colorfully reflected in the literature and drama of the period, also provided a means for Elizabeth's courtiers to demonstrate their loyalty and seek preferment.

Turning to visual and metaphorical depictions of the queen as elements of her ruling authority, Anna Riehl Bertolet's essay "Elizabeth I and the Heraldry of the Face" raises the question "How does an early modern subject describe the face of a living queen?" It was an exercise that posed particular difficulties when the queen's face did not conform to traditional standards of beauty. One answer was to combine portraiture and heraldry, allowing symbolic depictions that linked femininity and power. By overlaying her face with the royal coat of arms as a sign of her Tudor bloodline, writers of the period subtly turned aside claims, first made by her own father and later pressed by her Catholic enemies, that she was a bastard. Although heraldic metaphors allowed male writers to invest the queen's face with symbols important to her own assertions of governing authority, Riehl finds in them a strong undercurrent of hidden anxiety.

Nowhere was Elizabeth's rule perceived with more anxiety than in international affairs and matters of religion. The fourth section of essays considers representations of her both as a worldly potentate and as a godly ruler. As Vincent P. Carey argues in his essay "Elizabeth I and State Terror in Sixteenth-Century Ireland," the queen was aware of the brutal violence conducted in Ireland on her behalf. Examining incidents such as Shane O'Neill's trip to the English court in January 1561 and Elizabeth's letter of congratulation to Lord Grey de Wilton on his suppression of the Desmond rebellion in 1581, Carey relies on evidence provided by Elizabeth's own representatives in Ireland. Although her officials often expressed frustration at her characteristically hesitant approach to military intervention, Elizabeth sanctioned violence in Ireland because she recognized that her monarchical power required, in Carey's words, "humbling Gaelic ethnic pride." Moderate policies enacted early in the reign set precedents that paved the way for the more savage acts of suppression in the 1590s.

Unlike Elizabeth's often violent domination of Ireland, her approach to Catholic, mercantile Venice was patient and indirect, bearing fruit only in the final year of her life when she welcomed the first Venetian ambassador of her reign, Giovanni Carlo Scaramelli. In the essay "Elizabeth Through Venetian Eyes," John Watkins traces changing Venetian attitudes toward England's heretical queen — changes that reflect the similar diplomatic agendas of the two republics. Early in Elizabeth's reign, England and Venice maintained their distance, responding to the increasingly polarized religious climate that accompanied the Counter-Reformation. Then, late in the century, both states adopted increasingly bellicose tactics against Spain. Watkins devotes particular attention to Scaramelli's famous descriptions of Elizabeth in her final days, in which the Venetian represents the queen as a near-Catholic in order to downplay religious differences and gain English support for Venetian resistance to papal power.

Such emphasis on Elizabeth as a monarch who was moderate and willing to compromise informs Tim Moylan's discussion in "Advising the Queen: Good Governance in Elizabeth I's Entry into London, Bristol, and Norwich." Relating Elizabeth's coronation entry into London to less frequently studied receptions in Bristol and Norwich, Moylan points out ways in which all three pageants create an image of Elizabeth as a good governor. Not only do such depictions compliment the queen, but they also assert notions of shared authority between the crown and the people.

Like Moylan, Michele Osherow examines the Norwich pageant in her essay "'Give ear, O princes': Deborah, Elizabeth, and the Right Word." In associating Elizabeth with a heroine of singular capacity and scriptural authority, writers often interpreted the Old Testament account in ways that reshaped the image of Deborah and so attempted to confine Elizabeth to roles more traditional for her sex. Examining Deborah's story in the Book of Judges, Osherow shows that her power was grounded in her use of language—a source of authority that defied early modern strictures on women to be silent and obedient. In works by such writers as Thomas Bentley, Richard Vennar, Thomas Heywood, and Richard Mulcaster, references to Deborah register cultural cross-currents involving Elizabeth that are far more complex than scholars have hitherto recognized.

Elizabeth's role as a religious leader, specifically as Supreme Governor of the national Church, entered a particularly complicated phase in the late 1580s when the Elizabethan episcopacy intensified its policies of conformity amidst mounting Puritan criticism. Linda Shenk, in her essay "Elizabeth I's Divine Wisdom: St. Paul, Conformity, and John Lyly's *Endymion*," examines ways in which the queen and her supporters responded to the Puritan challenge by infusing her learned persona with notions of divine wisdom, as defined in St. Paul's first letter to the Corinthians. Shenk demonstrates that John Lyly's play *Endymion* is an early example of this strategy. In the play, Lyly uses Pauline theology to extol Elizabeth as a queen who possesses transcendent wisdom so virtuous that it makes all earthly wisdom appear foolish. In turn, Lyly's Pauline themes will echo throughout the rest of the reign in a cluster of texts that advocate acceptance of Elizabeth's divinely conferred authority and that of the Anglican Church. By examining Lyly's play alongside such texts, Shenk reveals the means by which the crown used divine wisdom as part of Elizabeth's public persona in order to gain support for its ecclesiastical policies.

In the final essay of the volume, Donald Stump takes up comparisons between Elizabeth and figures from the Bible, connecting changes in such characterizations to her deteriorating relations with strident Protestants of the period. In "Abandoning the Old Testament: Protestant Dissent and the Shift in Court Paradigms for Elizabeth," Stump explores the reasons that, during the last two decades of the reign, even forward Protestant writers turned from scriptural heroes and heroines such as Deborah, Solomon, Judith, and David to less religious paradigms for the queen, such as classical goddesses, pastoral shepherdesses, and the Fairy Queen. The paper argues that Elizabeth's negotiations to marry the duke of Anjou paved the way for this far-reaching cultural shift. In Elizabeth's delicate maneuvering over the marriage, pagan and classical sources were less politically sensitive and more in line with her increasingly hostile stance toward her Protestant critics, who, in seeking to influence the way she governed, were inclined to thump their Bibles.

In leading up to the anecdote with which we began this introduction, Sir Francis Bacon emphasized Elizabeth's interest in achieving fame, for she "was certainly good and virtuous, and so she desired to seem; she hated vices and took the way to fame by that of honor." In a subsequent paragraph, Bacon then returned to the idea of fame, noting that "if any had told her fitly in discourse, that the world would have taken notice of her admirable parts, though she had lived in some mean estate, she would have been well pleased with such insinuations, so much she desired that her virtue should stand alone unbeholding to her fortune for praise." Although the queen was famously vain, her concern to ensure not only that her virtues, like her governing arts, were without parallel but that they should be *seen* to be so should not distract us from her very real and remarkable attainments. When, for example, England's position in the world became alarmingly precarious in the 1580s, as the situation with Mary Queen of Scots came to a head, assassins plotted, and the long-threatened wave of Spanish invaders finally rolled up the Channel toward her, she demonstrated that her "sovereign arts" were indeed exceptional, worthy of the singularity that she claimed when she ordered that the comparison between her and Catherine de Medici be struck from her secretary's draft of the letter. The true basis of her fame appears in sharper relief when we examine her complex interactions with the many favorites, diplomats, counselors, ladies-in-waiting, court entertainers, poets, playwrights, and polemicists that surrounded her, shaping — and sometimes challenging — her authority.

To those whose primary interest is in the queen, turning so much of our attention to those she dealt with may seem a distraction. By examining the flawed but exceptional woman Elizabeth in relation to the many figures around her, however, we are able to see things that no solitary portrait could ever show us: her indomitable will to govern, the full range of arts that she relied on to govern well, the effects of those arts on her courtiers and countrymen, and, yes, her majesty.

Maternal Memory: Elizabeth Tudor's Anne Boleyn

Mary Hill Cole

Virgin Queen, bastard, the last of the Tudors: these popular references to Elizabeth I reflect an emphasis we have come to expect on her solitary, tenuous position as unmarried queen.[1] Although surrounded by scores of courtiers and government officials, and ladies in waiting who shared her private chambers, Elizabeth without husband or children seems, from the distance of four centuries, genealogically alone. Even her contemporaries saw her in solitary terms. To Francis Bacon, this isolation from family meant that Elizabeth had the "glory entire" to herself: "as she had no helps to lean upon in government, except such as she had herself provided; no own brother, no uncle, no kinsman of the royal family, to share her cares and support her authority," he observed, Elizabeth thus had to achieve her own greatness.[2] But Bacon's view of an Elizabeth without kin is as myopic as it is androcentric. For an orphan without husband, children, or living siblings, Elizabeth had a curious abundance of family.

An extensive Tudor and Boleyn presence—most notably, the Grey sisters, the numerous Careys, the Knollys, and the Sackvilles—revealed Elizabeth's use of her family at court and in her government. For a person who did not generate her own lineage, Elizabeth certainly enjoyed the fruits of other people's loins. She enjoyed, as well, the political benefits that came from her resemblance to Henry VIII: she had his coloring, his temper, his dramatic flair, and, through no little effort and good fortune, his crown. In portraits, words, and actions, she

---

[1] I would like to thank Carole Levin and Donald Stump for their invitation to discuss these ideas with such encouraging colleagues at the New Orleans conference. Conversations with Ken Fincham, Judy Klein, Russ McDonald, and Georgianna Ziegler shaped my research in crucial places, and Retha Warnicke and Betsy Walsh pointed me toward valuable sources. I especially appreciate the close commentary of Ralph Cohen on the entire project.

[2] Sir Francis Bacon, *Works*, ed. James Spedding, 14 vols. (London: Longman & Co., 1858), 3:310.

embraced the genetic inheritance of her by then popular father.[3] To heighten the contrast with her half-sister Mary, Elizabeth stressed her Englishness, a reference to their common father that distinguished Elizabeth's native-born mother from Catherine of Aragon, the Spanish mother of Mary.

But with few exceptions, Elizabeth preserved a notable, intriguing silence about her mother, Anne Boleyn, even though her reputation as an icon of Elizabeth's Protestant, English heritage might have proved useful on occasion to her daughter.[4] Is it possible, four hundred years later, to conjecture what Elizabeth thought about her mother, or, at least, to find remnants of her mother's life with which Elizabeth had contact? Was there any evidence, expressed indirectly or symbolically, of the bond between mother and daughter? As was often the case with Elizabeth, in the matter of her kin, a gap between words and actions characterized her response. While she publicly embraced her Tudor ancestors, she treated her Tudor cousins harshly. By contrast, she almost never mentioned her mother's name in public, but she bestowed favors on Boleyn descendants and discreetly honored her maternal ancestors. Her divergent responses to her paternal and maternal kin offer another avenue into the issue of her own legitimacy as queen. Through this odd contradiction in familial relations we can see how dangerous, yet necessary and important, were the kinship groups surrounding Elizabeth. Even as they conferred legitimacy on her monarchy, they had the potential to undermine it. In keeping silent about Anne Boleyn while acting with honor toward her memory, Elizabeth negotiated the shoals of her own birthright and, perhaps, cultivated a memory of the mother she had not known.

Elizabeth did not have much of a bond with Anne Boleyn during their brief time together. After her birth, Elizabeth lived most often in separate accommodations from her mother; in accordance with childrearing customs of the era, her daily care came from Lady Bryan, noble nursemaid to the Tudor children.[5] When Anne died in May 1536, Princess Elizabeth was two years and eight months old. Even had people later fed her memories of her infancy, Elizabeth

---

[3] For an analysis of Tudor familial portraits, see Louis Montrose, *The Subject of Elizabeth: Authority, Gender, and Representation* (Chicago: University of Chicago Press, 2006), 20–64.

[4] Alexander Ales and William Latymer, among other contemporaries, noted Anne's role in encouraging Protestantism. See J. Stevenson, ed., *Calendar of State Papers Foreign 1558–9* (London: Longman, Green, Longman, Roberts, & Green, 1863), no. 1303, and Retha M. Warnicke, *The Rise and Fall of Anne Boleyn* (Cambridge: Cambridge University Press, 1991), 148–60.

[5] Eric Ives, *The Life and Death of Anne Boleyn: 'The Most Happy'* (Oxford: Blackwell Publishing, 2004), 255–56. By December 1533, Elizabeth was at Hertford with Lady Bryan, by decision of the council. Anne seems to have visited Elizabeth and corresponded about her daughter's care. See also David Loades, *Elizabeth I* (London: Hambledon & London, 2003), 29–31.

had precious little on which to hang a sense of maternal closeness. The circumstances of Anne's death, however, had a lasting impact on her daughter. The public charges that resulted in Anne's execution meant that Elizabeth faced chronic battles against those who deemed her a bastard and the wrongful queen of England. On a personal and a political level, Anne's legacy to her daughter was fraught with pain and danger. No wonder that Elizabeth maintained a discreet silence about her mother.

She did, however, publicly honor her Tudor forebears, through whose paternal ancestry flowed her own claim to rule England. She visited the tomb of her "deere Uncle, late Prynce Arthur, all rycheley and bewtifully adorned" in Worcester Cathedral.[6] When she saw the derelict tombs of the dukes of York at Fotheringay, Elizabeth ordered reburial with new memorial monuments.[7] Without harping on the Wars of the Roses, which ended with her grandfather's martial assumption of the throne, Elizabeth leaned on Tudor dynastic pillars that, some eighty years after the war, evoked achievement and stability.

But she found dead Tudors easier to embrace than live ones. Henry VIII's two sisters had descendants who could threaten her crown. These royal replacements—some supported by European powers—Elizabeth could not help but view with concern. And she did. She kept her cousin Mary Queen of Scots imprisoned in England before executing her in 1587. She imprisoned her Grey cousins for secret marriages that could challenge the succession. As Elizabeth defanged her Tudor rivals while honoring Henry VIII's name, her actions underscored the harshness, luck, and skill involved in political survival in Renaissance England.

In contrast to Elizabeth's stated admiration of her father, her opaque attitude toward Anne Boleyn has hampered our understanding of their relationship. How do we interpret something that is not there, a negative, a silence? Most writers agree that Elizabeth kept her opinions of Anne Boleyn, if she had any, to herself.[8] Interpreting the reasons for her silence yields divergent Elizabeths: she did not care about her mother's fate; she was shocked by it; her father's execution of her mother psychologically harmed Elizabeth; she was too practical to focus on the past.[9] Such varied interpretations leave us with two impressions:

---

[6] John Nichols, *The Progresses and Public Processions of Queen Elizabeth*, 3 vols. (London: J. Nichols, 1823; repr. New York: Burt Franklin, 1961), 1:538–39.

[7] Nichols, *Progresses*, 1:410; see also David Starkey, *Elizabeth: Struggle for the Throne* (London: Perennial, 2000), 268.

[8] See, for example, Anne Somerset, *Elizabeth I* (London: Weidenfeld & Nicolson, 1991), 7–8, 96; Carolly Erickson, *The First Elizabeth* (New York: Summit, 1983), 36–37; Susan Bassnett, *Elizabeth I: A Feminist Perspective* (Oxford: Berg, 1988), 19; Starkey, *Elizabeth: Struggle for the Throne*, 23.

[9] J. E. Neale, *Queen Elizabeth* (London: Jonathan Cape, 1934), 18; Elizabeth Jenkins, *Elizabeth the Great* (London: Gollancz, 1958), 99–100; Maria Perry, *The Word of a*

that Elizabeth did not care about her mother, and so ignored Anne Boleyn, or that she did care about her mother but was traumatized into silence by Anne's execution.

Elizabeth broke that silence on two recorded occasions, both times to foreign ambassadors, both times before she became queen.[10] In 1553, in a conversation with the Spanish ambassador, Princess Elizabeth suggested that her mother had incurred the animosity of Catherine of Aragon and Mary. Several years later, in May 1557, the Venetian ambassador reported that Princess Elizabeth asserted her legitimacy, "alleging in her own favour that her mother would never cohabit with the King unless by way of marriage, with the authority of the Church, and the intervention of the Primate of England."[11] In noting the tortured family dynamics between Henry VIII's first two wives, Elizabeth was stating the obvious; its interest to us is that she said it at all. But in defending her mother, Elizabeth addressed the central issue that in later decades would dominate discussions of Anne Boleyn: the matter of Elizabeth's own legitimacy. She was defending herself as much as her mother.

As Carole Levin has noted, "Elizabeth was sensitive about any references to what her father had done to her mother."[12] That sensitivity had decades to fester as religious writers of the sixteenth century used the sins of Anne Boleyn to impugn the origins of the English Reformation and to blacken Elizabeth's sexual and political reputation. Catholic writers called Anne a whore, Elizabeth a bastard, and the English church an abomination. Whether she read these tracts, heard summaries of them, or dismissed them entirely, Elizabeth had a lifetime of exposure to Anne Boleyn's memory through a debate that united mother and daughter in their proclaimed moral turpitude.

Catholic critics argued that the invalid marriage of Anne Boleyn negated Elizabeth's title to the throne and that the mother's unbridled sexuality had

---

Prince (Woodbridge: Boydell Press, 1990), 55; L. J. Smither, "Elizabeth I: A Psychological Profile," *Sixteenth Century Journal* 15 (1984): 47–70, here 51; Bassnett, *A Feminist Perspective*, 5.

[10] Jenkins, *Elizabeth the Great*, 15; Christopher Hibbert, *The Virgin Queen* (Cambridge, MA: Perseus, 1991), 18; Somerset, *Elizabeth I*, 7; Erickson, *The First Elizabeth*, 148.

[11] Rawdon Brown, ed., *Calendar of State Papers and Manuscripts Relating to English Affairs Existing in Archives and Collections of Venice, Vols. V and VI* (London: Her Majesty's Stationery Office, 1873–1881), 5.2:1059. As Christopher Hibbert noted, Elizabeth was "not ashamed to be a Boleyn" (*Virgin Queen*, 18).

[12] Carole Levin, "'We shall never have a merry world while the Queene lyveth': Gender, Monarchy, and the Power of Seditious Words," in *Dissing Elizabeth*, ed. Julia Walker (Durham, NC: Duke University Press, 1998), 77–95, here 87.

reappeared in the daughter's lascivious court.[13] The 1570 papal bull excommunicating "Elizabeth the Pretended Queen" justified that action in part on grounds of her illegitimacy.[14] The English Jesuit Nicholas Sander wrote several tracts so savaging the reputations of Anne Boleyn and Elizabeth that Burghley decried him as an "odious, unnatural and pestiferous traitor."[15] What had Sander written? Telling the familiar story of Henry's affair with Mary Boleyn, prior to his incestuous marriage with her sister Anne, Sander claimed that Henry VIII had first slept with the sisters' mother, Elizabeth Howard, and that Anne herself was Henry's daughter as well as his concubine.[16] In this twisted family tree, Elizabeth would thus be both the daughter and granddaughter of Henry VIII, and the daughter and half-sister of Anne Boleyn. Sander's account influenced other Catholic writers. On the eve of the Armada's invasion, Cardinal William Allen urged Catholics to rise up against Elizabeth, the "incestuous bastard, begotten and born in sin."[17] In the eyes of her opponents, the bond that tied Elizabeth to her mother was entirely scandalous and illustrates the problematic legacy of Anne Boleyn: the corruption of the mother justified rebellion against the daughter.[18]

But Elizabeth had exposure to a different memory of her mother, one cultivated by defenders of the English church and its queen. In his early writings, John Foxe strove to praise Anne without condemning Henry VIII as a murderer. He later extolled Anne's reign as a time when "the religion of Christ most happily flourished, and had a right prosperous course."[19] For Foxe, as well as for John Aylmer, the Protestant achievement under Elizabeth had its origins in the court of Anne Boleyn. As Aylmer wrote in *The Harborowe for Faithfull Subjectes*, "Was not Queen Anne the mother of this blessed woman, the chief, first, and only

---

[13] On such views, not just among Catholics but Protestants as well, see Carole Levin, "All the Queen's Children," in this volume, 85-103.

[14] Jenkins, *Elizabeth the Great*, 157.

[15] Conyers Read, *Lord Burghley and Queen Elizabeth* (London: Jonathan Cape, 1960), 243; Thomas M. Veech, *Dr. Nicholas Sanders and the English Reformation, 1530–1581* (Louvain: Bureaux du Recueil, Bibliothèque de l'Université, 1935), 92.

[16] Veech, *Dr. Nicholas Sanders*, 245–51.

[17] Carole Levin, *"The Heart and Stomach of a King": Elizabeth I and the Politics of Sex and Power* (Philadelphia: University of Pennsylvania Press, 1994), 80.

[18] For more on this matter, see Sheila Cavanagh, "The Bad Seed: Princess Elizabeth and the Seymour Incident," in *Dissing Elizabeth*, ed. Walker, 9–29, here 22–23; Erickson, *The First Elizabeth*, 46, 50, 70, 110, 194–95; Levin, "'We shall never,'" 87; Levin, "Queens and Claimants: Political Insecurity in Sixteenth-Century England," in *Gender, Ideology, and Action: Historical Perspectives on Women's Public Lives*, ed. Janet Sharistanian (New York: Greenwood Press, 1986), 41–66, here 58.

[19] John Foxe, *The Acts and Monuments of John Foxe*, ed. George Townsend, 8 vols. (London: Seeley, Burnside, and Seeley, 1843–1849; repr. New York: AMS, 1965), 5:135.

cause of banyshing the beast of Rome, with all his beggerly baggage?"[20] Another Protestant, Bartholomew Clerk, wrote that "Anne's advent was a blessing from God as she was the mother of the Phoenix, Elizabeth."[21] This Protestant praise matched in its heightened tone the Catholic critique of mother and daughter, and that very exaggeration offered Elizabeth a counterpoint memory of her mother.

Traces of Anne Boleyn's life more tangible than religious debates offered Elizabeth contact with her mother's memory. These personal ties appeared by way of genealogy, patronage, images, places, and objects that evoked, in ways quite direct, the existence and legacy of Anne. These bonds suggest that Elizabeth quietly but consistently relied upon her Boleyn family, and she chose to surround herself with maternal memories. Despite the dynastic threat attached to Anne Boleyn's reputation, Elizabeth preserved—usually in small acts, often without comment—a place in her world for the mother whom she had barely known.

From her birth to her death, Elizabeth lived in a circle of her Boleyn relatives, some distant, some close. In her early years, her mother's relatives staffed her nursery and household.[22] As queen, Elizabeth had a supply of Boleyn cousins in her household and government courtesy of her mother's sister, Mary Boleyn, and her husband William Carey. These Boleyn cousins included Catherine Carey Knollys; Sir Francis and Sir William Knollys; Henry Carey, Lord Hunsdon;[23] Catherine Carey, later the Countess of Nottingham; Philadelphia Carey; George Carey, 2nd Lord Hunsdon; Sir John Carey; Sir Edmund Carey; and Sir Robert Carey. This last, Robert Carey, became a trusted messenger between James VI and Elizabeth. In 1587, she gave Robert the delicate task of conveying a letter about her execution of James's mother, Mary Stuart. Elizabeth wrote that she "sent this kinsman of mine, whom ere now it hath pleased you to favor, to instruct you truly of that which is too irksome for my pen to tell you."[24] Using a Boleyn

---

[20] Quoted in John King, *Tudor Royal Iconography* (Princeton: Princeton University Press, 1989), 246; see also Retha M. Warnicke, "Conflicting Rhetoric about Tudor Women: The Example of Queen Anne Boleyn," in *Political Rhetoric, Power, and Renaissance Women*, ed. Carole Levin and Patricia Sullivan (Albany: State University of New York Press, 1995), 39–54, here 42–43.

[21] Quoted in Veech, *Dr. Nicholas Sanders*, 93–94.

[22] Ives, *Life*, 194–97, 255–56, 381 n. 53; Warnicke, *Anne Boleyn*, 134, 237, 315; Starkey, *Struggle for the Throne*, 18, 75, 79; Paul Johnson, *Elizabeth I* (New York: Holt, Rinehart & Winston, 1974), 15–16; Smither, "Psychological Profile," 56.

[23] In the 1520s and 1530s, questions arose regarding the paternity of Henry Carey, considered by some to be the illegitimate son of Henry VIII and his mistress, Mary Boleyn. See Warnicke, *Anne Boleyn*, 46; Michael Riordan, "Carey, William (c. 1496–1528)," *Oxford Dictionary of National Biography* (Oxford: Oxford University Press, 2004), 10:89-90.

[24] *Elizabeth I: Collected Works*, ed. Leah Marcus, Janel Mueller, and Mary Beth Rose (Chicago: University of Chicago Press, 2000), 296; Emily Georgiana Susanna Reilly, comp., *Historical Anecdotes of the Families of the Boleynes, Careys, Mordaunts, Hamiltons,*

kinsman increased the weight of her message to the king. In calling James's attention to this family bond, Elizabeth left unsaid—but probably not unheard—another part of her message. Who better to deliver the news of a mother's beheading than the grandnephew of Anne Boleyn, whose family had recovered its place to thrive again at court? The subtext would not be lost on James.

Elizabeth also showed a sensitivity to her mother's family in the area of ecclesiastical patronage. She supported the church career of her illegitimate first cousin, George Boleyn, natural son and namesake of Anne Boleyn's brother. Between 1559 and his death in 1603, George Boleyn held various church offices, including that of dean of Lichfield, and it was rumored that Elizabeth "would have made him bishop of Worcester, but he refused it." In his will, Boleyn stated that "Her majestie gave me all that ever I have," eloquent testimony to the significance of her mother's memory for Elizabeth.[25] Given her own history, Elizabeth might also have sympathized with the challenges faced by an actual Boleyn bastard.

Suitors to the queen certainly felt that the memory of Anne Boleyn was a good card to play in soliciting patronage from her daughter. In 1559, William Barker wrote to the new queen seeking her continuation of her mother's generous support of his Cambridge studies. When he later became embroiled in the duke of Norfolk's treason, Barker invoked Anne Boleyn's memory in appealing for mercy from Elizabeth: "as by her majesty's noble mother I first began at Cambridge tasting of her munificence, so by her majesty's clemency I may end the rest of my sorrowful days there."[26] Elizabeth, whether because of her mother or Barker's incrimination of other plotters, did eventually pardon him.[27] Barker's appeals to the memory of Anne Boleyn suggested that some people were aware of how her mother's name resonated with Elizabeth.

Two chaplains, William Latymer and Matthew Parker, served both queens and personified the legacy of Anne Boleyn to her daughter. As Elizabeth's chaplain and clerk of her closet, William Latymer drew upon personal knowledge of her mother in writing his "Chronickille of Anne Bulleyne," which he dedicated

---

and Jocelyns (Newry: J. Henderson, 1839), 29. For Elizabeth's use of familial labels with James VI, see Lena Cowen Orlin, "The Fictional Families of Elizabeth I," in *Political Rhetoric*, ed. Levin and Sullivan, 85–110.

[25] Brett Usher, "Backing Protestantism," in *John Foxe: An Historical Perspective*, ed. David Loades (Aldershot: Ashgate, 1999), 105–34, here 115–16; *Dictionary of National Biography*, ed. Leslie Stephen, 66 vols. (London: Smith, Elder, & Co., 1885–1901), 2:783.

[26] Maria Dowling, "Anne Boleyn and Reform," *Journal of Ecclesiastical History* 35 (1984): 30-46, here 34; Thomas Freeman, "Research, Rumor, and Propaganda: Anne Boleyn in Foxe's Book of Martyrs," *Historical Journal* 31 (1995): 797–819, here 807–8.

[27] P. W. Hasler, *The History of Parliament: The House of Commons, 1558–1603*, 3 vols. (London: Her Majesty's Stationery Office, 1981), 1:396; Kenneth R. Bartlett, "Barker, William (*fl.* 1540–1576)," *Oxford Dictionary of National Biography*, 3:899-900.

to Elizabeth.[28] Maria Dowling, editor of the "Chronickille," speculates that because of Latymer's position and reputation (news of his project had reached Holinshed and Foxe), Elizabeth did see the finished text.[29] Had she read Latymer's reflections, she would have met a loving mother concerned with her daughter's linguistic and spiritual education. Addressing Elizabeth, Latymer wrote that "wee truste your highnes shall encrease to the whisshed desire of your most deare and naturall mother, the glorye of God, and joyfull comforte of all your noble happy realme."[30] In Elizabeth's success was the validation of her mother's life.

Another of Anne Boleyn's chaplains, one tied to her by family, was Matthew Parker. In the week before her execution, Anne asked Parker to assume the spiritual custody of her young daughter.[31] Some twenty years later, Elizabeth asked Parker to be Archbishop of Canterbury, and so reached out to a living representative of her mother. After resisting this request for several months, Parker made Anne's maternal love an issue in his eventual submission to her daughter. He did not forget, Parker wrote to Nicholas Bacon, "what words her grace's mother said to me of her, not six days before her apprehension."[32] He wrote to Elizabeth herself of "the great benefits which sometime I received at your grace's honourable mother's benevolence (whose soul I doubt not but is in blessed felicity with God)."[33] As Parker described his bond with Anne Boleyn, Elizabeth, in effect, heard her mother's voice from the grave. And he returned to that theme years later in 1572. In a pithy complaint to Burghley about Elizabeth's leniency to Catholics, Parker swore that "if I had not been so much bound to the mother, I would not so soon have granted to serve the daughter."[34] For the sixteen years he did serve her, Elizabeth had Anne Boleyn's spiritual surrogate by her side.

In addition to these Boleyn relatives and friends, Elizabeth had ceremonial reminders of her mother's legacy. The coronation of Elizabeth in January 1559 united mother and daughter in a symbolic display of the power of family. Given

---

[28] Maria Dowling, "William Latymer's Chronickille of Anne Bulleyne," in *Camden Miscellany*, 4th ser., 39 (London: Royal Historical Society, 1990): 23–65, here 28–29.

[29] Dowling, "Latymer's Chronickille," 27. See also Ives, *Life*, 50; Freeman, *Research, Rumor, and Propaganda*, 797–98.

[30] Dowling, "Latymer's Chronickille," 63–65.

[31] He also served as chaplain to the king. For more on Parker, see John Bruce and T. T. Perowne, eds., *Correspondence of Matthew Parker* (Cambridge: Parker Society, Cambridge University Press, 1813), vii; Edith Weir Perry, *Under Four Tudors, Being the Story of Matthew Parker* (London: George Allen & Unwin, 1964), 56, 57, 68, 171–72; V. J. K. Brook, *A Life of Archbishop Parker* (Oxford: Clarendon Press, 1962), 16, 66; William Haller, *Foxe's Book of Martyrs and the Elect Nation* (London: Jonathan Cape, 1963), 83; D. J. Crankshaw and A. Gillespie, "Parker, Matthew," in *Oxford Dictionary of National Biography*, 42:707–28.

[32] Bruce and Perowne, *Correspondence*, 59; Perry, *Matthew Parker*, 177.

[33] Bruce and Perowne, *Correspondence*, 70.

[34] Bruce and Perowne, *Correspondence*, 391–92; Perry, *Matthew Parker*, 51.

Elizabeth's parentage, the procession would have evoked, for some citizens, the memory of her mother's troubled entry twenty-six years earlier, when Londoners loyal to the displaced Catherine of Aragon supposedly turned the king and queen's initials—H.A.—into shouts of derision, HA.[35] But Anne's place in her daughter's entry was one of recognition and honor. The two creators of Anne's entry, John Leland and Nicholas Udall, instructed Richard Mulcaster, who designed Elizabeth's pageantry.[36] As Elizabeth went from the Tower through the city into Westminster, she stopped her carriage in front of a stage where child actors formed a living family tree. On the bottom level were Henry VII and Elizabeth of York, clasping hands, with red and white roses, crowns, and scepters. Above them, linked by rising branches, were Henry VIII and Anne Boleyn. Highest of all, joined to her parents by branches but alone at the top, was Elizabeth, proclaimed "the onelye heire of Henrye the Eighth."[37] To make that genealogical statement, Anne Boleyn needed to be honored as queen and mother; to emphasize the bond of succession between Henry VIII and daughter Elizabeth, the sibling interrupters, Edward VI and Mary I, had vanished. In a fascinating interaction, Elizabeth watched her grandparents and her parents as she listened to herself (as a child) give a speech on national unity residing in the two Queen Elizabeths. In this tableau of living monarchs, past and present, Elizabeth may have found continuity and legitimacy in the validation of her queen mother.[38]

To linger for a moment in the realm of intriguing possibility, it may be the case that the next day in her coronation one of the crowns used by Elizabeth was Anne Boleyn's.[39] Three crowns figured in Tudor coronations: St. Edward's, the

---

[35] Ives doubts that the shouts occurred, as was reported in Brussels (*Life*, 177–78).

[36] King, *Iconography*, 230. According to King, "Elizabeth actively involved herself in preparations for such spectacles" (228). Elizabeth issued instructions to Sir Thomas Cawarden, Master of the Revels, to lend apparel in his keeping to the Londoners participating in the street pageants. See Georgianna Ziegler, comp. and ed., *Elizabeth I: Then and Now* (Seattle: University of Washington Press, Folger Shakespeare Library, 2003), 31–32. David M. Bergeron conjectures that the actors performing in the family tree wore red and white gowns provided by the queen; see "Elizabeth I's Coronation Entry (1559): New Manuscript Evidence," in *The Mysteries of Elizabeth I: Selections from English Literary Renaissance*, ed. Kirby Farrell and Kathleen Swaim (Amherst: University of Massachusetts Press, 2003), 21–26.

[37] Nichols, *Progresses*, 1:41–44; James M. Osborn, ed., *The Quenes Maiesties Passage through the Citie of London to Westminster the Day before her Coronacion* (New Haven: Yale University Press, 1960), 18. Anne Boleyn's entry had no references to Tudor genealogy or family trees; see Sydney Anglo, *Images of Tudor Kingship* (London: Seaby, 1992), 49.

[38] On the inclusion of Anne and the exclusion of other Tudor relatives in the family tree displayed at Norwich on the pageant at Gracious Street, see Tim Moylan, "Advising the Queen," in this volume, 230–50, esp. 237–38.

[39] Catherine of Aragon reportedly refused to give up her crown, so the king had a new one made for Anne by Master Sadocho. See *Calendar of State Papers and Manuscripts*

Imperial crown, and a personal crown made for the new ruler.[40] For her personal crown, according to Janet Arnold, Elizabeth could have remodelled Edward VI's or Mary's or another one in the Whitehall jewel house; no evidence exists that she did.[41] But she might also have worn Anne Boleyn's crown, the appearance of which in a 1574 inventory of royal jewels indicates that Elizabeth, whether she used it at her coronation or not, had her mother's crown in her possession.

Elizabeth incorporated other symbols of her mother into her own panoply of royal references. She claimed Anne's motto, *Semper Eadem* (always the same), and made it her own throughout her reign.[42] In that mother-daughter context, the motto offered an expression of loyalty and constancy that placed Anne Boleyn in the symbolic center of her daughter's monarchy. Elizabeth also adopted her mother's falcon as a badge.[43] About the time of her marriage, Anne Boleyn took the white falcon of her Boleyn ancestors, the earls of Ormonde, and gave it her own dynastic spin. The new image had the raptor standing amid red and white roses on a tree stump, wearing a crown, and glaring proudly at the scepter clutched in its right talon.[44] The symbol communicated Anne's role in continuing the Tudor line through her own queenly authority. The special characteristics of the falcon, too, would have appealed to Anne: unique among hawks, the female peregrine falcon is larger and more skilled in hunting than its mate, the tercel.[45] Perhaps that idea resonated with Elizabeth, too, who appropriated the white falcon badge as a reminder of her mother's legacy and her own.

Decorative reminders of Anne Boleyn confronted Elizabeth in a variety of public and semi-public locations. Taken by itself, each example might seem minor, but in the accumulation of such contacts a larger meaning emerges. Henry VIII's nuptial enthusiasm had led him to blanket his palaces with emblems of

---

Existing in the Archives and Collections of Milan, Vol. I: 1385–1618, ed. Allen B. Hinds (London: His Majesty's Stationery Office, 1912), 558.

[40] Janet Arnold, "The 'Coronation' Portrait of Queen Elizabeth I," *Burlington Magazine* 120 (November 1978): 727–41. For a discussion of St. Edward's place in Elizabethan historical circles, see Janelle Greenberg, *The Radical Face of the Ancient Constitution: St. Edward's "Laws" in Early Modern Political Thought* (Cambridge: Cambridge University Press, 2001). Greenberg notes that the crown of St. Edward figured in English coronations since its discovery in the twelfth century (51). According to Ives, Anne Boleyn broke with the tradition that only reigning monarchs used St. Edward's crown when she used it as one of the crowns in her coronation (*Life*, 179).

[41] Arnold, "'Coronation' Portrait," 727–28, 732–35. Elizabeth's personal crown appears in Hilliard's coronation miniature and in the Mildmay Charter portrait. The habit of reusing coronation robes and the appearance of them in Elizabeth's coronation portrait (ca. 1600) suggests, to Arnold, that Elizabeth wore her sister Mary's robes.

[42] Cavanagh, "Bad Seed," 21.

[43] King, *Iconography*, 246; Ives, *Life*, 230, 399 n. 52.

[44] Ives, *Life*, 221–22, plate 31; King, *Iconography*, 51.

[45] *Oxford English Dictionary* (Oxford: Clarendon Press, 1989), s.v. "falcon."

his current wife. Although most of Anne Boleyn's badges, therefore, had a relatively short shelf life, some did survive for decades, even centuries. During her many visits to Hampton Court Palace, on summer progresses as well as the customary Christmas stay, Elizabeth saw her mother's initials and badges carved in the Great Hall.[46] At St. James's Palace, Elizabeth saw Anne and Henry's initials adorning the doorways of the gatehouse turrets.[47] On her 1564 visit to King's College Chapel, Cambridge, Elizabeth heard evensong and watched a pageant in close proximity to the choir screens carved with the falcon badge and her parents' initials, H.A.[48] In these subtle but definite reminders of Anne Boleyn, Elizabeth had contact with her mother's memory.

For Elizabeth, few places would have evoked Anne's memory as powerfully as the Tower of London, site of her mother's execution and burial. While both queens lodged there before their coronation entries, the growing reputation of the Tower as a place of death created a disturbing bond between mother and daughter. In the 1554 aftermath of Wyatt's revolt, Elizabeth had feared entering the Tower under Mary's orders. At her happier arrival there in 1559, Elizabeth "patted the earth and said, 'Some have fallen from being princes of this land to be prisoners in this place. I am raised from being prisoner in this place to be the prince of the land.'"[49] With her customary use of "prince" to include women, Elizabeth's words would allude as well to her mother.

Another site evocative of her Boleyn blood was the city of Norwich, which Elizabeth visited once, in July 1578.[50] That occasion turned into a civic homecoming as she traveled through the region where the Boleyns had flourished for generations. The town's acknowledgement of this family bond appeared in the ubiquitous display of Boleyn devices—in particular, the falcon that now signified both Anne and Elizabeth. Elizabeth entered Norwich through a gate emblazoned with her mother's falcon next to her own royal arms.[51] Reaching the

---

[46] Ben Weinreb and Christopher Hibbert, eds., *The London Encyclopedia* (London: Macmillan, 1983), 360. A gate at the palace was named for Anne Boleyn. Elizabeth would not have seen her mother's leopards there, however, because workmen had given them new heads and tails to turn them into Jane Seymour's panthers; see Anglo, *Images*, 37–38.

[47] H. M. Colvin, *The History of the King's Works, Vols. III-IV: 1485–1660* (London: Her Majesty's Stationery Office, 1975–1982), 4:26–27.

[48] King, *Iconography*, 86.

[49] Weinreb and Hibbert, *The London Encyclopedia*, 875. Other members of the ruling elite to die in the Tower included Henry VI; Edward IV's sons; Henry VIII's fifth wife, Catherine Howard; Henry Howard, earl of Surrey; Edward Seymour, duke of Somerset; John Dudley, duke of Northumberland; and Lady Jane Grey.

[50] See Mary Hill Cole, *The Portable Queen: Elizabeth I and the Politics of Ceremony* (Amherst: University of Massachusetts Press, 1999), 24, 32, 55, 77, 101–2, 109, 141–44.

[51] Nichols, *Progresses*, 2:143–45. Images from Elizabeth's 1559 London entry reappeared in the Norwich pageantry; see Anglo, *Images*, 89.

market, Elizabeth passed through another gate decorated with her mother's "falcon, with crowne and scepter, which is hir owne badge." Elizabeth proceeded into the cathedral grounds through the Erpingham Gate, freshly painted with the arms of Anne's grandfather, Sir William Boleyn, and her great-grandmother, Lady Anne Boleyn.[52] Inside the cathedral, Elizabeth sat on a special canopied throne, on the north side of the apse facing south, where she would have spent the service looking up at panels carved with Boleyn shields and bulls' heads (allusion to the family name "Bullen"), and across at the elaborate tomb of Sir William Boleyn, her great-grandfather.[53] As Zillah Dovey notes, Elizabeth "would have readily recognized [the tomb] from the heraldic devices."[54] In going to Norwich Cathedral, Elizabeth paid homage to her maternal ancestors and wrapped herself in their civic memory.

Other aspects of her Norfolk progress held Boleyn allusions. While in Norwich, Elizabeth received from James VI a present of "some falcons," a gift that, intentionally or not, aptly brought the shared mother-daughter badge to life.[55] One of the five Norfolk men who received a knighthood from Elizabeth was her host Edward Clere, a Boleyn descendant and owner of Blickling, perhaps the birthplace of Anne Boleyn.[56] She also visited the Woodhouses, distant Boleyn relatives, at Kimberley, where, to honor Elizabeth, they had built a throne, its valence embroidered with her parents' emblems and H.A. initials.[57] Both civic and private hosts put Elizabeth's maternal ancestors, and Anne Boleyn in particular, at the center of the hospitality they hoped would please her royal daughter. From Elizabeth's perspective, the Norwich visit brought her home.

Elizabeth's public contact with her mother's memory was, by definition, more apparent than any personal, private expression of that bond, but a few domestic objects allude to its existence. When she was eleven, Elizabeth chose to translate *The Glasse of the Synnful Soule*, written by Marguerite de Navarre, sister of Francis I and a friend of Anne Boleyn from her days at the French court. Marc Shell argues that Elizabeth made the translation "most likely from a 1533 edition" owned by her mother.[58] In a personal gesture acknowledging the falcon's symbolic resonance with Elizabeth, Robert Dudley gave her a "faire cup of

---

[52] Zillah Dovey, *An Elizabethan Progress* (Gloucester: Sutton, 1996), 72.

[53] Richard John King, *Handbook to the Cathedrals of England, Eastern Division* (London: J. Murray, 1862), 108, 124–26.

[54] Dovey, *An Elizabethan Progress*, 72.

[55] Dovey, *An Elizabethan Progress*, 74.

[56] Ives, *Life*, 3; Dovey, *An Elizabethan Progress*, 83, 103. On her route back to London, Elizabeth stayed with Clere at Thetford, conveniently located south of Norwich.

[57] Dovey, *An Elizabethan Progress*, 96. The valence probably came from Blickling.

[58] Marc Shell, *Elizabeth's Glass* (Lincoln: University of Nebraska Press, 1993), 3. Marcus, Mueller, and Rose, the editors of Elizabeth's *Collected Works*, agree with Shell (6). See also King, *Iconography*, 251. Made as a gift for her stepmother, Katherine Parr,

cristall fationed like a slipper, garnished with golde, and a cover of golde, enamaeled, with [a] white faulcone in the toppe."[59] That the gift came around the time of his secret marriage to Lettice Knollys, grandniece of Anne Boleyn, and Elizabeth's angry discovery of their union lends a certain intimacy to his choice of the present's design. He might also have hoped that the falcon's allusion to female strength would solicit Elizabeth's mercy in his time of disgrace.

Another object, smaller than these hand-held items, evoked the mother-daughter bond in an even more personal way. Elizabeth owned a ring, made around 1575, its mother-of-pearl band studded with rubies and in its center a monogram "ER" in block diamonds and gold tracing. Beside the diamond "ER" was a solitary pearl that covered a clasp, which, when released, opened the ring into a locket. Inside were two enamel portraits: one of Elizabeth in profile, and facing her across the hinge, Anne Boleyn, in a three-quarter view.[60] Whether opened, as such a ring would be in private moments, or closed, in public ones, the

---

the book discusses incest to such a degree that, Marc Shell argues, the topic itself must have weighed heavily in Elizabeth's thoughts.

[59] Nichols, *Progresses*, 1:527–28; 2:276.

[60] Plantagenet Somerset Fry, *Chequers: The Country Home of Britain's Prime Ministers* (London: Her Majesty's Stationery Office, 1977), 52–53; Ives, *Life*, 42–43; Somerset, *Elizabeth I*, 7. In 2003, the public could view the tiny locket ring when it was on display as part of the *Elizabeth* exhibition at Greenwich; see David Starkey and Susan Doran, eds., *Elizabeth: The Exhibition at the National Maritime Museum* (London: Chatto & Windus, 2003), 12–13, catalogue no. 7. Diana Scarisbrick notes that Robert Dudley gave jewels to the visiting queen on the occasion of her arrival at and departure from his house ("Elizabeth's Jewellery," in Starkey and Doran, *Elizabeth*, 184), and Felicity Heal examines the nature of royal gift-giving in "Giving and Receiving on Royal Progress," in Jayne Elisabeth Archer, Elizabeth Goldring, and Sarah Knight, eds., *The Progresses, Pageants, and Entertainments of Queen Elizabeth I* (Oxford: Oxford University Press, 2007), 46–61. In Ives' view, the ring "must have been made for her, or as an elaborate gesture of loyalty to her" (*Life*, 373 n. 29). Given the richness and intimacy of the ring, I think that it likely came to Elizabeth as a present from a courtier personally close to her. The dating of the ring coincides with her elaborate visits to Dudley at Kenilworth in 1572 and 1575, a time when he continued to press his matrimonial suit with the queen. With his deep knowledge of Elizabeth from their childhood, his public ambition to marry her, and his pattern of royal gift-giving, Dudley had sufficient presumption, wealth, and access to present Elizabeth with such a beautiful invocation of family and motherhood; whether he actually did so is uncertain. Elizabeth's inventories of jewels do not refer to the ring, but Somerset Fry states that the ring went from Elizabeth, to James VI, to the 1st Earl of Home, and eventually to Sir Alec Douglas-Home, who as Prime Minister had the use of Chequers in 1963–1964; see *Chequers*, 31–32, 52. For discussion of the difficulties in identifying jewels due to resetting, see Arnold, "The 'Coronation' Portrait," 731; Ives, *Life*, 252. It is unlikely that any of Anne's paraphernalia, her personal jewels inheritable by her daughter, reached Elizabeth. My thanks to Judy Klein for raising this point and to Marlena Hobson for her insights into the artistry of the ring.

dual, joined portraits created an intimate contact, face to face, enamel to flesh, between mother and daughter.

The intimacy with her mother and her Boleyn kin continued through Elizabeth's last years to her death. As her Boleyn relatives died, Elizabeth felt the loss, not just of their friendship but also of the familial link with the past. In February 1603, her cousin George Boleyn died, as well as her close confident, Catherine Carey Howard, the countess of Nottingham, whose loss had made Elizabeth's "heart . . . sad and heavy for ten to twelve days" before she herself died.[61] With Elizabeth at her death was Philadelphia Carey, Lady Scrope, grandniece of Anne Boleyn, and nearby awaiting the news of her death to carry north to Scotland was Philadelphia's brother, Sir Robert Carey, grandnephew of Anne Boleyn.[62] In her funeral procession, the Boleyn coat of arms joined other family icons accompanying the queen on her last journey.[63]

Elizabeth's divergent treatment of her Tudor and Boleyn extended family reminds us of the dual importance of kinship in English government. The virtue of appearing as Henry VIII's daughter encouraged Elizabeth to lay claim to an inheritance of his popularity, independence, and authority. The virtue of appearing as Anne Boleyn's daughter, however, was less obvious, when the public circumstances of her death served to undermine the legitimacy of Elizabeth's crown. And yet, whether through her own initiative or through the efforts of others, Elizabeth did have contact in public and in private with the memory of her mother, and in acts of patronage and loyalty, she recognized the significance of Anne Boleyn as queen and mother. Perhaps Elizabeth was sensitive to her mother's last words from the scaffold: "If any person wil medle of my cause I require him to judge the best."[64] While Elizabeth honored her mother's request not to "medle" in her cause, she did remember. In subtle and personal acts, Elizabeth found ways to recognize, even embrace, the memory of Anne Boleyn.

---

[61] F. H. Mares, ed., *The Memoirs of Robert Carey* (Oxford: Clarendon Press, 1972), 58; Jenkins, *Elizabeth the Great*, 323–24.

[62] Jenkins, *Elizabeth the Great*, 323–24; Reilly, *Historical Anecdotes*, 29–30.

[63] Anglo, *Images*, 103.

[64] George Wyatt, *Extracts from the Life of the Virtuous, Christian, and Renowned Queen Anne Boleigne* (London: Richard & Arthur Taylor, 1817), 20–24.

Elizabeth Tudor: Maidenhood in Crisis

Janel Mueller
with Linda Shenk and Carole Levin

Scholars of Queen Elizabeth have solid, objective reasons for being curious about why Elizabeth assumed the identity of a "Maiden Queen" and then stayed true to it. She came to the throne under the system of hereditary monarchy, and when she did so, she was the last direct descendant in the Tudor line. Both of these hard facts would seem to have required that she marry and bear children. Yet precisely the opposite occurred. Why did she steer a course contrary to the expectation that she, as queen, would also be a wife and a mother?

Various explanations have been proposed, especially in the last two centuries. Most of these have necessarily been speculative. Perhaps Elizabeth was traumatized by what she came to know of the treason trial, conviction, and beheading of her mother, Queen Anne Boleyn, by her father, King Henry VIII. These events occurred in the spring of 1536, when Elizabeth was only two-and-a-half years old. (Significantly, Anne's swift conveying to execution occurred after she miscarried of what would have been a son in January 1536.) Perhaps Elizabeth made her choice during the illness she suffered in the late summer and fall of 1548, as she grieved for her beloved stepmother, the dowager Queen Katherine Parr, who had died after giving birth to her only child. Katherine was thirty-six at the time of her death; Elizabeth was fifteen. Perhaps Elizabeth made her decision when her elder half-sister, Queen Mary, married Prince Philip of Spain, who was soon to become king, against the wishes of the English people. Mary thereafter faced some very public humiliations: her husband was with her only sporadically (Philip ruled actively in Spain and only visited England), and she had two false pregnancies (in August 1555 and April 1558) when she was thirty-nine and forty-two, respectively. Taking these developments singly or altogether, it might seem that the grave dangers of death or failure connected with childbearing, experienced by three English queens close to Elizabeth, are sufficient to explain why she did not wish to marry.[1]

---

[1] For a sensitive discussion, see Christine Coch, "'Mother of my Contreye': Elizabeth I and Tudor Constructions of Motherhood," *English Literary Renaissance* 26 (1996):

Donald Stump, Linda Shenk, and Carole Levin, eds., *Elizabeth I and the 'Sovereign Arts': Essays in Literature, History, and Culture*. MRTS 407. Tempe: ACMRS, 2011. [ISBN 978-0-86698-455-3]

I do not deny elements of truth or plausibility in these explanations; I simply object that there is no written evidence to support any of them. Each or all of these theories can co-exist with an explanation that I offer in this essay—a proposal for which there is, in fact, a sizeable amount of written evidence. I focus on a transformation in Elizabeth's self-representation that occurs over two sequences of letters that she wrote between the summer of 1548 and early winter of 1549. The first series occurs at the end of Katherine's pregnancy; the second, just following Katherine's tragic death. In these letters, we can see Elizabeth's tone changing from one of girlish, emotional immaturity to one that is more guarded and self-possessed. In the second series, written after the scandal of inappropriate conduct with Lord Thomas Seymour, Elizabeth—a princess only fifteen years of age—responds to this situation of grave political danger by adopting a starkly different persona. In these four letters, written during a time rife with danger to both her person and her reputation, Elizabeth makes clear that the crucial issue for her is selfhood, not sexuality. Elizabeth serves notice that she is taking charge of herself, assuming agency and accountability, and articulating what she will and will not allow others to make of who she is. This metamorphosis, grounded in the language of maiden selfhood, sheds new light, I suggest, on Elizabeth's later decision to live out her life as a maiden queen.

To understand both the gravity of the political danger that Elizabeth faced and her reasons for emphasizing her agency as a princess speaking alone involves acknowledging the inappropriate conduct of her guardians—the very people who should have protected her. At that time, her governess, Katherine Ashley, and her accounts manager (known as her cofferer), Thomas Parry, were actively promoting a marriage between Elizabeth and Lord High Admiral Thomas Seymour, young King Edward VI's uncle, without the knowledge or permission of the older uncle, the Protector, Edward Seymour, or of the Privy Council, or of the boy-king. This was risky and reckless business—to plot a marriage of a direct heir to the English throne without the knowledge and permission of the monarch then ruling. The very initiative smacked of disloyalty and forbidden unilateral action, possibly leading to usurpation or some other form of treason, which was a crime punishable by death.

The other source of danger facing Elizabeth was the increasingly devious and suspicious behavior of Lord Thomas Seymour himself. The history of his dealings at court attests to his considerable good looks (he was exceptionally fine-featured and well-groomed), his personal magnetism, high-spiritedness, ambition—especially vis-à-vis his older brother—and his persistent lack of sound judgment. Three days after Henry VIII died on 28 January 1547, Edward Seymour persuaded the Privy Council to accept him as Governor and Lord Protector of his

---

423–50; repr. in *The Mysteries of Elizabeth I*, ed. Kirby Farrell and Kathleen M. Swaim (Amherst: University of Massachusetts Press, 2002), 134–61. See also Retha Warnicke, "Elizabeth I and Mary Stewart" in the present volume, 53–68.

nephew Edward VI, the nine-year-old heir to the throne. Edward Seymour assumed the title of duke of Somerset. With the intent of containing his younger brother's ambitions, Edward Seymour had Thomas Seymour named to the peerage (as baron Seymour of Sudeley) and to the position of Lord High Admiral. Somerset hoped to ship Thomas Seymour out to sea, or at least to confine him to the coastal regions, away from the court.

But Thomas did not comply with his older brother's intentions. He began to woo an old flame, the thirty-five-year-old widow of Henry VIII, Katherine Parr, who very quickly showed herself responsive. An undated letter to Thomas Seymour in her handwriting, written in the spring of 1547, contains a revealing reflection on their previous plans to marry, which broke off when Henry decided to make Katherine his sixth wife. Katherine writes to Thomas Seymour as follows:

> My lord, I would not have you to think this mine honest goodwill to you to proceed of any sudden motion or passion. For as truly as God is God, my mind was fully bent the other time I was at liberty, to marry you before any man I knew. Howbeit God withstood my will therein most vehemently for a time, and through His grace and goodness made that possible, which seemed to me most unpossible. That was, made me to renounce utterly mine own will and to follow His will.[2]

Alluding to her marriage to Henry as compliance with God's will, Katherine stresses that this outcome was beyond her control. But now that the king her husband was dead, Katherine and Thomas were free to wed. By late April or May 1547, they had married secretly, without permission from the Protector, or the Council, or the young king.[3] Young Edward, who was very fond of his stepmother, was duped by his uncle Thomas's generous gifts of pocket money into trying to persuade her to make a marriage she had already made. Word of the marriage leaked out by June 1547, too late for preventing or undoing it. Seymour's furtive, near-treasonous actions in his marriage with Katherine, would—in less than two years—compound the political danger facing Elizabeth. She would be associated with a man who, as I will next demonstrate, contrived to manage the succession by gaining control over current heirs to the throne.

With Katherine's marriage to Thomas Seymour, Princess Elizabeth, who had lived at intervals with Queen Katherine prior to Henry VIII's death, essentially acquired a stepfather. It was certainly of interest to him to have a direct

---

[2] Dowager Queen Katherine Parr to Thomas Seymour, spring 1547 (portion of autograph letter exhibited at Sudeley Castle, Gloucestershire, transcribed by Janel Mueller in September 1996, with the kind permission of the owner, Lady Elizabeth Ashcombe).

[3] Besides its overtones of potentially treasonous insubordination, this was a very injudicious move on the part of Katherine Parr, who should have waited for nine months after January 1547 before remarrying, to establish that she was not carrying a child of Henry VIII's.

heiress to the throne in his household—epecially this one, for there had been rumors of his possibly marrying Elizabeth before his quick success with Katherine. However, Thomas Seymour had other self-promoting plans afoot at this time. He convinced Lady Jane Grey's father, the marquis of Dorset, to allow her to reside with him and dowager Queen Katherine, as his ward. Thomas hoped to engineer a marriage between Jane and young King Edward and, thus, to unseat his brother as the power behind the English throne, taking that role for himself.

In the course of 1548, Thomas Seymour's secret intrigues to replace his brother as Protector became more grandiose and more dangerous. He asked William Sharington, the under treasurer of the Bristol mint, to coin testoons for him (Sharington was already illegally coining some for himself), using this request as a bribe to keep these dealings secret. Using his position as Lord High Admiral, he extorted money from ships sailing to Ireland; he stockpiled a cache of arms at one of his country estates; and with his hospitality, generosity, and affable manner, he won supporters among the gentry and nobility in the West Country. In these same months, Katherine became pregnant. She bore a daughter, Mary, to Thomas Seymour on 30 August 1548, but by 5 September she lay dead of puerperal fever. Now, in the closing months of 1548, the handsome, personable Lord Thomas Seymour was a highly eligible widower, visibly in circulation, and, sometimes openly, sometimes covertly, promoting his alliances and his prospects of further advancement and greater power—the control of the boy-king, his nephew. All of this would unravel when Sharington's embezzlement of Crown money from the Bristol mint came to light, together with Thomas Seymour's complicity in the crime. Starting in mid-January 1549, on the order of the Privy Council, Thomas Seymour and a number of his suspected supporters were arrested, imprisoned, and interrogated about their involvement in high treason.

This, the winter of 1548–1549, became a season of life-threatening danger for Princess Elizabeth. Her governess, Katherine Ashley, and her accounts manager (or cofferer), Thomas Parry, had indiscreetly undertaken to foster a match between her and the new widower, her half-brother's uncle. Elizabeth, as we shall see, consistently rejected her governess's talk of marrying Lord Thomas Seymour, and she consistently refused to get involved in any action leading toward that end. Why did this whole thing happen, then, and what, in fact, did happen, to place the fifteen-year-old Elizabeth in such dire jeopardy of her own life?

Peeling back the layers of this historical onion involves using documents of the time to assemble a chronology of actions, conversations, and other developments. It is crucial to emphasize that we have these documents—most notably, the formal interrogations and testimony by Katherine Ashley, Thomas Parry, and Elizabeth herself—because Seymour did cross that fatal line and engage in criminal activities. We also have three handwritten letters by Sir Robert Tyrwhit, the court official dispatched by the Privy Council to interrogate Elizabeth and get her confession, as well as seven handwritten letters by Princess Elizabeth that bear directly on the history of her acquaintance with Thomas Seymour. The ultimate question in all this is the following: From what she wrote and from what others report of her, what can we gather about the net impact of this experience on Princess Elizabeth?

The earliest pieces of written evidence that we have are three letters by Elizabeth from the summer of 1548, two to Katherine Parr, who was in an advanced state of pregnancy, and one to Lord Thomas Seymour. The letters to Katherine Parr are girlish, even clingy, immature in their emotional dependency and their ready affection. They are obviously those of a young girl. It is clear from them that Elizabeth had been living with her and Thomas Seymour but that Elizabeth has now gone away. She is distressed at this arrangement—at the loss of her beloved stepmother's company and at Katherine's fragile health—but grateful for Katherine's demonstration of care for her:

> For truly I was replete with sorrow to depart from your highness, especially leaving you doubtful of health. And albeit I answered little, I weighed it more deeper when you said you would warn me of all evils that you should hear of me. For if your grace had not a good opinion of me, you would not have offered friendship to me that way that all men judge the contrary. But what may I more say than thank God for providing such friends to me, desiring God to enrich me with their long life, and me grace to be in heart no less thankful to receive it than I now am glad in writing to show it.[4]

From the second letter to Katherine, we gain a glimpse of the political danger that was mounting in regard to Elizabeth when we learn that Sir Anthony Denny (a member of the Privy Council) and his wife are now living in the same

---

[4] *Elizabeth I: Collected Works*, ed. Leah S. Marcus, Janel Mueller, and Mary Beth Rose (Chicago: University of Chicago Press, 2000), 17–19, parenthetically noted hereafter as *CW*, with page references following. Elizabeth's cryptic allusions to a swift departure and to Katherine's promise of warning the princess prompt us to ask: What caused Katherine to abruptly send Elizabeth from her household, after reassuring the princess of her continuing friendship, that she would warn Elizabeth of any evil she heard of her and maintain her own good opinion? The most direct answer we have comes from the confession that Thomas Parry, Elizabeth's cofferer, wrote in January 1549, during the Privy Council's formal investigation into Thomas Seymour's doings. Parry's account, however, takes a rather indirect form; he reports on several conversations he had with Elizabeth's governess, Katherine Ashley. Parry, very significantly, cannot remember whether Ashley said Elizabeth was dismissed or left of her own accord. For this report, see Samuel Haynes, *A Collection of State Papers, Relating to Affairs in the Reigns of King Henry VIII, King Edward VI, Queen Mary, and Queen Elizabeth, From the Year 1542 to 1570* . . . (London: William Bowyer, 1740), 1:96, parenthetically noted hereafter as Haynes, with page reference following. Spelling modernized by JM.

household with Elizabeth and her governess, Katherine Ashley.[5] The Dennys' residence with Elizabeth is the first warning sign that she has attracted the suspicions of the Lord Protector, Edward Seymour. In her letter to Lord Thomas Seymour, who obviously has taken the liberty of writing to her separately from his wife, Katherine, Elizabeth manifests a budding self-possession: she is cautious, courteous, and notably brief:

> You needed not to send an excuse to me. For I could not mistrust the not fulfilling of your promise to proceed for want of goodwill, but only the opportunity serveth not. Wherefore I shall desire you to think that a greater matter than this could not make me impute any unkindness in you. For I am a friend not won with trifles, nor lost with the like. Thus I commit you and all your affairs in God's hand, who keep you from all evil. (*CW*, 17)

Katherine Ashley, too, was interrogated as part of the formal investigation of Thomas Seymour, and her testimony takes the form of handwritten, signed recollections that she produced at several sittings. Ashley's account leaves a strong impression of her awareness that she and Parry were playing a dicey, high-stakes game in exploring prospects for a match between the Lord Admiral and the princess. Ashley is our source for a heavyweight piece of banter between herself and Thomas Seymour in the spring of 1547 and for a mealtime conversation she had with Parry and his frightened wife, resulting in a solemn promise from Parry to Ashley.[6] Ashley's other testimony supplies a circumstantial history of physical familiarity with Elizabeth. This testimony tells us that the familiarity began shortly after Thomas Seymour married dowager Queen Katherine around April of 1547. It also states that Elizabeth continued to reside in that household

---

[5] "Master Denny and my lady [Denny] with humble thanks prayeth most entirely for your grace, praying the almighty God to send you a lucky deliverance. And my mistress [Katherine Ashley] wisheth no less, giving your highness most humble thanks for her commendations" (*CW*, 20).

[6] Parry broke this promise when he reported Ashley's second-hand report of Elizabeth in Thomas Seymour's arms. Ashley describes this promise of secrecy between her and Parry in her testimony. This section in the testimony reads as follows: "after supper Parry's wife looked upon her husband, and wept, and spake to this examinate [Ashley] and said, 'Alas, I am afraid lest they will send my husband to the Tower, or what they will do with him.' Then said this examinate, 'Nay I warrant you, there is no such cause, but there was a certain private communication betwixt him and me. But I pray you, pray him that he will not meddle with that. For it doth not touch our examination.' Then the said Parry gave his word again before the said Lady Fortescue, his wife, that he would be torn in pieces rather than that he would open that matter" (National Archives, State Papers, 10/6/22, 10/6/20, in *CW*, 27–29). Documents preserved in the National Archives at Kew, Surrey, that were transcribed by Janel Mueller for *CW* are hereafter parenthetically noted as NA, with reference number following.

while coming up with strategies for protecting herself, since none of the adults about her—even Ashley—were doing this adequately. We also learn that there were observers of all of these incidents: Elizabeth and Thomas Seymour were not left alone together. From Ashley herself we again get the story of Elizabeth in a man's arms, but this time it is spun very differently from Parry's account of what Ashley said to him. Ashley indicates that Katherine made up this story to drive home a moral to Ashley: she should be more vigilant in caring for Elizabeth. She "should take more heed, and be, as it were, in watch betwixt her and my lord admiral."[7]

At this point we reach the questions that center on Elizabeth. Was Elizabeth attracted to the handsome, personable, highly placed Thomas Seymour? More importantly from a political perspective: did she involve herself in any way in a prospective marriage with Seymour that did not have (and would not receive) the king's and the Council's authorization? Put otherwise, did Elizabeth's behavior in any way parallel the politically and personally dangerous actions of her beloved stepmother, with regard to the same man? For potential insight into Princess Elizabeth's feelings about Thomas Seymour, our source is, once again, Ashley, her governess. After her dismissal (or departure), the shock of Queen Katherine's death, and her own sickness and grief, Elizabeth seems to have regained some of her vitality and spirits by late fall of 1548 and the subsequent festivities at court. Ashley's recollections of this time register some mild indications of adolescent impressionability on Elizabeth's part—putting her fingers to her eyes when the prospect of marriage with Thomas Seymour was broached, laughing and turning pale when she chose him as a dancing partner, blushing when he was mentioned.[8]

With regard to the crucial political question about whether Elizabeth did anything to entangle herself with Thomas Seymour, there is just one small possibility. Two weeks before Christmas 1548, Elizabeth was startled by the news that Durham Place, which she had understood would be available for her use as a London residence, had instead been turned into a mint. She decided to send Thomas Parry to London to ask Thomas Seymour if he could do anything to remedy the situation. Parry met with Seymour four times, each time finding

---

[7] "Confession of Katherine Ashley. From the original, written by Sir Thomas Smith [secretary to the Council], and signed Kateryn Aschyly," January 1549 (Haynes, 100). For the rest of this section of Ashley's testimony regarding Seymour's indiscreet actions towards Elizabeth, see 1:99–100.

[8] For Ashley's descriptions of Elizabeth's reactions, see "Examinations and Depositions of Katherine Ashley, Governess to Princess Elizabeth, Regarding Possibly Questionable Dealings with Thomas Seymour, Lord High Admiral, February 1549" (*CW*, 25–27; NA, State Papers 10/6/20, 10/6/22). Ashley also recalls Thomas Seymour's rather belated expression of concern that his earlier indiscreet behavior towards Elizabeth had affected his reputation.

himself more surprised and more drawn in by Seymour's bold behavior.[9] Thomas Seymour may have learned to keep his sexual advances in check, but his political designs on Elizabeth—in the form of marital designs—are patent in the questions he presses on Parry. How large is Elizabeth's household, and what are its expenses? How lucrative are her lands, and where are they located? Does she presently hold title to them—and is this for her lifetime, or are the lands hers to convey? When Seymour has his answers from the uncircumspect Parry, he then begins to think aloud: some of Elizabeth's lands could be exchanged for better lands—in fact, for ones bordering on his own. He will look into the matter. It is much more economical when two households are combined into one. He proposes to visit Elizabeth when she is at her manor of Ashridge, near one of his. Parry relates these suggestions to Ashley, who declares that she will speak with Thomas Seymour herself before there is any decision made about his seeing or speaking with Elizabeth. Elizabeth was not involved in any of Thomas Seymour's gross indiscretions regarding her, except to have sent Parry to ask his help with a place to stay at Christmas.

The crowning exhibits in the story of Thomas Seymour's treasonous ambitions and potentially fatal dealings with Elizabeth are the four letters in her own handwriting, written directly to the Lord Protector, Edward Seymour. Clearly she felt altogether alone and on her own, with no one to negotiate for her or defend her. But these very circumstances brought Elizabeth to understand what mattered most to her. She wanted to be in control of her person, her reputation, and her agency—the capacity to make her own decisions under her best informed and best thought-out sense of what she should do. This multiple self-control is so essential to her, she realizes—and shows she realizes—in these letters to Edward Seymour, that she will struggle for it with all the eloquence and all the arguments that she can muster. In exacting displays of consistency and firmness, Elizabeth documents how she took the lead in the political maneuverings of this episode and how she worked to determine what action would be taken where she was directly concerned.

These letters show a fifteen-year-old growing up quickly, undergoing a crash course in the Royal Tudor School of Hard Knocks, and addressing the supreme political authority of the realm from a position as a mistrusted and maligned underdog. These letters of Elizabeth display a sudden, intense character-building, a mastery of strong feeling, a superb capacity to reason in the clutch, and above all, a self-confidence that speaks truth to power.

Unlike a more vulnerable Elizabeth who wrote to Katherine to express her longing for companionship, the Elizabeth of these letters is poised and independent. As early as the first letter, Elizabeth adopts a simple, direct approach that underscores her claims of integrity.

---

[9] Parry's account comes from the section of his written confession entitled "My Communication with the Lord Admiral," January 1549 (Haynes, 97–98).

> Master Tyrwhit and others have told me that there goeth rumors abroad which be greatly both against mine honor and honesty, which above all other thing I esteem, which be these: that I am in the Tower, and with child by my lord admiral. My lord, these are shameful slanders, for the which . . . I shall most heartily desire your lordship that I may come to the court . . . that I may show myself there as I am. (*CW*, 24)

Elizabeth's directness emphasizes the connection she acknowledges between honesty and honor, and, significantly, she introduces her focus on virtue with a pious reflection about herself: "These be the things which I both declared to master Tyrwhit and also whereof my conscience beareth me witness, which I would not for all earthly things offend in anything, for I know I have a soul to save as well as other folks have, wherefore I will above all thing have respect unto the same" (*CW*, 24). By alluding to her conscience and to "earthly things," Elizabeth affirms that her actions are guided by ultimate priorities far more vital to her than the difficulties of the present scandal.[10]

Elizabeth returns to considerations of directness, honesty, and virtue in the third letter, when she defends herself again, saying,

> As concerning that you say—that I give folks occasion to think in refusing the good to uphold the evil—I am not of so simple understanding. Nor I would that your grace should have so evil a opinion of me that I have so little respect to mine own honesty that I would maintain it [a connection with Thomas Seymour] if I had sufficient promise of the same, and so your grace shall prove me when it comes to the point. (*CW*, 33)

Elizabeth's maturing poise and sense of selfhood evidently did not go unnoticed. In his letters, the Lord Protector seems to have remarked on her self-assurance, for Elizabeth responds to his comments in her third letter:

> And whereas I do understand that you do take in evil part the letters that I did write unto your lordship, I am very sorry that you should take them so. For my mind was to declare unto you plainly as I thought in that thing, which I did also the more willingly because (as I write to you) you desired me to be plain with you in all things. And as concerning that point that you write—that I seem to stand in mine own wit in being so well assured of mine own self—I did assure me of myself no more than I trust the truth shall try. (*CW*, 32)

In an instant that must have given her some satisfaction, Elizabeth seizes the chance to confront Edward Seymour's observations about her self-presenta-

---

[10] On other charges of fornication against the Queen during her reign, see Carole Levin, "All the Queen's Children," in this volume, 83–103.

tion—the self-possession that she, once again, bolsters by invoking the truth of the matter and the trueness of her own words and intentions.

In all four of these letters, Elizabeth employs a carefully modulated tone to defend her integrity, but at points she heightens this tone as she presents herself as a young woman who must defend herself single-handedly, without other support. In evoking this sense of isolation, however, she balances vulnerability with strength, and while acting alone, she would not act only for herself. Even in these dire circumstances, Elizabeth refused to abandon Katherine Ashley. In her final letter to Somerset, Elizabeth begs for mercy for her governess: "For Katherine Ashley, that it would please your grace and the rest of the Council to be good unto her." Elizabeth magnanimously proceeds to credit Ashley with her good upbringing—a greater achievement than that of Elizabeth's own parents, who had simply brought her into the world. This appeal for her governess brings underlying questions to the fore: What had Ashley (and Parry) permitted? arranged? agreed to on Elizabeth's behalf? In everybody's eyes, it seems, including our own, these two personal servants failed to sufficiently protect and respect their eminent young charge. If Katherine Parr had a moral for Ashley in her story of Elizabeth in Seymour's arms, Elizabeth had a moral for herself in all these proceedings. She had been cast into terrible jeopardy; she would now take charge of herself. It is the rapid appearance of such defining qualities of character, intelligence, and breadth of understanding that, taken together, persuade me that the Thomas Seymour crisis became the catalyst for Elizabeth's unbeholden, self-sufficient, self-determined identity as a "Maiden Queen."

Sir Robert Tyrwhit provides further confirmation of Elizabeth's maturing self-possession in his account of her interrogation, which the princess was compelled to face alone. As already noted, Thomas Seymour was arrested and sent to the Tower of London on 17 January 1549, on suspicion of treasonous dealings. Four days later, Ashley and Parry were arrested at Hatfield House, where Elizabeth was staying; they too were taken to the Tower. This left Elizabeth at Hatfield, without any adult guardian or adviser, to face repeated questioning by Tyrwhit, the Privy Council's designated agent. Tyrwhit's three letters of January and February 1549 provide a particularly detailed record because these letters served as progress reports to the Lord Protector. At first, Tyrwhit feels confident of getting incriminating evidence from Elizabeth—"I do see it in her face that she is guilty . . . concerning my lord admiral," he says—but by degrees she drains his confidence away. The clearest indication of the self-possession that Elizabeth is gaining as she copes with the uncertainties of her situation comes from her tears. In his first letter to the Lord Protector, Tyrwhit reports that Elizabeth "was marvelous abashed, and did weep very tenderly a long time" at the news that Ashley and Parry had been sent to the Tower, and he reports that she asked whether they had said anything taken to be incriminating. By the third letter, Tyrwhit is reporting that Elizabeth has so resisted the Protector's and the Council's instructions to accept Lady Tyrwhit as her governess "that she wept all that night and lowered all the next day." Tyrwhit then explicitly attests Elizabeth's display of self-possession with regard to who would rule her: "In the end of the matter, I perceived that she was very loath to have a governor; and, to avoid the same, she said the world would note her to be a great offender, having so hastily a governor appointed her."

Once the process leading to Seymour's trial was set in motion, its conclusion followed swiftly. On 24 February 1549, the boy-king Edward was persuaded by his uncle Edward, the Lord Protector, to authorize proceedings for high treason against his other uncle, Thomas. On 5 March, a bill of attainder against Thomas Seymour received the boy-king's assent. Fifteen days later, on 20 March, Thomas Seymour was beheaded on Tower Green.

The deadly suddenness of Thomas Seymour's fate taught Elizabeth a political lesson that she would not have to relearn. Five years later, in March 1554, Elizabeth again found herself in political danger as the potential Protestant heir to the throne. This time, she faced the prospect of imprisonment in the Tower. She wrote an urgent letter to her half-sister, the Catholic Queen Mary, begging to be allowed to see her in person and try to resolve the suspicion and mistrust that lay between them before any further action was taken. In pleading for a personal audience and a chance to show her true loyalty to her sister, Elizabeth invokes the Edward Seymour–Thomas Seymour precedent and its terrible conclusion as an outcome for both of them to avoid.

> I have heard in my time of many cast away for want of coming to the presence of their prince, and in late days I heard my lord of Somerset [Edward Seymour] say that if his brother had been suffered to speak with him, he [Thomas Seymour] had never suffered. But the persuasions to him were made so great that he was brought in belief that he could not live safely if the admiral lived, and that made him give his consent to his death. Though these persons are not to be compared to your majesty, yet I pray God as evil persuasions persuade not one sister against the other, and all for that they have heard false report, and not hearken to the truth known. Therefore once again, with humbleness of my heart because I am not suffered to bow the knees of my body, I humbly crave to speak with your highness. (*CW*, 41–42)

Elizabeth's first expressions of aversion to marriage were recorded during the reign of Queen Mary. She angered her half-sister by refusing to consider a political match with Emmanuel Philibert, duke of Savoy, in November 1556, explaining that "the afflictions suffered by her were such that they had . . . ridded her of any wish for a husband."[11] In April 1558, when King Erik of Sweden declared his desire to marry Elizabeth, she told Sir Thomas Pope, her guard-

---

[11] *Calendar of State Papers, Venetian*, 6.2:887, cited in Anne Somerset, *Elizabeth I* (New York: St. Martin's Press, 1991), 53.

ian appointed by Queen Mary, that she intended to stay true to a decision to remain unmarried—a decision that she had made "in my brother King Edward's time."[12] In my judgment, the Thomas Seymour affair is the likeliest incentive behind any such decision taken in Edward's reign.

With somewhat greater distance of time and perspective, negative and defensive considerations would recede from the terms of reference in which Elizabeth articulated her identity as England's "Virgin Queen." Her self-expression, particularly her prayers, recurrently voiced her political, religious, and personal sense of herself as God's handmaid—as she put it in her first speech before Parliament, 10 February 1559: "From my years of understanding, sith I first had consideration of myself to be born a servitor of almighty God, I happily chose this kind of life in which I yet live, which I assure you for mine own part hath hitherto best contented myself and I trust hath been most acceptable to God" (*CW*, 56). In such a confirmed state of self-knowledge and self-dedication, Elizabeth was able to accept and be pleased with the gift of a posthumous portrait of Thomas Seymour presented to her by John Harington, who had been a loyal servant to her from the years before she came to the throne. The portrait can be seen in the National Portrait Gallery, London, inscribed with an exonerating set of verses that I have transcribed as an epilogue, of sorts, to the present discussion:

> Of person rare, strong limbs and manly shape;
> Of nature framed to serve on seas and land;
> Of friendship firm, in good state and ill hap;
> In peace, heed, and in war, skill, greets bold band.
> On horse, on foot, in peril or in play,
> None could excel, though many did assay.
> A subject true to King, and servant great;
> Friend to God's truth; enemy to Rome's deceit;
> Sumptuous abroad, for honor of the land;
> Temperate at home, yet kept great state with stay,
> And gave more mouths more meat
> Than some advanced on higher steps to stand.
> Yet against native reason and just laws,
> His blood was spilt, justless, without just cause.[13]

---

[12] *Calendar of State Papers Domestic, Edward VI*, 101: "April 26, 1558. Answer of the Lady Elizabeth, given at Hatfield, to Sir Thomas Pope, as to the proposal of marriage made by the King Elect of Sweden" (Imperfect MSS, James I); BL, Harleian 4447; Cotton Vitellius xii.16.8: "Letter from Sir Thomas Pope to Queen Mary on Elizabeth's wanting to remain unmarried as she did in Prince / King Edward's days."

[13] According to Sir John Harington (1561–1612), his father gave the queen a picture of the Lord Admiral "with a pretty verse written on it, and it now hangs in the gallery at Somerset House." This portrait of Thomas Seymour, Lord Admiral, Baron Sudeley, by

Elizabeth could appropriately be presented with a portrait of Thomas Seymour as a memento. She could also accept it appropriately. The experience of the danger in which he had involved her was pivotal in her development of a sense of who she was and how she must conduct herself to survive and flourish. Though only fifteen at the time, Elizabeth found and claimed the identity that would sustain her during her long reign as the Virgin Queen.

an unknown artist, is National Portrait Gallery 4571, and the "pretty verse" inscription reads as modernized by Janel Mueller.

The Two Virgin Queens:
Embodying Queenship in the Reigns of Mary I and Elizabeth I

Sarah L. Duncan

The name Virgin Queen has long been attached to Queen Elizabeth I; it has not been as widely acknowledged, however, that her older sister Mary I attempted to manipulate her own identity in a similar fashion. Historians have traditionally portrayed Mary as a woman who did not possess the political skills to turn the handicap of her sex into an asset.[1] Her reign, therefore, has been compared unfavorably with Elizabeth's, and her actions as a ruler are most often described as merely providing a negative example for her younger sister.

Because Mary has for the most part been depicted as having failed to develop a satisfactory persona as queen, the use of language by Mary and her supporters to control her image has not been examined with the same attention paid to Elizabeth's expert manipulation. It is possible, however, to discern certain similarities between the two queens, specifically by tracing the use of two related contemporary political theories to define their identity as regnant queens: the theory of the king's two bodies, and the corporeal concept of kingship. First, analyzing the language used by Mary and those speaking in her behalf during

---

[1] For example, A. F. Pollard, *The History of England from the Accession of Edward VI to the Death of Elizabeth (1547–1603)* (New York: Greenwood Press, 1969), 158, wrote of Mary's "limited political capacity," and G. R. Elton, *Reform and Reformation: England, 1509 – 1558* (Cambridge, MA: Harvard University Press, 1977), 376, echoed this view, describing her as "devoid of political skill." Mary's leading biographer, David Loades, *Mary Tudor: A Life* (Oxford: Basil Blackwell, 1989), 8, 327, has agreed that "Mary was a profoundly conventional woman" and "incapable of political manipulation." John Guy, *Tudor England* (Oxford: Oxford University Press, 1990), 227, has written that "she was politically self-deceived" and "seemed limited, conventional, and stubborn," while more recently, A. N. McLaren has asserted that "the failures of Mary's reign" reinforced the sixteenth-century view that "defined women as spiritually deficient and lacking the capacity for political virtue." See *Political Culture in the Reign of Elizabeth I: Queen and Commonwealth 1558–1585* (New York: Cambridge University Press, 1999), 46.

her marriage negotiations in late 1553 and early 1554 sheds light on the similarities between Mary's and Elizabeth's self-representation and their shared ability to use the accepted theory of the king's two bodies to strengthen their royal image.[2] Second, examining how each queen and her supporters, as well as her detractors, used the corporeal concept of monarchy either to augment the queen's power or to attempt to deny her royal authority demonstrates the means by which a queen's identity could be manipulated. Such examination also traces underlying fears about sixteenth-century gynecocracy. The creation of Elizabeth's image would blur gender divisions by portraying her as both male and female: as Elizabeth herself put it, "I know I have the body but of a weak and feeble woman, but I have the heart and stomach of a king."[3] The origin of this dual-gendered depiction of regnant queenship, however, developed during Mary's reign when she was represented as embodying both masculine and feminine qualities in order to depict her as a queen with kingly powers, thus providing a model for Elizabeth to follow when she inherited her sister's throne.[4]

"A queen, and by the same title a king also"

Just as it has been demonstrated that the theory of the king's two bodies was of particular value to Elizabeth and her councilors in her reign, the same idea proved to be one of the most useful tools available to Mary and those who spoke for her during the course of her marriage negotiations.[5] By the reign of Elizabeth I the medieval concept of the king's two bodies had developed into the idea that

---

[2] Although Elizabeth was more inclined to point out differences between herself and her older sister, clear similarities between their use of language can be cited. Mary Hill Cole traces a similar "gap between words and actions" that characterized Elizabeth's response to other family members: see Cole, "Maternal Memory," in this volume, 1–14. To delineate the numerous ways in which Elizabeth demonstrated an adverse stance to Mary's iconography is beyond the scope of this essay. I address some of these issues, however, in S. L. Duncan, "'Most godly heart fraight with al mercie': Queens' Mercy during the Reigns of Mary I and Elizabeth I," in *Queens and Power in Medieval and Early Modern England*, ed. Carole Levin and Robert Bucholz (Lincoln, NE: University of Nebraska Press, 2009), 31–50.

[3] Elizabeth I, *Collected Works*, ed. Leah S. Marcus, Janel Mueller, and Mary Beth Rose (Chicago: University of Chicago Press, 2000), 326.

[4] For similar revisionist treatments of the gendering of monarchy during Mary's reign, see Judith Richards, "Mary Tudor as 'Sole Queen'?: Gendering Tudor Monarchy," *Historical Journal* 40 (1997): 895–924, and Charles Beem, *The Lioness Roared: The Problems of Female Rule in English History* (New York: Palgrave Macmillan, 2006), 63–100.

[5] Carole Levin, *The Heart and Stomach of a King: Elizabeth I and the Politics of Sex and Power* (Philadelphia: University of Pennsylvania Press, 1994), 121–48; Marie Axton,

the King has in him two Bodies, Viz., a Body natural, and a Body politic. His body natural . . . is a Body mortal . . . . But his Body politic is a Body that cannot be seen or handled, consisting of Policy and Government, and constituted for the Direction of the People, and the Management of the Public Weal.[6]

Elizabeth herself referred to the concept very early in her reign, stating on 20 November 1558 in her first speech as queen: "I am but one body naturally considered, though by [God's] permission a body politic to govern."[7] The theory and its characteristic language, however, were certainly current in Mary's reign. During Wyatt's rebellion, for example, the earl of Arundel wrote to the earl of Shrewsbury: "God be thankyd the quenes highnes is in good helth of her body but syke in certeyn nawghty members of her commonwelth."[8] The queen's two bodies here included her natural body and that of the nation or commonwealth, her body politic. Clearly a monarch could incorporate and rule the "body politic" even if that ruler's natural body was female.

Mary certainly made use of the concept of the king's two bodies, although during her reign the theory was complicated to some extent with the introduction of gender. Sometimes Mary made reference to her body politic as female, for example, by speaking of being "married to her realm" and by referring to the commonwealth as her "husband."[9] At other times, her body politic was male, as when Mary or her subjects referred to her as king or prince.[10] Mary herself did so when she answered objections raised to a foreign alliance by a delegation led by Sir John Pollard, the Speaker of the House of Commons, on 16 November 1553. The queen also spoke of herself as "prince" in the speech she gave at the Guildhall in London in February 1554 during Wyatt's rebellion, requesting Londoners

---

The Queen's Two Bodies: Drama and the Elizabethan Succession (London: Royal Historical Society, 1977), 38–39.

[6] See Edmund Plowden, *Commentaries or Reports* (London: S. Brooks, 1816), 212a, quoted in Ernst H. Kantorowicz, *The King's Two Bodies: A Study in Medieval Political Theology* (Princeton: Princeton University Press, 1957), 7.

[7] *Elizabeth I: Collected Works*, 52.

[8] Talbot Papers, Ms. 3149 (London, Lambeth Palace Library), fol. 5r.

[9] State Papers, Domestic Series, Mary, and Philip and Mary (London: Public Record Office, Kew Gardens), SP11 2 /9; State Papers, Foreign Series, Mary, and Philip and Mary (London: Public Record Office, Kew Gardens), SP69 2/95.

[10] Leah S. Marcus has pointed out of the word "prince" that its "most basic sixteenth-century meaning was ruler, especially male ruler; it was also applied to the eldest son of a reigning monarch." See Marcus, "Shakespeare's Comic Heroines, Elizabeth I, and the Political Uses of Androgyny," in *Women in the Middle Ages and the Renaissance: Literary and Historical Perspectives*, ed. Mary Beth Rose (Syracuse, NY: Syracuse University Press, 1986), 135–53, esp. 139–40. Carole Levin also discusses the use of "prince" as gender-specific in Elizabeth's reign: see *Heart and Stomach*, 121–24.

to "stand fast with your lawfull prince."[11] In the aftermath of the rebellion, Princess Elizabeth famously referred to Mary's masculine status after the queen had ordered her to be taken to the Tower. Elizabeth wrote: "If any ever did try this olde saying that a kinges worde was more than a nother mans othe, I most humbly beseche your Majesty to verifie it in me."[12] Similarly, after his arrest for his part in the conspiracy against the Anglo-Spanish marriage, the duke of Suffolk protested that he meant no harm to the queen herself, saying: "she is the mercifullest prince, as I have truly founde her, that ever reigned, in whose defence I am, and will be, readie to die at her foote."[13]

While Mary would not refer to herself as king or prince with the same frequency that Elizabeth later did, she, too, understood that her role as ruler had a masculine aspect to it and that she played a masculine part as sovereign. Early in Mary's reign, Grace, countess of Shrewsbury, wrote to her husband, the earl of Shrewsbury, to inform him that when she had met with the queen, "her hyghnes were so moche my good ladye that comaundid me whatsoever I laked [lacked] I shuld be bold to come to her grace, for she wold be my husbande unto your Lord retorne agen."[14] This statement was not supposed to be taken literally, nor does it suggest that Mary wanted a female partner. It is enlightening, however, in terms of Mary's comprehension of her status. She understood that she played a patriarchal role in her body politic even though she was a woman. To the countess of Shrewsbury, Mary was both "my good ladye" and "my husbande." Mary could play the part of "husband" to her subjects, even though she was "wife" to the realm, thus incorporating both masculine and feminine elements of the two bodies within her person. She understood, as Elizabeth later would during her reign, that as sovereign she played an androgynous role: in her sovereignty she was both masculine and feminine, king and queen.

Mary's understanding of the duality of her role, the knowledge that her kingly authority was incorporated into her natural female body, was particularly useful to her during the course of her marriage negotiations in 1553 and 1554. Like Elizabeth, Mary demonstrated an ability to assert both her kingly nature and her femininity in her use of language; in Mary's case this enabled her to take

---

[11] Raphael Holinshed, *Holinshed's Chronicles of England, Scotland, and Ireland*, ed. Henry Ellis, 6 vols. (London: J. Johnson, 1807–1808), 4:16–17.

[12] SP 11 4/2.

[13] *Chronicle of Queen Jane and of Two Years of Queen Mary*, ed. John Gough Nichols (London: Camden Society, 1849), 123.

[14] Talbot Ms. 3206, P223r. Elizabeth would later make a very similar remark about Philip II's widowed sister Juana, saying "how well so young a widow and a maiden would get on together, and what a pleasant life they could lead. She (the Queen) being the elder would be the husband, and her Highness the wife." See *Calendar of Letters and State Papers Relating to English Affairs, Preserved Principally in the Archive of Simancas*, ed. Martin A. S. Hume, 4 vols. (London: Her Majesty's Stationery Office, 1892–1899), 1:364.

charge of her marriage negotiations. When Mary confronted the speaker of Parliament after he had advised her to avoid a foreign marriage, she emphasized her kingly dignity, saying,

> Parliament was not accustomed to use such language to the kings of England, nor was it suitable or respectful that it should do so. Histories and chronicles would show that such words had never been spoken, for even when the kings had been in childhood they had been given liberty in questions of marriage, wherefore they ought always to enjoy the same.[15]

Mary represented herself to the Speaker as king in order to make it clear that, even though she was a female ruler, she now enjoyed the same prerogatives that previous kings had, and that like them she intended to exercise her free will on the subject of marriage. She considered the choice of a marriage partner to be a kingly prerogative. Elizabeth may have profited from Mary's insistence on this point. Although she conveyed a similar sentiment during her own reign in response to requests that she marry, she did not need to be as forceful: "But in this I must commend you, that you have not appointed me an husband. For that were unworthy the majesty of an absolute princess, and the discretion of you that are born my subjects."[16]

If Mary convincingly demonstrated her kingly will when addressing her subjects, she was equally adept at playing on her femininity in her dealings with Holy Roman Emperor Charles V's ambassador, Simon Renard. When Renard broached the subject of marriage in mid-August 1553, Mary admitted the necessity of marriage for the good of her realm. She told the ambassador to ask her council about their own intentions, since "it did not behove a lady to be the first to make overtures of marriage."[17] Throughout the marriage negotiations, she continually declared her willingness to marry the emperor's son Prince Philip of Spain while blaming her council for producing obstacles. By doing so, she was able to uphold the pretense that, as a lady, she was not fit to conduct negotiations while persuading the emperor to make numerous concessions. Once Charles V's

---

[15] *Calendar of Letters, Despatches and State Papers Relating to the Negotiations between England and Spain*, ed. Royall Tyler, 13 vols. (London: His Majesty's Stationery Office, 1916–1954), 11:363–64 [hereafter *CSP Spanish*].

[16] *Elizabeth I: Collected Works*, 59. Another version of this speech recorded Elizabeth as saying: "For the other part, the manner of your petition I do well like of and take in good part, because that it is simple and containeth no limitation of place or person. If it had been otherwise, I must needs have misliked it very much and thought it in you a very great presumption, being unfitting and altogether unmeet for you to require them that may command, or those to appoint whose parts are to desire, or such to bind and limit whose duties are to obey, or to take upon you to draw my love to your liking or frame my will to your fantasies" (*Collected Works*, 57).

[17] *CSP Spanish*, 11:171, 213.

ambassadors had arrived for the conclusion of the process, Mary asserted once again that "it was not seemly for a woman to speak of or negotiate her own marriage, so she would not meddle with it, but would depute her councilors to treat with us, and see that her kingdom's rights were respected."[18]

Mary used her femininity not only in dealing with Charles V's ambassadors but also in sidestepping the objections of her own council and others who opposed a foreign alliance. At times, she used accepted beliefs about the inherent physical weakness of women as a valuable tool. When in mid-November the speaker, John Pollard, and others petitioned her to take a subject as her spouse, she told them that "to force her to take a husband who would not be to her liking would be to cause her death, for if she married against her will she would not live three months, and would have no children, wherefore the Speaker would be defeating his own ends."[19] Later, to Renard, she admitted feigning illness in the days before she accepted Prince Philip as her prospective husband: "She had pretended to be ill for the last two days, but her illness was really the travail that this decision had cost her."[20] It also bought her time to deliberate her decision without any interference.[21]

Although Mary was willing to capitalize on contemporary views of female weakness, she, and her spokesmen, also promoted her status as an exceptional woman because she was an anointed queen—a claim Elizabeth later would make as well.[22] When King Henry II of France objected to the marriage on the grounds that it would provoke war between England and France, he used the familiar idea that Mary's position would be inferior to that of her husband. Once married, the queen would not abide by England's peace treaty with France because Prince Philip, son of Henry's chief enemy, would convince her otherwise. In response, Mary's ambassador Dr. Wotton pointed out that, as a queen, Mary was more than an ordinary woman. Wotton allowed that "wyves will be muche perswadid by their husbands, yet I take that to have more place yn pryvate personnes, than yn this cace which we ar yn." Mary was not like other women: she was a queen in a public position, and as such, she "is wyse of her self, so is she content to haue wyse counsell about her, so that neyther she her self, nor yet

---

[18] *CSP Spanish*, 12:11.

[19] *CSP Spanish*, 11:364.

[20] *CSP Spanish*, 11:328.

[21] Magdalena S. Sanchez has explored some of the ways in which both men and women used illness and melancholy "as a political ploy and as a negotiating tool." See *The Empress, the Queen, and the Nun: Women and Power at the Court of Philip III of Spain* (Baltimore: Johns Hopkins University Press, 1998), 157–58, 171.

[22] Elizabeth in 1566 claimed that "though I be a woman, yet I have as good a courage answerable to my place as ever my father had. I am your anointed queen." See *Elizabeth I: Collected Works*, 97.

her counsell can so lightlye by wordes be deceived."[23] Mary herself assured the French ambassador, Noailles, that she would remain true to the peace treaty with France and that neither "husband father kynsman nor any other person a lyve shuld (God assisting hir with his grace) cause her to change."[24]

Mary fashioned her image as that of an extraordinary woman to persuade the French that her powers would remain the same after her marriage and that "the government of the realm shall always remayn fully in hir highnes and nott in the prince."[25] In order to convince her own countrymen that the match was beneficial, however, she refashioned herself as being no more than ordinary. In January 1554, after the conclusion of the marriage treaty, and coinciding with the start of Wyatt's uprising in Kent, Mary sent copies of the marriage articles to be published in the counties. This would demonstrate the strength of her position in the marriage contract while proving the falseness of Wyatt's claims. She stated that the purpose of the rebels was "to take from us that liberty which is not denied to the meanest woman in the choice of husband."[26] Mary deserved the same right as any other woman in her kingdom to choose a marriage partner.[27] At the same time, her statement implied her regal stature as well: if the "meanest woman" could choose her husband, shouldn't a queen be able to do so as well? In constructing herself as both ordinary woman and extraordinary queen, Mary played both sides of the same coin.[28]

Mary combined these two versions of womanhood at other times during the negotiations, catering to traditional beliefs about female roles while at the same time highlighting her sovereign status. From the beginning of her reign, she entered into numerous discussions of marriage by protesting that marriage was against her will. She would marry out of duty, "as my progenitors have done before."[29] Elizabeth would later echo this sentiment in 1563, admitting she would for duty's sake forgo a chaste life: "For though I can think it best for a private woman, yet do I strive with myself to think it not meet for a prince."[30] Both Mary and Elizabeth made it clear that their willingness to wed rested on their

---

[23] SP 69 2/110.

[24] SP 69 2/109.

[25] SP 69 2/95.

[26] SP 11 2/8.

[27] Although non-royal women, particularly elite women, often were forced to marry husbands not of their own choosing, Lawrence Stone has argued that "Among the propertyless at the bottom of society, however, children even in the sixteenth century were probably very much freer to choose a spouse than their superiors." See *The Family, Sex and Marriage in England 1500–1800*, abr. ed. (New York: Harper, 1979), 135.

[28] Mary's language upholding her right to a husband of her own choice was echoed in John Christopherson's publication *An Exhortation to All Menne to Take Hede and Beware of Rebellion* (London, 1554; *STC* 5207), L3r.

[29] Holinshed, *Chronicles*, 4:16.

[30] *Elizabeth I: Collected Works*, 79.

sovereign status alone: Mary by asserting her commonality with her progenitors, the former kings of England, and Elizabeth by emphasizing that the unwedded state was not appropriate for a prince such as she. Mary would also attest that had she remained "a private individual she would never have desired it, but preferred to end her days in chastity."[31] Elizabeth would state in 1576 that "if I were a milkmaid with a pail on mine arm . . . I would not forsake that single state to match myself with the greatest monarch."[32] Mary's (and later Elizabeth's) statement acknowledged not only her special status as a ruling queen rather than a private individual but also her female nature. The queen showed her conformity to accepted images of chaste, virginal, single women.[33]

Mary elaborated on her image as a traditional woman by telling Renard that "she had never felt that which was called love, nor harboured thoughts of voluptuousness, and had never considered marriage until God had been pleased to raise her to the throne."[34] She echoed this in her speech to her London subjects during Wyatt's rebellion, protesting that "I am not so desirous of wedding, neither so precise or wedded to my will, that either for mine owne pleasure I will choose where I lust . . . I have hitherto lived a virgine."[35] While consistent with traditional ideals, Mary's representation of herself as virginal and chaste may have been designed to trigger comparison in the minds of her audience to her namesake, the Virgin Mary. The identification of Queen Mary with Mary, mother of God, was not new: similar connections had been made from the time she was young.[36] At her accession, William Forrest's broadside ballad compared her to the Virgin Mary.[37] In addition, Mary's coronation procession had portrayed her as a virgin queen, and at the end of August 1554 the emperor's ambassadors reported that, "Among the good and the faithful," sayings were circulating that "God will take pity on His people and Church in England, through the instrument of a virgin called Mary, whom He has raised to the throne."[38] Mary's identification of herself as a chaste virgin therefore capitalized on that recognition, promoting her status once again from ordinary, to extraordinary,

---

[31] *CSP Spanish*, 11:132.

[32] *Elizabeth I: Collected Works*, 170.

[33] Constance Jordan, *Renaissance Feminism: Literary Texts and Political Models* (Ithaca: Cornell University Press, 1990), 29.

[34] *CSP Spanish*, 11:213.

[35] Holinshed, *Chronicles*, 4:16–17.

[36] John N. King, *Tudor Royal Iconography: Literature and Art in an Age of Religious Crisis* (Princeton: Princeton University Press, 1989), 197–99.

[37] *Harleian Miscellany*, ed. T. Park and W. Oldys, 12 vols. (London: White & Cochrane, 1808–1813), 10:253–54.

[38] *CSP Spanish* 11:187.

and perhaps even saintly. She was not just a virgin, but a Virgin Queen, the first of that name.[39]

Mary's determination that she would marry "for the good of the country, though it was contrary to her inclination," also reminded listeners of her sovereign status. She would marry against her desire, only for the good of her realm: if not for the responsibilities of her position she would gladly remain single. This protestation on Mary's part was particularly effective when used in the presence of Charles V's ambassadors. The implication was that the queen would forsake her virginal status only if the marriage contract were favorable to her and her commonwealth. As a reluctant bride she would have to be wooed by concessions and full recognition of her own and her kingdom's status and independence. Again, Elizabeth would later determine that this sentiment was one worth repeating when she acknowledged in her first speech to Parliament in 1559 that if she did marry, she would "never in that matter conclude anything that shall be prejudicial to the realm."[40]

Although Mary portrayed herself as a Virgin Queen in some of her statements, she also made it clear on numerous occasions that she considered herself to be already married, in the sense of having wed her realm: "I am already married to this Common Weal and the faithful members of the same."[41] This was yet another statement that Elizabeth would later adopt as her own, although she would use it, rather, to suggest that she was not in need of another marriage: "I am already bound unto an husband, which is the kingdom of England, and that may suffice you."[42] Mary did not, however, see her symbolic marriage

---

[39] Cardinal Pole also reminded her of the connection, writing to the queen that "if ever woman had merciful grace for which to magnify and praise God in the words of his blessed mother, whose name the Queen bears . . .the Queen herself has more cause than anyone to sing." See *Calendar of State Papers and Manuscripts, Relating to English Affairs, Existing in the Archives and Collections of Venice (CSP Venice)*, ed. Rawdon Brown and G. Cavendish Bentinck, 38 vols. in 40 (London: HMSO, 1873–1890), 5:385. He later wrote: "Had the Lord wished it so to be, He would have established the reign of Northumberland. But such a government was not pleasing in His sight, and His hand destroyed it without the act of any man, and gave the crown into the hands of a virgin, because she was religious, pious, beloved of the Lord, and had placed all her trust in him" (*CSP Spanish*, 11:420).

[40] *Elizabeth I: Collected Works*, 57.

[41] From Mary's speech at the Guildhall in London during Wyatt's rebellion, quoted in John Proctor, *The Historie of Wyates Rebellion, with the Ordre and Maner of Resisting the Same* (London: Robert Caly, 1555; *STC* 20407), sig. 54r.

[42] *Elizabeth I: Collected Works*, 59. Elizabeth echoed this statement to the Scottish ambassador, William Maitland, laird of Lethington, in 1561 when she said: "So many doubts of marriage in all hands that I stand awe myself to enter in marriage, fearing the controversy. Once I am married already to the realm of England when I was crowned with this ring, which I bear continually in token thereof" (65).

as precluding her body natural from taking another spouse in order to provide her realm with a son and heir. The acknowledgment of her duty to wed someone who would benefit the realm usually "put her in mind of her coronation oath, as a reminder of which she wore a ring on her finger."[43] Mary made it clear to those listening—her people, councilors, ambassadors, and others—that she had a prior contract with her kingdom and that the welfare of her people would take precedence over that of her new husband. She spoke of the marriage to her realm as being the first, and of the commonwealth as being her first husband, saying "thatt God would never suffer hir to forgett hir other promise made to hur fyrst husband on the day of hir coronation."[44] Contracting a second marriage "shoulde greatly advaunce this realme"[45] but would in no way negatively affect the first one, for as Mary attested in her own words: "we have always preferred the benefit of our commonwealth before any cause of our own, and, being first married to our realm, do not mean by our second marriage to prejudice the commonwealth."[46]

Repeatedly bringing up the subject of her first marriage afforded Mary the opportunity to reaffirm her own sovereign status: she might be in negotiations to become a wife, but, as queen, she had already wed a kingdom. It also conveyed the message that while she might be cast in the role of subservient wife to her husband, Philip, a prior commitment existed, limiting her new husband's power over her. Mary put this bluntly to Renard, saying that

> She would wholly love and obey him to whom she had given herself, following the divine commandment, and would do nothing against his will; but if he wished to encroach in the government of the kingdom she would be unable to permit it, nor if he attempted to fill posts and offices with strangers, for the country itself would never stand such interference.[47]

Just as Elizabeth would prove adept at fashioning her image as queen during her long reign, Mary manipulated and refashioned her image a number of times during the months-long negotiations: as king and queen, prince and princess, husband and wife, Virgin Queen and ordinary woman. She changed her role to suit her audience: to her councilors, she depicted herself as king in order to convince them of her right to choose her husband; to appeal to her people's sense of justice, she chose to compare herself to an ordinary woman. She could also represent herself in ways that played on more than one of these images. She did so when she

---

[43] *CSP Spanish*, 11:297.

[44] SP 69 2/95.

[45] Proctor, *The Historie of Wyates Rebellion*, sig. 53v.

[46] SP 11 2/9; *Tudor Royal Proclamations*, ed. P. L. Hughes and J. F. Larkin, 3 vols. (New Haven: Yale University Press, 1964–1969), 2:28.

[47] *CSP Spanish*, 11:289.

portrayed herself to Speaker, John Pollard, and others first as a powerful male, a "king," then as a weak and mortal female. In her Guildhall speech, she combined all of these roles. First, she addressed her "loving subjects, what I am, you right well know. I am your queene, to whom at my coronation . . . ye promised your allegiance and obedience unto me." She reminded them that she was the "right and true inheritor to the crowne of this realme of England" and that this status had been confirmed by acts of parliament. Not only was she their queen but also she was truly Henry VIII's daughter: "And to him alwaies ye shewed your selves most faithfull and loving subiects, and him obeied and served as our liege lord and king," and she doubted not "but you will shew your selves likewise to me his daughter." She was virginal, yet married to the realm, with the ring to prove it. In addition, she was "prince and governor," "sovereigne ladie and queen," and even mother: "I cannot tell how naturallie a mother loveth her children, for I was never the mother of anie; but certeinlie a prince and governor may as naturallie and as earnestlie love subjects, as the mother dooth hir child."[48] Elizabeth, of course, would also present herself as the mother of the English populace during her reign,[49] saying in 1559, "And reproach me no more . . . that I have no children: for every one of you, and as many as are English are my children and kinsfolks," and again in 1563, "I assure you all that though after my death you may have many stepdames, yet shall you never have any a more mother than I mean to be to you all."[50] Both queens' statements emphasized that, although they were virgins and childless, they would prove to be true mothers to their people. They drew attention once again to their sovereign status: Mary's statement, overtly, by referencing herself as prince and governor, and Elizabeth, more subtly, by alluding to the rulers, or step-dames, who would rule England after her death.

Queen and prince, daughter, wife, and virgin-mother: like Elizabeth, Mary had the ability to present herself in different ways to different people (or in all ways to her subjects). Continually insisting on her "kingly" or royal dignity enabled Mary to draw strength from her supposed feminine weakness. Mary's manipulation of her royal image allowed her to craft what many would have considered impossible: a marriage contract favorable to England. The articles of the contract severely limited Philip's power as king-consort and prevented him from

---

[48] Holinshed, *Chronicles*, 4:16. The report given to Cardinal Pole also referred to Mary's self-presentation as mother: "[O]n the day of her coronation, when the ring which she wears was put on her finger, she purposed accepting the realm of England and its entire population as her children; and thenceforth she never intended to do anything but what was for their benefit" (*CSP Venice*, 5:459).
[49] See Carole Levin, "All the Queen's Children" in this volume, 85–103.
[50] *Elizabeth I: Collected Works*, 59, 72.

appointing foreigners to offices in England, changing the laws or customs of the country, or removing the queen from the kingdom unless she permitted it.[51]

Mary's ability to fashion and refashion her image is a skill more often ascribed to Elizabeth; it is clear, however, that Mary was the first to demonstrate this proficiency. Although difficult to prove, the similarities in their language suggest that Mary's manipulation of her image provided an example for Elizabeth to follow when she became queen.[52] In addition, in her marriage negotiations Mary's choice of language suggested a possible path for Elizabeth to follow if and when she chose to marry. At the beginning of Mary's reign, few believed that a ruling queen could retain power after her marriage. At her funeral in 1558, however, in spite of her marriage, Bishop White of Winchester defined the first Virgin Queen as having been "a queen, and by the same title a king also."[53] Similarly, John Aylmer could write in his *Harborowe for Faithfull and Trew Subiectes* (1559),

> Say you, God hath apoynted her to be subject to her husband . . . therfore she maye not be the heade. I graunte that, so farre as perteineth to the bandes of mariage, and the office of a wife, she muste be a subiecte: but as a Magistrate she maye be her husbands head . . .Whie may not the woman be the husbandes inferiour in matters of wedlock, and his head in the guiding of the commonwealth.[54]

Moreover, the outcome of Mary's marriage negotiations—a marriage contract that upheld Mary's autonomy and power as queen while strictly limiting the constitutional role her husband could play—would also provide a working model for Elizabeth. During the marriage negotiations in the mid-1560s between the queen and Archduke Charles of Austria, Elizabeth insisted that, if she were to agree to the match, "all the Articles would have to remain exactly as they had been agreed upon and attested between King Philip and Queen Mary."[55] Whether Elizabeth

---

[51] SP11 1/20; *Statutes of the Realm*, ed. Alexander Luders et al., 9 vols. (London: Eyre & Strahan, 1810–1822), 4.1:222–26.

[52] Certainly there were occasions when Elizabeth was present to witness the performance of Mary's iconography, such as Mary's first entry into London and her coronation; Elizabeth also spent some time at the royal court over the course of Mary's reign.

[53] John Strype, *Ecclesiastical Memorials, relating chiefly to religion . . . under King Henry VIII, Edward VI and Queen Mary I*, 6 vols. in 3 (Oxford: Clarendon Press, 1822), 3.2:546.

[54] John Aylmer, *An Harborowe for Faithfull and Trewe Subiectes, agaynst the Late Blowne Blaste, Concerninge the Government of Wemen* (London: John Day, 1559), C4v.

[55] Victor von Klarwill, ed., *Queen Elizabeth and Some Foreigners: Being a Series of Hitherto Unpublished Letters from the Archives of the Habsburg Family*, trans. T. H. Nash (London: John Lane, 1928), 250; Susan Doran, "Religion and Politics at the Court of Elizabeth I: The Habsburg Marriage Negotiations of 1559–1567," *English Historical Review* 104 (1989): 908–26, esp. 915.

considered this proposal seriously or not, it is clear that she would not contemplate marriage unless she could obtain a contract as favorable to her as Mary's had been. She would be her husband's head rather than his subject, just as the Anglo-Spanish marriage contract had defined Mary as Philip's head.

II
"Mooste lawfull heade and governesse"

During their respective reigns Mary I and Elizabeth I were either identified by their supporters, or identified themselves, as the head of the body politic in spite of the fact that they were ruling queens rather than kings. The corporeal concept of monarchy, like the related theory of the king's two bodies, was an important aspect of early modern political theory. This comparison of the kingdom with the human body — the people of the realm making up the body of the *corpus mysticum*, with the ruler as its head — was a widely understood metaphor in sixteenth-century England.[56] In 1533, Henry VIII had declared that the realm of England was an empire "governed by one supreme head and king, and having the dignity and royal estate of the imperial crown of the same, unto whom a body politic, compact of all sorts and degrees of people ... be bounden."[57] The idea of the ruler as head of the body politic was, however, more complicated for Mary and Elizabeth than for their male predecessors: contemporaries argued that a female head of the body politic left that body weakened and vulnerable to attack. In addition, the choice of a foreign spouse by either queen could also prove to be perilous to the *corpus mysticum*. Mary, Elizabeth, and their supporters, therefore, attempted to counteract those fears by depicting each queen at various times and ways as both masculine defender and feminine protector of the body politic.

The corporeal theory of monarchy could be a helpful concept for a female sovereign. During Mary's reign, John Christopherson in *An exhortation to all menne to take hede and beware of rebellion* (1555) identified Mary as Englishmen's "mooste lawfull heade and gouernesse" and characterized any man that rebelled against her as "an vnkynde subiecte ... that travayleth to destroye the prince." He warned that

> lyke as in a mans body, yf the fote shuld fight with the hand, the heade with the necke, the backe with the belye, and euery part with other, the bodye shuld vtterly perishe, so a contrye, where the inhabitants make warre one against another, & one seketh to destroye another, must nedes come to vtter confusion.[58]

---

[56] Kantorowicz, *The King's Two Bodies*, 218–30.
[57] *Statutes of the Realm*, 3:427f, quoted in Kantorowicz, *The King's Two Bodies*, 228.
[58] Christopherson, *Exhortation*, L2v, Dd3v.

Christopherson sought to bolster Mary's authority as queen by invoking the corporeal concept of monarchy, with Mary, in spite of her sex, as head of the body politic. During Elizabeth's reign, when Parliament demanded in 1566 that Elizabeth name an heir, she (famously) asserted her authority by responding, "A strange thing that the foot should direct the head in so weighty a cause." Continuing, she reassured Parliament members that "At this present, [your petition] is not convenient.... But as soon as there may be a convenient time ... I will deal therein for your safety and offer it unto you as your prince and head, without request. For it is monstrous that the feet should direct the head."[59] Elizabeth's sharp reminder that, as queen, she was the head of the body politic reinforced her status as monarch and communicated her intention that she alone would decide when to name an heir.

The corporeal concept of monarchy, however, could also prove to be problematic for a queen. According to Aristotelian and Galenic theory, commonly held throughout the sixteenth century, the head, the seat of reason, was associated with the masculine, while the feminine was situated lower in the body, the site of sinfulness and passion.[60] As the head of the mystical body, a woman ruler would be undone by her own paradoxical nature: ruled by her sexuality and insatiable desire rather than by reason, she challenged traditional hierarchies of power and gender and endangered the realm. A female sovereign thus threatened the political and social order, and her reign was more likely than that of a king to result in tyrannical rule. Either her lust for power would lead to disorder, leaving the kingdom vulnerable to conquest, or her lust for men would allow a superior male power to take control of the realm through marriage.

The perceived threats to the mystical body should a woman become the head were expressed by John Ponet, the author of *A Shorte Treatise of Politike Power*, in 1556, when he described a number of "monstrous marvailes on the earthe" signifying the "great wrathe and indignacion of God." These included the birth of a child in Oxford "with two heades and two partes of two evil shaped bodyes ioyned in one" and a child born at Coventry "without armes or legges."[61] According to Ponet, these "monstrous" births reflected the reality of what had befallen

---

[59] *Elizabeth I: Collected Works*, 96–98. All of this derives, of course, from 1 Corinthians 12:12–26.

[60] Merry E. Wiesner, *Women and Gender in Early Modern Europe*, 2nd ed. (New York: Cambridge University Press, 2000), 32. According to Wiesner, women were considered more disorderly than men "because they were unreasonable, ruled by their physical body rather than their rational capacity, their lower parts rather than upper" (307). For a discussion of the corporeal concept of monarchy during the reign of Isabel of Castile, see also Barbara F. Weissberger, *Isabel Rules: Constructing Queenship, Wielding Power* (Minneapolis: University of Minnesota Press, 2004), chap. 4, "The Neo-Gothic Theory and the Queen's Body," esp. 96–103.

[61] John Ponet, *A Shorte Treatise of Politike Power* (London, 1556; *STC* 20178), K3v.

England's body politic as a result of one of (what John Knox would later call) the "monstruous regiment of women" becoming the sovereign head of England. Regarding the Oxford child, Ponet wonders, "what did it betoken, but that our one swete head, king Edwarde should be taken away . . . and that ther should be in his place two headdes, diverse governours, and a towarde division of the people." Regarding the Coventry baby, he speculates that it "must nedes signifie, that the natural body, that is, the people of Englande, shalbe helpeles, ready to be trodden under the fote of every creature, and non to releve or succour it."[62] The natural "swete head" of the body politic, the masculine head of state as personified by Edward VI, was replaced with two heads representing Mary and her husband Philip, an unnatural occurrence leading to disorder within the kingdom. Likewise, the body of the *corpus mysticum*, as a result of Mary's queenship and subsequent marriage to a foreign prince, was left weakened, susceptible, and open to attack or invasion: the body politic was thus feminized by its vulnerability, unable to retain its masculine imperviousness. By its very nature, according to this view, female sovereignty threatened the health of the masculine body politic.

Ponet's reference to Mary's spouse, Prince Philip of Spain, also illustrates the fears that sixteenth-century Englishmen harbored about a queen's choice of husband. During both Mary's and Elizabeth's reigns, authors warned that the marriage of their female head to a foreign prince would have a negative impact on the body of the realm, bringing disease or the danger of Catholicism. In *How Superior Powers oght to be obeyd of their subicts: and Wherin they may lawfully by Gods Worde be disobeyed and resisted* (1558), Christopher Goodman warned the inhabitants of England: "no more shal you without speedie repentance escape the Spaynishe plague of adoulterous Philippe whom the Lorde will make his sworde and maul to beate down your townes and Cities, and to devoure the people therof."[63] Similarly, in John Stubbs's pamphlet *The Discovery of a Gaping Gulf* (1579) opposing Elizabeth's marriage with Francis, duke of Alençon, Stubbs not only attributed the spread of syphilis to the French but also warned of the plagues that God would send to punish the English should the queen take Francis as her husband.[64] In one instance, for example, he wrote: "It is no small

---

[62] Ponet, *A Shorte Treatise*, K4v.

[63] Christopher Goodman, *How Superior Powers Oght to Be Obeyd of their Suiects* (Geneva, 1558; *STC* 12020), I4r. It was rumored that Philip engaged in licentious behavior after leaving England for the first time, although David Loades has argued that "Whatever the English pamphleteers may have thought, he was never given to promiscuity." See Loades, *Mary Tudor*, 260.

[64] *John Stubbs's Gaping Gulf with Letters and Other Relevant Documents*, ed. Lloyd E. Berry (Washington, DC: Folger Shakespeare Library, University Press of Virginia, 1968), 3, 6, 19. See also Donald Stump, "Abandoning the Old Testament: Shifting Paradigms for Elizabeth, 1578–82," in this volume, 281–99.

matter for a queen, the head of the land, to join in any manner with that person over whom the inevitable plagues of the most true Lord do hang."[65]

During Mary's reign, Protestant authors warned of other dangers to the English populace if she chose to marry Philip of Spain. One of Wyatt's fellow rebels in 1554 thus warned that if Mary's proposed marriage to Philip went forward, Englishmen would suffer under the rule of Spaniards: they would "spoyle us of our goodes and landes, ravishe our wyfes before our faces, and deflower our daughters in our presence."[66] The rape of Englishwomen can be read as a metaphor for the conquest of the kingdom and the resultant loss of power and property belonging to Englishmen. In his *Discoverie of Guiana* (1596), urging England's conquest of that country, Walter Raleigh would later draw the analogy between Guiana and a woman's body ripe for the violation of invasion: "Guiana is a Countrey that hath yet her Maydenhead, never sackt, turned, nor wrought . . . It hath never been entred by any armie of strength and never conquered and possessed by any Christian Prince."[67] During Mary's reign, likewise, those who opposed the Anglo-Spanish union portrayed the body politic of the realm of England as metaphorically penetrable by outside forces. Philip was thus figured as a conquering tyrant, perpetrating on behalf of his countrymen the rape of conquest—the symbolic rape of the political and economic rights of Englishmen. Mary herself, they believed, allowed this political emasculation to take place: in "abhorring the Englishe nation" she "hath ioyned her self to adulterous Philip . . . to whom she hathe, and dothe continually labor to betray the whole kingdome."[68] Similarly, in 1579 during Elizabeth's marriage negotiations with Alençon, Stubbs charged that the queen would sacrifice her very Englishness by wedding a foreigner. According to Jacqueline Vanhoutte, Stubbs "makes Elizabeth's membership in the nation contingent on her rejection of Alençon's proposal . . . . Her marriage to a foreigner threatens to dissociate the queen from England, a potential rupture that Stubbs . . . reads as a prostitution of England and an unmanning of the English."[69] In spite of the fact that Elizabeth had fashioned her image, in contrast to that of her sister Mary, as wholly English ("Was I not born in the realm? Were my parents borne in any foreign country?"), she,

---

[65] Stubbs, *Gaping Gulf*, 72.

[66] *Chronicle of Queen Jane and Queen Mary*, 38–39.

[67] Sir Walter Ralegh, *The Discovery of the Large, Rich, and Beautiful Empire of Guiana* (1596), ed. Sir Robert H. Schomburgk, Hakluyt Society, 1st ser., 3 (London: Hakluyt Society, 1848; repr. New York: Burt Franklin, 1970), 115. See also Wiesner, *Women and Gender*, 310; Hackett, *Virgin Mother*, 115–18.

[68] Goodman, *Superior Powers*, G2v.

[69] Jacqueline Vanhoutte, "Queen and Country?: Female Monarchs and Feminized Nations in Elizabethan Political Pamphlets," in *Elizabeth I: Always Her Own Free Woman*, ed. Carole Levin, Jo Eldridge Carney, and Debra Barrett-Graves (Aldershot: Ashgate, 2003), 7–19, esp. 15.

like Mary, could not escape fears that a female head made the body politic, and Englishmen, vulnerable.[70]

Although Protestant writers were willing to use these kinds of warnings to encourage their fellow countrymen to overthrow what was in their eyes a tyrannical government, most apparently used this reasoning only in the case of Catholic rulers like Mary and Philip. John Aylmer, in *An Harborowe for Faithfull and Trewe Subiectes*, would reverse the same argument to encourage Englishmen to support the next regnant queen of England, Elizabeth I. Aylmer, in contrast to Protestant authors during Mary's reign, urged his readers to become "Goddes and the Quenes obedient subiectes." He asked, "Is it not better to healpe the mother and mistres of thy country, with thy goods and body: then by withholding thy hande, and nigging, to make her not hable to kepe out thine ennemy?" In this case, he warned, the enemy included nationalities other than the Spaniards, but they would perpetrate the same crimes if Englishmen did not rally to their queen: "haddest thou rather that thy auncient enemy, the proud French man, or untrusty scot, should come to ransake thy coffers, to deflour thy wife, to ravish thy daughters, to . . . enioy thine enheritaunce, cut thine own throte, and bring thy country to naughte[?]"[71] According to this argument, it was not the advent of a ruling queen that feminized the body politic and allowed its metaphorical rape; it was the failure of the body politic to give obedience to the head (whether male or female), here figured as the "mother and mistres," that would inevitably weaken the country. Aylmer was following the same logic that had been used by Christopherson to promote obedience to the Catholic Mary in 1555:

> And as the shepeherde is the defence of the shepe, the head of the fote, the captayne of the souldyar, so in very dede the Prince is the tuition and safegard of all his subiectes. And our prince and gouernesse the Quene, requireth nothing of vs agayne but gentle & obedient hartes, which if we shewe unfeynedly toward her grace, we shall saue our soules, our bodyes, our goodes, & our country therby.[72]

---

[70] *Elizabeth I: Collected Works*, 95.

[71] Aylmer, *An Harborowe*, M4r-M4v.

[72] Christopherson, *Exhortation*, Dd1v-Dd2r. Miles Huggarde used a somewhat different tactic in *The displaying of the Protestantes, [and] sundry their practices, with a description of diuers their abuses of late frequented* (London: Robert Caly, 1556; *STC* 13558), 130, arguing that the feminization of the realm was caused by Protestant believers. This would be cured only by the reunification of the kingdom under Catholicism: "Then shall we be inuincible & without feare of forein realms. Then shall we be impregnable without feare of any nacion."

Authors such as Christopherson in Mary's reign and Aylmer in Elizabeth's reign therefore encouraged their readers to obey the queen as the head of the body politic, suggesting that their obedience thereby strengthened the realm itself.

In addition to their supporters' published assertions that Mary and Elizabeth held authority and commanded obedience as head of the body politic, both queens themselves used language at times during their respective reigns to counter fears that a female head would weaken the body politic. Mary and Elizabeth, each in turn, actively bolstered her image as head of the *corpus mysticum* by portraying herself as protector or defender of the realm in the traditionally male role of military leader. Mary upheld this masculine identification in her Guildhall speech during Wyatt's rebellion in 1554 when she encouraged the citizens of London to stand with her against the rebels. She assumed a male persona by demonstrating her willingness to go into battle if necessary to defeat the enemy. When the queen was incorrectly informed that the rebels had overcome her forces, she replied "that she hir selfe would enter the field to trie the truth of hir quarrel, and to die with them that would serve hir, rather than to yeeld one iot unto such a traitor as Wiat was, and prepared hir selfe accordinglie."[73] To the people of London, Mary "promised constantlye not to depart from them, although by her counsel she had been muche moved to the contrarye, but would remaine nere & prest to adventure the Spence of her royall bloude in defense of them."[74] Elizabeth would later make similar statements, to Londoners during her coronation procession in 1559 when she urged them to "persuade yourselves that for the safety and quietness of you all I will not spare, if need be, to spend my blood." To the troops amassed at Tilbury in 1588 against the Spanish Armada, she said: "being resolved in the midst and heat of the battle to live and die amongst you all, to lay down for my God and for my kingdom and for my people mine honor and my blood even in the dust . . . I myself will venter [venture] my royal blood."[75]

Mary's, and later Elizabeth's, stated intentions to risk her body for her people called attention not only to her sovereignty—she would be shedding not ordinary blood but royal blood—but also to the Tudor bloodline, by virtue of which she was rightful queen.[76] It highlighted the fact that she had overstepped traditional gender boundaries by vowing to act as a male ruler rather than as a woman. The body she sacrificed for her country might be female, but by offering to lay

---

[73] Holinshed, *Chronicles*, 4:20.

[74] Proctor, *The Historie of Wyates Rebellion*, 54r. According to Proctor, the queen's words "so wonderfullye inamour the heartes of the hearers, as it was a world to heare with what shoutes they exalted the honour and magnanimitte of Quene Mary."

[75] *Elizabeth I, Collected Works*, 54, 326.

[76] Cardinal Pole would later also stress her English heritage in his speech to Parliament in November 1554, when he spoke of Mary as being "your lawful Quene and Governes, borne amonge you." See John Elder, *The Copie of a letter sent in to Scotlande* (January 1555), Yale University, Beinecke Library, D6v.

down her life in battle she reinforced the idea that, as monarch, she was king as well as queen. In another version of Mary's Guildhall speech, the representation of the queen as being more than female went even further. Her words represented her not as a woman acting out masculine abilities but rather as a man herself, as she encouraged Londoners to stand with her against Wyatt: "Wherefore now as good and faithfull subiects plucke up your harts, and like true men stand fast with your lawfull prince against these rebelles both our enemies and yours, and feare them not: for assure you that I feare them nothing at all."[77] Mary's inversion of her gender role by adopting a manly persona allowed her to enforce her own sovereignty in appealing to her male subjects' understanding of their masculinity. If they supported their fearless queen, here figured as prince, they acted as "true men," firm in their allegiance; if they refused, they not only forswore their ruler, they reversed their own gender identity by demonstrating their womanly fear, thus becoming cowardly or effeminate men. Similarly, in her Armada speech, Elizabeth also presented herself as male, saying "I know I have the body but of a weak and feeble woman, but I have the heart and stomach of a king and of a king of England too . . . I myself will be your general, judge, and rewarder of your virtue in the field." She continued: "Not doubting but by your concord in the camp and valor in the field and your obedience to myself and my general, we shall shortly have a famous victory."[78] By inverting her own gender identity Elizabeth symbolically rendered her kingdom impervious to invasion, taking "foul scorn that Parma or any prince of Europe should dare to invade the borders of my realm."[79] In addition, just as Mary had done, she challenged her male subjects to act as true men on the battlefield, their valorous actions to be judged worthy of reward by the queen alone, and their masculinity dependent upon their obedience to their queen.

In addition to adopting a male persona to develop her image as defender of the realm in times of battle and warfare, each queen was also depicted as a feminine protector of the body politic, with the ability to unite the realm after religious schism. Mary, for example, was linked to the female personification of Truth. She took *Veritas Temporis Filia* as her motto, and the phrase was placed upon her Great Seal in 1553.[80] During Mary's reign, Truth, the daughter of Time, symbolized the survival and return of Catholicism to England. In *Respublica*, an interlude attributed to Nicholas Udall and apparently performed at court during Christmas 1553, Truth made an appearance as Veritas, who was

---

[77] Holinshed, *Chronicles*, 4:17. Elizabeth I would later call attention to her own courage in a speech to Parliament, saying that "though I be a woman, yet I have as good a courage answerable to my place as ever my father had." See *Elizabeth I: Collected Works*, 97.

[78] *Elizabeth I: Collected Works*, 326.

[79] *Elizabeth I: Collected Works*, 326.

[80] Roy Strong, *Artists of the Tudor Court: The Portrait Miniature Rediscovered, 1520–1620* (London: Victoria and Albert Museum, 1983), 55.

joined by Misericordia, Justicia, and Pax to rescue the widow Respublica from the vices Avarice, Oppression, Adulation, and Insolence, disguised as Policie, Reformation, Honesty, and Authority.[81] The play was dedicated to Mary, who had been sent by God "to reforme thabuses which hitherto hath been, / And that yls whiche long tyme have reigned uncorrected / shall nowe forever bee redressed with effecte."[82] Elizabeth, of course, also took the same phrase as her personal motto during her reign, although the meaning was reversed to signify the survival of Protestantism.[83]

Both queens were also linked with the Virgin Mary in a number of ways. The use of the Marian metaphor had considerable resonance in the creation of a regnant queen's image. The Virgin Mary was the model of perfect womanhood—chaste, merciful, pure, and unthreatening—and as such she provided a useful symbol for a ruling queen in counteracting fears about female viragos, women rulers who had become too masculine and sexually threatening as a result of their power. In particular, the Virgin Mary's intercessory powers with God to save men's bodies and souls could also be used to define the image of a queen regnant. John Christopherson could therefore write of Mary I in 1555 that "almyghtye God of his mere goodnes hath sent vs such a vertous Lady to reygne ouer vs, and by her delyuered vs from bondage and tyrannie, and by her broughte vs from blindnesse and heresye, and by her reconciled vs to his spouse the Catholike Churche agayne, and so by her saved both our bodies & our soules."[84] John Proctor accorded Mary not only the ability to intercede with God in order to save the people of England but also the power to heal England itself. In his "A Prosopey of Englande unto the Degenerat Englishe," as the voice of England he wrote:

> And nowe that it hath pleased the highe God of his unspeakable mercie to appoint so virtuous a governesse over me, at the sounde of whose heavenlie and manifolde virtues, as He hathe hitherto compounded my quarrels abrode, and as it were holden forrene handes backe, beynge willinge to pursue me, and to make example of me by shameful ende, as I was example to the whole worlde of all disorder, impietie, and heresie; so nowe

---

[81] *Respublica: An Interlude for Christmas 1553 Attributed to Nicholas Udall*, ed. W. W. Greg, EETS, o.s. 226 (London: Early English Text Society, 1952), 1. Veritas emerged "owte of the earth" fulfilling the prophecy in Psalm 85:11: "Truth shall spring out of the earth; and righteousness shall look down from heaven." See *Respublica*, 59 (V.ix.1705). See also Donald Gordon, "'Veritas Filia Temporis:' Hadrianus Junius and Geoffrey Whitney," *Journal of the Warburg and Courtauld Institutes* 3 (1939–1940): 228–40.

[82] *Respublica*, 2–3 (prologue, lines 49–52).

[83] On the use of this device to legitimize Elizabeth's accession, see Tim Moylan, "Advising the Queen" in this volume, 233–50. See also King, *Tudor Royal Iconography*, 228–31.

[84] Christopherson, *Exhortation*, Dd6v-Dd7r.

by her ministery, and authoritie, He meaneth mercifully to cure and heale my mangled bodie, to repayre myne abased state, to restore my good and wholesome lawes, to reforme my disordered members.[85]

Through the agency of a virgin queen with heavenly virtues, the kingdom would be repaired and restored. The combination of Queen Mary's immaculate body and her intercession with God meant that the realm, which had suffered from "many sore sicknesses," could be healed, and the body politic made whole again, restoring its masculine integrity.[86] With less elaboration, John Aylmer would allude to Elizabeth in 1558 in the same role:

As for thys losse we haue nowe, I doubt not, but as the olde fathers are wonte to saye, that as by a woman came death: so by a woman was broughte fourthe life. In like manner as bi a womans (whether negligence, or misfortune, I wote not) we haue taken this wound, so bi a nothers diligence and felicitie, we shal haue it againe healed.[87]

Both Mary and Elizabeth were thus portrayed as providential queens who would return the kingdom to its rightful state. Mary was lauded as a reformer of religion, chosen by God who "hathe of late bene so mercyfull to us, and delivered us from mooste cruell tyrannye by hys dearlye beloved handmayde, our most noble queen."[88] Richard Mulcaster's account of Elizabeth's coronation procession likewise depicted her as a providential ruler who would rescue the realm from Catholicism. He counseled that "all English hearts and her natural people must needs praise God's mercy, which hath sent them so worthy a prince."[89] Elizabeth herself reminded the Commons in 1563 of her role in saving them from papal jurisdiction: "Do not forget that by me you were delivered whilst you were hanging on the bough ready to fall into the mud—yea, to be drowned in the dung."[90] Moreover, in a speech to Parliament in 1576, Elizabeth would similarly call herself God's handmaid: "And as for those rare and special benefits which many years have followed and accompanied my happy reign, I attribute to God alone, the Prince of rule, and count myself no better than His handmaid."[91] Such references to Mary and Elizabeth as a handmaid emphasized the connection between

---

[85] Proctor. *The Historie of Wyates Rebellion*, 95r–v.
[86] Christopherson, *Exhortation*, A2v. Similarly, Bishop White of Winchester made reference to Mary's healing abilities during the queen's funeral sermon, saying: "She found the realm poisoned with heresy, and purged it." See Strype, *Ecclesiastical Memorials*, 3.2:546.
[87] Aylmer, *An Harborowe*, L3r-L3v.
[88] Christopherson, *Exhortation*, Ee6r; *Elizabeth I: Collected Works*, 169.
[89] *Elizabeth I: Collected Works*, 55.
[90] *Elizabeth I: Collected Works*, 72.
[91] *Elizabeth I: Collected Works*, 169.

the queen and the Virgin Mary, the "handmaid of the Lord."[92] Later in Elizabeth's reign, her virginal status again became a useful symbol to depict her ability to defend and protect the realm although in a somewhat different way. Louis Montrose has explored how the queen's Armada portraits, as well as her Armada speech in 1588, emphasized her virginity in order to transform "the problem of the monarch's gender into the very source of her potency. The inviolability of the island realm, the secure boundary of the English nation, is thus made to seem mystically dependent upon the inviolability of the English sovereign, upon the intact condition of the queen's body natural."[93] Elizabeth's Armada speech, therefore, played on both her feminine and masculine roles as protector and defender of the *corpus mysticum*.

Mary I and Elizabeth I thus took advantage of the corporeal theory of monarchy, just as they had used the related theory of the king's two bodies, to bolster their power and authority as sole queen during their respective reigns. Although Protestant writers who portrayed female sovereignty as a danger to the body politic specifically targeted Mary in the mid-1550s, these anxieties clearly did not disappear when Elizabeth came to the throne. In the case of both Mary and Elizabeth the fears that a female head would prove to be harmful to the body politic were countered by manipulating the representation of each queen's gender and sexuality. The formation of each queen's identity supported the idea that a female ruler could be portrayed successfully as head of the body politic not only because she assumed the masculine qualities of kings but also because she demonstrated the feminine healing and protective qualities associated with the Virgin or with virginity itself, resulting in a dual-gendered depiction of queenship. As demonstrated by both queens, therefore, defining regnant queenship required embodying the virtues not only of the ideal male ruler but of ideal womanhood

---

[92] Luke 1:48.

[93] Louis Adrian Montrose, "The Elizabethan Subject and the Spenserian Text," in *Literary Theory / Renaissance Texts*, ed. Patricia Parker and David Quint (Baltimore: Johns Hopkins University Press, 1986), 303–40, esp. 314–16. Similarly, Peter Stallybrass, "Patriarchal Territories: The Body Enclosed," in *Rewriting the Renaissance: The Discourses of Sexual Difference in Early Modern Europe*, ed. Margaret W. Ferguson, Maureen Quilligan, and Nancy J. Vickers (Chicago: University of Chicago Press, 1986), 123–42, has argued that "The state, like the virgin, was a *hortus conclusus*, an enclosed garden walled off from enemies.... As [Elizabeth] ushers in the rule of a golden age, she is the imperial virgin, symbolizing, at the same time as she is symbolized by, the *hortus conclusus* of the state" (129). Virginity conferred upon a woman a higher status, both spiritually and physically, akin to that of a man. Her chastity and purity signified the transcendence of her natural, sinful state, as well as the impermeable nature of her body. The intact and thus masculinized state of the queen's body could therefore symbolize her realm's imperviousness to attack. See also Andrew Belsey and Catherine Belsey, "Icons of Divinity: Portraits of Elizabeth I," in *Renaissance Bodies: The Human Figure in English Culture c. 1540–1660* (London: Reaktion Books, 1990), 11–35.

as well. This approach, first fashioned by Mary during the few short years that she ruled England, was one that Elizabeth would later capitalize on to good effect during her own reign.

Elizabeth I and Mary Stewart:[1]
Two British Queens Regnant:
A Gender Comparison:
Rational or Romantic

Retha Warnicke

That Queen Elizabeth I and Mary, Queen of Scots, who never met face to face, have been compared in both fictional and non-fictional literature seems almost to have been inevitable. It was extraordinary that on the British Isles, which had not had an undisputed woman ruler since the Norman Conquest, two queens regnant, Mary, beginning her personal rule in 1561, and Elizabeth, succeeding her sister Mary Tudor in 1558, should reign during the same chronological period. That Mary also became Elizabeth's captive adds another dimension to any comparison. According to Sir James Melville, Elizabeth herself began this tradition. In 1564, she questioned him about the Scottish queen's appearance and then asked which one of them was the "fairest." He tactfully replied that they "were both the fairest ladies of their courts." After he heard her play upon the virginals and observed her dancing, Elizabeth asked which queen played and danced "best." Melville praised Elizabeth's musical talents and said his queen did not dance "so high and disposedly as she did."[2]

In modern studies of the queens, both historical and popular non-fiction writers have usually identified stereotypical gender differences between them. Elizabeth was rational and a politically astute ruler while Mary was romantically inclined and politically inept. As monarchs, by these standards, Elizabeth exhibited masculine strength and Mary feminine weakness, qualities that form part of the explicit gender roles and expectations of early modern society. A sampling of a few modern biographies of these two queens will indicate how ingrained in literature are these depictions of their characters. In 2005, Natalie Meers related

---

[1] The Stewart spelling is used here because most Scottish historians favor it. See, for example, Michael Lynch, ed., *Mary Stewart in Three Kingdoms* (London: Blackwell, 1988).
[2] Gordon Donaldson, *The Memoirs of Sir James Melville of Halhill* (London: The Folio Society, 1969), 38–39.

that recent academic historians have been portraying a "darker" side to Elizabeth's reign than did earlier biographers, such as Sir John Neale.[3] Even though these more critical scholars have sometimes described her reign as "troubled," particularly in the 1590s, they have agreed she ruled by consulting with her privy councilors and other advisors. Meers called this interaction "a collaborate exercise, although one in which ultimate supremacy lay with the crown."[4]

Two recent academic biographers of Elizabeth, Wallace MacCaffrey and David Loades, show the tendency to overdraw contrasts between the queens. Elizabeth, explained MacCaffrey in his 1993 study, exercised the considerable skills required to rule her realm, demonstrating all the arts of a politician. After criticizing some of her policies, he admitted that "Triumphantly disproving the doubts men had entertained about a woman's rule, she had imposed her will on her people as effectively as her father ever did." When he briefly turned to Mary's reign, he claimed that during Henry Stewart, Lord Darnley's courtship of her, she was "more ardent" than he. In a discussion of Darnley's death, MacCaffrey accused James Hepburn, fourth earl of Bothwell, of murdering him but also pointed to "unpleasant imputations" about the affair that threatened the queen's honor.[5] In his 2003 biography, Loades agreed with MacCaffrey that Elizabeth was pragmatic and intelligent. She ruled with procrastination, guile, and shrewdness, displaying good sense and enjoying longevity. When he turned to Mary, Loades claimed she wed Darnley because she "fell violently in love" with him and then married Bothwell, his murderer, who was "likely" already her lover. Later, as an English captive, Loades surmised that Mary "was losing such grasp of reality as she had ever possessed."[6]

Two twenty-first-century biographers of Mary, John Guy and Susan Doran, show similar tendencies toward stereotyping the queens.[7] The subtitle of Guy's 2004 volume summarizes his view of her: *My Heart Is My Own*. In May 1565, he explained, Mary "believed she was in love with Darnley," but this emotion was a "brief infatuation brought on by Darnley's sexual attractiveness." Later, within two or three days after Bothwell abducted her, she fell in love with him. She

---

[3] J. E. Neale, *Queen Elizabeth I: A Biography* (New York: Doubleday, 1957).

[4] Natalie Meers, *Queenship and Political Discourse in the Elizabethan Realms* (Cambridge: Cambridge University Press, 2005), 1, 101–2. One of the academic studies she discussed was Christopher Haigh, *Elizabeth I*, 2nd ed. (London: Longman, 2001). It is not included here because it is not a biography but a series of essays.

[5] Wallace MacCaffrey, *Elizabeth I* (London: Edward Arnold, 1993), 87, 103, 445.

[6] David Loades, *Elizabeth I* (London: Hambledon & London, 2003), xii, 161–62, 185, 221, 307, 319.

[7] Jenny Wormald, *Mary, Queen of Scots: Politics, Passion and a Kingdom Lost* (New York: Touris Parke Paperbacks, 2001) differs from the 1988 version basically in its updated bibliography. It also is not a true biography, covering very briefly the last twenty years of her life.

could have "barricaded the door" to her bedchamber to prevent his entering, but did not. Her subsequent marriage to him proves their relations were consensual since she would never have wed her rapist. Guy described her as a "fool for love," because she slept with this married man before he was divorced from his wife. "But she had deep emotional needs. She expected love and needed to be loved." When he turned to Elizabeth's decision to remain single, Guy noted that in 1560 she contemplated marrying Lord Robert Dudley and speculated that their lovemaking only went so far as "heavy petting." After his wife Amy Robsart died, Elizabeth decided that marrying him would be politically "too risky." Guy related she had a "genius for public relations" and she seemed to think that her "bouts of indecisiveness" offered her more time "to weigh her options."[8]

Susan Doran's short life of Mary in 2007 provides a context for introducing her readers to manuscripts housed at the British Library. She explained that when Mary learned Elizabeth refused to name her as her successor in 1565, she turned to Darnley, "evidently" having fallen in love with him while visiting his sickroom. After his death, Doran noted, Mary's activities brought her under some suspicion, because, for example, she seems to have indulged in a game of archery with Bothwell when she should have been privately mourning her husband's death. Doran agreed with most other modern biographers, except Guy, that Bothwell raped her but concluded that she had "serious weaknesses that affected her political judgement at crucial moments." Two of those decisions were "her poor choice of husbands." Extensive evidence about Elizabeth's character could obviously not be revealed in this short biography. Doran did point out during her discussion of Elizabeth's proposal for Mary to wed Dudley that earlier, in 1560, the French court was amused by the rumor that the English queen was "romantically linked" to him and then horrified by the gossip that he had his wife killed in order to marry her. A reader could, therefore, surmise that the unwed Elizabeth did not follow her heart in making marital decisions.[9]

Many popular historians have examined the lives of Elizabeth and Mary. One recent study will be highlighted here because it is a double biography and because it represents the viewpoints that the public knows best. According to Jane Dunn's study in 2004, Mary had a "reckless" heart and displayed so much determination in her quest to marry Darnley that she gained a reputation for preferring her bridegroom to her religion. "Her blood was up and an attractive young suitor was at hand." Without confirming that Mary actually colluded in Bothwell's abduction of her, Dunn gave equal attention to the disclaimers of her honor as well as to those of her defenders, one of whom, Sir James Melville, was

---

[8] John Guy, *The Life of Mary Queen of Scots: My Heart is My Own* (London: Fourth Estate, 2004), 156, 211, 330, 361.

[9] Susan Doran, *Mary Queen of Scots: An Illustrated Life* (London: The British Library, 2007), 75, 81, 114–15, 177. For her opinion about Elizabeth's courtships, see eadem, *Marriage and Matrimony: The Courtships of Elizabeth I* (London: Routledge, 1996).

a witness to the abduction. Dunn then referred to the "evidence of their mutual passion and jealousy" after their marriage. About Elizabeth, she opined that "life's hard lessons had left her better prepared for the artfulness" required in governing England. She "was revolutionary in ruling alone and inspired in her use of celibacy as a political tool."[10]

While these modern writers seem basically to agree about the rational versus romantic characters of the two queens, diametrically opposed opinions can be found in contemporary writings. Bishop Alvaro de la Quadra, the Spanish resident, disparaged Elizabeth's character in 1559 when discussing the possibility of her marrying Archduke Charles of Styria: "As she is a woman, and a spirited and obstinate woman, too, passion has to be considered. . . . She is, in short, only a passionate, ill-advised woman. . . ."[11] Her continuing, but frustrated, affection for Robert Dudley, whom she ennobled as earl of Leicester in 1564, led Elizabeth to express bitterness toward her cousin Lettice, dowager countess of Essex, whom he secretly married in 1578. In July 1587, when Leicester was in the Netherlands, his stepson, Robert, the heir of Lady Leicester and her first husband, Walter Devereux, earl of Essex, quarreled with Elizabeth concerning his mother. Essex informed a friend, Edward Dyer, about the incident at Northhall, Hertfordshire, the home of Leicester's brother, Ambrose, earl of Warwick. In response to his harsh statements about Sir Walter Raleigh to Elizabeth, she "came to speak bitterly against my mother," thus disgracing his house, and although it was almost midnight, he sent his sister, Dorothy, her maiden of honor, away, and left court, too.[12]

Observers sometimes commented positively about Mary's rational way of ruling. In a treatise written before 1603, Sir Thomas Craig, Scotland's crown advocate, recalled he had "often heard" her "discourse so appositely and rationally in all affairs which were brought before the privy council."[13] In 1564, Pietro Bizarri, an Italian Protestant who had recently visited her court, dedicated his *De Bello ac Pace* to her and later testified "she was beloved and esteemed in the highest degree by the whole kingdom and that the island enjoyed her most prudent and courageous government."[14] Obviously, equally positive contemporary comments about

---

[10] Jane Dunn, *Elizabeth & Mary: Cousins, Rivals, Queens* (New York: Alfred A. Knopf, 2004), 235–36, 242, 245, 297–98.

[11] *Calendar of Letters and State Papers Relating to English Affairs Preserved Principally in the Archives of Simancas: Elizabeth I*, ed. Martin A. S. Hume, 4 vols. (Nendeln, Liechtenstein: Kraus Reprint, 1971), 1–101.

[12] David Starkey, ed., *Rivals in Power: Lives and Letters of the Great Tudor Dynasties* (London: Macmillan, 1990), 273.

[13] Thomas Craig, *The Right of Succession to the Kingdom of England*, trans. J. Gatherer (London: M. Bennet for D. Brown et al., 1703), 84.

[14] George Barwick, "A Side-Light on the Mystery of Mary Stuart: Pietro Bizzari's Contemporary Account of the Murders of Riccio and Darnley," *Scottish Historical Review*

Elizabeth and equally negative aspersions of Mary can also be found in contemporary documents. Their existence makes the overwhelming modern consensus that Elizabeth was rational and Mary was romantic all the more puzzling. These queens were actually more complex individuals than these stereotypes allow. A brief examination of their upbringing and education, their leisure activities, and their marital decisions will offer insights into that complexity.

Their upbringing differed considerably. Elizabeth's family might be described as dysfunctional since her father, Henry VIII, married six times, seeking to sire male children. His marital choices provide an odd mixture of romantic inclination and political astuteness. Elizabeth would have probably heard that he married for love her mother, Anne Boleyn, who was executed for adultery and incest. At the age of eight years, she must have heard about his great anguish when he assented to the execution of the fifth wife, Katherine Howard, for sexual crimes. This was clear evidence that love marriages could go astray. Since the fourth wife, Anne of Cleves, whom he divorced shortly after their marriage, remained in England until her death in 1557, that Henry's diplomatic marriages also failed would have been reinforced in Elizabeth's mind. When her father married his sixth wife, Catherine Parr, in 1543, he certainly must have been attracted to her, but not much evidence has survived about the depths of his feelings for her. If John Foxe can be believed, the king definitely did not like her religious instruction.

When Henry died in January 1547, Elizabeth was living in the household of Catherine, who ignored the widow's usual mourning customs by remarrying some three or four months after his death. Her new husband was Thomas Seymour, Lord Seymour of Sudeley, the uncle of Edward VI, Henry's heir and successor. This union usually is described as a love marriage. Historians have often lauded Catherine Parr's role as mother of Henry's children, but as his widow, she seems to have failed in parenting Elizabeth. When some of the princess's servants were interrogated by agents of Seymour's older brother, Edward, duke of Somerset, the young king's Lord Protector, they gave evidence of Seymour's having physically and emotionally abused Elizabeth. Often individuals confess to official interrogators the information they want to hear, especially when torture might be used against them. Although their responses must, therefore, be viewed with some skepticism, it seems clear that Catherine did not at first protect her stepdaughter from Seymour, who had assumed the role of Elizabeth's father figure.[15] After Catherine's death in 1548, Seymour attempted to promote a match

---

21 (1924): 115–27, here 121–22.

[15] For a detailed discussion of the conduct of Parr and Seymour and its effects on Elizabeth, see Janel Mueller, "Elizabeth Tudor: Maidenhood in Crisis," in this volume, 15–27.

with Elizabeth.[16] This sordid business led the fifteen-year-old princess to write a letter to the Lord Protector, denying that she was carrying his brother's child.[17] Through her experiences during her brother's and sister's reigns, Elizabeth honed the political survival tactics that would benefit her as queen regnant. Certainly, in her youth and young adulthood, both romantic and politically-arranged marriages did have some extremely negative political connotations. Neither seems to have been an attractive model to follow.

Her academic education also reinforced any negative ideas she might have developed toward romantic alliances. She received, as would Mary Stewart, the instruction mostly reserved for young aristocratic men. Both studied classical languages and literature on the Erasmian model, which emphasized rhetoric and viewed classical values as inspirations for social reform. Erasmus, a Christian humanist, also taught that classical values should be judged by Christian ethics. This instruction, he believed, would lead monarchs to become rational, moral rulers. One of Elizabeth's most important tutors was the noted scholar Roger Ascham, with whom she studied Greek, as well as Latin. Like Erasmus, he criticized the reading and writing of romance literature. After her accession, Ascham praised her classical learning in his book *The Schoolmaster,* claiming that "few in nomber in both the universities or els where in England, that be in both tonge, comparable with her majesty."[18] Later, Sir Robert Naunton was to comment: "She was learned, her sex and time considered, beyond common belief."[19] Her academic education, therefore, disparaged romantic notions.

Mary's upbringing, like Elizabeth's, is important for understanding her later marital decisions as monarch, which, as will later be shown, were not love matches. Her mother was a member of the Guise family, whose most obvious domestic success was the important marriages they arranged. The model they established for her was one of politically and financially advantageous unions, sometimes with individuals with whom they were strangers or barely acquainted. In 1538, Mary, the eldest daughter of Claude, duke of Guise, wed James V of Scotland. Although disappointed that her only surviving royal child was female, her Guise relatives still utilized her offspring to their advantage. In 1548, her five-year-old namesake

---

[16] At Seymour's trial, John Russell, second earl of Bedford, reported he had tried to persuade him not to marry the king's sister because that would cause Edward VI to be suspicious about his future goals. See M. L. Bush, "The Tudors and the Royal Race," *History: Journal of the Historical Association* 53 (1970): 38–39.

[17] *Elizabeth I: Collected Works,* ed. Leah S. Marcus, Janel Mueller, and Mary Beth Rose (Chicago: University of Chicago Press, 2000), 33–35.

[18] *The English Works of Roger Ascham,* ed. James Bennet (London: T. Davis and J. Dodsley, 1761), 272.

[19] Sir Robert Naunton, "Fragmenta Regalia . . . 1641," in *Harleian Miscellany,* ed. William Oldys, 10 vols. (London: J. White, J. Murray, and J. Harding, 1808–1813), 2:80.

daughter, the Scottish queen regnant from her infancy, was matched with Francis, the heir of Henry II, king of France, before they were acquainted.[20]

Subsequently, Mary moved to France where she learned from her Guise relatives but also from Catherine de Medici, her future mother-in-law, the importance of arranging and maintaining dynastic unions to achieve their family's political ambitions. Catherine, for example, remained absolutely loyal to her husband, Henry II, despite his public and private favoring of his mistress, Diane de Poitiers. Clearly, Mary's relatives never offered romantic marriages as models for her to follow.

Although Mary studied humanism on the Erasmian model, she, unlike Elizabeth, did not learn Greek. This pedagogy, of course, condemned medieval romanticism. She studied Latin and wrote into a book, which has been published, her Latin translations of some French letters. In them she referred to a "prince's duty... to administer the benefits of the commonwealth to his subjects" and concluded that, therefore, she should "take pains to be very wise." Thus she was trained to behave as a rational ruler, as a prince.[21] After she returned to Scotland, in a 1562 decree consistent with her education, she also forbade her subjects from dressing up as Robin Hood and Little John, as they usually did during rather raucous May Day celebrations. When she herself went incognito, unlike Henry VIII, she did not dress up in medieval costume but dressed like either a bourgeois woman or a man.

The Frenchman with the most influence on Mary's upbringing after she left the nursery was her mother's brother, Charles, cardinal of Lorraine. He taught her skills for ruling rationally and successfully. She learned to protect her honor by maintaining secrecy about her personal matters at court, where spies operated, and to use ciphers for sensitive correspondence. He insisted that her mother fund her separate household at court when she was eleven years old to permit her to leave the nursery. This move gave her opportunities to observe the operations of the court on a daily basis. In addition, her mother, serving as her regent in Scotland, communicated with her about governmental issues. Unlike Elizabeth's, Mary's relatives nurtured her and taught her how to survive the hazards of court politics. When Mary returned to Scotland in 1561 to begin her personal rule, she was as well equipped as any prince, by education and experience, to rule rationally and to marry advantageously to continue her dynasty.

How the two queens occupied themselves in their leisure moments can also offer insights into their personal inclinations. If either viewed marriage as a romantic undertaking, surely in her creative works some references to the romantic tradition could be found. Elizabeth sometimes represented herself as a king, such

---

[20] For biographical information about Mary, see Retha M. Warnicke, *Mary Queen of Scots* (London: Routledge, 2006).

[21] P. Stewart-MacKenzie Arbuthnot, ed. and trans., *Queen Mary's Book: A Collection of Poems and Essays by Mary Queen of Scots* (London: George Bell & Sons, 1907), 44.

as turning in her free time to classical translations. Among her surviving translations are works by Boethius, Plutarch, and Horace.[22] Elizabeth emphasized that she was learned, associating herself thereby with male academic achievements. She gave Latin orations during her three progresses to all-male university communities, albeit with disclaimers such as her educators had "put their efforts into barren and unfruitful ground," and "I am worthy of no praise at all."[23] Linda Shenk has argued that these orations reveal that she "sought to contain the power humanism gave to educated men and to assert a position of her own indisputable supremacy."[24] Indeed, Sir John Oglander noted, after recalling she was a "favorer of learning," that "There was nothing wanting that could be desired in a prince, but that she was a woman."[25]

Elizabeth's orations did not please all her subjects. Francis Osborne, who was born in 1593, published a treatise in 1658 in which he stated:

> Her sex did bear out many impertinences in her words and actions, as her making Latin speeches in the universities and professing herself in public a Muse, then thought something too theatrical for a virgin prince.[26]

Unlike Elizabeth's, Mary's favorite indoor leisure activity was embroidering, not studying classical literature, although it is true that when she first returned to Scotland she continued to read Latin with her tutor, the Scottish humanist George Buchanan. As an English prisoner, she later wrote "An Essay on Adversity," citing examples from the lives of Socrates, King Herod, and less ancient individuals, such as the German Emperor Frederick II, but no translations of classical works from her captivity are extant.[27] These activities built on her early training in humanism.

---

[22] *Queen Elizabeth's Englishings of Boethius, Plutarch, and Horace*, ed. Caroline Pemberton, EETS o.s. 113 (London: K. Paul, Trench, Trübner, 1899; repr. Millwood, NY: Kraus Reprint, 1981); Harold Kaylor, Jr., and Philip Edward Phillips, eds., *The Queen's Translation of Boethius's "De Consolatione Philosophiae,"* MRTS 366 (Tempe, AZ: Arizona Center for Medieval and Renaissance Studies, Renaissance English Text Society, 2009); *Elizabeth I: Translations, 1592-1598*, ed. Janel Mueller and Joshua Scodel (Chicago: University of Chicago Press, 2009).

[23] *Elizabeth I: Collected Works*, 91.

[24] Linda Shenk, "Turning Learned Authority into Royal Supremacy: Elizabeth I's Learned Persona and Her University Orations," in *Elizabeth I: Always Her Own Free Woman*, ed. Carole Levin, Jo Eldridge Carney, and Debra Barrett-Graves (Aldershot and Burlington, VT: Ashgate, 2003), 78-96, here 93.

[25] Francis Bamford, ed., *A Royalist Notebook: The Commonplace Book of Sir John Oglander, Kt.* (London: Constable, 1936), 192.

[26] Francis Osborne, *The Works of Francis Osborne* (Ann Arbor: University Microfilms International, 1977), 441.

[27] Arbuthnot, *Mary's Book*, 116.

Much evidence, however, has survived about her embroidering, which seems to have been devoid of romantic themes. As an English captive, Mary had plenty of time to sew and often employed embroiderers to draw designs with birds, beasts, and fish copied from sixteenth-century emblem books. Some were Christian designs, as, for example, one representing resignation to suffering. It displays a sickle descending from the sky to prune a vine and includes the motto "Virtue Flourishes by Wounding." At least on one occasion, her embroidery had a role to play in her courtships. At various times during her captivity, she sought to marry noble and royal men she had never met, requesting them to obtain armies to release her from prison. From 1568 to 1571, she considered herself the betrothed of Thomas Howard, fourth duke of Norfolk, who was beheaded in 1572 for involvement in the Ridolfi Plot. During those years, she wrote to him and also sent him a cushion with the Christian pruning emblem. Perhaps to ingratiate herself with Elizabeth, Mary even presented some of her handiwork to her cousin, who seems never to have embroidered after reaching adulthood. Specimens of her childhood endeavors are available, but as queen, she distanced herself from that employment, so closely associated with the female sex.[28]

Another pastime they both pursued was the writing of poetry; a study of their verses indicates the insufficiency of accepting the stereotypes of rational Elizabeth and romantic Mary. Although Elizabeth, of course, wrote religious poetry, she also composed verses about courtship and love. Historians agree that she had four favorites: the earl of Leicester, Sir Christopher Hatton, Sir Walter Raleigh, and finally the earl of Essex. In about 1587, she wrote a verse in response to Raleigh's piece expressing his fear that he had lost her love. The two compositions are a "surviving instance of sophisticated poetic banter that took place between the queen and her favorites." Her response to Raleigh begins:

> Ah, silly Pug, wert thou so sore afraid?
> Mourn not, my Wat, nor be thou so dismayed.
> It passeth fickle Fortune's power and skill
> To force my heart to think thee any ill.[29]

Most of Mary's extant poetry, which she composed in French, explores issues concerning death and religion. No light-hearted love poetry survives. The two authenticated verses addressed to men include one to John Leslie, bishop of Ross,

---

[28] Susan Frye, "Sewing Connections: Elizabeth Tudor, Mary Stuart, Elizabeth Talbot, and Seventeenth-Century Anonymous Needleworkers," in *Maids and Mistresses, Cousins and Queens: Women's Alliances in Early Modern England*, ed. Susan Frye and Karen Robertson (New York: Oxford University Press, 1998), 165–82.

[29] *Elizabeth I: Collected Works*, 307 n. 1, 308.

about his release from an English prison in 1574 and a sonnet to Pierre de Ronsard in about 1583, in which she eulogized the life of Henry II:[30]

> Since pride and hate he knew not I will claim
> The title of good prince to grace his name.[31]

On the same paper as the poem to Ronsard, Mary composed "Poem on Resignation." It begins

> O Lord, My God, do Thou this prayer receive,
> As I submit me to Thy Holy Will;
> And, while my soul to this sad earth shall cleave
> O grant me power to yield in patience still![32]

She did not use private compositions, therefore, to vent her alleged romantic bent.

One of the most obvious differences between Elizabeth and Mary, which had the greatest impact on their realms, is that Elizabeth remained single and Mary chose to marry. Both had sound political reasons for their decisions even though some writers have identified psychological or biological reasons for Elizabeth's failure to wed and romantic impulses for two of Mary's choices. Evidence of the dangers awaiting queens regnant who married were readily available to Elizabeth. In 1554, Mary Tudor had her half-sister imprisoned after Thomas Wyatt the younger and other rebels attempted to prevent her wedding to Philip II.

Nevertheless, after causing a scandal by her attentions to Robert Dudley in 1559, Elizabeth is usually believed to have considered marrying him, following his wife's death in 1560. She was well aware of the risks for queens regnant of marrying and probably, as Susan Doran maintains, "the active opposition of some leading councilors convinced her that it would definitely be unwise and perhaps disastrous to proceed with the match."[33] In November 1579, when Leicester was in disgrace with her because of his marriage to the countess of Essex, he referred to the queen's "bitterness" in a letter to William Cecil, Lord Burghley, and acknowledged having carried himself as a "bondman" toward Elizabeth while "hope" was left.[34] One indication of the queen's feelings might be found in a draft of a personal letter written to him while he was in the Netherlands in July 1586. In it she dropped the royal 'we.' It begins: "Rob, I am afraid you will

---

[30] Questions exist as to whether she wrote "Verses on the Death of Francis II." See Arbuthnot, *Mary's Book*, 88.

[31] Arbuthnot, *Mary's Book*, 131.

[32] Arbuthnot, *Mary's Book*, 129–31.

[33] Doran, *Marriage and Matrimony*, 210.

[34] Simon Adams, "Queen Elizabeth's Eyes at Court: The Earl of Leicester," in *Leicester and the Court: Essays on Elizabethan Politics*, ed. eadem (Manchester: Manchester University Press, 2002), 133–50, here 146.

suppose by my wandering writings that a midsummer moon hath taken large possession of my brains this month, but you must take things as they come in my head, though order be left behind me. . . ." Then she turned to governmental issues and ended the letter with:

> Now will I end that do imagine I talk still with you and therefore loathly say farewell [here she made the symbol of eyes, her nickname for him] though ever I pray God bless you from all harm and save you from all foes with my million and legion of thanks for all your pains and cares. As you know, ever the same, E.R.[35]

Her continuing, almost irrational, hostility to the countess of Leicester, whom she never forgave for marrying him, seems another indication of the depth of her feelings for him. After his death in 1588 and his widow's remarriage to Sir Christopher Blount, Elizabeth agreed to receive the countess, her former maiden of honor, at court only once, in 1598, despite Essex's intercession.[36]

Mary Stewart's unfortunate experiences surely also had an impact on Elizabeth's decisions. Mary's marriage in 1558 to Francis, the French dauphin, generated opposition in Scotland to the regency of her mother, Mary of Guise. After the regent died of natural causes in June 1560, the Lords of the Congregation succeeded in effecting the Protestant Reformation and abolishing the mass. Following the December death of Mary's husband, who had succeeded as Francis II, Elizabeth sent Francis Russell, second earl of Bedford, to condole with her widowed cousin on her loss and to alert her that the Scottish rebellion and Reformation were reactions to her marriage; many Scots feared French annexation of their kingdom.

Thus, when Elizabeth spoke to her first Parliament in 1559 about the possibility of her own marriage, stating that she preferred to remain single,[37] she was aware of the rebellion against her sister's betrothal to Philip and an erupting one against her cousin's French marriage. Elizabeth's claim to value singleness was not original, for her sister announced at her accession that she preferred not to marry but would do so for her realm and the continuation of the dynasty.[38] Meanwhile, in 1565, Mary's wedding to Henry, Lord Darnley, heir of Matthew Stewart, fourth earl of Lennox, led to a rebellion, the Chaseabout Raid. Her il-

---

[35] Adams, *Leicester and the Court*, 148.

[36] Arthur Collins, ed., *Letters and Memorials of State in the Reigns of Queen Mary, Queen Elizabeth, King James, King Charles the First. . . .Written and Collected by Sir Henry Sidney. . . .*, 2 vols. (London: T. Osborne, 1746), 1:ii, 359 and 2:91, 93, 95.

[37] *Elizabeth I: Collected Works*, 56–60.

[38] C. V. Malfatti, ed. and trans., *The Accession, Coronation, and Marriage of Mary Tudor, As Related in Four Manuscripts of the Escorial* (Barcelona: Malfatti, 1956), 37. On this and other ways in which Elizabeth learned from her sister Mary, see also Sarah Duncan, "The Two Virgin Queens," in this volume, 29–51.

legitimate half-brother, James Stewart, earl of Moray, joined with the Hamilton family, headed by James, duke of Châtelherault, who had the best claim to the Scottish throne after Mary, to denounce her marriage to Darnley. The uprising, the third in about a decade against a queen regnant's marital choice, failed, and the rebels fled to England, where Moray met with Elizabeth. Why Mary decided to wed Darnley will be discussed below.

Mary's union with Darnley was complicated because, besides his descent from Margaret Tudor, he was also the scion of a family with Scottish royal blood. The Lennox Stewarts had long maintained that their succession claims were superior to those of the Hamiltons. Mary's unwillingness to surrender regal authority to Darnley, as he had expected, led him to attempt a palace coup. In March 1566, only eight months after their wedding, he permitted armed allies to enter her supper room at Holyrood Palace and murder David Riccio, her secretary. Darnley's plan was to keep his wife, pregnant with their son James, under house arrest while he ruled Scotland. Somehow she managed to convince Darnley that he was in as much danger as she, and they escaped together. Marriage, her experience proved, made a queen politically vulnerable to her husband's whims.

In February 1567, a group of men who had been at Holyrood House when Riccio was murdered and who were alienated by the perceived armed threat to their lives combined with other malcontents to cause Darnley's death. Mary herself seems to have thought initially that she was also their target. Two months later, the earl of Bothwell, one of the assassins, abducted and raped Mary. She subsequently ennobled him as the duke of Orkney and married him. Sir James Melville, a member of her train during the abduction, claimed "she could not but marry him, seeing he had ravished her and lain with her against her will."[39] Early modern heiresses usually wed their abductors to protect their honor.

In Mary's case, some contemporary concerns about a queen regnant's marriage to a native-born subject were realized, for the union with Bothwell led to civil war because of fears that he would privilege his family and allies. No matter the choice, foreign or domestic, at least in the case of the two Marys, they each faced rebellions because they decided to wed.[40]

When Elizabeth's decision to remain single is assessed in the context of the reactions to her sister's and cousin's marriages, perhaps the question should be "Why should she have married?" instead of "Why did she not marry?"[41] The answer to the query as to why she should have wed lies in her contemporaries' es-

---

[39] Donaldson. *Memoirs of Sir James*, 64.

[40] Jacqueline Vanhoutte, "Queen and Country?: Female Monarchs and Feminized Nations in Elizabethan Political Pamphlets," in *Elizabeth I: Always Her Own Free Woman*, ed. Levin et al., 7–19, related that some advisors recommended that queens marry their subjects.

[41] For further examination of Elizabeth's decision to remain single, see Mueller, "Elizabeth Tudor: Maidenhood in Crisis," in this volume, 15–27.

teem for family, lineage, and dynasty. Her rejection of those priorities must have been based in great part upon political concerns about rebellions and civil war and not on personal psychological issues. In her childhood, her adolescence, and her adulthood, she had seen both romantic marriages and arranged diplomatic unions either fail or generate problems for her family and the realm. Certainly, for her to remain single was a most rational choice.

Indeed, Elizabeth, at the age of forty-six, chose not to wed Francis, duke of Anjou and Alençon, because, Susan Doran argued, her male privy councilors would not recommend this alliance to her.[42] Anne McLaren has also explained that the councilors debated "the likelihood" of Elizabeth's having children when she married. This factor became extremely important as she entered her forties. Without the possibility of offspring, her marriage took on the perception of a "conquest of the crown and realm." McLaren pointed out that John Stubbs raised this issue in a pamphlet that was published and for which the government had him arrested. He was convicted of seditious libel, and as Elizabeth refused to reduce the penalty, an executioner cut off his right hand.[43]

Furthermore, these negotiations with Anjou occurred in the late 1570s. At that time her Scottish cousin was her prisoner, and Elizabeth was aware of the three rebellions that Mary's marriages had caused. Elizabeth could also recall the armed challenge to her sister's intended marriage. It can be suggested that when Elizabeth presented a ring to Anjou, who arrived in England to pursue their match, she did so to gauge her courtiers' reactions and not out of some romantic impulse to seal a pact with him. Had her councilors recommended his candidacy, it is impossible to determine what her final decision would have been. From the beginning of her reign, the question of her marriage posed quite a dilemma, as Alexander Nowell, dean of St. Paul's, expressed on 11 January 1563. In a sermon before the queen at her second Parliament, he said that the marriage of Mary Tudor was "a terrible plague to all England" but the "want of your marriage and issue is like to prove as great a plague."[44]

In Catholic countries, vocations existed for both men and women wishing to remain single. In Protestant countries, women were viewed as achieving adulthood or maturity only when they married and assumed domestic responsibilities and family duties. Singleness was, therefore, considered socially an unacceptable, almost an irrational, life choice for women. Even so, there was not a lack of single women. Amy Froide has determined that from 1574 to 1821, single women, ex-

---

[42] Doran, *Marriage and Matrimony*, 9, 211.

[43] Anne McLaren, "The Quest for a King: Gender, Marriage, and Succession in Elizabethan England," *Journal of British Studies* 41 (2002): 259–90, here 269.

[44] *A Catechism Written in Latin by Alexander Nowell, Dean of St. Paul's . . . Together with the Same Catechism Translated into English by Thomas Norton. Appended is a Sermon Preached by Dean Nowell Before Queen Elizabeth. . January 11, 1563*, ed. G. E. Corrie, Parker Society (Cambridge: Cambridge University Press, 1853), 228.

cluding widows, comprised on average about 30% of adult women. Viewing their singleness as a temporary pre-marital phase, civic leaders treated them as though they were youths, regardless of their age, in need of male discipline.[45]

Although Catholic women could more appropriately remain single and some possibly even join nunneries, Mary probably never seriously considered maintaining her widowed status, especially in Scotland, where she returned in 1561, after Francis's death, and began to seek a new husband. Concerned that Mary might wed a foreign Catholic prince and assuming she was seeking a political alliance and not a romantic liaison,[46] Elizabeth requested that her Scottish cousin accept Leicester as her husband. Besides his inferior status, some critics denounced this offer because of rumors that he was Elizabeth's cast-off lover. Even so, Mary agreed to marry him if Elizabeth would gain legislative recognition of her place as her successor. In mid-March 1565, however, Randolph gave her the following message: Until Elizabeth decided not to marry, she would refuse to name anyone as her successor.[47]

Meanwhile, the earl of Lennox, who returned home from English exile to recover his estates in 1564, requested the presence in Scotland of his heir, Lord Darnley. In February 1565, one month before Mary learned that Elizabeth would not recognize her succession rights, Darnley reached Scotland. In early April, as Mary was planning to send her principal secretary, William Maitland of Lethington, to London to discuss with Elizabeth's advisors the Leicester marriage, she astonished Randolph when she honored Darnley, ailing with measles, by sending him food from her own table, thus singling him out for special attention. For the previous two months, Randolph had observed no sign that she had any special interest in him. Unlike Elizabeth's favorites, Darnley apparently did not enjoy a public and romantic flirtation with his queen.

Later in April, when Lethington arrived in London, he learned that Elizabeth was still refusing to validate Mary's succession claims. Meanwhile, Sir William Cecil was reading Randolph's dispatch which revealed Mary's plan to wed Darnley. It is likely Mary hoped to use the threat of this alliance to leverage Elizabeth's recognition of her as her successor and thus revitalize the Leicester match. If Elizabeth still would not concede her succession rights, Mary would wed Darnley, a native Englishman, and secure his claims. This union would pre-

---

[45] Amy Froide, *Never Married: Singlewomen in Early Modern England* (Oxford: Oxford University Press, 2005), 2, 31; Cordelia Beattie, *Medieval Single Women: The Politics of Social Classification in Late Medieval England* (Oxford: Oxford University Press, 2007); and *The Single Woman in Medieval and Early Modern England*, ed. Laurel Amtower and Dorothea Kehler, MRTS 263 (Tempe: Arizona Center for Medieval & Renaissance Studies, 2003).

[46] The candidate she preferred was actually Philip II's son, Don Carlos, but those negotiations ended in 1564.

[47] National Library of Scotland, MS. 3657, fols. 18–20.

vent him from returning to England, possibly converting to Protestantism, and emerging as Mary's competitor for the crown. Marrying an English-born subject was also attractive because one of Mary's alleged weaknesses with regard to the English succession was her foreign birth. She later told Randolph that she chose Darnley because he possessed English succession rights and Leicester did not.

Mary's biographers, who have described this as a romantic match, have overlooked a manuscript disputing the assertion that she fell in love with him while nursing him.[48] Cecil related in an official document dated in late April 1565 that Lethington had denied the rumors about her sickroom visits with Darnley, which were spread in England by his relatives.[49] Although women had the major responsibility for informal medicine, for example nursing their close relatives, it would have been inappropriate for the young, unmarried queen to nurse a young, unmarried man, especially one with an infectious disease.[50] Nursing was not a romantic endeavor. After their marriage, he expressed gratification when she nursed him during an ailment. In her old age, even Elizabeth took on this female role when she offered nourishment to Lord Burghley when he was seriously ill.

Another issue concerning the Darnley marriage, indicating that it was not a romantic liaison, is the fact that in response to Elizabeth's protest against it, Mary postponed their wedding. She dispatched John Hay to England to request an Anglo-Scottish conference concerning her marriage.[51] Mary was likely still hoping to pressure Elizabeth into recognizing her as her successor. In July, Hay returned with Elizabeth's negative response and her demand that Mary wed Leicester. Mary then resumed the arrangements for marrying Darnley, granting him the title of king on 28 July, the eve of the wedding. Her uncle, the cardinal of Lorraine, believing it was a politically advantageous union, assisted her in obtaining a papal dispensation to wed her kinsman.

In assessing the rational versus passionate characterization of the two queens, in some sense the statement about Elizabeth is more accurate than the one about Mary. Although Elizabeth certainly permitted herself to be courted by foreign princes, flirted with her male favorites, responded to Raleigh's love poem, and was bitter about Leicester's marriage, her enjoyment of academic studies and her language facility led her to turn to the essentially male pastime of translating classical works and giving Latin orations. She chose not to marry, probably for political reasons, and although her advisors did not think so, it was undoubtedly a wise decision. That she remained unwed was an anomaly only because of dynastic concerns, for 30% of her female subjects never married. Her singleness

---

[48] Wormald, *Mary, Queen of Scots*, 152.
[49] Manuscript NA, SP 52/10 no. 38.
[50] Caroline Bingham, *Darnley: A Life of Henry Stuart, Lord Darnley, Consort of Mary Queen of Scots* (London: Constable, 1995), 98.
[51] *Lettres, Instructions, et Mémoires de Marie Stuart, reine d'Écosse*, ed. A. I. Labanoff, 7 vols. (London: C. Dolman, 1899), 1:266–75.

did, however, lead her occasionally to present herself publicly as a ruler within a masculine, that is to say, rational, framework.

Although the Scottish queen, unlike Elizabeth, did wed, she did not impulsively do so for romantic reasons. Facets of her culture privileging family, dynasty, and honor explain her spousal choices. Her reign was terminated because she was a queen regnant whose abductor-husband had taken control of her government. As a wife, a widow, and the mother of a son, she did represent society's familial expectations for women. Her life was, however, somewhat more complex than this characterization. Because of her education and her concern for governing her kingdom, occasionally alluding to herself as a prince, there was, by the standards of her culture, a masculine or rational quality to her behavior. Even her embroidery, a female occupation, and her poetry lack evidence of romanticism.

Both Elizabeth and Mary were attempting to maintain control over their realms at a time when men held the dominant social and political roles. Occasionally, they fashioned themselves with masculine qualities, for there was no long tradition of female rule, as they were two of the first three queens regnant in the British Isles since the Norman Conquest. Their major problem was that their advisors wanted them to marry and give birth to a male child, as the future Lord Burghley said in 1561: "Well, God send our Mistress a husband, and by time a son that we may hope our posterity shall have a masculine posterity."[52] Mostly, however, their advisors and subjects could not agree on which candidates they should wed. Mary chose to marry following the cultural and political ethos of her society and, as a result, faced three rebellions and felt it necessary to flee her realm in 1568. Elizabeth, ironically, chose to deny the dynastic expectations concerning marriage, preserving her control and living long enough to ensure the succession of Mary's child. The decisions they made about marriage, although quite different, were thus rooted in their political experiences and in their upbringing. It is ironic that the queen regnant who denied dynastic imperatives concerning marriage was the one to survive adversities and to rule for almost forty-five years.

---

[52] Philip Yorke, second Earl of Hardwicke, ed., *Miscellaneous State Papers, From 1501 to 1726*, 2 vols. (London: W. Strahan & T. Cadel, 1778), 1:174.

Grave Histories:
Women's Bodies Writing
Elizabethan History

Catherine Howey Stearn

Far in the back of Salisbury Cathedral stands an enormous family tomb. This soaring monument revolves around four marble figures. The two effigies on the tomb commemorate Edward Seymour, earl of Hertford, and a woman who, as the huge marble plaque above them declares, is Catherine Grey, his wife. These peacefully and eternally resting spouses are flanked by two kneeling figures, their adult sons, Edward Seymour, Lord Beauchamp (the figure on the left) and his younger brother Thomas Seymour (on the right). This grand scene of family devotion suffers from one minor flaw: legally, this family never existed.

Many who read histories of Elizabeth I's reign will encounter the tragic love story of the courtiers Catherine Grey and Edward Seymour, earl of Hertford. Catherine Grey was a maid of honor to Elizabeth I and a great-granddaughter of King Henry VII, which made her a potential heir to the throne. In 1560, Grey secretly married Edward Seymour, who also had connections to the Tudor dynasty.[1] In less than a year, the earl had been sent abroad; the one witness to the marriage, Lady Jane Seymour, Grey's fellow maid of honor and the earl's sister, was dead; and Catherine Grey was pregnant. When Grey could no longer conceal her pregnancy from the queen, Elizabeth I responded by imprisoning Grey in the Tower and recalling her husband from Europe so that he might join his wife there, though in separate rooms. Despite their official separation in the Tower, sympathetic guards allowed Grey and Seymour to welcome their first son into the world and to produce another. Now Grey's claim to the throne was bol-

---

[1] Seymour's royal connection was his aunt, Queen Jane Seymour, thus making him a first cousin to Edward VI. Furthermore, courtiers were supposed to get the queen's permission to marry, and under Henry VIII, a law had been passed that required individuals with a potential claim to the throne, such as Grey, to get the Privy Council's permission to marry. Technically, Grey and Hertford committed treason by secretly getting married; see J. M. J. Fletcher, *The Hertford Monument in Salisbury Cathedral: A Lecture* (Devizes: George Simpson & Co., 1927), unpaginated.

Donald Stump, Linda Shenk, and Carole Levin, eds., *Elizabeth I and the 'Sovereign Arts': Essays in Literature, History, and Culture*. MRTS 407. Tempe: ACMRS, 2011. [ISBN 978-0-86698-455-3]

Figure 1: The Hertford Monument, c. 1621, design attributed to William Wright, Salisbury Cathedral.

stered by the production of a male heir and a spare. To secure her shaky throne, Elizabeth I moved against the Grey-Seymour alliance by calling for an investigation into the validity of the marriage. By February 1563, the Ecclesiastical High Commission declared the union illegal.[2] Grey was deprived of a husband, and her children were denied any legitimate status; bastards did not threaten Elizabeth's right to rule.[3]

Although Grey and Seymour were released from the Tower in 1563, they were kept under house arrest in different locations. Furthermore, Grey was deprived of the custody of her elder son, who had been given to his father. Grey and her younger son lived under house arrest away from court until her early death in 1568. She was buried in Yoxford Church, Suffolk, until many years later, when her remains were removed to join the earl in his resting place at Salisbury.[4] Seymour was released shortly after Grey's death, and eventually he and Elizabeth I reconciled. The earl married twice more and outlived his two sons, finally dying in 1621 in his early eighties. And there the story traditionally ends, with Elizabeth triumphant over the heartbroken Catherine.[5]

However, that is not the end of the story. In the back of Salisbury Cathedral, Catherine Grey rests in stone cold triumph over Elizabeth I as she and the

---

[2] M. A. E. Green, ed., *Calendar of State Papers, Domestic Series, Addenda, 1566–1579* (London: Longman, Brown, 1871), 535. The proceedings of the ecclesiastical commission can be followed in Bodelian Library, Oxford University, Tanner MS. 84, fols. 105–197.

[3] Eventually under James, the children were able to inherit their father's lands and titles, but James upheld the bastardy judgement. See Susan Doran, "Seymour, Edward, first earl of Hertford," *Oxford Dictionary of National Biography*, 60 vols. (New York: Oxford University Press, 2004), 49: 870. The amateur, unpublished family history of the Seymour family, *Annals of the Seymours*, in the Folger Shakespeare Library, Washington, DC, MS. W.b.262 fol. 177r, claims that the children's legitimacy was also restored. The mistake is understandable, since bastards of noblemen were usually prohibited from inheriting their titles and estates.

[4] Fletcher, *The Hertford Monument*. I owe many thanks to Suzanne Eward, Librarian and Keeper of the Muniments of Salisbury Cathedral, who sent me both Canon Fletcher's piece on the Hertford Monument and his published essay on the Gorges Monument.

[5] For a traditional telling of the Grey-Seymour drama, see Violet Wilson, *Queen Elizabeth's Maids of Honour and Ladies of the Privy Chamber* (London: John Lane, Bodley Head, 1923), 69, n. 2, where Wilson states,"Lady Catherine died of decline whilst in the custody of Sir Owen Hopton at Yoxford in Suffolk. She and her husband never met again after they parted in the Tower." Norman Jones, in his chapter on marriage in *The Birth of the Elizabethan Age* (Cambridge, MA: Blackwell, 1993), discusses the Grey-Hertford marriage, its trial, and its subsequent annulment, but does not mention the tomb in Salisbury Cathedral. David Starkey, in *Elizabeth: The Struggle for the Throne* (New York: HarperCollins, 2001), 319, barely mentions the failed Grey-Hertford marriage: "Elizabeth also used the amorous adventures of the surviving Grey sisters . . . to put them under lock and key as well."

family that she struggled to create stand eternally together for all visitors to see. This tomb reconstructs the struggle between the Greys-Seymours and Elizabeth I, telling a story in stone: one with an ending different from the version passed down in ink by historians. This funerary monument can be read as a history, and, moreover, as a history written in body language: Catherine Grey's memorialized body, not just her life, is at the center of this alternate history. Grey's story and her tomb are permanent reminders that Elizabeth I was not the lone woman at her court surrounded only by men. Elizabeth I was at the center of a court inhabited by both men and women, some of whom tried to protect her while others threatened her political survival. Indeed, this essay will not only attempt to return women to the history of the last Tudor monarch but also discuss how women's bodies were central in shaping histories of Elizabeth I's reign. In addition to the case study of the Grey-Hertford tomb, I will also discuss the tomb of Helena, marchioness of Northampton and her second husband, Thomas Gorges, as well as the strategy behind James I's program of royal tomb-building at Westminster Abbey. These three case studies present the various ways families constructed their family histories by either appropriating or separating themselves from the queen, strategies which, in turn, constructed an alternate history of Elizabeth I's reign.

The need to re-populate the histories of the Elizabethan court with women was made glaringly apparent at the 2003 exhibition on the queen held at the National Maritime Museum in Greenwich, England. In the introduction to the exhibition catalogue, David Starkey writes that, "Elizabeth is extraordinary. She looks extraordinary. . . . And as a woman moving in a man's world, she is doubly extraordinary."[6] Yet Elizabeth, a queen regnant, was neither singular nor alone. Indeed, she succeeded a female monarch, her half-sister; moreover, women surrounded Elizabeth throughout her long reign, even past her death when her maids of honor and ladies and gentlewomen of her privy chamber watched over the queen's body before it was laid to rest. The few scholars who have worked on Elizabethan court women have limited themselves to determining whether or not the women of Elizabeth I's privy chamber exercised any political agency in terms of patronage networks and the women's (in)ability to influence political decisions and appointments to governmental offices.[7] However, this piece

---

[6] David Starkey, "Introduction," in *Elizabeth: The Exhibition at the National Maritime Museum*, ed. Susan Doran (London: Chatto & Windus, National Maritime Museum, 2003), 3.

[7] The work on Elizabethan female courtiers' power has been involved in a debate about the nature of the Tudor Privy Chamber and how a female monarch with female attendants did or did not change the space from which so much power and influence was wielded. David Starkey first worked out his model of the Henrician arrangement in "The King's Privy Chamber, 1485–1547" (Ph.D. diss., Cambridge University, 1973). For the scholarship that has tested Starkey's model with the case of Elizabeth I's privy chamber,

will connect the court to other spaces to see how women and their family members used the monumental bodies, activities, and memories of court women to construct family histories—histories connected to the larger national history.[8] Indeed, the political events of the country at large are central to the stories individuals and families created.[9] In turn, these tomb monuments can be read as historical records that speak to the fact that Elizabeth I's power as monarch was at times both limited and extended by her female courtiers.

Before returning to the Grey-Hertford tomb, let us turn to another large, early seventeenth-century funerary monument also in Salisbury Cathedral. This is the tomb of Helena, marchioness of Northampton, and her second husband,

---

see Philippa Berry, *Of Chastity and Power: Elizabethan Literature and the Unmarried Queen* (New York: Routledge, 1989); Elizabeth A. Brown, "'Companion Me With My Mistress': Cleopatra, Elizabeth I, and Their Waiting Women," in *Maids and Mistresses, Cousins and Queens: Women's Alliances in Early Modern England*, ed. Susan Frye and Karen Robertson (New York: Oxford University Press, 1999), 131–45; Natalie Mears, "Politics in the Elizabethan Privy Chamber: Lady Mary Sidney and Kat Ashley," in *Women and Politics in Early Modern England, 1450–1700*, ed. James Daybell (Aldershot and Burlington, VT: Ashgate, 2004), 67–82; Charlotte Merton, "The Women Who Served Queen Mary and Queen Elizabeth: Ladies, Gentlewomen and Maids of the Privy Chamber, 1553–1603" (Ph.D. diss., Cambridge University, 1992); and Pam Wright, "A Change in Direction: The Ramifications of a Female Household, 1558–1603," in *The English Court: From the Wars of the Roses to the Civil War*, ed. David Starkey (New York: Longman, 1987), 147–72.

[8] The term "monumental body" was coined by Nigel Llewellyn in *The Art of Death: Visual Culture in the English Death Ritual c.1500–c.1800* (London: Reaktion Books, Victoria and Albert Museum, 1991), 101.

[9] The idea that manuscript family histories, especially those written by women, did not exist in a domestic vacuum but connected the personal to the larger political/cultural/social/economic milieu comes from the argument made by Natalie Zemon Davis, "Gender and Genre: Women as Historical Writers, 1400–1820," in *Beyond Their Sex: Learned Women of the European Past* (New York: New York University Press, 1980), 153–82. There has also been a growing body of scholarship that has identified tomb building as an act of constructing a family history and family identity, whether it was royal, aristocratic or gentry. See M. Bryan Curd, "Constructing Family Memory: Three English Funeral Monuments and Patriarchy in the Early Modern Period," in *Framing the Family: Narrative and Representation in the Medieval and Early Modern Period*, ed. Rosalynn Voaden and Diane Wolfthal, MRTS 280 (Tempe, AZ: Arizona Center for Medieval and Renaissance Studies, 2005), 273–92; David Howarth, *Images of Rule: Art and Politics in the English Renaissance, 1485–1649* (Berkeley and Los Angeles: University of California Press, 1997), 153–90; Llewellyn, *The Art of Death*; idem, *Funeral Monuments in Post-Reformation England* (New York: Cambridge University Press, 1991); Peter Sherlock, *Monuments and Memory in Early Modern England* (Aldershot and Burlington, VT: Ashgate, 2008); and Daniel Woolf, *The Social Circulation of the Past: English Historical Culture 1500–1730* (New York: Oxford University Press, 2003).

Thomas Gorges.[10] On the sides of the tomb, under their respective effigies, is a list of the ancestry and accomplishments of each spouse. For example, on Helena's side, the Latin epitaph states, "Here are placed the remains of Hellen Snacenberg of Sweden, who accompanied the Lady Caecilia, daughter of Eric King of the Swedes into this Kingdom. On account of her beauty and modesty, for which she was renowned, she was pleasing to Queen Elizabeth, by whom she was placed among the maids of honor who served her sacred person in the Privy Chamber."[11] Thomas Gorges' side tells readers that he was a "Knight, 5th son of Sir Edward Gorges of Wraxall. . .Knight," who spent most of his life "in the service of Queen Elizabeth and King James, both of blessed memory." Both spouses listed their royal service as an important aspect of their lives that they wanted preserved for others to read, making their epitaphs sites where personal histories intersected with larger national histories. It is their very connection to the court that made these individuals and their families important and powerful. Their tomb is both evidence of and a record to that power and prestige.

---

[10] For details about the Gorges Monument, see J. M. J. Fletcher, "The Gorges Monument in Salisbury Cathedral," *Wiltshire Archaeological and Natural History Magazine* 50 (1932): 16–43, and Sherlock, *Monuments and Memory in Early Modern England*, 231–48. For more about Helena of Schnachenberg, see Charles Bradford, *Helena Marchioness of Northampton* (London: George Allen & Unwin, 1936).

[11] I am grateful to Rod Stearn and to Suzanne Eward, Librarian and Keeper of the Muniments of Salisbury Cathedral, for their assistance in translating this and other Latin inscriptions on the monument. I have not corrected the Latin found on the tombs but have kept the original spellings and abbreviations. Helena's entire epitaph reads: HIC SITA SVNT OSSA HELLENÆ SNACHENBERG/ SWEDANÆ QVÆ DOMINAM CÆLLIAM FILIAM / ERICI REGIS SWETIÆ IN HOC REGNVM COMITATA/ PROPTER VENVSTATEM PVDICITIAMQVE QVA/ CLARVIT GRATA REGINÆ ELIZABETHÆ. PER EAM/ INTER HONORARIAS MINISTRAS SACRÆ SVÆ/ PERSONÆ INTIMO CVBICVLO ATTENDENTES ASSITA/ FVIT ET LOCATA IN MATRIMONIO GVILLIELMO/ D'NO PAR DE KENDALL MARCHIONI NORTHAMP/ TONIÆ QVO SINE PROLE MORTVO NVPSIT/ THOMÆ GORGES EQVITI AVRATO CVI 4: FILIOS/ ET 3 FILIAS PEPERIT: CVIVS POST OBITVM/ VIDVITATE VITAM EGIT PER ANNS 25 QVIBVS PIE/ PERACTIS EXCESSIT E VIVIS PRIMO DIE APRILIS ANNO/ ÆTATI 86. ANNOQ DOM'NI 1635. Thomas Gorges' epitaph reads: IN HOC MONVMENTO SEPVLTVM iacet CORPVS/ THOMÆ GORGES DE LANGFORDE IN HOC TRACTV/ SEVERIANO EQVITIS AVRATI QVINTI FILII/ EDOVARDO GORGES DE WRAXALL IN AGRO/ SOMERSETENSI EQVITI AVRATO: QVI POST/ MAXIMAM VITÆ PARTEM SERVITIO REGINÆ/ELIZABETHÆ ET REGIS IACOBI BEATÆ/ MEMORIÆ PRINCIPVM IN SANCTIORE PENETRALI CV̄/ FIDELITATE IMPENSAM RESIGNAVIT ANIMAM IN/ MANVS REDEMPTORIS SVI 30°DIE MARTII A° /ÆTAT 74to:A°: DO: mi 1610.

Figure 2: The Gorges Monument, c. 1631, designer unknown, Salisbury Cathedral.

What is not mentioned on the tomb is Elizabeth I's wrath when Helena and Thomas married without her consent in 1576.[12] However, Helena's monumental history counters the image of Elizabeth as a vindictive Virgin Queen capable of trying to keep her courtiers from enjoying the state of marital bliss that she denied herself. Helena's epitaph continues with "bestowed in marriage on William Lord Parr of Kendal, Marquess of Northampton." Queen Elizabeth made it very clear that she approved of the 1571 marriage between Helena and the brother of her final stepmother, Catherine Parr, because she was present at their wedding, which took place in the Queen's Chapel Royal.[13] The reasons why Elizabeth reacted badly to Helena's second marriage were twofold: they had married without Elizabeth's consent, and Helena had married a man beneath her social station. As the epitaphs make clear, Helena was a Swedish noblewoman who had first married a highly positioned English nobleman, whereas Thomas Gorges was but a gentleman knight.

Not surprisingly, the rest of Helena's inscription makes no allusion to the fact that Thomas ended up serving a brief amount of time in the Tower as a result of their marriage.[14] Instead, Helena's epitaph constructs a smooth transition from her widowhood to her remarriage; she was "bestowed in marriage to William Lord Parr . . . who dying without issue she married Sir Thomas Gorges, to whom she bore four sons and three daughters, after whose death she lived 25 years a widow piously." Ultimately, Helena and her husband's period of royal disfavor was short because their crime was far less serious than that of Grey and Seymour, who had not only married without the queen's consent but also had created a union that could have potential consequences concerning the succession to the English throne. Eventually, Helena and Thomas regained Elizabeth's favor and were able to remain married and establish a family. Whereas Catherine Grey died in disgrace and disfavor, Helena acted as Elizabeth I's chief mourner at her funeral, and Thomas Gorges was able to continue his service to the crown under James I.[15]

---

[12] Bradford, *Helena*, 65–67, is vague on the year they married but declares that, in 1576, Helena was in disfavor, and Gorges was imprisoned for their clandestine marriage. The entry for Helena, Marchioness of Northampton in the *Oxford Dictionary of National Biography* says that they were married "about 1576." See Paul Harrington, "Gorges [née Snackenborg], Helena, Lady Gorges," *Oxford Dictionary of National Biography*, 22:994.

[13] For the record that the marriage of the marquess and marchioness took place in the Chapel Royal, see *The Old Cheque-Book or Book of Remembrance, of the Chapel Royal from 1561 to 1744*, ed. Edward F. Rimbault (London: Camden Society, J. B. Nichols & Sons, 1872), 160, and Bradford, *Helena*, 57–58. The marriage was very short, as William Parr died six months later in 1571.

[14] Bradford, *Helena*, 63.

[15] TNA, LC2/4/4, the account book of Elizabeth I's funeral.

Figure 3: detail of the effigies of Helena, marchioness of Northampton and Sir Thomas Gorges.

The Gorges tomb forms an interesting family history because it demonstrates two important ways in which a family could edit and create such a history: through their choice of words and use of women's bodies. The editing work is clear as there is no mention of any period of royal disfavor and punishment. Moreover, the body language of the tomb erases the crime of a social status mismatch. The two effigies of husband and wife are laid side by side, resting as equals, even though Helena's social status was technically higher. The deliberate placement of the monumental bodies is not meant to erase Helena's status or degrade it in any way, but to raise Thomas's. Even though they lie side by side, Helena's effigy is given sartorial markers to allude to her rank as marchioness. Her effigy's carved outfit includes a mantle lined with ermine, and the sleeves of her dress have ermine cuffs, reminiscent of the outfit recorded in portraiture which she probably wore at the coronation of Elizabeth I's successor, James I.[16] Her

---

[16] I found this image and a copy of it in the Heinz Library, the picture archive of London's National Portrait Gallery. One portrait was at Shadwell Park, Thetford, Norfolk, until it was sold at Sotheby's in the 1990s; the other portrait is currently located at Rousham House, which houses part of the Ashton collection. More than likely it was painted in the style of Robert Peake shortly after James I's coronation because the

husband's effigy, by contrast, wears his knightly armor, but no ermine, which would have been reserved for the nobility, not the gentry. Therefore, a social balance is created between spouses, but not at the expense of Helena's rank and accomplishments. Helena is not marginalized in this history, but rather her high standing and accomplishments are yoked to her husband so that their children might inherit a joint patrimony of past royal service and noble blood.

The Gorges' eldest son commissioned and paid for this tomb in 1635, four years after Helena's death in 1631 and twenty-five years after Thomas's.[17] While Helena may not have commissioned the tomb, the significance of her monumental body and memorialized life are not lessened if we apply to them Natalie Zemon Davis's work on early modern European family strategy. According to Davis, early modern European families appropriated their past to ensure their future survival. Families utilized their past to create ties to ancestors, re-enforcing continuity and sentiment by recounting past family accomplishments. These stories provided a means to naturalize any present social privileges.[18] Although Davis' work focuses upon manuscript family histories, early modern people also utilized portraiture and funerary monuments to construct their histories. Significantly, these histories were by their very nature collaborative enterprises. Even if women themselves did not commission the works that commemorated them and their accomplishments, current or future generations often saw their role as important in establishing a glorious family patrimony. Family members then deliberately incorporated their female relatives into the family history. Whether women were the authors or the subjects, family strategy kept these women from fading into the family history as mere ghosts.

The monument that recorded the Gorges family's high social standing did so by creating a family history that was attached to a positive depiction of Elizabeth I. Helena's epitaph implies that being hand-picked by the queen was a testament to Helena's virtue and beauty. If Elizabeth's virtue as a ruler was besmirched, then so too would be Helena's royal employment. Her husband's epitaph more explicitly reminds his audience that Elizabeth, along with her successor James I, were good monarchs, since they and their reigns were of "blessed memory." However, in order to attach the "memory" of Helena and that of her husband

---

marchioness is dressed in the red velvet associated with coronation dress. There are other portraits of both men and women dressed in all, or part of, their coronation finery, such as Lucy Russell, countess of Bedford, whose coronation portrait was also painted by a follower of Robert Peake c.1603 and is currently held by the London National Portrait Gallery: see Janet Arnold, *Queen Elizabeth's Wardrobe Unlocke'd* (Leeds: W.S. Maney & Sons, 1988), 64–65.

[17] Fletcher, *The Gorges Monument*, 16l; Susan Brown, *Sumptuous and Richly Adorn'd: The Decoration of Salisbury Cathedral* (London: Stationery Office, 1999), 146.

[18] Natalie Zemon Davis, "Ghosts, Kin and Progeny: Some Features of Family Life in Early Modern France," *Daedalus* 106 (1977): 87–114.

Figure 4: detail of the effigies of Catherine Grey (rear) and Edward Seymour, earl of Hertford.

to the positive one of Elizabeth, the Gorges family had to edit their family history in order to share more fully in the glory of Elizabeth's memory. This tomb monument mutually constructs the political glory of the Gorges family and that of Elizabeth I, and Helena's court career played an integral part in connecting the family to a glorious reign.

Whereas the monumental body and past of Helena, marchioness of Northampton, were placed side by side with her husband's, Catherine Grey's effigy and ancestry are at the forefront of her funerary monument. In spite of the fact that the monument including her is known officially as the Hertford Monument, the entire structure revolves around her effigy. She is placed above Seymour, not side by side as on the Gorges Monument. The most obvious explanation for this placement is that her lineage was superior to that of the earl.[19] Their lineages are carved out in Latin in the large plaque above them. The earl was "Son and heir of the most illustrious, most noble Edward Duke of Somerset, Earl of Hertford, and Viscount Beauchamp and Baron St. Maur, K[night of the] G[arter], Uncle and Guardian of King Edward VI and Lord Protector of the Kingdom, Commander in Chief...Treasurer and Earl Marshal of England

---

[19] Fletcher, *The Hertford Monument*.

and Governor of Guernsey and Jersey by Ann his wife descended from an ancient and noble family."[20]

As esteemed as this lineage might have been, it did not quite equal the family ancestry of Grey, Seymour's "dearly beloved wife Catherine, daughter and heiress of Henry and Frances Grey, Duke and Duchess of Suffolk, [the latter who was] daughter of Charles Brandon, Duke of Suffolk and Mary his wife, sister of Henry VIII and Dowager Queen of France and endowed as her granddaughter and the great-granddaughter of Henry VII."[21] Whereas Seymour's claim to greatness was that his father held high positions of power, the closest he

---

[20] The full inscription on the plaque in its original Latin is M.S./EDOVARDO HERTFORDIÆ/ COMITI BARONI BEL: CAMPO.&c/ILVSTRISSIMI PRINCIPIS EDOVARDI. DVCIS SOMERSETÊSIS/COM: HERTFORDIÆ, PROCOMIT:s BEILICAMPI. & BARONIS DE SANCTO/ MAVRO GARTERIANI ORDINIS EQVESTRIS CELEBERRIMI SODALIS./ EDOVARDI.VI. REG: AVVUNCVLI & GVBERNATORIS, EIVSQ: REGNORV̄/ DOMINIORV̄ AC SVBITORV̄ PROTECTORIS DIGNISSIMI. EXCERCITV̄Q/PRÆFECTI & LOCV̄ TENENTIS GENERALIS. THESAVRARIJ .& COMITIS/ MARESCAILI ANGLIÆ. GVBERNATORIS, & CAPITANEI INSVLARV̄ DE GARSNEY/ & JERSEY.&c EX ANNA VXORE SPLENDIDISS: ORTA NATALIB, & PERANTIQVIS./ FILIO ET HÆREDI/ NEC NON CONIVGI SVÆ CHARISS. DILECTISS./CATHARINÆ/ HENRICI & FRANCISCÆ GRAI DD SVFFOLC FILIÆ & HÆREDI/CAROLI BRANDON D. SVFFOLC EX MARIA HEN: VIII SORORE, & GAILIAR/ REGIN.DOTAZIA [sic] PRONEPTI. & HEN: VII. ABNEPTI./ INCOMPARABILI CONIVGVM PARI / QVI ALTERNANTIS FORTVNÆ VICES, SVBINIDE EXPERTI/ HIC TANDEM QVÂ VIXERE CONCORDIÂ REQVIESCVNT SIMVL/ ILLA/ SINGVLARIS EXEMPLI PROBITATIS, FORMÆ, AC FIDEI FÆMINA,/ NON SÆCULI SVI, SED OMNIS, ÆVI, OPTIMA, CLARISSIMA/ XXII IANVA ANN: CIƆ.IƆ LXIII. PIE AC PLACIDE EXPIRAVIT. / ILLE/ VIR INTEGERRIMVS. NOBILITATIS NORMA./ MORVM, AC DISCIPLINÆ PRISCÆ CONSERVATOR./ ELOQVIO, PRVDENTIA, INNOCENTIA, GRAVITATE,/NEC MINVS VIRTVTE, & DOCTRINA QVAM GENERIS SPLENDORE NOBILIS./ VT QVI VNA CV̄ EDOARDO PRINCIP: REG: HEN: FIL: IN STUDIJS ADOLEVERAT./ RELIGIONIS ACERRIMVS VINDEX./ RECTI AC IVSTI PERPETVVS ASSERTOR/ IN ADMINISTRANDIS PROVINCIJS SIBI CREDITIS SVMMÆ FIDEI AC AVCTORITATIS./ AMPLISSIMA AD ARCHI D.D. PRO IAC: M:B:REG: OPT: LEGATIONE FVNCTVS/ DOMI, FORISQVE, MVNIFICENTIA MAGNVS./ ET VT OPIBVS EXCEILENS, SIC ANIMO QVAM DIVITIIS LOCVPLETIOR./ NEC VNQVAM POTENTIA SVA. AD IMPOTENTIAM, IN CLIENTES, VSVS./ PLENVS HONORIBVS PLENVS ANNIS/ OCTOGESIMV̄ SVV̄ & TERTIV̄ AGENS AN°: CIƆ.IƆ CXXI VI APRIL: NATVRÆ CONCESSIT./ FILIOS EX HEROINA SVSCEPIT DVOS.

[21] The translation of the Latin inscriptions comes from Fletcher, *The Hertford Monument*. The details of the Grey-Hertford story and tomb also come from this lecture.

comes to royalty is that he is the cousin of a king. Grey, on the other hand, is the great-granddaughter of a king, as well as granddaughter of a queen. Her lineage is of greater genealogical value, which elevates her physically on the tomb.[22] The Hertford Monument illustrates a different strategy from the one demonstrated by the Gorges tomb. Instead of trying to equalize the spouses, the monument highlights Catherine Grey's royal blood and separates her from the body and blood of her husband. This royal princess's lineage augmented the Seymour family's claim to royalty that the earl's own could not as effectively provide. Moreover, this royal blood, although stemming from King Henry VII, had been transmitted exclusively by women: his daughter Mary passed it on to her daughter Frances, who in turn gave it to her daughters, one of whom was Catherine Grey.[23]

It was not only the body language that was deliberately crafted, but so too was the inscription. The omissions here, as in the Gorges Monument, are just as interesting as what was presented. Nowhere on the tomb are the names of the two other wives of the earl of Hertford. He had provided his first legally recognized wife, Frances Howard, daughter of Lord Howard of Effingham, with a monument at Westminster Abbey—but neither she nor his last wife, another Frances Howard who outlived him, is mentioned anywhere on the one in Salisbury Cathedral. As demonstrated by the Gorges Monument, the practice of including references to other spouses was quite common. Indeed, husbands who married more than once were sometimes buried with both wives at their sides. However, the bodies of the earl of Hertford's subsequent wives were edited out of this family history. Another woman erased from this text is Queen Elizabeth I. Grey's position as maid of honor to Elizabeth I is not stated, and Seymour's service to James I as ambassador is mentioned only briefly in a paragraph after the one in which Catherine Grey's life is recounted.[24] As we saw with the Gorges Monument, tomb texts often modified the histories of those being commemorated, making it easy to list the honors and leave out any dishonor. And yet, here the honor of Grey's royal service was completely ignored and that of her husband was marginalized. Instead, both Seymour and Grey, and consequently their descendants, stand apart from and independent of Elizabeth I and James I.

It is understandable why Elizabeth I would be banished from this space, but why would James I receive similar (though not as harsh) treatment? To answer this question, the authorship of this tomb must be discussed. William Seymour,

---

[22] Fletcher, *The Hertford Monument*.

[23] An even more famous daughter was Jane, who was queen for nine days, before Mary I took back the throne. Eventually Mary ordered the execution of Grey, her husband, and Grey's father-in-law, the duke of Northumberland, who had engineered Grey's accession.

[24] Another omission of Catherine Grey's life was her divorce from a husband to whom she had been betrothed as a young child; see Fletcher, *The Hertford Monument*, and Wilson, *Queen Elizabeth's Maids of Honour*, 107.

the earl's grandson, is credited with commissioning the tomb shortly after the death of his grandfather. Seymour inherited both his grandfather's title of earl of Hertford and the first earl's penchant for secretly marrying heiresses to the English crown. In 1610, he married Arabella Stuart, first cousin to King James I. Like his grandparents, they too were arrested, separated, and imprisoned. A failed escape attempt left Arabella Stuart to die of grief and starvation while under house arrest and William Seymour free but in exile on the Continent.[25] When Arabella Stuart died in 1615, Seymour made peace with the king and returned to court, where he earned a knighthood and continued in royal service.[26] Six short years later, his grandfather died, and William Seymour commissioned the tomb. Although Seymour had returned to the court of James I, the wounds of his failed attempt to gain power by marrying a royal heir had apparently not completely healed. William Seymour rehabilitated his family at the expense of the two sources that had forcefully stopped the family's further ascent up the social and political ladder. By leaving out the name of Elizabeth I and by barely acknowledging James I, the Seymour family connections to those monarchs were minimized, allowing the Seymours' claims to royalty to stand on their own. By commemorating a family Elizabeth sought to destroy, this monument challenges her royal authority and records the limitations of her power.

Both the Hertford and the Gorges monuments serve as examples of how women's lives and activities were the linchpin that connected family histories to larger national histories. Families acknowledged that women participated in national politics and appropriated that fact to establish the importance and social standing of the family. Even royal families utilized their female relatives' monumental bodies to construct their family histories. Indeed, the central example of women's tombs used in writing family histories and, consequently, British national history can be seen in James I's royal program of monument-building at Westminster Abbey.

As Julia M. Walker has discussed extensively, Elizabeth I's present tomb at Westminster Abbey is not her original resting place.[27] In 1603, she was interred

---

[25] Ruth Norrington, *In the Shadow of the Throne: The Lady Arabella Stuart* (London: Peter Owen, 2002), 106, discusses the secret wedding; 119–33, the plan to escape; 135–42, her further imprisonment; 147, her refusal to eat and the date of her death, 25 September 1615. For a more recent biography on Arabella Stuart, see Sarah Gristwood, *Arbella: England's Lost Queen* (New York: Houghton Mifflin, 2003).

[26] Fletcher, *The Hertford Monument*.

[27] Julia M. Walker has written on this subject in three different articles. See "Reading the Tombs of Elizabeth I," *English Literary Renaissance* 26 (1996): 510–30; "Bones of Contention: Posthumous Images of Elizabeth and Stuart Politics," in *Dissing Elizabeth: Negative Representations of Gloriana*, ed. eadem (Durham, NC: Duke University Press, 1998), 252–76; and the chapter "1603–1620: The Shadow of the Rainbow," in eadem, *The Elizabeth Icon 1603–2003* (New York: Palgrave Macmillan, 2003), 6–48. See also Peter

with her grandfather Henry VII under the altar in the abbey chapel bearing her grandfather's name. When James I came to the English throne, he needed to smooth over some rather messy familial and national history: the execution of his mother, Mary Stuart, Queen of Scots, Elizabeth's dying childless, and his own accession, as a Scot, to the English throne. The way he tackled this problem was to reconstruct the dynastic history of the English crown through a program of building royal tombs at Westminster. James built a grand tomb for Elizabeth, but it was built over the site where Elizabeth's half-sister, Mary I, lay interred. The two sisters were buried together, but the large monument on this spot depicts only Elizabeth's effigy.

Walker argues that, by deliberately moving Elizabeth in 1607 from the center of the chapel to the north aisle (literally to the side), James physically marginalized Elizabeth from the Tudor-Stuart succession story. James put two barren women together, consigning them to the margins and making it clear that childless women have no important place in a family history. Pride of place was reserved for the reproductive female relatives who had ensured James I's place on the English throne. The woman to whom he did give a prominently placed tomb was his mother, Mary Stuart. Her monument cost almost three times as much as the one he built for Elizabeth (£2000 vs. £765), and it is both taller and wider. James carefully chose the site of his mother's tomb; she is buried directly behind King Henry VII's mother, Lady Margaret Beaufort, and in front of the monument of Margaret, countess of Lennox, James's paternal grandmother. James's careful placement of his mother's tomb situates her in a fruitful dynastic line that both rehabilitates Mary Stuart's position in the dynastic history and bolsters his own claim to the crown.[28]

James then claimed Elizabeth's original resting place as his own. By placing himself in the same grave as his great-great-grandfather, King Henry VII, James makes clear that his ascendance to the throne represents a continuation and not a rupture in the history of the English crown. The positioning of his grave, those of his cousins Elizabeth and Mary, and that of his mother declare that he is the direct descendant of King Henry VII. James's displacement of Elizabeth I

Sherlock, "The Monuments of Elizabeth Tudor and Mary Stuart: King James and the Manipulation of Memory," *Journal of British Studies* 46 (2007): 263–89. Sherlock also does a close reading of James I's building campaign in Westminster Abbey, but he disagrees with Walker that James's removal of Elizabeth I from her original resting place was an act of disrespect.

[28] Walker, *Elizabeth Icon*, 29. Sherlock, "The Monuments," 271, also declares that the tomb-building program of James I did divide the Tudor and Stuart women into sections based upon their fertility or barrenness. However, he later states (287) how these distinct lines became blurred later on in James's reign when he buried three of his unmarried children in the same vault as their grandmother, Mary, Queen of Scots. See also Howarth, *Images of Rule*, 169–70.

from her original tomb also displaces her from the dynastic history: James I was king of England, not because a childless woman bequeathed the throne to him, but because he was the great-great-grandson of King Henry VII.[29] Despite the fact that James's royal tomb program celebrated patriarchy, the deliberate use of women's monumental bodies subtly reminds us that James I, like William Seymour, received his kingly blood from his female relatives.

The tombs James I commissioned at Westminster Abbey and the Hertford and Gorges monuments at Salisbury Cathedral demonstrate that manipulating female bodies and deciding whom to include or exclude changes the history the monuments tell. Funerary stonework, like manuscript histories kept by families, recorded the ways in which both men and women participated in court life. Such histories and those of the reign of Elizabeth I mutually shaped each other. Family members, including women, acted as links to the larger political arena for a family, and these links enhanced a family's record of itself. However, the family could either construct a positive image for itself by tying its success to that of the queen, or it could tell a story at the expense of the queen's image and memory. In both life and in death, women could either support Elizabeth as queen, or they could challenge the queen's authority. It is time for modern histories to reflect what people knew in the sixteenth and seventeenth centuries, that women played an important part in the life and the reign of Elizabeth I. The Virgin Queen was not the lone woman at court during her reign; rather, she ruled with women, over women, against women, and was ultimately laid to rest eternally among women.

---

[29] Walker, *Elizabeth Icon*, 29. Sherlock, "The Monument," 282–83, also argues that putting his own heraldry on Elizabeth's tomb monuments subverts Elizabeth's memorial—it not only speaks to her memory, but is used as a platform to demonstrate that James I was directly descended from Henry VII, and thereby a rightful heir to the throne.

All the Queen's Children: Elizabeth I and the Meanings of Motherhood[1]

Carole Levin

I. "offspring ... perhaps ungracious"

Henry IV of France once said there were certain things to which one would never know the answer. While one was what was his own religion (Henry being the man who is said to have claimed, "Paris is worth a mass"), another was the answer to the question, whether or not "Queen Elizabeth be a maid or no."[2] If Elizabeth were not a virgin, then, many would argue, she was instead a mother. In 1559 Elizabeth herself is said to have proclaimed that she would be known for having "lived and died a virgin."[3] Yet in conjunction with this trope, as Christine Coch points out, throughout her reign she used the rhetoric of motherhood when she spoke about her people.[4] Despite the fact that in the end she never married, she did at least consider the possibility of marriage for a number of years as well having several favorites at court, most notably Robert Dudley, earl of Leicester.[5] During her reign there were frequent rumors that she had had children; a number of people were arrested for slander for talking about her pregnancies and the babies she destroyed. And at least one young man, calling himself Arthur Dudley,

---

[1] A version of this paper was presented at Southern Illinois University, Edwardsville, March 2003. I am grateful to John Pendergast for inviting me. I am most appreciative of Jo Carney, Ilona Bell, Steven May, Pamela Nickless, and especially Carolyn Biltoft for their support of this essay. Carolyn's French translations as well as other research support were of immense help. For more on Elizabeth's reputation in the sixteenth century, see Carole Levin, *The Heart and Stomach of a King* (Philadelphia: University of Pennsylvania Press, 1994).

[2] Francis Osborne, *Works*, 9th ed. (London, 1689), 383–84.

[3] *Elizabeth I: Collected Works*, ed. Leah S. Marcus, Janel Mueller, and Mary Beth Rose (Chicago and London: University of Chicago Press, 2000), 58.

[4] Christine Coch, "'Mother of my Contreye': Elizabeth I and Tudor Constructions of Motherhood," *English Literary Renaissance* 26 (1996): 423–51.

[5] See Susan Doran, *Monarchy and Matrimony: The Courtships of Elizabeth I* (New York: Routledge, 1996).

claimed in the 1580s to be Elizabeth's son. Today, serious scholars of the period are in agreement that Elizabeth bore no children, never experienced pregnancies. But the counterparts to the scandal-mongers of the sixteenth century are the romance novelists on the one hand, and those of the far shore of the Shakespeare authorship controversy on the other. For them, what is most important about Elizabeth and the secret key to her personality is the fact of motherhood. This essay examines Elizabeth's own use of language to imply her motherhood in a metaphorical sense, the rumors about her during her reign and soon after about her sexuality and fertility, and the theories about her that are still bandied about today. The comments about her sexual behavior and supposed children, both then and now, also open a curtain to people's attitudes toward powerful women, especially ones, like Elizabeth, who ruled unmarried.

From the beginning of the reign Elizabeth was under great pressure to marry and name an heir. Sir Thomas Gargrave, speaker of the House of Commons, informed Elizabeth in February of 1559 that it was the prayer of all Englishmen that she marry forthwith and have children. But Elizabeth already had a response ready that gave a new meaning to her role as mother. "Whensoever it pleases God to incline my heart" to marriage then she would do so, but until that time she would remain a virgin but also mother to her people, demonstrating at least rhetorically that the venerated Mary was not the only one who could be both virgin and mother.[6] "And do not upbraid me with miserable lack of children," she stated, "for every one of you, as many as are Englishmen, are children, and kinsmen to me."[7]

I am certainly not suggesting that when Elizabeth became queen in 1558 she knew that she would never marry and had already mapped out the image of herself as "Virgin Queen." For years she played at courtship and in 1566 told her Parliament "I will marry as soon as I can conveniently."[8] But it does seem clear that marriage was not something she wanted, and she even questioned just what kind of children she might have. While most people expect to have children whom they will love and who will make them proud, she stated that "such offspring as may come of me . . . may . . . become, perhaps, ungracious."[9] In 1561 Elizabeth informed the Scottish ambassador that "Princes cannot like their own children, those that should succeed unto them."[10]

It seems that only very briefly did Elizabeth's "biological clock" perhaps give a timorous tick tock when she considered marrying Francis, duke of Alençon, later Anjou, in the very final marriage negotiation of her reign. And she

---

[6] On the precedent set by her sister Mary, who also described herself as a mother to her people, see Sarah Duncan, "The Two Virgin Queens," in this volume, 29–51.

[7] *Elizabeth I: Collected Works*, 57, 59.

[8] *Elizabeth I: Collected Works*, 95.

[9] *Elizabeth I: Collected Works*, 58.

[10] *Elizabeth I: Collected Works*, 65.

was appalled to find that after twenty years of being urged to marry and have children, now people were opposed, not only because of deep distrust of the French but more importantly because of the fear that the queen was now too old to make having a child a safe possibility. In 1579 at the age of forty-five she told her council in tears of frustration because they opposed her, that it was "doubtful whether there could be any more surety for her and her realm than for her to marry and have a child of her own body to inherit."[11] But this moment, if sincere, was fleeting.

II. "nothing other than a wicked stepmother"

When Elizabeth became queen in 1558 at the age of twenty-five, she was the last of her immediate family. Her mother had been beheaded before she was three and all her stepmothers were dead. She had survived the reigns of her father, her younger brother, and her older sister. Elizabeth was ruling not only as an unmarried woman—a virgin—but also as a woman not under the control of any man. By presenting herself as both virgin and mother, Elizabeth was also carefully implying that she could rule with no man at her side, needing no male power to support her. As Lena Cowen Orlin points out, Elizabeth frequently supplemented her rhetoric of motherhood to her people by the way she used the language of close familial relationships, especially in her correspondence with other monarchs—cousin, sister, *and* mother. Elizabeth alone could create family relations as she needed to.[12]

This mix of potential connections was especially true in the way she spoke to and about her cousin Mary Stuart. Though only nine years older than Mary, she not only did on occasion give her advice as an older sister would to a younger one, but as a mother might to a daughter.[13] Elizabeth was particularly concerned for Mary after the spectacular murder of her second husband Henry Lord Darnley and Mary's hasty marriage to Lord Bothwell, whom many concluded was Darnley's murderer, and she wrote to Mary a number of warning letters:

> How could a worse choice be made for your honor than in such haste to marry such a subject, who besides other and notorious lacks, public fame

---

[11] *Calendar of the Manuscripts of the . . . Marquis of Salisbury . . . Preserved at Hatfield House*, ed. Robert Cecil, Marquis of Salisbury, et al., 15 vols. (London: Her Majesty's Stationery Office, 1883–1976), 2:272.

[12] Lena C. Orlin, "The Fictional Families of Elizabeth I," in *Political Rhetoric, Power, and Renaissance Women*, ed. Carole Levin and Patricia A. Sullivan (Albany: State University of New York Press, 1995), 85–109.

[13] On Mary's response to Elizabeth's overtures to her as a "sister," see Retha Warnicke, "Elizabeth I and Mary Stewart," in this volume, 53–68.

hath charged with the murder of your late husband, besides the touching of yourself also in some part, though we trust that in that behalf falsely.[14]

While she was always ambivalent about her younger, more sexually available cousin, her feelings about Mary changed vividly once she became aware of Mary's plotting against her once Mary was in custody in England. In 1569 Elizabeth told Bertrand Fénélon, the French ambassador, "that she had taken great pains to be more than a good mother to the Queen of Scots," but, in somewhat the language of fairy tales, "she who uses and plots against her mother, deserves to have nothing other than a wicked stepmother."[15] Some may well have considered Elizabeth in this role when in 1587 she signed Mary Stuart's death warrant.

As well as the rhetoric she used in writing to and talking about other monarchs and in her comments to her people, Elizabeth frequently agreed to be a godmother. She served this function not only to Mary Stuart's only son James VI, who eventually became her successor, and to some other foreign children, but to many of the children of her courtiers; Elizabeth had well over one hundred godchildren.[16]

III. "that I may show myself . . . as I am"

Yet despite Elizabeth's efforts to demonstrate herself as 'mother' in positive, rhetorical ways, from the time she was fifteen rumors circulated that she was pregnant or had had children. The first time the rumor surfaced was in 1549 when Elizabeth was being questioned about her connections with Thomas Seymour, who was in the Tower.[17] When Sir Robert Tyrwhitt examined Elizabeth, he warned her in a hectoring manner that there were rumors she was with child by Seymour, perhaps hoping that such news would break her spirit. Instead, Elizabeth took as much control of the situation as she could, writing to Edward Seymour, the Lord Protector, demanding that she come to court where she could show the world that she was not pregnant:

> Master Tyrwhit and others have told me, that there goeth rumors abroad which be greatly both against mine honor and honesty . . . which be these: that I am . . . with child by my lord admiral. My lord, these are shameful

---

[14] *Elizabeth I: Collected Works*, 118.

[15] Bertrand Fénélon, *Correspondance diplomatique*, ed. Charles Purton Cooper, 7 vols. (Paris: Panckoucke, 1838–1840), 2:169.

[16] Steven W. May, *The Elizabethan Courtier Poets: The Poems and Their Contexts* (Columbia, MO: University of Missouri Press, 1991), 27 n. 2.

[17] On this incident and its effects on the Princess, see Janel Mueller, " Elizabeth Tudor: Maidenhood in Crisis," in this volume, 15–27.

slanders. . . . I shall most heartily desire your lordship that I may come to the court after your first determination, that I may show myself there as I am.[18]

When she was not allowed to come to court, Elizabeth quickly moved on to a new strategy.

It might so seem good unto your lordship and the rest of the Council to send forth a proclamation into the countries that they refrain their tongues, declaring how the tales be but lies.[19]

While Elizabeth did not get her proclamation, Leah Marcus, Janel Mueller, and Mary Beth Rose suggest that she did get "a more local order or declaration to the same effect," since she subsequently thanked the Lord Protector for it.[20]

Elizabeth also learned from this dangerous situation that she had to take care to protect her reputation while she was an heir to the throne; she was far more careful about the way she presented herself. Despite this, several years later, in her sister's reign, the rumor surfaced again, started by Elizabeth's Catholic enemies. In 1554, when Elizabeth was brought to London under suspicion of involvement in Thomas Wyatt's rebellion, she was under great stress and unwell. She insisted on traveling as slowly as possible. The Spanish ambassador wrote to the emperor and presented his own interpretation of the reasons why:

The Lady Elizabeth, who is so unwell that she only travels two or three leagues a day, and has such a stricken conscience that she cannot stand on her feet and refuses meat or drink. It is taken for certain that she is with child.[21]

Once she became queen in 1558 and chose Robert Dudley as her Master of the Horse and closest companion, the rumors became louder and louder. Dudley was married to Amy Robsart until her mysterious death in 1560. The whispers become a rush of noise that Elizabeth had children by Dudley, and many claimed these babes had then been gruesomely killed. As Adam Fox suggests, "It was clearly widespread from the earliest years of the reign and . . . over the succeeding years these rumours continued to spread, growing larger and more elaborate."[22]

---

[18] *Elizabeth I: Collected Works*, 24.
[19] *Elizabeth I: Collected Works*, 32–33.
[20] *Elizabeth I: Collected Works*, 32 n. 2.
[21] *Calendar of Letters, Dispatches, and State Papers, Relating to the Negotiations between England and Spain, Preserved in the Archives at Simancas and Elsewhere*, ed. Royall Tyler (London: Longman, Green, Longman & Roberts [etc.], 1862–1954), vol. 12, *Mary, January – July 1554*, 120.
[22] Adam Fox, *Oral and Literate Culture in England, 1500–1700* (Oxford: Clarendon Press, 2000), 361–62. On Catholic propaganda attacking Elizabeth's sexual reputation, see also Mary Hill Cole, "Maternal ," in this volume, 1–14.

Here is a sampling of such rumors by various English people of the time. In 1560 Mother Amy Dowe openly asserted "that the Queen was with child by Robt. Duddeley." Three years later Edmund Baxter's wife claimed that when she saw Elizabeth at Ipswich "she looked like one lately come out of child-bed." Men as well as women participated in spreading this gossip. In 1570 a man named Marshame had to pay a fine of £100 or lose his ears for saying Elizabeth had two children by Dudley. Two years later Robert Blosse was arrested for claiming that now the number of children was up to four, a claim later made by Robert Gardner in 1582. In 1580 the number was back to two, claimed the laborer Thomas Playfere, though in 1598 Edward Fraunces thought it was three. In 1600 Robert Fowler, a blacksmith, proclaimed that Essex was one of Elizabeth's sons, while the other was, bizarrely enough, the brother of the former vicar of the local parish. But Henry Stanford was convinced that Elizabeth did not have sons; instead, it was three daughters. In 1581 Henry Hawkins explained why Elizabeth so liked to go on progresses; it was a way for her to leave court and have her illegitimate children: five all told. A number of those who spoke of Elizabeth's illegitimate children were also emphatic that, once they were born, they were then destroyed. So claimed Robert Gardner, Dionisia Deryck, and Hugh Broughton.[23] I have argued elsewhere that these rumors suggest both the wish for an heir and also anxiety and concern over an unmarried woman ruler.

IV. "My life is in the open"

It is hardly surprising amidst all these rumors of children that in the late 1580s a young man appeared who called himself Arthur Dudley, and claimed to be the son of Elizabeth and Robert. The young man made his appearance in Spain in 1587. He was taken into custody as a spy. The story he told Philip II's English secretary Sir Francis Englefield was certainly arresting.

He claimed he had only recently learned that, when he was born, the man he had thought was his father—Robert Southern, a confidante of Katherine Ashley who had been close to Elizabeth since the Queen was a child—had been summoned to court and given an infant child named Arthur to raise as his own. But Arthur never really felt that he was part of the family, and when he was fourteen or fifteen he had an argument with his supposed father, Robert Southern, and left to see the world. After some years of travel abroad, he received a letter from Southern in 1583 begging him to return to England. When Arthur came home,

---

[23] Fox, *Oral and Literate Culture in England*, 362–63; Levin, *The Heart and Stomach of a King*, 75–78, 83–84; Marcy L. North, "Queen Elizabeth Compiled: Henry Stanford's Private Anthology and the Question of Accountability," in *Dissing Elizabeth: Negative Representations of Gloriana*, ed. Julia Walker (Durham, NC: Duke University Press, 1998), 185–208, here 186.

he found Southern to be very ill, and with many tears Southern confided that Arthur was not his son, nor had he paid for his upkeep. Arthur begged to know who were his real parents; Southern finally told Arthur secretly that he was the son of the earl of Leicester and the queen. Arthur managed to see his real father Robert Dudley, earl of Leicester, who expressed great affection for him, but when Leicester sent Arthur to Sir Francis Walsingham, supposedly so that he could have a certificate that would protect him from arrest, Walsingham examined him very curiously and he deferred giving Arthur the paper. This conversation made Arthur afraid to return to Walsingham, and he again fled England, this time for Spain.

Englefield reported this story to Philip, along with Arthur's offer to be a spy for the Spanish against his supposed parents, Elizabeth and Leicester. But Englefield was highly doubtful. "I think it very probable that the revelations that this lad is making everywhere may originate in the queen of England and her Council, and possibly with an object that Arthur himself does not yet understand." But just in case Arthur *was* Elizabeth's bastard son, Englefield continued, "I am of opinion that he should not be allowed to get away, but should be kept very secure to prevent his escape." The king of Spain concurred, noting it would be "safest to make sure of [Dudley's] person until we know more about it." This is the last mention of "Arthur Dudley," kept "safe" by the Spanish, never to be heard from again.[24]

So does the appearance of Arthur Dudley prove that Elizabeth was a mother? I hardly think so. Certainly the young man had a number of convincing details to offer. But Elizabeth's life was closely observed; there is no way she could have hidden a pregnancy. As she told the Spanish ambassador, Guzman de Silva, in 1564, "My life is in the open, and I have so many witnesses that I cannot understand how so bad a judgement can have been formed of me." De Silva, who observed her closely, came to accept her protestations. In a letter to the duchess of Parma the same year, he wrote that his experiences at court "make me doubt sometimes whether Robert's position is so irregular as many think. It is nothing for princes to hear evil, even without giving any cause of it."[25] Also, though the evidence is overwhelming that Elizabeth did not have a child, even if she did, it is, as Martin Hume suggests, "beyond belief that a boy in the condition represented would have been allowed to run about the world at his own free will."[26] Hume argues that Dudley was a spy and the story was cover in case he were caught. While this may well be the case, it is also possible that "Arthur Dudley,"

---

[24] *Calendar of the Letters and State Papers, Relating to English Affairs Preserved in, Originally Belonging to, the Archives of Simancas*, ed. Martin A. S. Hume, 4 vols. (London: Her Majesty's Stationery Office, 1892–1899), 4:101–12.

[25] *Calendar Simancas*, 1:381, 387.

[26] Martin A. S. Hume, *The Courtships of Queen Elizabeth* (London: E. Nash & Grayson, 1926), 341.

with what Freud would dub a "family romance," really believed that he was Elizabeth's son.[27] As the author of the 1572 text *Of Ghostes and Spirits* suggests, some men "bycause they have ben long weried with sicknesse, or else bycause they love extremelie . . . thinke them selves great Princes . . ."[28] There are a number of recorded cases in sixteenth-century England of people confused about their identity and perceived as "frantic" or "frenzied." A number of them even had some connections with Elizabeth. William Cartwright, brother of the Puritan Thomas, caused such uproar when he claimed he was the rightful king that he had to be committed to Bedlam.[29]

There is an irony about the Arthur Dudley story. In 1584, only a few years before the young man's appearance in Spain, a scurrilous anti-Dudley pamphlet, *Leicester's Commonwealth*, was published. As well as calling Leicester a murderer, the pamphlet suggested that he planned to subvert the succession with an illegitimate son, "Whereby he might be able after the death of her Majesty to make legitimate to the crown any one bastard of his own by any of so many hackneys as he keepeth, affirming it to be the natural issue of her Majesty by himself."[30] The anonymous author of *Leicester's Commonwealth* did not believe that Elizabeth had had a child but feared that an impostor could be brought forth. A half-century after Elizabeth's death, Francis Osborne referred to stories he had heard about Elizabeth's children, "a son bred in the state of Venice, and a daughter, I know not where nor when," but Osborne dismissed these stories as "fitter for a romance than a history."[31] In the seventeenth century there were a number of "secret histories" written that were romances about Elizabeth and her sexual / romantic relationships.[32]

---

[27] Sigmund Freud, *Collected Papers*, ed. James Strachey, 5 vols. (New York: Basic Books, 1959), 5:74–78. Freud used the term "family romance" to discuss a particular phenomenon, one where people thought they were the children of someone famous instead of the child of their parents. For more on the term "family romance," see Reuben Fine, *A History of Psychoanalysis* (New York: Columbia University Press, 1979), 425; and Henri F. Ellenberger, *The Discovery of the Unconscious: The History and Evoluton of Dynamics Psychiatry* (New York: Basic Books, 1970), 507–8.

[28] Lewes Lavater, *Of Ghostes and Sprirites Walking By Nyght, 1572*, ed. J. Dover Wilson and May Yardley (Oxford: Oxford University Press, 1929), 11.

[29] Andrew Forest Scott Pearson, *Thomas Cartwright and Elizabethan Puritanism* (Cambridge: Cambridge University Press, 1925), 393, 483.

[30] *Leicester's Commonwealth: The Copy of a Letter Written by a Master of Arts Cambridge (1584) and Related Documents*, ed. D. C. Peck (Athens, OH: Ohio University Press, 1985), 130.

[31] Osborne, *Works*, 384.

[32] See John Watkins, *Representing Elizabeth in Stuart England: Literature, History, Sovereignty* (Cambridge: Cambridge University Press, 2002), 150–87.

V. "She was, simply, a woman."

We hear the echoes of the sixteenth-century slander in the writings of romance novelists and those convinced that the man William Shakespeare was not the author of the plays that bear his name. In the sixteenth century the rumors about Elizabeth's sexual conduct and her illegitimate children represented a variety of anxieties: concern about political insecurity, worry about the succession, fear of a woman ruler and a desire to cut her down to size by emphasizing her lack of ability to control her emotional behavior, arguing that for women, sex and romance, rather than power, are the key desires. While in the twentieth and now twenty-first centuries the belief that Elizabeth had children is brought forth by romance novelists on the one hand and anti-Stratfordians on the other, their contention is the end of a continuum that is part of the popular view of Elizabeth.[33] If we examine the twentieth-century films about Elizabeth, from Sarah Bernhardt's in 1912 to Cate Blanchett's in 1998, most of them focused almost entirely on Elizabeth's romantic entanglements. The result of all of these is to dismiss Elizabeth and, by extension, powerful women. The Elizabeth of *Fire Over England* (1937) and *Shakespeare in Love* (1998) are among the few film versions not concerned with her romances, and not coincidentally the few to show a powerful queen.

Elizabeth is certainly one of the most popular historical figures in the world. Both scholarly and popular studies of her are being published every year and many, many novels are being produced. In *The Queen's Bastard* (1999), Robin Maxwell writes about Arthur Dudley, accepting the story that he was indeed the son of Elizabeth and Leicester. This is Maxwell's Elizabeth, madly in love with Robert Dudley:

> My God, thought Elizabeth, how beautiful he is! She wished for nothing more than to fly into Robin's strong embracing arms . . . [He] kissed her hungrily on the mouth. She yielded to the kiss and moaned with the familiar pleasure of his touch . . . . Then in Robin Dudley's kingly bed, he made long awaited and passionate love to the Queen of England.[34]

Maxwell asserts that Dudley meant everything to Elizabeth: "For only with Robin was her heart truly safe. In his presence alone was Elizabeth other than queen. She was, simply, a woman."[35]

---

[33] For more on that subject, see Martha Tuck Rozett, "Fictional Queen Elizabeths and Women-Centered Historical Fiction," in *Constructing a World: Shakespeare's England and the New Historical Fiction* (Albany: State University of New York Press, 2003), 103–42, and Frances E. Dolan, "How a Maiden Keeps Her Head: Anne Boleyne, Elizabeth I, and the Perils of Marriage," in *Marriage and Violence: The Early Modern Legacy* (Philadelphia: University of Pennsylvania Press, 2008), 132–63.

[34] Robin Maxwell, *The Queen's Bastard* (New York: Scribner, 1999), 7–8, 10.

[35] Maxwell, *Queen's Bastard*, 53.

Elizabeth had light and irregular periods,[36] and Maxwell has her character Elizabeth assume as a result that she cannot get pregnant. When she finds that she is, she is convinced that marrying Robert or letting the world know of the pregnancy would be a mistake. Elizabeth's only confidantes are her lover, his sister Mary Sidney and Mary's husband Henry Sidney, William Cecil, Principal Secretary, and her dear old governess Katherine Ashley. Elizabeth tells Robin that she loves him and will marry him later, though she knows she is lying to him, having promised on her mother's grave, which is historically problematic given she did not have one, never to marry or share her power. Elizabeth's plan is to keep the baby a secret until the time is right to announce him as the heir to the throne. But William Cecil and Katherine Ashley have a different scheme, convinced it will never be safe for the world to know that Elizabeth has had a bastard son. Kat Ashley exchanges Elizabeth's son for a stillborn child that she hands to the mourning Queen, who proclaims: "I must hold him till his father . . . Oh, where is Robin, where is my love . . . ?"[37] This is almost too much for Kat Ashley:

> Kat has never seen such copious tears from Elizabeth, not at the death of her father, of her beloved brother Edward, of the only woman she'd called mother, Catherine Parr. It was breaking Kat's heart to see Elizabeth so distraught . . . It was, she told herself over and over again in a solemn litany, 'for her own good'. . .[38]

Then Kat hands the boy to Robert Southern, an old lover of Kat's, to raise.

Many years later, since Elizabeth indeed has refused ever to marry Robin, he marries her cousin Lettice Knollys, widowed countess of Essex. Elizabeth is devastated when she hears about it. "The Queen's body heaved and she commenced weeping . . . She, no longer the Queen but merely a wronged and wretched woman."[39] Robin and Lettice have a son who dies in childhood, and eventually Robin and Elizabeth reconcile, still not knowing the truth about *their* son.

After a difficult childhood Arthur flees home and travels through Europe. During one of his visits back to England, Robert Southern, on his deathbed, finally lets Arthur know who he really is. Soon before the Armada, Arthur decides he must confront his real father with the truth. And luckily he has proof. Like his maternal grandmother Anne Boleyn, he also has a rudimentary sixth finger — one, incidentally, that Retha Warnicke has thoroughly disproved as being

---

[36] *Calendar of State Papers and Manuscripts Relating to English Affairs, Existing in the Archives and Collections of Venice, and in Other Libraries of Northern Italy*, ed. Rawdon Brown and G. Cavendish Bentinck, 38 vols. (London: Her Majesty's Stationery Office, 1864-1947), 1:105.

[37] Maxwell, *Queen's Bastard*, 60.
[38] Maxwell, *Queen's Bastard*, 60.
[39] Maxwell, *Queen's Bastard*, 265.

a legend developed by Catholic propagandists after Anne Boleyn's death.[40] Dudley and Arthur weep in each other's arms, but Dudley laments that they cannot at that moment tell Elizabeth: "She is in a state of such appalling . . . fragility that I fear the sudden shock of your existence might kill her . . . . We shall have to wait for a more opportune moment."[41] At a time of crisis for the realm, Maxwell's Elizabeth is most known for her fragility.

Arthur heads back to Spain to work as a spy; when captured he admits his true name and is imprisoned, but the English Catholic Sir Francis Englefield secretly arranges his escape and he returns to England to help against Spain as the Armada is being defeated. As the reconciled Robin and Elizabeth celebrate the English victory in their rooms at court, Arthur comes to finally meet his mother. Like Leicester, she is at last convinced:

> There in front of her eyes was the tiny nub of flesh and nail. She could only stare at the extra finger and then at the face. The eyes. The black, fathomless eyes. Her mother's eyes.
>
> "Dear God, dear God!" she wailed and suddenly her arms went round the young man.[42]

Elizabeth promises Arthur that she will acknowledge him as her successor "come what may."[43] But Arthur refuses. "You were brought up on a diet of . . . responsibilities, and you craved to rule. I crave adventure!"[44] The novel ends with Arthur on board ship on his way to the New World.

While as a professional historian I may be critical of this novel, what seems more significant is the way in which non-academics respond. Here is a sampling from amazon.com. Clare: "I loved this novel! Robin Maxwell is a master storyteller . . . . I like her premise, the plot is intelligent, her characterizations of all the historical characters is right on. This novel was hands-down one of the best I have ever read." Chip agrees: "Whether Elizabeth was indeed the Virgin Queen is open for debate, but almost 500 years of speculation about her supposed affair with her horseman, Robin Dudley, lends a plausible air to this novel . . . . Reading her interactions with her court, her relatives, and her supposed lover are an exercise in devouring truly brilliant prose." Cloudia is equally impressed: "Maxwell is brilliant in that she only takes advantage of the room for speculation and never alters the facts themselves which she presents with seemless [sic] accuracy."

---

[40] Retha Warnicke, *The Rise and Fall of Anne Boleyn* (Cambridge: Cambridge University Press, 1989), 3.
[41] Maxwell, *Queen's Bastard*, 296.
[42] Maxwell, *Queen's Bastard*, 419.
[43] Maxwell, *Queen's Bastard*, 422.
[44] Maxwell, *Queen's Bastard*, 424.

But not everyone who posted on amazon loved the book. Margaret was very disappointed. "Elizabeth in 'The Secret Diary of Anne Boleyn' [Maxwell's earlier novel] is headstrong, thoughtful and deep. The Elizabeth you are shown is this book is quarrelsome, selfish and annoying. 'Robin' Dudley is also a detestable character once you get down to it." One reader from Illinois was upset with the historical inaccuracies: "I don't have much respect for historical fiction that blatantly disregards facts to make the book more exciting for modern audiences. I do NOT recommend this."

But for many of the readers, that the book is fiction does not stand in the way of their believing it *might* all be true. As Jen says, "I realize this book is fiction, but that it MAY have some basis in fact. . . . I would highly recommend it." So would a reader from Milwaukee: "[It] is wonderful!!! I couldn't put it down! I love the way Maxwell took a tiny, barely mentioned historical 'fact' and created a story with it. . . . While the basic history is accurate, keep in mind that this is a work of historical fiction and will not be as accurate as a textbook." Kat disputes this statement, arguing that the novel may be more true than the "serious biographies" that she has read: "Many 'serious' biographies would make you believe that only they tell the truth and that there are no holes in history. Well there are holes, and this novel uses them. . . . The author has done an excellent job of this in this novel to make a very interesting alternative history story. She also provides what 'facts' she was able to dig up on the real Arthur Dudley . . . because this man really existed, even if some of the details of the story are a fabrication." And Karen likes it so much that she can't understand why it's not a college textbook: "What yummy history! . . . What if Elizabeth, the Virgin Queen DID have an illegitimate son? Robin Maxwell originates a most superb tale about such a speculation with enough history woven through to see it's [sic] inclusion in college history courses."

This is why I find *The Queen's Bastard* so problematic. It is self-admittedly a novel, but one with pretensions toward historical accuracy, and clearly many readers see it as a correct depiction of Elizabeth's character and as quite possibly true. In her afterword, this is certainly the point Maxwell herself makes. "I found as I researched *The Queen's Bastard* . . . the scenario was entirely plausible. In fact, nothing in his story conflicted with any part of Elizabeth's or Leicester's minutely documented lives."[45] In her afterword Maxwell is a bit careless with her discussion of historians, leading the unwary reader to believe that David Howarth believed in the authenticity of Arthur Dudley. Howarth actually concluded that "one has to believe he was the son of some lady of the court, and that he and Southern sincerely believed his mother was the queen."[46] Maxwell is convinced that most historians scoff at the idea of Arthur Dudley because of their view of

---

[45] Maxwell, *Queen's Bastard*, 433.
[46] David Howarth, *The Voyage of the Armada: The Spanish Story* (London: Collins, 1981), 40.

Elizabeth as "the Virgin Queen she purported to be." Maxwell, however, argues "My own opinion is that the two were intimate in the fullest sense of the word . . . . Perhaps readers of history as well as historical fiction should finally be made aware of Arthur Dudley's existence so that they might decide for themselves if he was, in fact, the bastard child of Lord Leicester and the Virgin Queen."[47]

VI. "the Eternal Feminine strong within her"

In *The Queen's Bastard* a strong and successful historical woman gets reduced to behaving as the heroine of a romance novel with her great love, her passionate emotions, and her secret son. While Maxwell claims her story is "entirely plausible," Orville Ward Owen, Alfred Dodd, and Paul Streitz go further; each claim their theory as fact. All of these men are absolutely committed to the idea that the man named William Shakespeare was not the author of the plays, and all are also convinced that the true author was the son of Elizabeth I, but that is where, as we shall see, their agreement ends.

In the late nineteenth century, the Detroit physician Dr. Orville Ward Owen argued that by breaking a cipher he could prove not only that Sir Francis Bacon wrote Shakespeare's plays, but that he was the secret son of Elizabeth I and Robert Dudley. Alfred Dodd furthered the idea in his 1949 book, *Francis Bacon's Personal Life-Story*, where the love affair of Elizabeth and Dudley begins during the reign of Mary while the two are in the Tower, clearly a perfect "pick up place." "He was just the type of man to appeal to a lonely maiden, loveless, forlorn, friendless."[48] But even though as queen she could hardly be described as forlorn, her intimacy continued unabashedly; she not only did not want the world to know, but she was afraid of what we later historians might think as well: "She began to pose as the VIRGIN QUEEN. There was a fixity of purpose, the better to cloak her real life, to throw dust in the eyes of posterity."[49] Though we know that hundreds of years later many of us are studying Elizabeth, it seems doubtful that as she began her reign she would have been wasting her time worrying about how to fool posterity. Nor does Dodd explain why it was so critical for her to outwardly present herself so completely differently than in "real life."

Three years into the affair Elizabeth became pregnant. And she was desperate, since of course Amy Robsart was still alive and, suggests Dodd, she knew that if she were to "have a bastard son, there would be a Roman Catholic reaction, and even the Protestants would have declared for Mary of Scotland."[50]

---

[47] Maxwell, *Queen's Bastard*, 434, 436.
[48] Alfred Dodd, *Francis Bacon's Personal Life-Story* (London and New York: Rider, 1949), 41.
[49] Dodd, *Francis Bacon*, 41.
[50] Dodd, *Francis Bacon*, 41.

Luckily Amy came to the rescue by committing suicide. Elizabeth and Robert were married privately at the home of Lord Pembroke in late September. The witnesses to the marriage were Nicholas Bacon and his wife, and on 22 January they became the queen's son's foster parents. Even though Amy's death had saved her from having a bastard child, Elizabeth decided to keep the birth a secret. She did not want it known she was married to Dudley because her husband "would be forever England."[51] But Francis was not their only secret child. In November 1567 they had another son, this time adopted by Lettice Knollys. Of course, Dodd is referring to Robert Devereux, second earl of Essex, which means that when Elizabeth had Essex executed in 1601, she was killing her own son.

Dodd's evidence is highly questionable as he relies on the work of Deventer von Kunow: "After much research in British and Continental archives, she found evidence of the Queen's marriage and the birth of their two children." Unfortunately, Dodd does not provide any citations from von Kunow's book, *Francis Bacon, Last of the Tudors*. The letters of the Spanish Ambassador de Quadra "clearly prove, in my opinion, Elizabeth's passion, [and] that there was a undoubtedly a secret marriage between Dudley and Elizabeth."[52] But many scholars have read the same letters and found no such implication. Finally, what clinched the matter for Dodd was that he had broken the cipher of the sonnets, demonstrating Bacon wrote them and knew he was Elizabeth's son. Most, however, might find it most improbable that the sonnets contain secret codes at all. Perhaps more interesting than the "evidence" is Dodd's evaluation of Elizabeth's character:

> The tragedy of Elizabeth has never been truthfully told by the fanciful writers of history, who are adepts at skirting the surfaces and ignoring the deeps. . . . The Truth is, these writers forgot the prime thing in remembering she was our greatest English Queen. They forgot that she was at heart a simple woman of primal instincts with the Eternal Feminine strong within her . . . that the desire for love in the most intimate sense as sweetheart, companion, wife and mother beat quite as fiercely in her breast as in the heart of the average maiden longing and dreaming of the arrival of Prince Charming.[53]

VII. "a myth . . . perpetuated by noncritical historians"

Dodd's Elizabeth, at heart a simple woman, is quite a contrast to the depiction by Paul Streitz in his tedious, brief, tragical, and occasionally mirth-filled *Oxford: Son of Queen Elizabeth I* (2001). The book is riddled with historical errors.

---

[51] Dodd, *Francis Bacon*, 41.
[52] Dodd, *Francis Bacon*, 27.
[53] Dodd, *The Marriage of Elizabeth Tudor* (London: Rider & Co., 1940), vii-viii, 26, 27.

Here are just a few of many, many examples: that the marriage of Henry VIII's older brother Arthur and Catherine of Aragon took place in 1500 and lasted two years (it was in 1501 and lasted five months), that Henry Fitzroy was given the title duke of Buckingham (it was duke of Richmond), that Sir Thomas Cranmer was the bishop of Winchester and Stephen Gardiner archbishop of Canterbury (Cranmer was never knighted and Streitz has their titles reversed).

Streitz is convinced that "The more one reads, the more the Virgin Queen becomes a myth built by the Tudor monarchy and perpetuated by noncritical historians."[54] Streitz's contempt for the professional historians he believes are "noncritical" may be because his training is so different. His advanced degree is an MBA. He is the director of the Oxford Institute, which sponsors events to promote the acceptance of the belief that the Earl of Oxford was the author of the plays. The Institute also runs the Oxford Institute Press, and the only author it publishes is Streitz. His other books are *The Great American College Rip-Off* and *America First: Why Americans Must End Free Trade, Stop Outsourcing and Close Our Open Borders*. Before embracing the Oxford controversy he co-authored musicals such as *Oh, Johnny*, *Connie and the Cowgirls*, and *Madison Avenue, the Subliminal Musical*.

Streitz argues that Elizabeth gets pregnant for the first time at fourteen. A few years later she falls in love with Robert Dudley, and though she conspires with him to murder his wife, she still does not marry him herself even though they sleep together for years and probably have at least four children together. The father of her last child is her own oldest son. As far as I can understand, reading this truly incoherent, if at times hilarious, book, Elizabeth got pregnant by Thomas Seymour and had a son whom William Cecil managed to get John de Vere to take in and pretend was his own. Then when Elizabeth became queen, Cecil and Dudley murdered de Vere; Cecil "was in a position to control the future of Edward de Vere, while Robert Dudley stood to control many of John de Vere's lands."[55] But Dudley and Cecil were not allies—indeed they were enemies. "Robert Dudley had to be implacably opposed to the very existence of Edward de Vere. Robert clearly had designs to marry Elizabeth, but Edward de Vere was the first male child of Elizabeth and stood between Robert and the throne. That Edward de Vere survived at all can only be thought of as a miracle engineered by William Cecil."[56]

Streitz argues that "the idea that Elizabeth never had any true intention of marrying anyone is yet another myth."[57] Elizabeth meant to wed Robert after they had murdered Amy Robsart, but William Cecil prevented her from

---

[54] Paul Streitz, *Oxford: Son of Queen Elizabeth I* (Darien, CT: Oxford Institute Press, 2001), xiii.
[55] Streitz, *Oxford*, 111.
[56] Streitz, *Oxford*, 115.
[57] Streitz, *Oxford*, 123.

marrying him and making him the king by fabricating a Catholic plot. Since, in his version of events, Dudley had planned to marry Elizabeth and ally England with Catholic Spain, the marriage plan was ruined.

Amy's murder was neither Robert Dudley's first nor his last. His father John had risen to the position of duke of Northumberland and de facto ruler in the reign of the young Edward VI. But Northumberland became "anxious . . . [since he] could only lose influence as time passed . . . Poisoning the young king was a method to ensure that this did not happen. A likely suspect for poisoning the young king was [Dudley's] son, Robert."[58] Here is the evidence Streitz presents: Dudley later poisoned Lettice's husband, the earl of Essex, and "from the similarity in symptoms between this incident and the death of King Edward VI, one would suspect that the same poison was used . . . [revealing] Robert Dudley as the murderer of the young king, Edward VI."[59] However, while it was widely believed in sixteenth-century England that Leicester poisoned Essex, in fact we have no evidence that Essex was murdered at all. Furthermore, the deaths of Essex and Edward VI were utterly dissimilar.

Streitz's Elizabeth was quite a wild woman but at least her first son was a genius. "Oxford was the first person of the English Renaissance, and perhaps the last person in the world who knew everything there was to know . . . From his earliest years, his output was enormous, and when the final list of Oxford's works is compiled, it may be most of the literary production of the Elizabethan period"[60]—not just Shakespeare but Spenser as well. Since Oxford was her oldest son, readers may wonder who the rest were. Her children by Dudley were Mary Sidney, Robert Cecil, Robert Devereux, and Elizabeth Leighton. After breaking with Dudley she seduced her own son; her incestuous union with de Vere produced Henry Wriothesley. Streitz argues that the real way to understand Elizabethan politics is to see it as a struggle among the queen's children.

In *Curled Up With a Good Book* Dean Warren states that "This reviewer couldn't put the book down." While Warren admits that Streitz's assertions are at first "hard-to swallow," his theories are "fiercely argued with the aid of quotes from ancient documents, impressive research. . . . As one reads, Streitz carries one along" (http://www.curledup.com/oxford.htm). *The Midwest Book Review* concurs. "In this persuasively presented account, William Shakespeare is proclaimed to be in fact Edward de Vere, the 17th Earl of Oxford and the illegitimate son of Queen Elizabeth I. A gripping historical construction of incest, betrayal, and murder in the royal family as well as a new look at the origin of some of the greatest classics of Western literature, *Oxford: Son Of Queen Elizabeth I* is a highly compelling, iconoclastic and challenging read for anyone with an interest in English history" (http://www.midwestbookreview.com). Most of the post-

---

[58] Streitz, *Oxford*, 105.
[59] Streitz, *Oxford*, 105.
[60] Streitz, *Oxford*, 131.

ings of amazon.com also found Streitz absolutely convincing both in the authorship controversy and in his characterization of Elizabeth. For example, Faran has "read many books about Edward, the Queen, etc. . . . and I am convinced he WAS Shakes-speare and that she had him just after she turned 15. . . . Good show sweet prince!! Loved the book. I hope others will look at your facts and realized how we all have been duped by the very very cunning/beautiful/enigmatic Queen Elizabeth, a once in a lifetime woman." Carl agrees: "Paul Streitz's research and argumentation are superb. . . . The book is indispensible [sic] reading for anyone willing to go that deeply into such a sensitive matter. . . . I do expect . . . to revisit its pages often, and I am looking forward to every intellectually-stimulating minute." Gary is also overwhelmed: "I just finished reading this masterful book, *Oxford*, and I wanted to say how much I enjoyed it. . . . I can honestly say that I have never read anything of the magnitude, depth, or thoroughness of this important book. Quite honestly, I couldn't put it down. . . . The book demands to be read by all [and] gives plausible explanations for most of the nagging problems surrounding the authorship question, the life of Edward de Vere, and, in general, Tudor England. . . . I don't know how the author was able to achieve this where others, by comparison, have failed, but it is a monumental accomplishment." Another posting by Peter argues that "the greatest need is to find more professors of English renaissance literature and Tudor history willing to break ranks and finally give attention to the mounting evidence in favor of Oxford as the author; they have relied on professorial hauteur long enough." There appears part of the American psyche, the intense need to prove that experts are wrong, that the accepted story is actually a conspiracy. We see the same tendency in the many, often wild, theories about the Kennedy assassination or 9/11. In many cases part of the theory is that those in authority deliberately falsified what happened to protect themselves from what they had done.[61] But not all amazon posters were so impressed with Streitz. Mrs. J. H. Pick states: "I'm sorry but this sort of dangerous nonsense goes beyond the ridiculous. Anyone with no knowledge of English history or a basic acquaintance with English literature might actually take it seriously! It is unmitigated, meretricious nonsense."

---

[61] 70 percent of Americans who think there was some sort of plot behind the killings, 68 percent think there was "an official cover-up" to hide the truth about the assassination from the public. ABC NEWS POLL: WHO KILLED JFK? – 11/9/03. "September 11 Conspiracy Theories"
http://www.rotten.com/library/conspiracy/september_11_conspiracy_theories/

VIII. "ever her own mistress"

The connection between the authorship controversy and the characterization of Elizabeth is a strange one that combines the need for social status as a part of genius with the denigration of a powerful woman. If Shakespeare was a country bumpkin buffoon who was too low-class to write the plays, how high-class is it to have the author an aristocrat who was the secret son of the Queen herself? It is also interesting that in the 1940s the Baconian Dodd viewed the Queen as "a simple woman of primal instincts," perhaps a statement on how all women of the time should be understood. Oxfordian Streitz, however, at the turn of the twenty-first century, has an Elizabeth who had her first illegitimate son at the age of fourteen and then went on to have another five with various men, one of whom was not only her eldest son but the secret author of the Shakespearean canon. One can only wonder about Paul Streitz's attitudes toward modern women.

Elizabeth as secret mother feeds the bizarre notion that a man of high status wrote the plays attributed to William Shakespeare. But there is certainly more to this belief system than the much-written-upon "authorship controversy," and we might wonder why in both her century and our own there is such interest in the possibility of Elizabeth I having love affairs and children. We can certainly move beyond the fact that everyone loves gossip, especially about famous people. While this may be true, when the rumors and accusations are aimed at someone who had a formative role in shaping society, then they become steeped (whether intentionally or unintentionally, consciously or unconsciously) in a discourse of power. Every harmful secret divulged or invented has the capacity to call a leader's legitimacy into question. This is especially poignant with women leaders, who are typically already under close scrutiny and have a far narrower range of acceptable behavior. As I have elsewhere argued, either they are questionable leaders because of their femininity or they are exceptional leaders only because of their lack of such femininity, which is in itself questionable. For men in the early modern period one way to prove their honor was success on the battlefield. For women, their honor was centered in their reputation: to have that questioned, even if unfairly, would mean the loss of honor. While Elizabeth might "have the heart and stomach of a king," she also admitted to "the body of a weak and feeble woman," and her woman's body could betray her in the ways people spoke of it.

The root '*vir*' in 'virgin' is the same as it is for the derogatory term 'virago,' and means simply "man." The former term, which can be roughly translated as "untouched by a man," has traditionally denoted a very positive attribute, especially for young and pious women. The other word, which means "like a man, or manly," could be a very negative term. In the sixteenth century, while it could denote a female warrior or amazon, it could also be used to mean "a bold, impudent (or wicked) woman; a termagant, a scold," indeed "shamelesse double sex'd."[62] The connection between these two words, however, goes far beyond their shared linguistic root. Historically, the term 'virago' has been applied to strong women who, in one way or another, refused to be controlled by men. Yet the term 'virgin' only retains its positive connotation in reference to a woman who is in some way under a man's control (a young docile maiden who is soon to be married, a nun who is subservient to God and church). Indeed, virginity, when it remains outside a man's designs and jurisdictions, can result, ironically, in a woman being dubbed a virago. This is especially true for women in power, and particularly for Elizabeth, who refused to share her rule with a man. Because of her refusal to marry and have a child, or even name an heir, Elizabeth attempted rhetorically to convey that the she was the mother of all the citizens of England. But many in both her times and ours attempted to say that she had lost her honor and independence by not really being a virgin, and by either destroying or refusing to openly acknowledge her children she was also a "monstrous mother." Sixteenth-century slanderers and many modern writers have attempted to diminish Elizabeth; I think, however, with quite imperfect success. Despite these characterizations, Elizabeth both then and now remains "ever her own mistress."[63]

---

[62] *Oxford English Dictionary* (online version, accessed January 2009), def. 3 and def. 4.a, example 1621 J. Taylor.

[63] Francis Bacon, *Works*, ed. James Spedding, 14 vols. (London: Longman & Co., 1858), 4:310.

Elizabeth Tudor: Poet

Ilona Bell

During her lifetime and in the decades following her death Elizabeth I was celebrated as a most excellent poet. Not only did George Puttenham dedicate *The Art of English Poesie* to Elizabeth, but he addressed her throughout, quoting her poems, mixing encomium with instruction, assuming that she would actually enjoy reading and using his three-hundred-page tome: "my most Honored and Gracious: if I should seeme to offer you this my deuise for a discipline and not a delight, I might well be reputed . . . the most arrogant and injurious: your selfe being alreadie, of any that I know in our time, the most excellent Poet."[1] No doubt this was an extravagant courtly compliment, crafted to win Elizabeth's patronage, but it may not have been as incredible as it seems today because Puttenham's treatise and many of Elizabeth's poems were written during the 'drab age' of English poetry, before Sidney, Spenser, Shakespeare, and Donne raised it to such magnificent heights.[2]

Elizabeth I reigned over the English poetic imagination far longer than she reigned over the realm. Elizabeth was still being lauded as a great poet long after she was in a position to reward anyone—when worms had tried her long-preserved virginity and her quaint honor turned to dust. "Before many, or most, I may iustly and without flatterie preferre the famous Queene *Elizabeth*," John Heywood wrote in *Gunaikeion*, "Of whose pleasant Fancies, and ingenious Ditties, I haue seene some, and heard of many."[3] By the middle of the twentieth century Elizabeth's reputation as a poet had declined precipitously. When Leicester Bradner published *The Poems of Elizabeth I* in 1964, he excluded "When I was fair and young" on the grounds that he did not believe Elizabeth could have

---

[1] George Puttenham, *The Arte of English Poesie* (Kent, OH: Kent State University Press, 1970), 21.

[2] For an illuminating account of the Drab age of English poetry, and Elizabeth's place in it, see Steven May, *The Elizabethan Courtier Poets: The Poems and Their Contexts* (Columbia: University of Missouri Press, 1991), introduction, 1–68.

[3] John Heywood, *Gunaikeion* (London, 1624), 398.

written such a fine poem.[4] By the end of the twentieth century Elizabeth was the subject of more historical, biographical, and artistic productions than anyone in the United States except Abraham Lincoln. Yet literary scholars were more interested in how the Elizabethans represented their queen than in how Elizabeth represented herself. Elizabeth's reputation as a writer and poet is now in recovery. I hope this essay will help spark further interest in Elizabeth Tudor as poet, for the work of analyzing, annotating, and reevaluating her poems and their significance has just begun.[5]

Like most Elizabethan lyric poetry, Elizabeth Tudor's poems were written not for print but for a private manuscript audience, but that only increased their value, as Heywood reveals when he boasts that "I haue seene some, and heard of many." Elizabeth may have written additional poems that were not signed or preserved, as Puttenham's fulsome tribute to her seems to suggest: "the Queene our soueraigne Lady, whose learned, delicate, noble Muse, easily surmounteth all the rest that haue written before her time or since, for sence, sweetnesse and subtillitie, be it in Ode, Elegie, Epigram, or any other kinde of poeme Heroick or Lyricke, wherein it shall please her Maiestie to employ her pen."[6] This is often cited as evidence that Elizabeth wrote more poems in more genres than surviving manuscripts indicate, but that is not what Puttenham meant. His mid-sentence shift to the future tense—"wherein it *shall* please her Maiestie to employ her pen"—reveals that this list is not a compendium of Elizabeth's collected works; rather it is an advertisement for the kinds of poems Elizabeth would be able to write if she chose to apply her proven poetic skills to the genres set forth in Puttenham's treatise.

Elizabeth's English poems are short, ranging from two to thirty-two lines. The poems that have survived are occasional poems or posies designed to be circulated in manuscript, recited in person, sent as messages, or left where they would be seen by someone known to the queen. Elizabeth wrote both the first and second half of poem-and-answer sets. She wrote a posie in her French Psalter. She wrote a lover's complaint and a response to a lover's complaint, thereby helping to transform the monologic male voice of Petrarchan poetry into a characteristi-

---

[4] Leicester Bradner, *The Poems of Elizabeth I* (Providence: Brown University Press, 1964).

[5] Thanks to the editorial labors of Bradner, Marcus, Mueller, Rose, May, Stump, and Felch, we are now in a much better position to study the language, textual variants, dates, and historical circumstances of Elizabeth's writing. The best study of Elizabeth's poetry is Jennifer Summit, *Lost Property: The Woman Writer and English Literary History, 1380–1589* (Chicago: University of Chicago Press, 2000), 163–202. For a more complete study of Elizabeth as writer, see Ilona Bell, *Elizabeth I: The Voice of a Monarch* (New York: Palgrave, 2010).

[6] Puttenham, *Arte of English Poesie*, 77.

cally Elizabethan lyric dialogue of courtship.[7] Since she wrote courtly lyrics and occasional verse, the original, private lyric situation was deeply embedded in the poem's language and is still an intrinsic part of its meaning and purpose.

Elizabeth discovered the power of poetry even before her accession to the throne, when, defenseless and suspected of treason, she wrote an epigram "with her diamond in a glass window" at Woodstock. Elizabeth had been imprisoned in the Tower of London for two months following Wyatt's plot to assassinate Queen Mary. When the government failed to find any evidence proving Elizabeth's direct involvement, she was sent to Woodstock Castle where she was held for eleven months under the ever-vigilant custody of Sir Henry Bedingfield. Bedingfield, a precise and conscientious man, was afraid to make even the smallest decision without approval from the queen or the Privy Council. Fortunately, he kept a record of all correspondence to and fro. Upon arriving at Woodstock, Bedingfield was instructed by Mary not to allow Elizabeth to have "conference wth anye suspected p[er]son oute off his heryng, nor that she dooe by eny menes eyther receyve or sende eny message, l[ett]^{re}, or token."[8] Bedingfield asked how he was to know who was "suspected." The Council responded that he "must forsee that nooe p[er]sons suspecte have anye conference wth hyr at all; and yet to p[er]mitte such straungers whom [he] shall thynke honeste and not suspicious . . . to speke wth hyr In yor heryng onlye."[9] That was no help; Bedingfield responded that he had no idea how to "foresee" or "perceive" who was "suspect" or who was "honest." The council resolved the problem by deciding that Elizabeth should not be allowed to see or communicate with anyone without special permission. The decision shaped Elizabeth's day-to-day existence, and severely curtailed her power to defend herself.

Locked up inside a decrepit, drafty old castle, allowed to walk in the small private garden but refused permission to wander in the park or to study with her tutor, unable to see anyone but Bedingfield without special permission, these were the conditions under which Elizabeth carved the epigram with a diamond on a window at Woodstock:

Much suspected by me,
Nothing proved can be.
Quod Elizabeth the prisoner.[10]

---

[7] See Ilona Bell, *Elizabethan Women and the Poetry of Courtship* (Cambridge: Cambridge University Press, 1998), esp. 108–13, and Arthur F. Marotti, *Manuscript, Print, and the English Renaissance Lyric* (Ithaca: Cornell University Press, 1995).

[8] C. R. Manning, ed., "State Papers Relating to the Custody of the Princess Elizabeth at Woodstock in 1554," *Norfolk Archaeology* 4 (1855): 133–231, here 158.

[9] Manning, ed., "Custody of Elizabeth at Woodstock," 164.

[10] Unless noted otherwise, Elizabeth's writing is quoted from *Elizabeth I: Collected Works*, ed. Leah S. Marcus, Janel Mueller, and Mary Beth Rose (Chicago: University of

This two-line couplet, with a total of twelve syllables, is about as short as an epigram can be. The brevity and compactness of the poem is central to its meaning for it shows how much Elizabeth's life and words were circumscribed by the role she had been assigned, the role of prisoner and suspected traitor. Of course, the traditional challenge of an epigram, and to some extent any lyric, is to see "what man can say / In a little," as Ben Jonson's lovely little "Epitaph on Elizabeth, L.H" avers. In some ways, Elizabeth's challenge was just the opposite, to show how little could be made out of anything she was prepared to speak or write. The terse poetic diction epitomizes what the poem asserts: Elizabeth's opponents can elicit only what she chooses to speak.

The oppressive constraints of Elizabeth's incarceration and the ominously unresolved charges against her pervade the poem. The passive construction captures Elizabeth's situation: as prisoner, her only recourse is constant vigilance and continued resistance. The rhythm and syntax focus attention on the first word of each line, "Much" and "Nothing," suggesting that "much" had been made of "nothing."[11] The Woodstock epigram provides only the barest facts. It does not say Elizabeth has done nothing; it only says that nothing can be proven. If "by" is taken in the older sense of "concerning," the couplet declares that although much is suspected *about* or concerning Elizabeth, nothing can be proven against her. She could still be condemned and executed without due cause, but, the poem implies, that would be an injustice. If "by me" is read as the implied subject of the passive verb "suspected," the lines contain a second meaning: Elizabeth's accusers are also suspected by her. The two meanings coexist, complicating and reinforcing each other.

But why engrave the poem on a window? First of all, Elizabeth's access to writing materials was carefully controlled because the Council had repeatedly warned Bedingfield to take every precaution to prevent Elizabeth from sending tokens, letters, or messages to her friends and supporters. The window and diamond were there, ready to be used, and Elizabeth was clever enough to make them a symbolic part of the poem's meaning. Elizabeth could see herself reflected and represented in the window, which could so easily shatter under pressure but did not, and in the diamond, one of the few remaining vestiges of her privileged status, valuable now not for its beauty or net worth but for its hard core and sharp edges. The multifaceted form of the diamond symbolizes the hermeneutic challenge the poem poses: Elizabeth's epigram, like her situation, looks totally different depending on one's point of view.

Chicago Press, 2000).

[11] Elizabeth continued to lobby for permission to write to Mary and the Privy Council, clearly believing that her rhetorical skills would convince them of her innocence. When Mary responded coldly to Elizabeth's first letter, and Bedingfield refused to forward her pleas to the Council, Elizabeth complained that she was worse off than a common prisoner at Newgate.

Elizabeth's words would have been easily legible from within, but the indefinite pronouns, cryptic diction, and ambiguous syntax could be fully understood only by those who were willing to see the situation from Elizabeth's point of view. When seen from outside the letters were reversed, but the epigram was short enough to be deciphered and remembered by anyone who cared enough to do so. The mirror text invites Elizabeth's foes to pause and consider how they would feel if the situation were reversed. To Elizabeth's supporters, it says: be vigilant and patient, the situation *may* soon be reversed.

The epigram served a number of different functions. First of all, it provided consolation for Elizabeth herself, and reminded her, every time she looked out the window, that constant vigilance was required if she was to avoid incriminating herself. Second, it was a message to her accusers, warning them not to confuse suspicion with proof. Third, I think, it was a message to Elizabeth's supporters. Elizabeth's old ally Thomas Parry had taken up lodging at a local inn where he managed Elizabeth's finances, arranged provisions for the castle, and received visits from scores of Elizabeth's supporters. Although no one was allowed to visit Elizabeth, Parry was permitted to bring funds to the kitchen staff and to send servants bearing provisions. The epigram was a way of informing her friends that she was safe, that the Marian government had no evidence against her, and that her allies must be exceedingly careful not to say or do anything to incriminate themselves or her. Finally, the epigram addressed posterity.[12] If Elizabeth had been executed, it would have become an emblem of her innocent martyrdom. When she was finally released, it became a famous emblem of her ability to outwit and outbrave her enemies.[13] The final line, "*Quod* Elizabeth the prisoner," could have been added when the poem was later copied onto the wall where it was seen and transcribed by visitors to England in the 1590s, but I think it was written by Elizabeth herself because it frames and recasts the epigram, much as the signature frames and recasts the posie written in the book at Windsor which we shall examine shortly. By writing the poem, Elizabeth reconstructs the situation, giving it a form and meaning of her own. Just as the artful doubleness of "Much suspected by me" enables Elizabeth to transform herself from the object of others' designs to the critic and judge of their actions, the narrative frame turns her from a helpless victim to a character in a narrative that she herself constructs and enacts. By choosing poetic language that is as artfully evasive as it is

---

[12] For information about Woodstock Castle, see Simon Thurley, *The Royal Palaces of Tudor England* (New Haven: Yale University Press, 1993). Elizabeth was lodged in the gatehouse rather than the castle, so her window would have been more easily visible from without.

[13] Visitors began to make pilgrimages to the site during Elizabeth's reign, and, Dunlop reports, "[r]ight into the eighteenth century, sightseers could remember this room, retaining the name of 'Queen Elizabeth's Chamber'." See Ian Dunlop, *Palaces and Progresses of Elizabeth I* (New Haven: Yale University Press, 1993), 15.

bluntly assertive, Elizabeth outmaneuvered her interrogators, thwarted her enemies, and gained a measure of control over her situation.

Elizabeth also wrote another, somewhat longer epigram while imprisoned at Woodstock:

> O Fortune, thy wresting, wavering state
> Hath fraught with cares my troubled wit,
> Whose witness this present prison late
> Could bear, where once was joy flown quite.
> Thou causedst the guilty to be loosed
> From lands where innocents were enclosed,
> And caused the guiltless to be reserved,
> And freed those that death had well deserved.
> But all herein can be naught wrought,
> So God grant to my foes as they have thought.
> *Finis.* Elisabetha a prisoner, 1555

The poem begins with a direct expression of personal feeling, "Hath fraught with cares my troubled wit," but here too the focus is less on physical suffering than mental constraint. The first four lines offer a terse but surprisingly powerful glimpse of Elizabeth's distress, but it is only a glimpse, not a full-fledged narrative, because she is not soliciting pity, she is demanding justice. Elizabeth finds solace in the thought that Woodstock Castle bears witness to a long line of injustice that traces its history back to an originary moment, "where *once* was joy flown quite" (my emphasis). The original Woodstock castle was built by Henry II to conceal and confine his mistress, Rosamond Clifford. The medieval castle had been destroyed by Elizabethan times, but Rosamond's story was well known, and it was widely believed that Henry's wife discovered the underground labyrinth leading to Rosamond's apartment and poisoned her. The vagueness of the reference ("Where once was joy flown quite") protects Elizabeth from any direct association with Rosamond's sexual dishonor while expressing sympathy with her plight, much as the other Woodstock epigram protects Elizabeth from any direct association with Wyatt's political dishonor while leaving open the possibility that his actions were justified.[14]

Elizabeth's final couplet imagines that Woodstock's history of releasing the guilty and restraining the innocent "can be" reversed, if fortune's random acts are overturned by God's justice. The final rhymes, "wrought" and "thought," strengthened by the internal rhyme, "naught wrought," echo and imagine a

---

[14] The variant, "bands," confirmed by Waldstein's accompanying Latin translation, meaning chains, seems to make more literal sense, but I prefer "lands" because it extends the injustice from the grounds of Woodstock itself to all the "lands" of England where the "guilty" executioners of Mary's will were free to wreak their vengeance upon "innocent" Protestants.

release from the constraint that "Hath *fraught* with cares my troubled wit" (my emphasis). The conclusion, "So God grant," provides a much-anticipated answer to the prayer the poem itself constitutes. The liberation the final couplet foresees could take a number of different forms, depending on how one interprets the words, "all herein can be naught wrought." All that remain imprisoned "herein," i.e., "here in" Woodstock Castle, can be made "naught" if God grants her foes what they want: the opportunity to convict and execute her. From the perspective of eternity, that would be a welcome liberation because it would free Elizabeth's troubled wit from the cares of this world, retrospectively giving a more positive spin to the previous line, "And freed those that death had well deserved." "[A]ll herein can be naught wrought" could also mean, all I've said "here in" the poem will be turned to "naught" if God grants my foes what they have "thought," i.e., if God does to my foes what they have thought about doing to me. In that case, Elizabeth will be released, her opponents will be "naught" as will the poem's argument, for it will no longer be true that the guilty are "freed" while the "guiltless" are "reserved" in prison. By warning her enemies that God will punish them for treating her unjustly, Elizabeth exercises some measure of control over her fate, much as she would later warn the members of her first parliament that they could not force her to marry because her decisions were guided by God, "who hath hitherto therein preserved and led me by the hand."[15]

A final, even more veiled epigrammatic turn suggests that if God grants what her foes have thought—if the treason plots she has been accused of should come to pass—then her foes will be rendered "naught," Elizabeth will be crowned queen, and everything they "wrought" will be undone. Highly conscious that anything she writes or says "can be" used against her, Elizabeth can only prophesy her foes' defeat by concealing it, as an amphibolous subtext, beneath the more obvious image of her own destruction. As it draws to a close, the poem makes a self-reflexive move, meditating on its own enigmatic form: since her foes have "caused the guiltless to be reserved" (in the sense of close-mouthed), Elizabeth remains as tersely self-protective as she is morally outspoken, using the epigram's twists and turns both to protest her bondage and to have her say without giving her foes anything to hold against her. With that, the ending takes its final epigrammatic turn, recapitulating the message of the other Woodstock epigram: "But all herein can be naught wrought." If "naught" can be made of "all" that is written "herein," then "Nothing proved can be."[16]

The moral discrimination, incisive verbal wit, enigmatic multiplicity of meaning, and self-reflexive form developed in the two Woodstock epigrams became a hallmark of Elizabeth's poetic style—and her prose style as well. They recur in poem #4 where the concrete physical images of the opening lines pose

---

[15] *Elizabeth I: Collected Works*, 57.
[16] The version printed in *Collected Works* has the two-line epigram following the signature of the longer epigram; clearly, they are closely related but discrete compositions.

deeper questions of perception, judgment, trust, and the process of interpretation itself:

> No crooked leg, no bleared eye,
> No part deformèd out of kind,
> Nor yet so ugly half can be
> As is the inward, suspicious mind.
> Your loving mistress, *Elizabeth*[17]

Compared, for example, to Ben Jonson's epigrams, this language sounds generalized and impersonal. The initial physical traits provide a foil for the final moral judgment, but the poem does not deny the importance of physical attraction or repulsion. Rather, the final epigrammatic twist declares that mental and moral ugliness are far worse. Yet despite the generalizing diction, Elizabeth clearly intended the poem for a particular person because the autograph text, written in her French psalter, is signed, "your loving mistress, Elizabeth." The puzzling disjunction between the impersonal judgment and the intimate signature constitutes the poem's primary interpretive crux. The signature complicates the poem substantially, making it not only trenchant but also conciliatory. "Mistress" meant both lady-love and a woman with power over someone else; hence the signature reminds Elizabeth's private lyric audience that she has the power to decide whether he is attractive or repugnant to her, and whether she is, and will continue to be, his "loving mistress." The signature reveals, moreover, that the epigram was written to and for someone Elizabeth cares about so deeply and knows so intimately that she can read—and hope to sway—his inward mind.

By hiding the posie at the end of the psalter rather than inscribing it on the opening pages, Elizabeth made it into a secret missive.[18] As was characteristic of posies, she discreetly omitted the name of her private lyric audience, or any identifiable references to his person; therefore, if anyone else happened to come upon the poem, it would seem like an abstract, ethical speculation on the relative importance of body and mind rather than her judgment of a specific person. But if Elizabeth showed her private lyric audience the poem, or more likely if she handed or sent him the psalter with a hint to look at the final pages, the words would almost certainly have contained a more pointed, private reference to events, or thoughts and feelings, known to them both—to some sort of unspecified tension or disagreement between them. Elizabeth clearly wanted to reassure him that

---

[17] *Collected Works* mistakenly prints the signature as Elizabeth R.

[18] Puttenham explains that posies, or short epigrams, were extremely fashionable—"made as it were vpon a table, or in a windowe, or vpon the wall or mantell of a chimney in some place of common resort, where it was allowed euery man might come," but also "put in paper and in bookes, and vsed as ordinarie missives." See *Arte of English Poesie*, 68.

she was still his "loving mistress," even as she felt compelled to warn him that his thoughts and actions could easily destroy her good opinion of him.

The editors of Elizabeth's *Collected Works* suggest that "[t]his may be the "obscure sentence" referred to by Burghley as written by the queen in 'a book at Windsor' when she was 'much offended with the earl of Leicester' in August 1565."[19] That seems likely for a number of reasons. First, the epigram is a sentence in both senses of the word: both a single grammatical sentence and a *sententia*, a pithy moral saying. Second, it *was* actually written by Elizabeth in a book, a French psalter, which is still extant in the Royal Library at Windsor Castle.[20] Third, the handwriting suggests an early date,[21] and Dudley is one of the few people the youthful Elizabeth loved and chastised in this way. Burghley's journal entry is also a single rather obscure sentence, but the actual wording contains a valuable clue to the function the epigram may have served: "The Queen Majesty semed to be much offended with the Erle of Lecester, and so she wrote an obscure sentence in a Book at Wyndsor."[22] The logical connective, "and *so* she wrote," suggests that Elizabeth wrote the "obscure sentence" because she had been, and still "seemed to be," much offended with Robert Dudley, the earl of Leicester. But are the epigram and the "obscure sentence" one and the same?[23]

---

[19] Marcus, Mueller, and Rose, and Doran all believe the epigram was written in the first part of Elizabeth's reign. See Susan Doran, *Monarchy and Matrimony: The Courtships of Elizabeth I* (London: Routledge, 1996). May thinks the poem was written while Elizabeth was still princess because the signature ends with a knot (similar to the one her father used in his signature). According to May, *Elizabethan Courtier Poets*, there are no extant examples of this signature after Elizabeth became queen when she signed her letters Elizabeth R. David Starkey provides a wonderfully detailed account of Elizabeth's early years in *Elizabeth: The Struggle for the Throne* (New York: Harper Collins, 2001), but I could not find a situation before her coronation that fits the poem's complex mixture of tones and concerns. We cannot know for certain that Elizabeth stopped using the knotted signature after she became queen because, as Doran commented in response to my query, virtually all of the extant autograph letters written by Elizabeth as queen are official correspondence. Most of her more intimate letters to Leicester have disappeared; the ones printed in *Collected Works* are copies and thus lack a signature. As Carol Levin suggested, Elizabeth may have chosen the more intimate signature on this particular occasion, using a knot instead of an R for Regina, to strike a more reassuring and less regal note.

[20] The possibility that Elizabeth gave the psalter to Dudley (or whomever the poem was addressed to) is strengthened by the fact that the book did not remain at Windsor Castle, although it has since been acquired by the Royal Library and resides there today.

[21] Doran, *Elizabeth I*, 201.

[22] William Cecil, Lord Burghley, *A Collection of State Papers . . . 1542 to 1598*, ed. Samuel Haynes, 2 vols. (London: W. Bowyer, 1740–1759; repr. Ann Arbor: University of Michigan Press, 1991), 2:760.

[23] The psalter was exhibited at the National Maritime Museum and reproduced in the catalogue. See David Starkey and Susan Doran, *Elizabeth: The Exhibition at the Na-*

Do the events Burghley cites match, and shed light on, the Windsor epigram? More importantly, what role might the poem have played in the historical drama unfolding at Windsor Castle in August 1565?

Burghley's journal entry offers no further information, but the reports of the Spanish ambassador, Don Diego Guzmán de Silva, provide a detailed account of what was happening at the time.[24] The queen arrived at Windsor on 10 August 1565, more preoccupied than ever with perturbing questions of courtship and marriage. To Elizabeth's great consternation, Mary Queen of Scots had recently married Darnley, a decision as rash as it was disastrous. While the court anxiously awaited news from Scotland, Elizabeth was being actively courted by several suitors of her own.[25] The French ambassador was pressing for an immediate answer to a marriage proposal from Charles IX. The sister of the king of Sweden was on her way to England, presumably to urge Elizabeth to reconsider her brother's suit. Elizabeth thought the French match would make her look ridiculous because Charles was only fourteen years old, and she showed little interest in reviving the Swedish courtship. She was much more attentive to the Austrian envoy, Adam von Swetkowich, Baron von Mitterburg, who had been sent to England to negotiate a marriage contract between Elizabeth and Archduke Charles.[26] "She will have no lack of husbands," de Silva commented laconically.[27] But in mid-July Emperor Maximilian sent an uncompromising letter, demanding that Elizabeth rather than Charles should provide a dowry, declaring that Charles' household expenses must be paid by the English treasury, asking for certain political prerogatives, and, most problematic of all, insisting that Charles

---

tional Maritime Museum (London: Chatto & Windus, 2003). Natalie Mears, who wrote the commentary, thought that Elizabeth may have written the poem "to Robert Cecil who was a hunchback," but the logic of the poem suggests that the private lyric audience had an inward, suspicious mind, not a deformed body.

[24] This is the first journal entry for August, and atypically, the day is not noted. The second entry is dated 10 August. De Silva reports that the queen arrived at Windsor from Richmond on 8 August. If Burghley wrote his journal entries singly, in sequence, that would mean Elizabeth wrote the obscure sentence on 9 August, but Burghley may have made all the August entries at one sitting, omitting the date because he did not know exactly when Elizabeth wrote the obscure sentence. De Silva first mentions the tiff between Elizabeth and Dudley on 27 August. On 3 September he writes again, having learned "[t]he real ground of the dispute between Lord Robert and Heneage"; see *Calendar of Letters and State Papers Relating to English Affairs Preserved Principally in the Archives of Simancas*, ed. Martin A. S. Hume, 4 vols. (London: Her Majesty's Stationery Office, 1892–99; repr. Nendeln, Liechtenstein: Kraus, 1971), 1:472. It could easily have taken de Silva two to three weeks to find out what happened.

[25] For an invaluable account of the financial, religious, and political issues surrounding Dudley's and Charles's courtships, see Doran, *Monarchy and Matrimony*, 40–98.

[26] *Calendar Simancas*, 1:456.

[27] *Calendar Simancas*, 1:445.

must be allowed to practice his Catholic religion. Meanwhile, Robert Dudley, the earl of Leicester, began jockeying to see whether Elizabeth might still be persuaded to marry him. While doing everything he could to support the archduke's suit, de Silva believed that Elizabeth would marry Robert Dudley or no one.

On one level, the Windsor epigram explores the difficult judgments that courtship and courtiership entail. While the English and Austrian governments were trying to hammer out a marriage agreement, Elizabeth was pondering what qualities were important in a potential husband. She repeatedly assured parliament that she would never make a match that was detrimental to the country (as her cousin Mary, Queen of Scots had just done), but she also insisted from the start of her reign that she would not be compelled to marry for pragmatic reasons alone. Indeed, she went so far as to take a vow that she would marry no man whom she had not seen.[28] True to her word, in August 1565 Elizabeth refused to make a commitment to marry the archduke—even if the religious, financial, and political differences could be resolved—until he came to England, so they could find out, as she put it, "whether they will be mutually satisfied personally." Sexual attractiveness and physical deformity may have been on Elizabeth's mind because she had once been told that Charles "had a head bigger than the Earl of Bedford's."[29] She was much relieved to learn that his head was not, in the words of the epigram, "a part deformed out of kind." On 13 July de Silva reported that "we spoke of the archduke's person, his age, his good parts, and she evidently felt pleasure in dwelling upon the subject."[30] Elizabeth may also have been thinking about misshapen body parts and marriage because Jane Grey's sister Mary, whom de Silva described as "little, crookbacked, and very ugly," was living at Windsor when, on August 20, it "came out that she had married a gentleman named Keyes. . . . They say the Queen is very much annoyed and grieved thereat. They are in prison."[31]

Relations between Elizabeth and Dudley were strained during the entire month of August. Towards the end of July, de Silva noted that Dudley "seems lately to be rather more alone than usual, and the Queen appears to display a certain coolness towards him. She has begun to smile on a gentleman of her chamber named Heneage, which has attracted a great deal of attention."[32] Dudley became increasingly jealous, and an argument broke out between the two men. Meanwhile, Throckmorton urged Dudley to find out whether he was still a lively

---

[28] For a more detailed discussion of Elizabeth's vow and its ramifications, see Ilona Bell, "Elizabeth I—Always Her Own Free Woman," in *Political Rhetoric, Power, and Renaissance Women*, ed. Carole Levin and Patricia A. Sullivan (Albany: State University of New York Press, 1995), 57–82.

[29] *Calendar Simancas*, 1:72.

[30] *Calendar Simancas*, 1:448.

[31] *Calendar Simancas*, 1:468.

[32] *Calendar Simancas*, 1:454.

candidate for the queen's hand by pretending that he had fallen in love with one of the ladies of the court and observing Elizabeth's response when he then requested permission to return to his own lodgings. Dudley began ostentatiously flirting with the viscountess of Hereford, "one of the best-looking ladies of the court," according to de Silva. "The queen was in a great temper and upbraided him" for fighting with Heneage and flirting with the viscountess.[33] Heneage was sent away, and Dudley returned to his own apartments where he remained for three days while Cecil and Sussex sought to bring about a reconciliation. At the beginning of September de Silva wrote that "Robert and the Queen shed tears, and he has returned to his former favor."[34]

The reference to the "inward, suspicious mind" would have struck Dudley with particular force. By flirting with the viscountess and fighting with Heneage, Dudley had not only displayed an "inward, suspicious mind," but he had made himself "suspicious" to Elizabeth. ("Suspicious" means not only open to or deserving of suspicion but also disposed to suspect evil, mistrustful.[35]) Indeed, his whole life had been clouded by suspicions. To begin with (since the word "kind" could refer to birth or family), "No part deformèd out of kind" refers to lingering feelings that Dudley's honor was tainted because both his father and grandfather had been attainted for treason. Then too, Dudley, like Elizabeth herself, had been imprisoned in the Tower of London on suspicion of treason. But even more to the point, suspicions about Dudley's mind and character were the principal reason Elizabeth had not married him. After Amy Robsart's death in 1560, rumors that Dudley had his wife killed so that he could wed the queen were so rampant and far-reaching that Elizabeth decided she simply could not marry him, even though she was physically attracted to him, and seemed to love him. By 1565 the gossip had subsided, but many of Elizabeth's subjects and allies continued to harbor their own inward suspicions about Dudley's mind and character.

There is also good reason to associate the "inward, suspicious mind" with Elizabeth herself since the very word "suspicious" alludes to and builds upon the key term in the Woodstock epigram, "Much suspected by me, / Nothing proved can be." While at Woodstock, Elizabeth outwitted her foes by countering their suspicions with inward suspicions of her own. The Windsor epigram confronts Elizabeth's fear of being plagued by the inward suspicious thoughts that both tormented and protected her at Woodstock and that recurred, to her consternation, whenever she faced a potential betrayal.[36] By writing the Windsor epigram

---

[33] *Calendar Simancas*, 1:472.

[34] *Calendar Simancas*, 1:472.

[35] All definitions taken from the *Oxford English Dictionary Online* (Oxford: Oxford University Press, 2000).

[36] Given the verbal similarities and the knotted signature, it is tempting to think that this epigram was also written when Elizabeth was at Woodstock; however, the only Psalter she had was in Latin (Manning, "Custody of Elizabeth at Woodstock," 161), and

and suggesting that Dudley (or whoever the poem was intended for) was the object of her suspicion, Elizabeth was expressing her own suspicious or mistrustful thoughts. That's precisely what makes this brief little posie at once so multifaceted a piece of writing and so intriguing an outward and visible sign of Elizabeth's inward preoccupations. But, one might well ask, was it fair for Elizabeth to admonish her private lyric audience for a quality of mind that she herself shared, and that her own behavior may well have provoked? If Dudley's schemes incited Elizabeth's suspicions, she had herself given him good reason to be suspicious: after all, she had been showering attention on Heneage and encouraging the archduke to come to England to meet her. Upon learning that Dudley had been trying to provoke her jealousy by flirting with the viscountess, Elizabeth "was in a great temper and upbraided him." Their reconciliation, complete with tears (or "bleared eyes") on both sides, reaffirmed their mutual affection. As de Silva's account illustrates, Elizabeth herself had behaved badly, but she was not wont to apologize. If, as the signature suggests, Elizabeth wrote the epigram to confront and work through her anger, the implicit acknowledgement—both to herself and to her private lyric audience—that her own inward, suspicious mind had led her to behave in an "ugly" way probably helped bring about a reconciliation.

Since the poem neither attributes "the inward, suspicious mind" to any particular individual nor addresses a private lyric audience directly, Elizabeth may have originally written the poem about Dudley but not for Dudley; however, it seems more likely that she was thinking about how it would strike him because the abstract language is a tactful way of admonishing him without criticizing him directly. The choice of the penultimate verb, "nor yet so ugly half can be," suggests that "the inward, suspicious mind" is a danger to beware, a condition, unlike a crooked leg or a deformed body part, that "can be" resisted even if it cannot be entirely avoided. While the poem raises objections that "can be" made in the past or future, its formal structure, when read along with the "loving" signature, implies that Elizabeth is no longer as "offended" as she "seemed to be" before writing the epigram. In the autograph copy the rhyme words appear at the beginning of lines 2 and 3, and in the middle of line 4. Elizabeth was not a professional scribe. Most likely, she miscalculated the space needed, but the result is interesting. Like the mirror text written on the window at Windsor, the outer deformity of the apparently unrhymed lines conceals an internal pattern that the poem invites the reader to discover. Despite appearances, there is an inner harmony that secretly links Elizabeth and her private lyric audience together, much as the internal rhymes transform the sentence of four and a half lines into a quatrain.

Although questions about the signature and the date remain, the remarkably close correlation among the language of the poem, events at Windsor in August

---

she was not allowed to communicate with anyone whom she would have addressed as "Your loving mistress."

1565, and Elizabeth's ongoing concerns about Dudley makes it highly likely that this was indeed the obscure sentence Elizabeth wrote in a book at Windsor. If Elizabeth wrote the poem in her French psalter when she "semed to be much offended" with Dudley as Burghley notes, the pointed critique of the epigram's final lines, tempered by the loving signature, could have been a pivotal intervention in the historical situation: a way of telling Dudley (without recommencing the quarrel) that his attempts to manipulate and deceive her by pretending to be in love with the viscountess were uglier than any sort of physical deformity, but that she was ready to forgive him as long as he didn't make it a regular habit of mind. If so, the epigram would have served a dual function: at once gentle admonition and tacit apology, it offered a face-saving rhetorical strategy that made reconciliation possible.

When we reconsider the epigram as a whole, the apparent dichotomy between physical and mental traits becomes a continuum that interrogates the very distinctions upon which the poem rests. This larger hermeneutical challenge pivots on the word "ugly" which alludes back to the physical deformity of the previous images, even as it anticipates the morally offensive loathsomeness of "the inward, suspicious mind." The "blearèd eye" refers initially to someone whose eyes are inflamed with infection or swollen with tears; upon rereading, the "blearèd eye" also refers proleptically to someone who is mentally blinded or deceived by mistrust (as both Dudley and Elizabeth were wont to be). Similarly, "[n]o part deformèd out of kind" evokes, first of all, a body part twisted out of its natural shape, but in retrospect, it also describes a part of one's mind or character that is "deformed out of kind"—deformed as a result of birth, or family, or a manner that is natural or habitual to a person, or an obsession with a single part of a much larger problem—a mind haunted by the kind of anxieties that troubled both Dudley and Elizabeth in August 1565 and throughout their courtship. Even "[t]he crooked leg" begins to look less straightforward, embodying the twisted movements of an "inward, suspicious mind," suggesting that his gestures of obeisance (for crooking the leg was a synonym for bowing) are marred by his inward suspicions.[37] The penultimate line suggests that the distinction between body and mind is a matter of magnitude rather than kind: "[t]he inward, suspicious mind" is related to but much worse than any of those previous traits because it encompasses them all, perverting all one's actions and distorting all one's perceptions, even at times causing physical ailments. As the literal and figurative meanings merge, the "blearèd eye" begins to perceive—even as it comes to symbolize—just how easily the process of perception, judgment, and interpretation "can be" distorted by distrust and deceit. Thus even if the epigram is rooted in events at Windsor in August 1565, it transcends them.

---

[37] I am grateful to Donald Stump for suggesting this alternative reading.

The exchange of lyrics between Walter Ralegh and the queen provides another example, probably the best example, of the way in which Elizabeth's poetry moves from historically situated lyric dialogue, designed to resolve a private disagreement or misunderstanding, to literary and intellectual critique. The dialogue begins with Ralegh's lyric to the queen in which he fashions himself as a noble knight errant, the allegorical figure of sorrow, who has searched the heavens and earth, armed with sighs and tears, trying to rescue his "Love," his "princess," his "true fancie's mistress," from "fortunes hands."[38] Ralegh's lyric is so carefully veiled in allegorical abstractions that it is impossible to know, on the basis of the poem alone, exactly what provoked his complaint that "Fortune hath taken thee away . . . Fortune hath taken all by takinge thee." These huge and rather vague claims take on real weight when we remember that Ralegh was an ordinary gentleman who became an extraordinarily wealthy and powerful courtier owing to the queen's personal favor. Based on the date of the manuscript, May argues convincingly that the poetic exchange took place almost certainly in the first half of 1587 when Ralegh's position as Elizabeth's preeminent favorite was challenged by the rise of the Earl of Essex.[39] But whatever the exact circumstances, Ralegh's poem is courtly, coterie verse, addressed directly to the queen, written in the hope of regaining Elizabeth's favor.

Ralegh's poetic persuasion had its desired effect, for Elizabeth's lyric response reassures him of her continuing affection and regard:

Ah silly pugg, wert thou so sore afrayd?
Mourne not my Wat, nor be thou so dismaid;
It passeth fickle fortune's powre and skill
To force my harte to thinke thee any ill.

The intimate, teasing banter, the opening question which invites an answering response, the affectionate terms of endearment, "pugg" and "Wat" (Elizabeth's pet name for Walt), and the reference to "my harte," instantly dissolve the distance Ralegh bemoans, implying that the lyric dialogue is part of an intimate conversation that predated Ralegh's complaint and that will continue after Elizabeth's reply. The adjective "silly" has an intriguing range of sympathetic and

---

[38] I quote May's carefully edited text of this poetic exchange (*Elizabethan Courtier Poets*, 318–19) because the version of Elizabeth's response selected by the editors of the *Collected Works* has a missing line.

[39] For further information see the introduction to May's *Elizabethan Courtier Poets*. See also Leonard Tennenhouse, "Sir Walter Ralegh and the Literature of Clientage," in *Patronage in the Renaissance*, ed. Guy Fitch Lytle and Stephen Orgel (Princeton: Princeton University Press, 1981), 235–58, here 240. As Tennenhouse explains, "the poetic fiction presumes that the lover is a victim through the accident of birth or class, and not through some fault or error on his part," nor, I would add, due to any choice or error on Elizabeth's part.

critical meanings (deserving of pity; defenseless; weak, sick; lacking in judgment; weak or deficient in intellect; foolish; poor; of humble rank) which encapsulate Elizabeth's complex response to Ralegh's poetic plea.

Ralegh has traditionally occupied a more important place in English literary tradition than Elizabeth, so it is not surprising that his poem has received more attention and regard than hers, and perhaps that is appropriate since he originated the lyric form and argument that Elizabeth adopted and recast. Stephen Greenblatt, who finds "something vast and heroic in [Ralegh's] sorrow," does not take Elizabeth's poem seriously. "From heroic love and despair," Greenblatt writes, "we descend to reassuring but demeaning pleasantries."[40] I don't think Greenblatt does Elizabeth's poem justice; "[t]he question that he frames in all but words / Is what to make of a diminished thing" (Frost, "The Oven Bird"). Instead, I want to argue that Elizabeth's deflationary rhetoric constitutes a witty and withering but nonetheless affectionate critique of Ralegh's conventional poetic persona, disingenuous rhetoric, and contradictory reasoning.

The very fact that Elizabeth takes the trouble to match Ralegh's poem, thought for thought, quatrain for quatrain, is a tribute not only to his place in her imagination and regard but also to the seriousness which she accorded his rhetorical strategies and lyric form.[41] Elizabeth reuses in order to interrogate many of Ralegh's rhymes. Yet the initial rhyme words, "afrayd" and "dismaid," do not appear in Ralegh's poem; they disclose what Ralegh hoped to conceal. His poetic complaint is motivated not by the elevated Petrarchan sentiments of his opening couplet ("My live's Joy and my sowle's heaven above") or the heroic suffering Greenblatt admires in the following stanzas ("Ded to all Joyes, I onlie Live to woe") but by much less noble and impressive emotions: fear and dismay.

Alluding to the Woodstock epigram on fortune, Ralegh attributes his loss of favor not to Elizabeth herself but to Fortune, that blind goddess whose arbitrary acts neither recognize nor reward "vertue right." Elizabeth reminds Ralegh that her earlier epigram resisted fortune's power and prayed God to punish the guilty and free the innocent: "No fortune base, thou saist, shall alter thee; / And may so blind a wretch then conquer me? / No, no, my pug, though fortune weare not blind / Assure thie selfe she could not rule my mind." The blunt, straightforward diction, softened by the endearing reassurances ("my pug," "assure thyself"), as-

---

[40] Stephen Greenblatt, *Sir Walter Ralegh: The Renaissance Man and His Roles* (New Haven: Yale University Press, 1973), 58. Helen Hackett, "Courtly Writing by Women," in *Women and Literature in Britain 1500–1700*, ed. Helen Wilcox (Cambridge: Cambridge University Press, 1996), 169-89, here 176–77, discusses Elizabeth's verse exchange with Sir Thomas Heneage.

[41] May comments, "Elizabeth's response, carefully coordinated with Ralegh's lines, develops its own remarkably tender, coaxing tone" (*Elizabethan Courtier Poets*, 122). I agree that Elizabeth is at once attentive and "tender," but I think the tone is more trenchant than "coaxing."

serts Elizabeth's powerful independence of mind and reminds Ralegh that his rise at court was due not to fortune but to Elizabeth's appreciative recognition of his intelligence and wit.

To show that her thoughts and actions are no more controlled by "fickle fortune's powre" than her feelings and attitudes are controlled by Ralegh's words, Elizabeth offers a detailed and thoughtful critique of Ralegh's logic. By wallowing in self-pitying pride ("And onlie love the sorrowe Due to me") and pledging allegiance to sorrow ("Sorrowe hencefourth that shall my princess bee"), Ralegh betrayed his own initial protestations of love and loyalty to Elizabeth ("my Love," "my princess"). Worse yet, having described Elizabeth as "my live's Joy," Ralegh's lyric takes an invidious pleasure in proclaiming Elizabeth's subjection to fortune: "And onlie Joy that fortune conquers kings, / Fortune that rules on earth and earthlie things." From Elizabeth's point of view, this is not only disingenuous, but it is also insulting and "silly" or foolish. Ralegh concludes his poem by boldly proclaiming, "No fortune base shall ever alter me"; but as Elizabeth's reply implies, fortune has already altered him, turning his witty, incisive intelligence to self-pitying fear and irrational despair.

The heart of Elizabeth's poem is a discriminating, measured critique of fortune's power which implies that Ralegh's logic—both his initial premises and his conclusion—is pretentious, dishonest, and internally inconsistent. Here, as in the Woodstock epigram, Elizabeth carefully weighs the extent and limits of fortune's power.

> Fortune I grant *somtimes* doth conquer kings,
> And rules and raignes on earth and earthlie things,
> But never thinke that fortune can beare sway,
> If vertue watche and will her not obay. (my emphasis)

Elizabeth's active verbs give "vertue" the power Ralegh denied it. While Ralegh's poetic persona wallows in self-pity and refuses to take responsibility for his situation, his imagery and rhetoric offer an implicit critique of Elizabeth's wisdom and judgment: "With wisdome's eyes had but blind fortune seen," Ralegh claims, "Then had my love my love for ever bin." When you stop to think about it, this is really presumptuous, as Elizabeth's response pointedly reminds Ralegh. Just because she is "Thie Love, thie Joy," that doesn't mean he is *her* love or joy. As a courtly poet addressing a private female lyric audience, or a courtier addressing his queen, he is certainly free, if he wishes, to declare his love for her in poetry; however, it behooves him to remember, poetry of courtship, whether amorous or political, depends for its success upon an answering response.

Having begun with a series of questions, Elizabeth ends with a series of imperatives that urge Ralegh to show some spirit and wit: "Plucke up thie hart, suppresse thie brackish teares." Elizabeth's directive speech acts command their own answers, for she is undoubtedly in a position of power over Ralegh. Her poem culminates in a performative speech act: "The lesse afrayde the better shalt thou spead." Elizabeth clearly has the power to make it so by saying so. Her playful, teasing language not only laughs at Ralegh's self-aggrandizing, self-indulgent sorrow, it also offers an astute literary critique of his conventional Petrarchizing: "But must thou neads sowre sorrowe's servant be, / If that to try thie mistris jest with thee."[42] Elizabeth's impatience with "sowre sorrow" and her offer to "jest with thee" suggests that Ralegh could make both his courtship and his poetry more effective if he replaced his weary, woebegone abstractions with some fresh imagery, colloquial diction, and incisive, spirited wit.

As we have learned from the Woodstock epigrams, Elizabeth's poems are generally written not only to clarify and articulate her own thoughts and feelings but also to make an impact: to shape or alter the immediate situation; to inform and sway the private lyric audience. Even when Elizabeth was as powerless as a future monarch could be, she realized that poetry "can be" a means of action. When she became queen, poetry became not only admonitory but also performative and efficacious, for she was clearly in a position to make it so by saying so. Throughout her reign, Elizabeth I continued to write poetry, or to deploy the rhetorical strategies of poetry, whenever the situation demanded not only blunt assertion but also inference, discrimination, deft persuasion, and discreet intervention. Elizabeth's poems expose and conceal, threaten and cajole, edify and deride, placate and stonewall. They not only reflect the private circumstances that comprise the poem's dramatic situation, they also alter the historical situation. Elizabeth developed rhetorical strategies in her poetry, which she then translated into other, more explicitly political modes of speech and writing. The prophecies and warnings developed in the Woodstock epigrams reappear in her early parliamentary speeches, even as they find their way into later proclamations directed against the Catholic insurgents. In her public speeches as in her private negotiations with foreign ambassadors, courtiers, and suitors, whenever she was faced with a particularly nettlesome political situation, Elizabeth used the rhetorical figures described in Puttenham's *Art of English Poesie*: "*Enigma*, or the Riddle," when "[w]e dissemble againe vnder couert and darke speaches"; *Amphibologia*, "the *ambiguous*, or figure of sence incertaine"; "the Courtly figure *Allegoria*, which is when we speake one thing and thinke another."[43]

Although the letters, speeches, and prayers far outnumber the fifteen poems contained in *Elizabeth I: Collected Works*,[44] the significance of Elizabeth's

---

[42] The awkward demonstrative pronoun "that" alludes to the key moment in Ralegh's argument—"And onlie Joy that fortune conquers king"—where a syntactical sleight of hand transforms joy from a noun to a verb, betraying Ralegh's own initial claim that Elizabeth herself is "my live's Joy."

[43] Puttenham, *Arte of English Poesie*, 196–98, 267.

[44] This tally does not include the twenty-seven stanzas written in French around 1590, which may or may not be a translation.

poetry far outweighs its volume. Elizabeth wrote poems that are more masterful and intricate than they may seem, and she encouraged or inspired her subjects to write some of the most powerful, complex, witty, and multifaceted poetry in the English language. Like many of the greatest Elizabethan lyrics, Elizabeth's poems move from enigmatic epigrams, coded posies, and witty self-dramatizations to abstract meditations on fortune, justice, and the very process of interpretation itself. Even in the few short poems examined here, Elizabeth mastered many of poetic tropes and rhetorical strategies that were later used so brilliantly by Sidney, Spenser, Shakespeare, and Donne: sharp, colloquial speech and deeply personal feeling; epigrammatic wit and ironic critique; enigmatic ambiguity, multiplicity of meaning, and veiled references intended to mean different things to different members of her private lyric audience; abstract moral judgment and hermeneutical self-reflexiveness. Perhaps that is why when Mary Sidney dedicated the Sidney psalter "To the Thrice-Sacred Queen Elizabeth," she posed her ultimate tribute as a rhetorical question: "For in our worke what bring wee but thine owne?"[45] By then, the answer was self-evident: "What English is, by many names is thine." Elizabethan English was the Queen's English.

---

[45] Mary Sidney, *The Triumph of Death, and Other Unpublished and Uncollected Poems*, ed. G. F. Waller, Elizabethan & Renaissance Studies 65 (Salzburg: Institut für Englische Sprache und Literatur, University of Salzburg, 1977), 89.

Queen Elizabeth to Her Subjects: The Tilbury and Golden Speeches

Steven W. May

The speeches attributed to Queen Elizabeth at Tilbury Camp in 1588 and to her last Parliament in 1601 rank among her most influential as well as her most admired public orations. One version of the Tilbury address was reported by the earl of Leicester's chaplain, Dr. Leonell Sharpe,[1] who was an eyewitness to the royal visit. However, the authenticity of this text has been seriously challenged by doubts about Sharpe's account of the surrounding circumstances and by the discovery of a rival version of the speech. In contrast, there is no doubt that Elizabeth actually delivered her "Golden Speech"—the problem is, which one? T. E. Hartley's superb edition of the relevant documents identifies five very different states of the text, only one of which (at most) can represent what the queen actually said on that November afternoon in 1601.[2] I contend that Elizabeth actually did address the troops at Tilbury in something like the fashion reported by Sharpe. I also offer an explanation of how the differing texts of her "Golden Speech" came into being, and which version most accurately preserves her words to her House of Commons.

---

[1] Sharpe (1559–1631) took his B.A. from King's College, Cambridge, in 1581, his M.A. in 1584, and D.Th. in 1597. He received an honorary D.D. from Oxford in 1618. After Leicester's death he became chaplain to the earl of Essex, and was appointed one of the queen's chaplains by 1602. He was appointed chaplain to Prince Henry about 1605. With John Hoskins and Sir Charles Cornwallis he was imprisoned in the Tower in 1614 for satirizing the Scottish influence at the Stuart court; Sharpe was released a year later. Sir John Chamberlain twice refers to him as "little Dr. Sharpe." See P. E. J. Hammer, "Sharp, Leonell," in *Oxford Dictionary of National Biography*, 60 vols. (Oxford and New York: Oxford University Press, 2004), 50: 51–53; Norman Egbert McClure, ed, *Letters of John Chamberlain*, 2 vols. (Philadelphia: American Philosophical Society, 1939), 1:478, 540.

[2] T. E. Hartley, ed., *Proceedings in the Parliaments of Elizabeth I*, 3 vols. (London and New York: Leicester University Press, 1995), 3:289–97, 412–14.

I

In late July 1588, an English army commanded by the earl of Leicester as Lieutenant and Captain General assembled at Tilbury to repel the anticipated Spanish invasion. At peak strength, about 20,000 men were encamped on the Essex coast near the mouth of the Thames.[3] The site was officially designated as ". . . the Camp appointed for the guard of her Majesties person . . ."[4] On 8 August Elizabeth traveled downriver by barge from St. James's Palace, arriving at Tilbury that afternoon. She rode through the army, then continued north about four miles to spend the night at Ardern Hall, the home of Thomas Rich.[5] On the following day she returned to the camp for a more extensive review of the troops, during which she allegedly delivered the address we know as her Tilbury speech. Scholars have cast doubt on the authenticity of this speech for several reasons. First, if the queen addressed the army, how many of those assembled could possibly have heard her speak? How could Sharpe have copied down her words verbatim even if he could hear them? And why do eyewitness reports from the camp fail to mention a specific royal oration? This last objection is answered in Lord Burghley's account of the royal visit. During the Armada crisis Cecil, a gout victim, enjoyed the ironic appointment "Colonel General of the Footmen." He visited the camp a few days after the queen, but his report (albeit written as a propaganda piece) was based on eyewitness accounts. Elizabeth, he asserts, "beyng a woman, she went to that army, she viewed it, she passed thrugh dyvers tymes, she lodged in the borders of it, she retorned ageyn and dyned in the army, she saw all the men quartered in ther severall camps, she viewed them from place to place . . . being accompanyed but with the Generall and some Certen officers of the feld."[6] This summarizes Elizabeth's two-day visit, with the important detail that she reviewed the troops accompanied only by Leicester and his immediate staff. As we shall see, firsthand accounts of the royal visit confirm Burghley's statement: Elizabeth dismissed her entourage of courtiers when she rode through the army, thus reducing the number of potential witnesses to any speech she might have delivered on the occasion. As Leices-

---

[3] On 1 August the Privy Council charged Leicester to be ready to move with his force of 25,000 foot and 3000 horse anywhere the enemy might attempt a landing. On 5 August the Council urged him to reduce the force at Tilbury from 20,000 to 6000 men insofar as there was "no apparaunt danger from th'enemies." See *Acts of the Privy Council of England*, ed. John Roche Dasent, 32 vols. (London: Her Majesty's Stationery Office, 1890–1949), 16:209, 222.

[4] *Acts of the Council*, 16:197.

[5] E. K. Chambers, *The Elizabethan Stage*, 4 vols. (Oxford: Clarendon Press, 1923), 4:103; Miller Christy, "Queen Elizabeth's Visit to Tilbury in 1588," *English Historical Review* 34 (1919): 43–61, here 52.

[6] *Acts of the Council*, 16:196; Lord Burghley's Papers, London, British Library, Lansdowne MS. 103, fols. 142r-142v.

ter's chaplain, however, Sharpe might well have been included among those who accompanied Elizabeth for the express purpose of recording the event. Sharpe also acknowledged that only some of the troops heard what the queen said, for Leicester, he explained, ordered him to "redeliver" her words to the camp on the following day. This is consistent with Janet M. Green's discovery of a manuscript text of the speech which, she argues, is in Sharpe's handwriting. It is subscribed, "Gathered by one that heard it, and was commanded to utter it to the whole army the next day, to send it gathered to the Queen herself."[7] More than three decades after the fact, Sharpe presented a copy of this text to the duke of Buckingham whence it made its way into the *Cabala* of 1654.[8]

Susan Frye's important article on the Tilbury speech nevertheless undermines much of Sharpe's testimony.[9] Frye shows that his letter to Buckingham adapts, but also distorts, events of 1588 in order to attack the government's pro-Spanish policy of the 1620s. The authenticity of the speech he ascribes to the queen is contested as well by Frye's discovery of a rival speech attributed to her on the same occasion. It survives in two texts, one incorporated into a sermon published by Thomas Leigh in 1612, the other subscribed to a painting in Gaywood Church, Norfolk.[10] Frye notes that these texts may represent another speech that Elizabeth gave at Tilbury or a very differently worded version of the same speech recorded by Sharpe. In any event, the emphasis in these texts differs markedly from Sharpe's version. Frye analyzes the essentially autobiographical focus of Sharpe's *Cabala* text: the queen is here concerned with her role in defense of her realm. The Leigh/Gaywood version, however, emphasizes the *enemy* as a force opposed to God and God's people, Elizabeth's own subjects. I shall return to the problem of the rival texts in a moment, but wish to consider now other contemporary accounts of the Tilbury speech and its context.

Three writers produced verse narratives of what happened that afternoon. Two of them rushed back to London to publish what they had seen and heard

---

[7] London, British Library, Harleian MS. 6978, fol. 87rv, identified in Janet M. Green, "'I My Self': Queen Elizabeth I's Oration at Tilbury Camp," *Sixteenth Century Journal* 28 (1997): 421–45.

[8] *Cabala, sive Scrinia sacra. Mysteries of state & government* (London: G. Bedel and T. Collins, 1654), sig. 2L2v.

[9] Susan Frye, "The Myth of Elizabeth at Tilbury," *Sixteenth Century Journal* 23 (1992): 95–114, here 104.

[10] Frye prints the rival speech from William Leigh's 1612 sermon (*STC* 15426), with the transcription of a similar text from the painting in St. Faith's Church, Gaywood. In "Provenance and Propaganda," Frances Teague joins Frye in casting doubt on Sharpe's testimony; see "Provenance and Propaganda as Editorial Stumbling Blocks," in *New Ways of Looking at Old Texts*, ed. W. Speed Hill (Tempe, AZ: Medieval & Renaissance Texts & Studies, Renaissance English Text Society, 1998), 119–23. Teague extends this argument in "Queen Elizabeth in Her Speeches," in *Gloriana's Face*, ed. S. P. Cerasano and Marion Wynne-Davies (Detroit: Wayne State University Press, 1992), 63–78, here 67–69.

as broadside ballads. Thomas Deloney is no doubt the T. D. whose initials are subscribed to the ballad entitled *The Queenes visiting of the Campe at Tilsburie with Her entertainment there*.[11] Deloney's presence at Tilbury has been called into question solely from the internal evidence of his ballad,[12] yet that text agrees in many substantive details with the other eyewitness accounts. Deloney records that she rode through the camp upon her arrival on 8 August, then spent the night at "maister Riches." She returned to Tilbury the next day riding a palfrey and preceded by trumpeters in scarlet coats. Her Lord General, the earl of Leicester, escorted her, according to Deloney, into the camp, where both infantry and cavalry paraded for her inspection. Elizabeth then left her ladies in waiting but, still accompanied by the Yeomen of the Guard, reviewed the troops. In this Deloney confirms the essence of Lord Burghley's account although he does add the Queen's Guard to her entourage. Deloney then summarizes her address to the army as follows:

> And then bespake our noble Queene,
> My loving friends and countrimen
> I hope this day the worst is seene,
> That in our wars ye shall sustain.
> But if our enimies do assaile you,
> never let your stomackes faile you.
> For in the midst of all your troupe,
> we our selues will be in place:
> To be your joy, your guide and comfort,
> even before your enimies face. (lines 161–170)

Deloney's one-stanza summary of the queen's speech bears some striking features in common with Sharpe's version. Deloney apparently transferred his sovereign's boast about having the "stomach of a king,"[13] to the exhortation to her soldiers, "never let your stomackes faile you." Certainly, her vow to serve "in the midst of all your troupe" echoes her pledge in Sharpe's text to join them "in the midst and heat of the battle to live or die amongst you all." Her concluding

---

[11] Thomas Deloney, *The Queenes visiting of the Campe at Tilsburie with Her entertainment there* (London: John Wolfe, 1588), *STC* 6565.

[12] Christy argues that Elizabeth could not have landed at Gravesend and then have proceeded across the estuary to Tilbury as Deloney relates, but this is a misreading. Deloney says instead that Elizabeth landed "ouer against that prettie towne," meaning directly across from or facing Gravesend. Christy's conclusion that the ballad includes "no information which he might not have derived by hearsay from someone who was present" is another way of saying that Deloney's narrative was, at worst, based on a firsthand report. See Christy, "Queen Elizabeth's Visit," 49.

[13] Steven W. May, ed., *Queen Elizabeth I: Selected Works* (New York: Washington Square Press, 2004), 77.

promise "to be your joy, your guide and comfort" resembles her offer, according to Sharpe, to be "your general, judge, and rewarder of every one of your virtues in the field."[14]

A second, and by far the longest, account of what happened during the queen's visit is found in James Aske's *Elizabetha Trivmphans*. This is a blank-verse narrative of the events surrounding the Armada's defeat, phrased in the Elizabethan high style. Although Aske's poem is filled with errors and literary fictions, he too notes that Elizabeth did "her trayne forbid" to follow as she reviewed the troops.[15] Aske included in his pamphlet a summary of the royal address. His source, however, was Elizabeth's "message from her mouth" to Captain Nicholas Dawtrey as she departed the camp for London.[16] This versified rendition of her remarks is described in a marginal note as "The effect of the Queenes speach," yet its central topics dovetail with Sharpe's account. Aske credits Elizabeth with volunteering to lead her army into battle and offering to reward them handsomely for their service:

> Yet say to them that we in like regarde,
> ....
> Wilbe our selfe their noted Generall.
> ....
> But in the midst and very heart of them
> Bellona-like we meane as then to march;
> On[e] common lot of gayne or losse to both,
> They well shall see we recke shall then betide.
> And as for honor with most large rewards,
> Let them not care they common there shalbe[17]

Meanwhile, a second ballad had been entered in the Stationers' Register on 10 August and printed by John Wolfe, who likewise printed Deloney's ballad. This verse account has not heretofore been studied for what it tells us about the queen's alleged speech to her army. *A Joyful Song of the Royal Receiving of the Queen's most excellent Majesty...at Tilbury* is subscribed T. I./J. The initials perhaps identify the hack writer Thomas Johnson, who published several books of 'conceits,' and

---

[14] May, *Elizabeth I: Selected Works*, 77.

[15] James Aske, *Elizabetha Trivmphans* (London: Thomas Orwin, 1588), *STC* 847, sig. D4r.

[16] Aske identified Dawtrey as the Sergeant Major in his list of camp officers. See *Elizabetha Trivmphans*, sig. C4v. Before coming to Tilbury, Dawtrey was primarily occupied with training the Hampshire musters. See *Calendar of State Papers Domestic Series, of the Reigns of Edward VI, Mary, Elizabeth, 1547–1625*, ed. Robert Lemon and Mary Anne Everett Green, 12 vols. (London: Longman, Brown, Green, Longmans, & Roberts, 1856–1872), 2:458, 464.

[17] *Elizabetha Trivmphans*, E1v.

another ballad in iambic tetrameter in 1595. T. I/J., whoever he was, describes Elizabeth receiving "A martial staff" on the second day of her visit, a detail also mentioned by Aske,[18] in Leigh's sermon text of the speech, and in Camden's *History of . . . Princess Elizabeth*,[19] but not by Deloney. On the second day of her visit, T. J.'s ballad continues, the queen spent two hours riding through the camp reviewing her army. T. J. also affirms that she "left her traine farre off to stand," and that she spoke "princely words" to the troops. T. J. thus becomes the fourth witness, with Sharpe, Leigh/Gaywood, and Deloney, to testify that the queen addressed her army on the second day of her visit. He records only one aspect of the speech, but it is a telling detail. The ballad states that Elizabeth gave her ". . . princely promisse none should lacke / Meate or drinke, or cloth for backe, / Golde and siluer should not slacke, / to her marshall men of England." Here, T. I/J. echoes and expands the passage from the *Cabala* text where Elizabeth promises her soldiers "rewards and crowns" for their service.

Taken in conjunction, these five accounts of what Elizabeth said at Tilbury bear witness, I think, to a single speech rather than two. The Leigh/Gaywood text is admittedly "the effect" of what she said, and it was no doubt written down from memory after the fact. Yet as Frye notes, it parallels Sharpe's account with such common elements as its defiance of the enemy, its acknowledgment of her feminine sex, and its assurance that the English fight on God's side against His foes. Notably, however, it lacks any reference to rewarding the soldiers and it dismisses Elizabeth's participation with them on the field of battle by merely exhorting them to "come and let us fight the battell of the Lord."[20] It is perhaps predictable as well as appropriate that the version of the speech that survives both on a church painting and in a sermon emphasizes the struggle between God and His foes in which the English are, conveniently, on the side of the Almighty. It is just as appropriate that the text reported by the earl of Leicester's chaplain stresses his worth as Lord General of the camp.

Given the circumstances of the alleged speech, the discrepancies among these five versions result, I believe, from omissions and selective emphasis on different topics in the address. Even if all witnesses to the event had furnished themselves with pen and ink, only a favored few could have been close enough to their sovereign to jot down on site even the gist of what she said. Deloney may have heard just as much as did Sharpe, but he was necessarily selective in choosing to versify only highlights of the address for his ballad. And Dawtrey apparently told Aske what he remembered of the queen's oration despite the contradiction in this text as to when she delivered it. T. I/J., meanwhile, heard, or chose to include in his ballad, only the promise of rewards that Elizabeth made toward

---

[18] *Elizabetha Trivmphans*, E1r.

[19] William Camden, *History of the most Renowned and Victorious Princess Elizabeth* (London, 1675), 2H2v.

[20] *STC* 15426, sig. G7v.

the end of her speech. The key distinction among the accounts concerns the emphasis on Elizabeth's willingness to reward her troops and to join them in battle. Deloney, Aske, and T. I/J. testify unanimously to a speech with these elements. The Leigh/Gaywood version of the speech, however, downplays the queen's offer to join her troops in battle and makes no mention of their rewards.

There is good reason to believe, however, that Elizabeth did in fact offer to accompany her soldiers into battle. To understand why, we must consider in more detail the military situation on the second day of her visit to Tilbury. In a letter of 5 August, the Privy Council had invited Leicester to reduce the number of troops in the camp as there was no apparent danger from the enemy.[21] Yet Sir Edward Ratcliffe, who actually spoke with Elizabeth during her visit, estimated that perhaps 16,000 soldiers remained in arms there at the time.[22] The English commanders feared that remnants of the Armada might return to cover a channel crossing by Parma and his battle-tested army. On 9 August, the same day that Elizabeth spoke to her troops, Lord Admiral Howard wrote from Canterbury to Sir Francis Walsingham, then attending on the queen. Howard assured Walsingham that the Armada, now dispersed in the North Sea, would necessarily return: "they dare not go back with this dishonour and shame," he wrote, "for we have marvellously plucked them."[23] As if to confirm his prediction, Walsingham reported to Burghley from "the court, in the camp" an occurrence at Tilbury on that same day:

> at noon, her Majesty, dining with the Lord Steward [Leicester] in his tent at the camp, had advertisement sent unto her from Sir Thomas Morgan ... that the Duke of Parma was determined this spring tide to come out, and that he looked that by that time the Spanish fleet would be returned.[24]

According to Walsingham, Elizabeth responded to this threat by resolving to stay in the camp and face the Spanish landing rather than go back upstream to London: "A conceit her Majesty had that in honour she could not return, in case there were any likelihood that the enemy would attempt anything. Thus your Lordship seeth that this place breedeth courage."[25]

Elizabeth's "conceit," spawned apparently by Morgan's false alarm, dissipated later that afternoon. She returned to London as planned. Yet her specific resolve to face the enemy on the field of battle with her troops crops up in the speech as recorded by four of its witnesses. Furthermore, the prospect of

---

[21] *Acts of the Council*, 16:222.
[22] London, British Library, MS. Cotton Otho E.9, fol. 205v.
[23] *State Papers Relating to the Defeat of the Spanish Armada Anno 1588*, ed. John Knox Laughton, 2 vols. (Bungay, Suffolk: Navy Records Society, 1987), 2:292.
[24] *State Papers*, 2:82–83.
[25] *State Papers*, 2:283.

imminent battle makes her emphasis on rewards to her soldiers that much more appropriate and likely. Accordingly, Sharpe's text, with its emphasis on both topics, is the one that probably comes closest to what Elizabeth said to her army that ninth of August 1588.

With Sharpe's version of the queen's speech established as more nearly authentic than Leigh/Gaywood, the choice of copy text is simple. All reprints of Sharpe's version that I have been able to trace through 1740 descend from its initial publication in the 1654 *Cabala*. Two manuscripts vie with this imprint for primacy as copy text, the Harleian version discovered by Green and a heretofore unexamined text among Chancery documents in the Public Record Office.[26] This manuscript is written in a mixed secretary-italic hand which at first dated the speech, '1686.' The same hand then replaced this date with 'August, 1688.' I can only speculate that this deliberate misdating of the address was meant to comment on the events of 1688 as a photo-negative replay of the Armada crisis. In this instance the Catholic regime of James II faced a Protestant invasion from the Netherlands under William and Mary. The Chancery manuscript of the speech diverges significantly from all other texts, but it repeats one error that links it to the other manuscript. Both the Harleian and Chancery texts quote Elizabeth as saying that she has come to Tilbury "but for my recreation." Now, there is a limit to royal *sprezzatura* even as displayed by Queen Elizabeth. The whole point of this section of her address is that she is there to endure with her soldiers the hardships of battle. She is prepared, she assures them, "to live and die amongst you all." She was manifestly not there to recreate herself while her hastily-levied recruits prepared to face Parma's battle-hardened veterans. The descent of the Chancery manuscript of the speech from a source related to Sharpe's Harleian MS. version points, I believe, to some limited circulation of the text in manuscript. In his letter to Buckingham Sharpe admits, after all, that his lordship is not the only recipient of the speech. Sharpe affirms that others, "such as I have given it to," also possess copies of it.[27] Ironically, the extant witnesses to this scribal tradition of textual transmission are flawed. The printed *Cabala* text, however, lacks demonstrable error and thus serves as copy text in my edition.

II

Some thirteen years after the Armada victory, on the afternoon of 30 November 1601, a delegation from the House of Commons some 150 strong entered Whitehall Palace for an audience with their sovereign. That autumn a Spanish army had landed in Ireland to support Tyrone's rebellion against the English. In response, Elizabeth convened her tenth Parliament on 27 October for the primary purpose of granting the Crown the extra income it needed to repel

---

[26] London, Public Record Office, *Duchess of Norfolk's Deeds*, C 115/101.
[27] *Cabala*, sig. 2L2v.

the invasion. In all, the House agreed to a grant of four subsidies; in return, Elizabeth curtailed her royal prerogative by rescinding a long list of monopolies. Unlike the Parliamentary subsidies, these royal privileges imposed continuous taxation on all classes of people for purchasing such everyday necessities as salt, vinegar, and starch, or practicing such trades as tanning leather and selling wine. Elizabeth cancelled these letters patent with a proclamation issued on Saturday, 28 November. She then invited the Lower House to meet with her in the Council Chamber at Whitehall on the following Monday.

That afternoon, the assembly kneeled before their sovereign as Speaker of the House John Croke addressed the queen, thanking her profusely for allowing their access to her royal presence and for her recent proclamation. Elizabeth replied with her "Golden Speech," and here, where we would most like to know exactly what was said, the record is obscured by an overabundance of evidence. My analysis of these texts suggests that Hartley's fourth version of the speech, the one based on Hayward Townshend's *Journal*, is probably the most accurate record of Elizabeth's words on this occasion. My argument pursues the neglected problem of how contemporary scribes might have copied down what was said in Parliament. The different versions of Elizabeth's "Golden Speech" offer us intriguing and heretofore unstudied evidence about the copying process which leads, I think, to recognition of Townshend's text, with all its warts, as the preferable one.

While historians often quote journals and diaries that claim to report Parliamentary proceedings verbatim, no one imagines that these texts provide more than outlines of what was said. G. R. Elton described these texts as "a notorious problem." "If," he continues, "they were recorded by a listener, accuracy is out of the question."[28] In general this must be true in an age before workable shorthand or mechanical recordings were in use. Worse yet, the official journal of the House is missing from 1584 to 1601.[29] Had it survived, however, it would allow us to test only the general accuracy of the various accounts of Elizabeth's speech. The clerks of Parliament and their deputies prepared summary notes of what took place in each session but they did not, so far as is known, attempt verbatim transcripts of the proceedings. If Townshend worked alone to produce his *Journal* of the 1601 Parliament, including the queen's "Golden Speech," he could have done no more than approximate her wording, as Elton affirmed. It is curious, however, that Townshend's 1601 journal is, overall, the fullest account of any Elizabethan parliamentary session, and far more complete than his 1597 journal. While

---

[28] G. R. Elton, *The Parliament of England 1559–1581* (Cambridge: Cambridge University Press, 1986), 10. See also A. F. Pollard, "Queen Elizabeth's Under-Clerks and Their Commons' Journals," *Bulletin of the Institute of Historical Research* 17 (1939–1940): 1–12, here 7: "before the elaboration of shorthand, which was still in its infancy, no report of debate could be adequate or trustworthy."

[29] Pollard, "Queen Elizabeth's Under-Clerks," 8.

I have not attempted a thorough analysis of his entire text, my comparison of Townshend's version of the "Golden Speech" with the two versions from which it was compiled suggests that he was not working alone. My hypothesis as to just how his account came into being emerges from a comparison of the five competing texts of the speech.

At just over 1,350 words, Townshend's account, the fourth in Hartley's organization of the texts, is the longest. Fourteen extant seventeenth-century manuscripts of this version testify to its wide circulation before it reached print with the entire *Journal* (under the title *Historical Collections*) in 1680. Closest to Townshend's wording is Hartley's third version of the speech. This state was published about 1628[30] and saw several reprints by the end of the century. Its appearance in at least eleven manuscripts suggests that it was almost as widely known as Townshend's state of the speech. Version three, however, is more than 250 words shorter than Townshend's copy. Although versions 3 and 4 organize the parts of Elizabeth's address very differently, they also agree word for word in many passages. This is because Version 4 is actually a somewhat truncated state of Version 3 conflated with an account of the speech that occurs as an appendix to a number of the manuscript copies of Townshend's *Journal*. Put another way, Hartley provides five texts of the speech, two of which were combined to produce Version 4. The Appendix, at just under 700 words, is the shortest account of Elizabeth's speech. The question is, how do the Appendix and Version 3 texts represent the address she delivered? Are they properly combined to form Version 4, or is this hybrid text largely or wholly redundant? And why should we choose any of these related texts over Hartley's first two witnesses to the speech?

Much can be learned about the relative authority of these five texts by comparing them with the queen's proclamation for "Reforming Patent Abuses." Specific content and phrasing in five passages of this document crop up in all but one of Hartley's five versions of the speech. The proclamation insists that Elizabeth granted the monopolies for "the common good and profit of her subjects . . . whose public good she tendereth more than any worldly riches." She assures them that she "never ceaseth to preserve her people in continual peace and plenty." The patents "granted to her majesty's ancient domestical servitors" have, however, been "notoriously abused . . . contrary to her highness' intention and meaning therein expressed."[31]

Hartley's first version of the speech, a unique text in British Library Harleian MS. 4808, echoes three of these passages: it mentions her servants, her concern for the "common good to the subject," and her desire to "preserve them in

---

[30] *STC* 7579.

[31] *STC* 8288; *Tudor Royal Proclamations*, ed. Paul L. Hughes and James F. Larkin, 3 vols. (New Haven: Yale University Press, 1964–1969), 3:no. 812, issued on 28 November.

peace."[32] The Appendix version picks up two of these excerpts: it cites Elizabeth's affirmation that she granted the patents to "servants of mine," thinking these measures "both good and beneficial to the subject." Versions 3 and 4 of the speech, however, echo the wording in all five excerpts. These specific echoes of the proclamation in four states of the text show that Elizabeth drew on that document for the wording of her "Golden Speech." Accordingly, what her MPs heard two days later may well have been a prepared address that Elizabeth wrote out in advance. This would also explain how she was able to send a draft of her speech to Sir Henry Savile that same afternoon, a draft she then forbade him to circulate.[33]

Broadly speaking, the process of combining Townshend's Appendix with the third state of the speech produced three substantive changes. It replaced Version 3 wording in two passages: one described how members of the House spoke against the monopolies because they understood how these grants estranged the queen from her subjects' love. The other dealt with Elizabeth's assertion that she was never afraid despite all the dangers and conspiracies that threatened her reign. The third change deleted from the Version 3 text her offer willingly to resign her throne were it not for her duty to God. Otherwise, the Appendix insertions connect, expand, and augment the queen's words as recorded in Version 3.

The most intriguing clue about the relationships among these three texts is the systematic way Townshend's Appendix was combined with Version 3 to create the fourth state of the text. Along with some duplicated content, the Appendix and Version 3 each records a number of topics not found in the other. In the Appendix, for example, Elizabeth refers to her subjects' love as a jewel, she vows to punish those who led her to grant the monopolies, and she mentions the danger of repealing them. Version 3 omits these topics, while it alone mentions the queen's promise to spend the subsidies wisely, her inability to rest until she had reformed the abuses of her letters patent, and her willingness to resign her throne were it not for her duty to God. Some overlapping phrases and interruptions aside, Appendix wording was superimposed on the Version 3 text in seven well-defined passages that range from 29 to 96 words apiece. Moreover, these passages alternate with seven Version 3 segments of roughly equivalent lengths.

Before attempting to explain this symmetrical alternation of parts to form the fourth version of the speech, we should consider another characteristic of all five witnesses to the address. All of them present the contents of the address in radically different order. This is not just a matter of added or deleted topics; corresponding topics appear in totally different places in the speech in all five versions. I have been unable to discern any pattern of agreement in these different organizations of content. To deepen the mystery, four of the five versions appear

---

[32] Hartley, *Proceedings*, 3:289.

[33] J. E. Neale, *Elizabeth I and Her Parliaments 1584–1601* (London: Jonathan Cape, 1957), 392.

to have been transcribed by eyewitnesses to the address.[34] Only the Appendix, which may or may not be Townshend's own notes on the speech, lacks explicit evidence of firsthand transcription. Still, its association with his *Journal* and the fact that it was integrated with Version 3 in most copies of that document suggest that Townshend considered it an authoritative source.

How could five copyists have transcribed the queen's words in such different sequences of the subjects she addressed? We can dismiss Version 2, the official, printed account of the speech, at the outset. However it came about, this text bears little relation to what Elizabeth said that afternoon. The Parliamentary historian J. E. Neale concluded that it was "entirely the Queen's composition" after the fact, yet its florid style little resembles that of Elizabeth's other orations. As Neale admits, it "deservedly sank from memory under the leaden weight of its euphuistic artifice and obscurity."[35] Hartley contends that the queen revised it until it was "polished into dullness and even opacity."[36] A sure sign that it was revised after the fact is its emphasis on several issues unmentioned by the other four versions, above all the queen's absolute prerogative to grant monopolies. Meanwhile, in this text the dozens of verbal echoes that resonate among the other states of the speech dwindle to a half dozen phrases. A. B.'s supposedly careful transcription is as dubious as the unimaginative choice of his initials from the first two letters of the alphabet.[37] Elizabeth may have approved this text, but its wording is remote from what she said on 30 November.

This leaves us with four apparently synoptic versions of the queen's address, each presenting its topics in a completely different order. What does this disorder coupled with the alternating pattern of Appendix and Version 3 passages in the combined text of Version 4 suggest about the creation and transmission of these texts? If Townshend (or whoever did the combining) supposed that he worked with two relatively complete summaries of the speech, why would he piece them together in this banded pattern of similar-sized passages? The answer, I think, is that these states of the text were drafted by three scribes working in tandem

---

[34] The scribe of version 1, which survives in a single manuscript, laments, "Many things through want of memory I have omitted without setting down many of her Majestie's gestures . . . ." See Hartley, *Proceedings*, 3:291. Version 2, the government's official, published account of the speech, is prefixed with the assurance that it was "taken verbatim in wrytinge by A. B. as neer as he could possiblie set yt downe." See Hartley, *Proceedings*, 3:292. The All Souls College, Oxford, manuscript of Version 3 claims that the text was "set downe by Mr Phillips" (Hartley, *Proceedings*, 3:295), a possible reference to one of two House members of this name. And Version 4 interrupts the queen's narrative to explain that "all this while we kneeled," adding that they stood up when she gave them permission to do so. It is clearly the work of someone present at the time.

[35] Neale, *Elizabeth I*, 392.

[36] Hartley, *Proceedings*, 3:xxx.

[37] Neale comments that if the scribe was not a fiction, the initials could apply to only one member of the House in 1601, Anthony Blagrave. See Neale, *Elizabeth I*, 392.

to record Elizabeth's words. Each writer jotted down about 30 to 50 words at a time. As one copyist reached the limit of his memory and penmanship, the next scribe took up the task. The Appendix scribe, perhaps Townshend himself, began the transcription, for the Appendix offers the most complete opening to the queen's address. A Version 3 scribe completed the task, for this state of the speech preserves the fullest account of Elizabeth's conclusion. This system of copying in tandem led to some textual overlap, of course, as the task proceeded and no copyist could be sure just where his predecessor would leave off; yet the system allowed these scribes to capture every key topic of the address.

Evidence that such a system was actually in place for transcribing speeches in Parliament on special occasions occurs in *Nobilitas politica et civilis* (1608), edited by the antiquary Thomas Milles from manuscripts he inherited from his uncle, Robert Glover, Somerset herald (d. 1588). An engraving between signatures M3 and M4 in this book (pp. 126 and 127) [38] depicts Queen Elizabeth enthroned in Parliament. Seated at a table in the foreground are four scribes who face their sovereign, heads bowed, busily transcribing the proceedings.

The same or a very similar engraving appeared in the 1680 edition of Townshend's *Historical Collections*. There is no reason to doubt that this is an authentic representation of the queen in Parliament, for *Nobilitas* is a serious work. Milles incorporated his English translation of it into his *Catalogue of Honor* (1610), with the same engraving on p. 69 (sig. G5). He assures us that this illustration "most truely and liuely" depicts the opening of Elizabeth's fifth Parliament, 23 November 1584. After identifying the locations in the engraving of the lords and officers in attendance, he notes that "lowest of all, sitteth the clark of the *Parlament*, with the Clark of the *Crowne*, behind whom the other Clarks writt, resting vpon their knees" (sig. G4v). These "other Clarks" are the four scribes who appear in the middle of the scene slightly below the center of the engraving. Granted that four scribes may have worked more efficiently than three, the key evidence of this engraving for my argument is that it seems to depict the scribes copying in tandem, a technique that three scribes could also accomplish whether or not the results would be as accurate as with four.

In either case, at the end of their task, scribes who copied in tandem faced the problem of reordering their fragments of the speech into the proper chronological sequence. After transcribing Elizabeth's "Golden Speech," the second and third scribes simplified this reconstruction by combining their drafts to produce Version 3. The result is necessarily rather incoherent. At one point Elizabeth is made to say that she has revoked the monopolies in order to maintain her subjects' love for her, for she never ruled with any other intent but her people's well-being. But she then digresses into a self-pitying lament: "what dangers, what practices, and what perils I have passed, some, if not all of you know." She ends

---

[38] Robert Glover, *Nobilitas politica vel ciuilis Personas scilicet distinguendi* . . ., ed. Thomas Milles (Londoni: Gulielmi Iaggard, 1608), after sig. M3v.

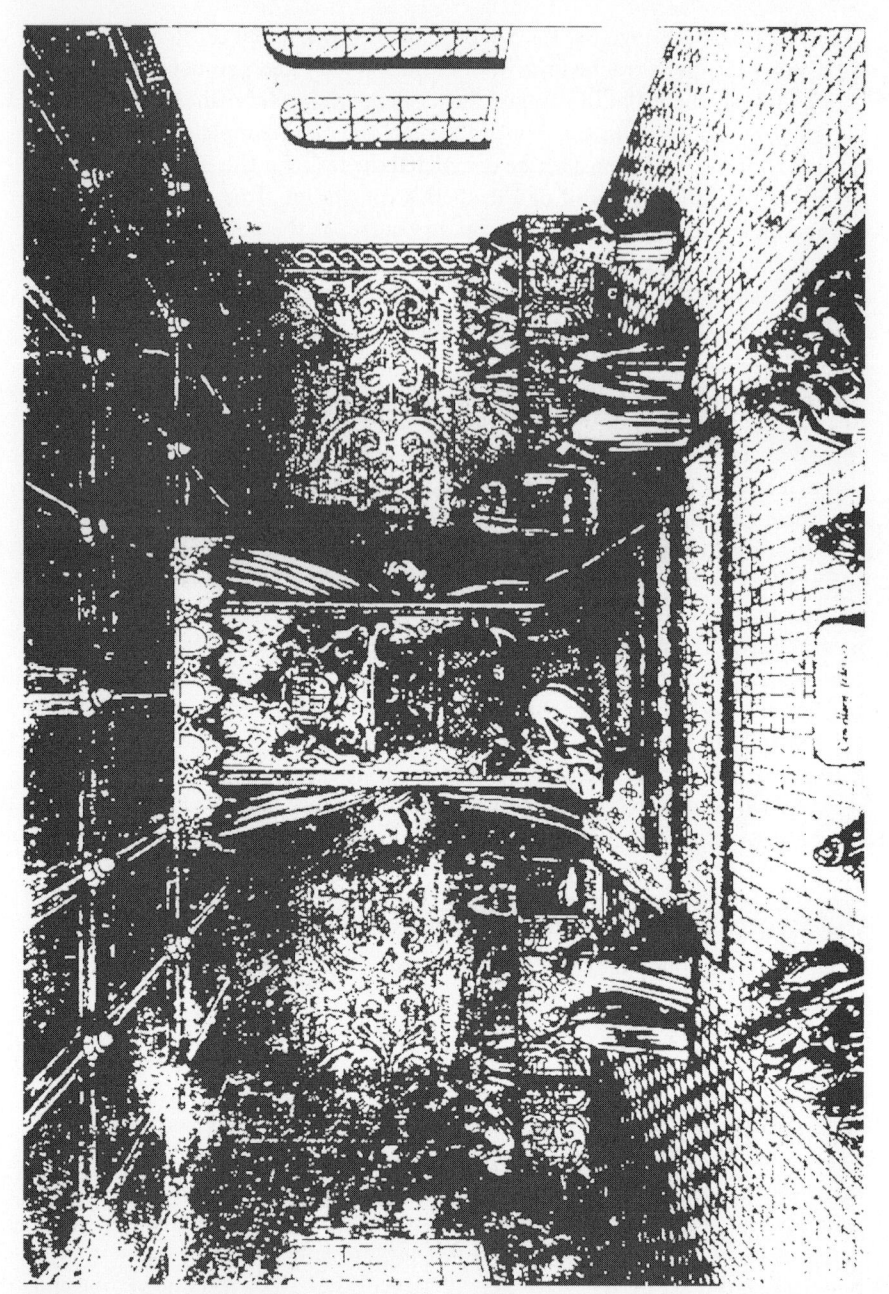

Figure 8.1. Queen Elizabeth in Parliament, 1584.
Published with permission of ProQuest.

with the pious affirmation that "it is God that hath delivered me." There is little meaningful connection between her repeal of the patents of monopoly and the dangers God has saved her from throughout her reign. Version 3's placement of the simile about physicians and their aromatical drugs is similarly disjointed—it is perhaps the most glaring error in this text. Fortunately, an overlapping Appendix passage correctly applies this analogy to the suitors who persuaded the queen to grant them monopolies, those seemingly attractive measures which were actually harmful to her subjects: "But I perceive," she complains, "they dealt with me like physicians who, ministering a drug, make it more acceptable by giving it a good, aromatical savor." Version 3 retains both the aromatical savor and the pills, but applies the simile to "The cares and troubles of a Crowne." Elizabeth here complains that she was somehow deceived about the nature of becoming a ruler. The problem with this reading, of course, is that no one lured her into her queenship or deceived her about its nature, nor was this topic wholly appropriate in a speech that emphasized her profound love for her subjects. Clearly, the compilers of Version 3 had Elizabeth's wording of the simile but could not remember where to place it in the text. Their mistake crops up, surprisingly, in Version 2, the government's official printed text of the speech. Thus, the published text probably derived, with much interpolated revision, from Version 3. The misplaced simile suggests, however, that Elizabeth did not scrutinize the revision if she had anything to do with it at all. Guided by the Appendix reading, the comparison and its referent are properly aligned in Version 4.

The Appendix is, nevertheless, as disjointed an account of Elizabeth's words as Version 3. For example, it quotes the queen asking the Speaker to thank the House on her behalf, but her gesture makes sense only when it follows her reference to the subsidies ("your intended helps"), a passage unique to Version 3. These remarks too are properly aligned in Version 4. Other gaps in the Appendix narrative include Elizabeth's threat of "condign punishment" for those who tricked her into granting the patents. She then, however, declines to sweep to her revenge rather "for conscience sake than for any glory or increase of love that I desire." How could such punishment either be impeded by conscience or redound to Gloriana's credit by its omission? Overall, the Appendix fragments of the address gained coherence when they were melded with the Version 3 text.

With a little tinkering, however, Version 3 was at some point modified to circulate independently. The revision amounted to little more than adding some brief opening remarks and a few transitions between the most disordered passages. Yet one Version 3 manuscript seems to have been explicitly prepared to receive the missing excerpts from the Appendix. Oxford, Bodleian Library, Rawlinson MS. D.1045 lacks more than 10% of the standard third state of the speech. What is most unusual about this manuscript, however, is its layout on the page.

It is copied in passages of various lengths separated by seven blank spaces varying from roughly half an inch to some two inches in width. These seven bands of blank paper within a single prose text are very unusual, paper-wasting anomalies in scribal practice of the time. They serve no purpose with regard to clarity of layout or the setting off of one part of the speech over another. What they suggest instead is the scribe's awareness that parts of the queen's speech were missing. He deliberately left room on each page to add these passages when they came to hand.

In summary, I propose that the Appendix and Version 3 texts are the work of three copyists who attempted to transcribe the queen's every word that November afternoon. The combined labors of two of them circulated as Version 3 of the speech, while the third scribe's text, which is just over half the length of Version 3, circulated as an Appendix to a number of the manuscript copies of Townshend's *Journal*. The resultant fourth version of the "Golden Speech" is probably the most complete and authentic record of what Elizabeth said, yet it leaves us with many doubts. Its parts still seem disorganized in places, and it may lack or misrepresent some key phrasing. Both Versions 1 and 2 of the address repeat, for example, the Version 3 passage in which Elizabeth contends that, were it not for her conscience and sense of duty she would "willingly resign the place I hold to another."[39] Version 4 merely approximates this sentiment: it has the queen affirm that "neither do I desire to live longer days than that I may see your prosperity," and later, "it is not my desire to live nor reign longer than my life and reign shall be for your good." Yet the cumulative evidence of three other witnesses argues that Elizabeth said something much more definite about her willingness to abdicate. This subject was diluted at best when Version 3 was combined with the Appendix. The similar passages I have just quoted also suggest that Version 4 includes some duplicated but misplaced excerpts from its source documents.[40]

The overarching purpose of my analysis is to move us closer to what Elizabeth said in both her speeches. But even if the *Cabala* text is closer to what she said at Tilbury Camp than the Leigh/Gaywood account, the odds are astronomically against Sharpe's transcription of the speech verbatim. And while Hartley's fourth version of five different states of the "Golden Speech" seems more complete and accurate than any of the others, its apparent redundancies and lapses argue that it too conveys the queen's words imperfectly. Unfortunately, then, Elizabeth's most celebrated public orations, those most carefully analyzed by scholars for all that they might tell us about her attitudes and beliefs, and her skills as an orator, are among the least reliable texts in her canon. For the moment, this is as close as I can get as an editor to what Elizabeth said on these oc-

---

[39] In Version 1, Harleian MS. 787, this becomes, "I could well be content that another had my charge." In Version 2, the official, published speech, we find "I would willingly yeild an other my place." See Hartley, *Proceedings*, 3:291, 293.

[40] May, *Elizabeth I: Selected Works*, 84, 87.

casions. With luck, it will not be as close as we ever get to her exact words. New evidence may come to light, and better students than I may draw more convincing conclusions from the evidence I have examined. If I have given them something to work with, I consider my time well spent.

Elizabeth, Burghley, and the Pragmatics of Rule: Managing Elizabethan England

Norman Jones

In 2000, Alan Axelrod published a "how to" book on management entitled *Elizabeth I CEO: Strategic Lessons from the Leader Who Built an Empire*. Axelrod held up Elizabeth as a role model for "would-be builders of contemporary empires."[1] As the *Investor's Business Daily* proclaimed, "Whether you're just beginning your corporate climb or you've reached the top and want to stay there, you can learn leadership from Queen Elizabeth I."[2]

Axelrod establishes a set of leadership principles that, he says, Elizabeth epitomized. Elizabeth, using these skills, turned the English corporation around. Finding it a failing mess in late 1558, by 1603 she had led it to become one of the greatest states in human history. Axelrod enumerates nineteen things Elizabeth did to manage the miracle, including developing leadership skills and a leadership image, setting objectives and goals, inspiring others, creating loyalty, building a team, minimizing micro-management, nurturing creativity in others, knowing the competition (enemies), and creating maximum performance and quality.[3]

Anyone knowledgeable about the Elizabethan world would have a problem with Axelrod's conclusions about Queen Elizabeth. The reader finds little doubts come creeping in, followed by great, towering doubts, concluding with snorts and sometimes guffaws. However, Axelrod is suggesting questions that deserve answers. We can agree that Elizabeth did make a success of her reign, and we have a tendency to do as Axelrod did and give her great credit for leadership, for she clearly was a leader. But was she the kind of leader Axelrod portrays—a sort of CEO for all seasons? What did management look like in the Elizabethan state, and how was it conducted? Most importantly, did Elizabeth have a "grand

---

[1] Alan Axelrod, *Elizabeth I CEO: Strategic Lessons from the Leader who Built an Empire* (Paramus, NJ: Prentice Hall, 2000), xii.
[2] Axelrod, *Elizabeth I CEO*, jacket blurb.
[3] Axelrod, *Elizabeth I CEO*, xii-xiii.

strategy" that she imposed on her commonwealth, or was her leadership as much about accepting and using governmental structures as it was a reflection of her values? How was her power limited and shaped?

There is a series of problems attached to these questions, problems that can be labeled, loosely, as those of authority, honor, and relationship. Early modern politics depended on formal legal systems and informal patronage systems. The two systems had to work together to make the state run, and they each delimited the scope of power. Each worked on the other, and they constantly and intentionally overlapped.

Let's begin with the issue of royal authority. In legal theory, Henry de Bracton's great dictum applied: the king was under God and the law. In practice, of course, the law was made by the king in Parliament, and Elizabeth was very aware of the authority of statute. We can often see this in the negative sense, when she had Members of Parliament arrested for addressing issues (such as religion) reserved to her prerogative. In the positive sense, however, she leaned heavily on statutes to ensure her authority. After all, it was statute law that changed religion, made her supreme governor of the church, and recognized her title to the throne.

The best available bulwark against the chaos lurking at the nation's door was law and order, and Elizabeth's ministers concentrated on making parliamentary statute paramount over theological truth. The verities of religion, Elizabeth knew, were many and contradictory, leading to dissension. Law, on the other hand, could be enforced as a common value of the nation.[4] Only if the law of the land was victorious over the laws of foreign popes could there be peace and security. As Elizabeth told the earl of Sussex, "Our laws do not make search of man's conscience . . . . without occasion manifestly given by outward deeds committed against the laws."[5]

Law was the cloak that masculated her, in that the Crown as an entity was distinct from person and immune from gender. Consequently, she clung to the law very carefully. But, of course, she brought to her use of the law her understanding of her job. As she told the scholars at the University of Cambridge in 1564, "the words of superiors, as Demosthenes said, are as the books of their inferiors, and the example of a prince has the force of law. If this was true in those city-states, how much more so in a kingdom?"[6]

---

[4] G. R. Elton, "Lex terrae victrix: The Triumph of Parliamentary Law in the Sixteenth Century," in *The Parliaments of Elizabethan England*, ed. D. M. Dean and N. L. Jones (Oxford: Blackwell, 1990), 15–36.

[5] PRO SP 70/91 fol. 83, quoted in Susan Doran, "Elizabeth I's Religion: The Evidence of her Letters," *Journal of Ecclesiastical History* 51 (2000): 699–720, here 704.

[6] *Elizabeth I: Collected Works*, ed. Leah Marcus, Janel Mueller, and Mary Beth Rose (Chicago: University of Chicago Press, 2000), 87–88.

Sitting at the top of the legal and social pyramids, the queen exercised authority that encompassed all the institutions beneath her, but she did not have a formal organizational mechanism for directly using them. What she had was power that grew from respect for law, deference to hierarchy, greed, and fear of disgrace and dishonor. Under those conditions, rather than making official pronouncements, she exerted her will through words and actions that rippled through the system. A letter from her or an audience with her could have tremendous effect, but she seldom used those tools directly. She sat at an imperious remove, a distance that made her interventions even more impressive. As the Spanish ambassador once remarked, she knew everyone worth knowing—which meant she knew which ears to box and which to whisper into. She exerted leadership by expressing her will, or falling into a rage, or rewarding a courtier, letting others actually pull the levers of government.

Of course, the Privy Council pulled those levers in her name, but she did not attend meetings of the Council. She let those in close contact with her carry her will to her councilors. Her leadership style was to relate closely with her courtiers and councilors and let them divine what was to be done in her name. This is why William Cecil and her favorites were so important. Through them, she could extend her power into the masculine world of law courts and councils. As a woman, she had little standing in the culture, but as a monarch under law she had immense *auctoritas*. That authority, in turn, gave her great *potestas*—but only insofar as her officials felt duty bound to carry out orders in her name.

The queen's authority was delegated to her officers, who were expected to communicate her will and execute it. At the apex of this system sat the Privy Council, the primary organ of administration and communication. Members of this body were the chief bureaucrats and some great magnates. These men occupied multiple positions in the central government and in local governments as well, their overlapping positions serving as conduits for messages from the center and information from the localities. Of course, they sat in Parliament too, where they could participate in the creation of the laws that they helped to enforce. This sort of overlapping delegation went all the way down the organizational chart, creating the informal network that allowed a government with rudimentary central agencies to function.

These gentlemen carried out what Steven Hindle has labeled "self-government by the King's command."[7] The key to this sort of self-governance was obedience arising from honor. The local magistracy had to be obedient to its betters, and, in theory, ultimately to the queen. Since it was a voluntary system, willingness to obey had to be maintained. Concepts of honor and self-interest mixed

---

[7] Steven Hindle, "County Government in England," in *Companion to Tudor Britain*, ed. Robert Tittler and Norman Jones (Oxford: Blackwell Publishers, 2004), 98–115, here 99.

into this obedience because it concerned one's place in society and one's duty, *noblesse oblige*.

The glue that bound the magistracy to their mistress was the deference due to a woman of high degree, destined by birth and divine destiny to a rule ratified by Parliament. All of this tied into the conceptions of personal honor that went along with an hierarchical society. Although the society was certainly patriarchal, obedience and deference were essential parts of its social psychology. Elizabeth, as she often reminded people, was a "prince" and her father's daughter. As such, she commanded reverence and expected obedience. Balancing the deference, however, was the issue of aristocratic honor. The gentlemen who were expected to run local government were very aware that lineage and service made one gentle, and it was this sensibility that created the interface of government. Service was expected as a duty, but honor had to be maintained.[8]

Listen to the way in which William, marquis of Northampton tried to negotiate obedience to a Privy Council order for a general muster in 1560. Writing to his deputies, the marquis gently reprimanded them for excusing their failure to hold proper musters because of old precedents and for sending in old certificates of musters. Wondering if they were legalistic or just forgetful, he expatiated on how he knew their loyalty to the queen and their country; he explained that their disobedience "toucheth me in estimation," and he urged them to consider how appreciative the queen would be of their good service. Of course, if they did not do good service, he would rather hide their behavior from her than have her know of their dishonor. Pleading and shaming, he tried to get the command carried out.[9]

Mervyn James stressed the importance of concepts of lineage and honor to governance in the north, but William Palmer argues that this was a two-way street. The magistracy was in a neo-Platonic universe in which honor and duty flowed both toward and away from the center. They may have had duties to their betters and their queen, but they also had duties to their families and localities that made their responses much more a matter of self-interest than is sometimes admitted. Concepts of honor, obedience, lineage, and service certainly motivated people. Honor and slight were, however, in the eyes of the beholder, just as when to serve and how enthusiastically was a calculation that related to values that were more localized than general. As Palmer says, ultimately it was about survival. Honor was a "discourse tool" that could be used to justify behavior.[10]

---

[8] Felicity Heal and Clive Holmes, *The Gentry in England and Wales 1500–1700* (Stanford: Stanford University Press, 1994), 24–33.

[9] Royal Commission on Historical Manuscripts, *Report on the Manuscripts of Lord Montagu of Beaulieu*, ed. Henry John Douglas Scott-Montagu and Sophia Crawford Lomas (London: HMSO, 1900), 9–11.

[10] William Palmer, "Scenes from Provincial Life: History, Honor, and Meaning in the Tudor North," *Renaissance Quarterly* 53 (2000), 425–48, here 448.

It was in this web of relationships that the fulcrum of early Elizabethan politics was located. Networks of relationships mediated between the center and the periphery, using the languages of law, deference, and patronage. However, those radiations from the center were delivered by humans and interpreted by self-interested locals. Orders were often not understood, or were acted on in ways that had not been imagined when they were sent. Of course, local magistrates were often expected to interpret them as befitting local conditions. Moreover, the complex, interlocking, and confusing layers of authority in many places meant that instructions from the center often entailed a negotiation.

National law did not operate everywhere in the same way. Justices of the Peace did not have authority over chartered towns, which chose their own magistrates. Bishops had a separate set of duties and authority, as well as a different legal system over which they presided. The Duchy of Lancaster, the Duchy of Cornwall, and the Palatinate of Durham had separate legal status, and were not always bound by Acts of Parliament, while the Stannaries Parliament and courts ruled the tin miners of Cornwall and had the right to overturn Westminster statutes. In the Marches and in Ireland, things were different again, so that only the individuals whose personal ties crossed these boundaries really bound the operational government together. As Ian Archer has documented for London,[11] these overlapping, multiple jurisdictions were made workable only by having many offices filled by the same person, or by a group of people who shared other things in common, whether it be kinship, parish life, or guild membership.

It was these local, regional, and national authorities, be they JPs, aldermen, guild masters, churchwardens, or judges, who, in their daily governmental activities, mediated the orders, made decisions, and interpreted their orders and the laws. Most of our political histories and our histories of political culture tend to see these people as inert, but they were not.

In this world of multiple, overlapping, formal, informal, and confusing governmental structures, it was difficult for a monarch to be effectively imperious. Elizabeth had to work within this structure or fail. And it was difficult to work within it because of her gender and her lack of a husband. After years of thinking about Elizabeth, I have concluded that she probably agreed with the broader culture about the place of a woman, allowing her gender to shape her reign in her own mind as well as in the minds of her courtiers. As some of the tracts about her marriage pointed out, as a woman she could not go out into the world, let alone lead in war. She had to delegate these activities to someone else. Sir Thomas Smith's character "Lovealien" put the case succinctly when he noted that princes, and most of all a queen, could not be a "strayer abroad" like a common man. A

---

[11] Ian Archer, "Government in Early Modern London: The Challenge of the Suburbs," in *Two Capitals: London and Dublin 1500–1840*, ed. Peter Clark and Raymond Gillespie, Proceedings of the British Academy 107 (Oxford and London: British Academy, Oxford University Press, 2001), 133–47.

queen needed a male helper who, because he was a man, could see, hear, and do on her behalf.[12] Smith, of course, meant that she needed a husband.

Elizabeth rejected the option of taking a husband, but she still needed a man to go abroad on her behalf. That man was, for Elizabeth, Sir William Cecil, later Lord Burghley, who embodied her authority in places like the Privy Council. She called him her "Spirit," and in many ways, it was an accurate description of his role. Cecil became her eyes, ears, and hands, while she remained the head. She added to his skills those of a number of other powerful men who brought their own virtues. In particular, Robert Dudley possessed something Cecil did not: birth. Son of a duke and brother of an earl, soon to be an earl himself, Dudley supplied the queen with entrée into places Cecil was less able to penetrate, and he supplied his clients with a different sort of influence with the queen. Then, too, Dudley could have ambitions that Cecil could not. He could aspire to marry the queen, and he could be her close friend. Their cooperative rivalry benefited the queen, even as it perhaps complicated their lives. They brought complementary forms of influence to bear on alternative networks, different men of influence, and different parts of the country.

Elizabeth's ability to choose and use men of political intelligence from various social hierarchies is a key to her rule. But did she make the policies carried out by Cecil, Leicester, and others she favored to carry her communications to the ruling gentlemen? I believe that she did set their forms, although she did it with a pragmatic political savvy that makes it hard, at times, to tell her from her councilors, on whose political skill she depended to carry them out. To test this, let us take the case of her management of the church.

One group of English leaders was even more patriarchal than the run-of-the-mill Englishman in the middle of the sixteenth century: the clergy. Although they accepted her as Supreme Governor, they did not hold that it was Elizabeth's place to actively run the church or indeed to interfere with it. Women could not hold sacramental authority, they had a clearly inferior position in God's eyes, and it was not their business to tell God's anointed how to run His church. The fact that Elizabeth was entitled "Supreme Governor" instead of "Supreme Head" of the Church underscores their resistance, for it is clear that the title given her by Parliament was a compromise forced as much by Protestants as by Catholics. All agreed that no woman could claim the title of "head" of Christ's church.[13]

Elizabeth did not have the title, but she felt that she had been put in her place by God and the law. She was *auxilia domini*, the helper or handmaiden of the Lord, a phrase full of biblical resonance (alluding to *ancilla domini*, Luke

---

[12] "Sir Thomas Smith's orations for and against the Queen's marriage," quoted in Appendix III in *The Life of the Learned Sir Thomas Smith*, by John Strype (Oxford: Clarendon Press, 1820), 210.

[13] Norman Jones, *Faith by Statute: Parliament and the Settlement of Religion* (London: Royal Historical Society, 1982), 130–32.

1:38). In her prayers, we see this theme again and again. Moreover, she believed that God had given her duties and had set limits on her. She prayed for the ability to administer justice with equity, keeping the peace: "And thus I shall feel, with my subjects, Thy most holy benediction, from the which I know peace to have come . . . which until now, to Thy honor and the comforting of Thy Church, I have enjoyed while my nearest neighbors have felt the evils of bloody war."[14] It was a prayer repeated in various forms throughout her reign, as she reminded herself in her petitions to God concerning her duties as queen.

Elizabeth's vision of her divinely appointed role convinced her that her primary duty was to secure domestic peace, no matter what religious leaders pressed her to do. As Supreme Governor, she sought order and peace first, seeing them as God's expectation of His handmaiden. Of course, peace and order could occur only if her subjects recognized their duty to their monarch's authority as Supreme Governor of the Church in England. As God's handmaiden, the Supreme Governor had total responsibility for the church, and she expected its leaders to bow to her authority. Honoring God meant honoring her.

Elizabeth's bishops, however, had a strong, inherited sense of their duty to God, too. Protestant though they were, they believed that the bishops had a key place in God's hierarchy and that they had to manage the spiritual lives of the their flocks. This required taking whatever steps were necessary to instill discipline and enforce theological purity. They believed they had the God-given duty to correct those that needed correcting. In keeping with ancient Christian tradition, many of them believed their authority was distinct from, and of a higher order than, the authority of the queen.

The bishops' duty to God collided with the queen's belief in her authority in the early 1560s. Clashes would continue for many years, as the bishops, caught between Protestant enthusiasts and the queen's prerogative, were battered from both sides. This battle created managerial problems. The bishops could not be dismissed or ignored, so the queen had to work with them without seeming to remove their authority. This is where Cecil came in. He had friends, connections, and savvy that were magnified by his connection to the queen. He lacked nobility, but he was in the center of a network of the men who made things work, the *togati*. He could lend the queen strength through his connections.

We can watch this process at work in the letters exchanged by Archbishop Matthew Parker and William Cecil in the 1560s and 1570s. Theirs was an old friendship, stretching back to their youth in Cambridge. Parker once described Cecil as "of long time my special good friend and master," and it is clear that they had known one another since the time Sir John Cheke had been their friend and tutor. Other members of this circle of friends included many of the new Elizabethan bishops, as well as Lord Keeper Sir Nicholas Bacon. They had all

---

[14] *Elizabeth I: Collected Works*, 314.

been acquainted in the 1540s, and Bacon and Cecil had married sisters. It was a tight little group that Winthrop Hudson once described as the "Cambridge connection."[15]

Archbishop Parker and his fellows were dependent upon Cecil and Bacon for their appointments, and they used them as their mediators with the queen. We see Parker's reliance upon Cecil in numerous letters in which he lets his hair down about the frustrations of his office. In 1563 we find him writing to Cecil "I cannot be quiet till I have disclosed to you, as to one of my best willing friends, in secrecy, mine imperfection, which grieveth me not so much to utter in respect of mine own rebuke, as it grieveth me that I am not able to answer your friendly report of me."[16]

All of this becomes important when we remember how Elizabeth related to Parker and his fellow bishops. She depended upon the terror of her office to keep them obedient to her supremacy. The bishops knew that the Reformation, their jobs, even their lives depended upon the success of the Elizabethan Settlement, and they were born into a society that held the majesty of monarchy in great awe. As ministers of the church, they also held that the queen was their spiritual child and that they were heirs of a very long history of ecclesiastical independence from secular rule. Putting all this together could produce moments like Archbishop Grindal's famous rebuke of the queen that got him suspended from office. Consequently, Elizabeth and her bishops sparred over their conflicting roles.

In the 1560s, this relationship was tested in a series of moves made by the bishops and rescinded by the queen after startling scenes of her anger sent them running to Cecil for solace and help. When, in 1561, Elizabeth declared that she would not tolerate married clergy in colleges and cathedral closes, Parker was horrified. The queen, he told Cecil, "expressed to me a repentance that we were thus appointed in office, wishing it had been otherwise." He was "in horror to hear such words to come from her mild nature and Christianly learned conscience." Convinced that the Devil must be at work, he turned to Cecil for help. To him he felt he could pour out his anguish—he even wished he could die, "*in amaritudine animae meae*" ["in the bitterness of my soul"]. But he also felt he could tell Cecil that the clergy were duty-bound to serve their consciences before God, commenting "I would be sorry that the clergy should have cause to shew disobedience, with *oportet Deo obedire magis quam hominibus*" ["it behooves one to

---

[15] Winthrop Hudson, *The Cambridge Connection and the Elizabethan Settlement of 1559* (Durham, NC: Duke University Press, 1980), 105–7.

[16] John Bruce and T. T. Perowne, eds., *Correspondence of Matthew Parker, D.D., Archbishop of Canterbury: Comprising Letters Written by and to Him, from A.D. 1535, to his Death, A.D. 1575* (Cambridge: Parker Society, 1853), 199–201: Parker to Cecil, ascribed to 1563, Lansd. 6, no. 89.

obey God more than men"].[17] It is striking that he could talk to Cecil this way, and he clearly expected that the prayers he was offering God to change Elizabeth's heart were also for the ears of the Principal Secretary. Cecil, he knew, had influence with the source of all authority in England.

The bishops' belief in their right to discipline the church was disabused as they learned to their shock that, in the queen's eyes, they did not have the right to continue the Reformation by enacting a new discipline. The Convocation, led by Archbishop Parker, prepared a slate of further reforms in discipline and a set of articles of faith in 1563, but, when they were introduced, they were met with royal wrath. The attempt to have them passed in 1566 met with the same fate. A petition from the bishops to the queen, begging her to allow the bills to proceed in Parliament, stressed that they advanced the cause of Almighty God and identified "divers and sundry errors . . . such as have been in this realm wickedly and obstinately by the adversaries of the Gospel defended." The passage of these Articles of Religion would allow her to reduce all her subjects to unity in religion. It was signed by all the bishops.[18]

Elizabeth was not impressed. Ignoring the issue of ecclesiastical discipline, she demanded of Parker and his brethren whether they had introduced the bills without her permission, against her express order. The archbishop denied it to the queen and immediately wrote Cecil, commenting that "Your presence with the Queen's Majesty wanteth; whereby her Highness may be the more disquieted with informations."[19] In the speech from the throne at the closing of Parliament, the Lord Keeper, speaking in the queen's name, announced that it was the queen's job to make sure that God was truly worshiped, to see that her subjects "do no injury one to another, and specially to make quietness among the ministers of the church."[20]

Quietness continued to be her goal. When Parker died in 1575 he was replaced by Edmund Grindal, promoted from the archbishopric of York to be primate of all England at Canterbury. Burghley, who had been his patron throughout his career and who would be an executor of his will, was behind his promotion, but it seems Elizabeth was not so certain that he was the right choice. He was unmarried, which she liked, but would he stick to the *via media*? In a letter telling Grindal of his impending election, Burghley waxed voluble about the need for a middle ground between ecclesiastical administration and puritan resistance. "I wish," he told the future archbishop, "there was more caution and circumspection in all their canonical jurisdictions and consistories, that the exercise thereof

---

[17] Bruce and Perowne, *Correspondence of Matthew Parker*, 156–60. Parker is quoting Job 10:1 and Acts 5:29.

[18] Bruce and Perowne, *Correspondence of Matthew Parker*, 293–94.

[19] Bruce and Perowne, *Correspondence of Matthew Parker*, 291.

[20] T. E. Hartley, ed., *Proceedings in the Parliaments of Elizabeth I, 1558–1581* (London: Leicester University Press, 1981), 169.

might be directly *ad edificationem* ["for edification"], and not to make gain of that which was meant to punish or prevent sin."[21]

Grindal, however, was soon caught between loyalty and duty. The queen, agreeing, perhaps with the recently deceased Parker, saw the popular clerical gatherings known as prophesyings as a threat to good order and her authority. When, in 1576, a report of troublesome prophesying in Northamptonshire and Warwickshire reached the queen, Burghley and Leicester both tried to warn Grindal, but he did not listen carefully. Even when ordered by the queen herself to suppress the meetings, he demurred. Instead, he wrote her a "schoolmasterly reproof" defending the gatherings and asserting that he could not in good conscience suppress them. "Bear with me," he wrote, "if I choose rather to offend your earthly Majesty than to offend the heavenly majesty of God."[22] "Remember Madam," he lectured, "that you are a mortal creature," who must appear before the divine tribunal. In the bowels of Christ, he besought her to put God's majesty before her eyes when dealing in religious matters.[23]

She did not bear with him. Leicester delivered his letter, and for the next five months, the queen's storm against him mounted. Burghley told him to stay away from the court, pleading sickness if necessary. Burghley and Leicester both tried to help him, but Elizabeth sequestered him in Lambeth Palace in May of 1576 and suppressed the prophesyings by a royal order directed to the bishops.

Elizabeth's anger was so great that she wanted Grindal removed. Burghley, Leicester, Bacon, and other men of influence attempted to protect him, but the queen's anger only grew, and now she turned it on them. She had been crossed in her policy and would not let her servants undermine her position. Sir Thomas Wilson informed Burghley that Elizabeth disliked his dealing with Grindal, "whom she would have deprived for his contempt committed." Burghley suffered from her anger and could not work his usual trick of being the queen's reasonable voice, since Grindal was not interested in being reasonable. Burghley wrote him a long letter in which he tried to demonstrate to Grindal how to approach the queen for forgiveness without necessarily admitting she was correct. The Archbishop was instructed to "good speeches of her majesty as a prince that in all her public doings hath shown her wisdom, in doing nothing without good cause."[24] He invited him to set down his answer to the queen in writing so that Burghley could correct it, but Grindal refused to follow his advice. To make matters worse,

---

[21] Quoted in Patrick Collinson, *Archbishop Grindal, 1519–1583: The Struggle for a Reformed Church* (Berkeley: University of California Press, 1979), 223, quoting ITL, Petyt MS. 538/47, no. 267, fol. 502.

[22] Collinson, *Archbishop Grindal*, 233–42.

[23] William Nicholson, ed., *The Remains of Edmund Grindal* (Cambridge: Cambridge University Press, 1843), 389.

[24] Quoted in Conyers Read, *Lord Burghley and Queen Elizabeth* (New York: Knopf, 1960), 184–85, quoting British Library, MS. Lansd. 103, no. 8.

Leicester had disgraced himself by marrying and, thus, had also diminished in the queen's favor. With or without his friends' support, Grindal could not escape the consequences of thwarting the queen's policy.[25] Although he was never deprived of his office, he died before she forgave him.[26]

Elizabeth clearly stood firm on her beliefs that God had given her sovereignty and that it was her duty to keep the peace in the church, suppressing any who would challenge her God-given authority. At the same time, she demonstrated the limits of moderating influence from prized courtiers. Neither Burghley nor Leicester, working behind the scenes, could deliver Grindal's obedience. Nor, therefore, could they protect him from the queen's consistent strategy of requiring ecclesiastical obedience.

Grindal was in trouble because he was tolerating exercises that were associated with Presbyterianism and Puritanism. To Elizabeth, the threat from people who saw ecclesiastical authority arising from below was just as great as the threat from people who thought it resided in Rome. The early Elizabethan church contained many clergy who had more Genevan ideas of ecclesiology than their queen liked. To give the laity power in the church was to undermine the authority that God had given his handmaiden and her bishops. Consequently, Elizabeth was not tolerant of Protestants who did not promote her rule. They were a threat to the peace of the realm, not unlike the dissidents in Scotland who had brought Presbyterianism there and run their queen out of the country. Elizabeth's religion was primarily about her place in God's plan; it was only secondarily about theology. Conformity was her watchword.

In a speech to her bishops in 1585, Elizabeth used her chief weapon, rhetoric, to demanded compliance from men who had great independence. Upbraiding them for suffering ministers to preach whatever they wanted and to minister the sacraments "according to their own fancies ... to the breach of unity," she demanded that they be brought to "conformity and unity." "And we require you," she went on, "that you do not favor such men being carried away with pity, hoping of their conformity and inclining to noblemen's letters and gentlemen's letters; for they will be hanged before they will be reformed." She knew, she said, that some of her Protestant subjects "of late have said that I was of no religion, neither hot [nor] cold, but such a one as one day would give God the vomit."[27] These Protestants were to be treated as strictly as papists because they were enemies of the realm and the state of religion. Private conventicles, she pronounced, were destroying good order.

In place of erring sermons and servants with too much learning, Elizabeth recommended the reading of the *Book of Homilies*. Her bishops were clearly

---

[25] Collinson, *Archbishop Grindal*, 249–77.

[26] On the implications of this dispute for the queen's representation in literature in the latter half of the reign, see Donald Stump, "Abandoning the Old Testament," in this volume, 281–99.

[27] *Elizabeth I: Collected Works*, 179. The allusion is to Revelation 3:15–16.

perturbed by this, since one sign of a properly reformed church was learned preaching, but they protested a shortage of educated men, instead. When the archbishop of Canterbury pointed out that there were 13,000 parishes in England and little hope of finding learned preachers for them all, Elizabeth was shocked. "Jesus!" she exclaimed, "thirteen thousand! It is not to be looked for. I think the time hath been there hath not been four preachers in a diocese. My meaning is not you should make choice of learned ministers only, for they are not to be found, but of honest, sober, and wise men, and such as can read the Scriptures and Homilies well unto the people."[28] As usual, she attacked and then moderated her attack, one of her managerial tricks.

Unity of doctrine and orderly service were clearly her political goals, and she was willing to sacrifice the evangelical religious ideal to get them. If maintaining unity and concord required silencing preachers or reading homilies, she was willing to take those steps. To those of her subjects who advanced God's cause above that of God's handmaid, she offered only gall and wormwood. Her purpose is summed up in another of her prayers:

> Father most high . . . who hast appointed me as monarch of the British kingdom, favor me by Thy goodness to implant piety and root out impiety, to protect freely willed religion, to destroy superstitious fear by working freely to promote divine service, and to spy out the worship of false idols; and further, to gain release from the enemies of religion as well as those who hate me—Antichrists, Pope lovers, atheists, and all persons who fail to obey Thee and me.[29]

It is hard not to include presbyterians and puritans in the class of people who failed to obey their queen.

From the standpoint of an administrator trying to keep her state from exploding into civil war, Elizabeth deserves some sympathy. She could hardly expect papists to support her, and it must have been terribly frustrating that the very people whose religion she was trying to establish did not understand the political necessity behind her political middle way.

As one reads the evidence that remains, one can see a pattern, even a strategy, emerging from all this. Elizabeth made obedience her watchword, and she publicly made her anger clear when the fathers of her church failed to obey and deliver obedience. Once that anger had been aired, Burghley was expected, in most cases, to mollify the bishops, keeping them working towards the ends the queen wanted. She was pursuing a strategy that demanded obedience, and it was Burghley's job to mediate with the bishops to get it. The bishops, however, had other duties besides that maintenance of ecclesiastical discipline. They were ad-

---

[28] *Collected Works*, 178–81.
[29] *Collected Works*, 163.

ministrators with multiple tasks assigned by the Crown, and part of Burghley's job was to see that they performed their duties, even when quarreling with directions in royal policy. To do this, he used the power lent him by the queen in conjunction with his ties of friendship and patronage.

For instance, Archbishop Parker was officially ordered by the queen to provide hospitality to the French ambassador. The draft of the queen's letter to Parker is in Burghley's hand, and it is clear from subsequent correspondence that Parker was responsible to Burghley for carrying out the charge. In a long report written about the visit, Parker gave Burghley intelligence of their conversations, looking into the intention of the embassy and warning that they intended to present the queen with a letter urging her to convert to Catholicism.[30]

Parker was clearly acting as the official representative of the Crown in this instance. In other cases, the Crown expected the bishops to take an active interest in good government in their dioceses. The well-known episcopal reports on the reliability of Justices of the Peace is a good example. Burghley invited the bishops to suggest actions to be taken by the Council that would improve conformity. The advice included suggestions that the lawyers should be suppressed, and, importantly, the observation that local patronage networks made it very hard to make the tenants of powerful people obedient if their lords were not willing to obey.[31] This sort of cooperation with the Privy Council over the selection of secular officers continued across the reign, with bishops promoting, and sometimes hindering, the operation of local government by using their influence. In the late 1580s, Bishop Scambler of Norfolk sought the dismissal of ten Puritan Justices of the Peace and then stacked the Commission of the Peace with people sympathetic to his ideas about church property. These interventions did not always work well, and they could polarize local politics, but they suggest the power bishops could exert over local government.[32] Consequently, they had to be managed carefully.

But if bishops were able to exert influence, there was an expected *quid pro quo*. Orders flowing to the bishops from Burghley were passed on the road by letters to Burghley from the bishops asking his help in all sorts of matters over which he had influence. Appointments to various kinds of offices, complaints about the behaviors of towns and clergy, plaintive requests for relief and help were all sent to the man who could act in the queen's name and who had her ear.

How he used that ear is an interesting question. Parker clearly believed that Burghley could control the kinds of information reaching the queen, which probably means that some of the demands for ecclesiastical conformity occurred because of what he told her. As her leading source of knowledge, Burghley and

---

[30] Bruce and Perowne, *Correspondence of Matthew Parker*, 215–17.
[31] Mary Bateson, "A Collection of Original Letters from the Bishops to the Privy Council, 1564," *Camden Society Miscellany* 9 (1893): individually paginated, vi, 83 pp.
[32] Alison Wall, *Power and Protest in England 1525–1640* (London: Arnold, 2000), 58.

a few other courtiers had considerable ability to maneuver her policy within the structure of her strategy of conformity.

That this was assumed to be true by the larger world is obvious, then and now.[33] Once again, the issue of gender comes into the equation. The men she was close to were assumed to be guiding her; the man she might marry would replace them all. In 1561, when it was thought that Dudley was near to marrying her and that he would trade the nation's religion to the pope in exchange for her hand, Cecil launched a very effective plot to demonstrate that she had to fear the evil machinations of papists, messing up the Spanish diplomacy that was designed to support Dudley.

To return to Axelrod's assessment of Elizabeth as queen of the CEOs, we can ask whether his list of managerial traits does match Elizabeth the real queen. Did she have traits that demonstrate that she had a strategy and the leadership skills to carry it out?

In the case of the bishops, she certainly conformed to Axelrod's expectations in several important areas, while deviating in others. She had clarity of vision. She knew the authority God had given her over the church and would not give it away. This looks like inflexibility, though I suppose that her inflexible sense of her prerogative over the church was required by the inflexibility of some of her clergy.

The leadership skill that Elizabeth most clearly demonstrates is a strategic sense of where authority was and how it could be exerted, given the limitations of the system. As a woman, she needed powerful men whose own networks of influence could be bent to her strategy. She instilled both fear and loyalty in her servants by demonstrating that she knew what was going on and by insisting, sometimes with hard words, that they carry out her strategy. She knew her enemies because she understood the implications of belief systems that discounted her royal power, and she would not tolerate them. Lastly, she was smart enough to surround herself with men who could be trusted to use their intelligence and power in her service. Maintaining their devotion through ties of honor and patronage was a sure sign of her leadership skills.

Elizabeth I was not like a modern executive. She was playing a game in which her head, not just her job, was on the line. Whatever lessons we can take from her must be in the context of royal power in an age when the average monarch had considerably less information and communication than the modern executive. Therefore, she needed, and had, a different, but equally significant, leadership style.

---

[33] Brett Usher has recently argued that Cecil did his best for the episcopal bench, and "almost invariably" got his way with Elizabeth on matters concerning the bishops. What I believe he underestimates is how necessary it was to get his way most of the time to ensure that Elizabeth got her way on the main points. Brett Usher, *William Cecil and Episcopacy, 1559–1577* (Aldershot: Ashgate, 2003), xii.

Elizabeth and Her Favourites: The Case of Sir Walter Ralegh

Susan Doran

Some time after 1572 Lord Treasurer Burghley presented Elizabeth with a "memorial" against favourites.[1] Adopting a conventionally obsequious tone, he assured his royal recipient that she did not of course need to heed the warning and advice contained in the document, since she was "one of the Wisest and Best of Princes" on whom the flattery of favourites could have no effect and who always considered the public good. Yet, despite this paradoxical protestation, Burghley wrote his tract for the queen, presumably because he thought she could benefit from it.

A royal favourite, claimed Burghley, had power that was incompatible with both the public good and the prince's advantage. The king was "the Father of his Country, whose Eye should watch over the Good of all and every one of his Subjects." This responsibility, however, could be fulfilled only when the king listened to "a Multitude of Counsellors." If in their place he relied upon "one particular Favorite" and "his immediate Creatures," the king would receive limited, partial, and flawed counsel about his subjects' needs that would be dangerous to follow. Burghley gave a number of reasons why this was so. First, a favourite's rise was through his good fortune in securing royal favour and not his own merits. Second, a favourite's sources of information could not be trusted: his informants "represent things to him, as he wou'd have them" and not as they were, for they sought the favourite's patronage "for which they daily pay the Adoration of so much Flattery." Third, a favourite's advice could only be self-interested. Even if he "shou'd attain a true knowledge of the state of things, . . . it is Forty to One, that these clashing with his private Aims, he gives them another Face to the Prince, a turn more agreeable to his separate Interest, tho' equally destructive of his Master's and Country's Good."

---

[1] William Cecil, Lord Burghley, *A Memorial Presented to Queen Elizabeth against Her Majesty's being Engros'd by an Particular Favourites*, 2nd ed. (London, 1708), 211–30. Published together with Sir William Cavendish's *Memoirs of Cardinal Wolsey*.

To demonstrate his argument, Burghley decided not to plunder examples from classical history. The cases of the infamous Sejanus and "any other of the Roman Minions" he considered to be too well known for further review. Instead he chose to expatiate on a favourite closer to home: Thomas Wolsey.[2] The cardinal's example, he wrote, "may warn your Majesty against all those, who wou'd engross not only your Majesty's Ear but all the Gifts and Places your Majesty can bestow." Listing Wolsey's faults, Burghley described Henry VIII's minister as a "Subject of the lowest and most plebeian Rise" who through his ambition and pride maintained a huge retinue, was profligate with royal revenues, and taxed illegally. Like all favourites, Wolsey offered his prince flattery not truth, and in the process did him immeasurable harm.

Burghley's disapproving attitude towards favourites was hardly unusual during the second half of Elizabeth's reign, while the negative characteristics he attached to Wolsey in particular and to favourites in general—lowly origins, pride, ambition, untruthfulness, and sycophancy—were widely treated as a favourite's stock in trade. As early as 1579 (in what some historians think was the first use of the noun 'favourite'),[3] John Stubbs's *The Gaping Gulph* contained the criticism that princes too often listened to chief favourites who "study rather for smooth, delicate words than for plain rough truth."[4] The painful punishment inflicted on Stubbs (his hand was chopped off!) may have inhibited other commentators from penning forthright criticisms of policies and favourites within a contemporary context, and it was left to English Catholic polemicists abroad to denounce in print the men who they believed enjoyed and abused Elizabeth's ear. Although referred to as "evil councillors," these upstarts who put their private interests before the public good were indistinguishable in their attributes from Burghley's "favourites."[5] Ironically, the men selected for their scorn included Burghley himself, although the earl of Leicester was attacked too.

During the 1590s, hostility towards favourites also came to be expressed in the coded discourse of historians, poets, and playwrights who were Protestant. Here too the favourite became merged with the evil councillor, and in at least one of these works Burghley was again the butt of criticism. Edmund Spenser cast the Lord Treasurer as the fox who controlled all patronage and oppressed the creatures of the forest in his beast-fable *The Mother Hubberds Tale*, published in

---

[2] Wolsey also appeared in the 1587 edition of *A Mirror for Magistrate*s in the guise of court favourite.

[3] Blair Worden, "Favourites on the English Stage," in *The World of the Favourite, c.1550–c.1675*, ed. John Elliott and Laurence Brockliss (New Haven: Yale University Press, 1999), 160–83, here 168.

[4] Lloyd E. Berry, ed., *John Stubbs's Gaping Gulph with Letters and Other Relevant Documents* (Charlottesville, VA: University Press of Virginia, 1968), 30.

[5] See, for example, Richard Verstegan, *A Declaration of the True Causes* (London, 1592; repr. in facsimile, Ilkley, Yorks.: Scolar Press, 1977).

1591. The poem was judged to be so politically sensitive that it was called in and not printed again until after the death of Robert Cecil.[6]

It has been suggested that Burghley was equally targeted for criticism in Sir Henry Savile's 1591 translation of Tacitus. In this work, a critique of evil councillors and, by implication, favourites can be found buried in both the epistolary dedication to the reader and a learned footnote on the life of Agricola. The dedication pronounced that readers could learn from the history of Galba that "a good Prince governed by evill ministers is as dangerous as if he were evil himself."[7] The annotation referred to the "suttle, ready, and pernicious means" that the enemies of "a greate man" used to put him "in disgrace with his Prince."[8] Blair Worden is convinced that Savile intended his readers to connect Essex with the "great man" in danger from his enemies and associate Burghley with the evil ministers who speak out against him, but, as will be discussed later, I suspect Savile had someone else in mind.[9]

Burghley was plainly not the target of a number of other literary treatments of favourites written in the early 1590s. If their authors did have contemporary figures in mind, they were evidently thinking of young courtiers rather than an elderly statesman with monopolistic tendencies. In the anonymous play *Woodstock*, Richard II is not dominated by one evil councillor but comes under the malign influence of a number of young, base-born men, referred to as "mignons" and "rash unskilful boys," who spend their money on "strange fashions . . . French hose, Italian cloaks, and Spanish hats."[10] Significantly, Richard's real-life older minister-favourites, Michael de la Pole and Simon Burley, were omitted from the play. In both Christopher Marlowe's play *Edward II* and Michael Drayton's epic poem *Peirs Gaveston* (1593), the homoerotic relationship portrayed could hardly have been further removed from the partnership of Elizabeth and Burghley. Edward, wrote Drayton, was originally attracted to Gaveston's beauty, a beauty that

---

[6] Written a decade or so earlier, during the debates on the Anjou marriage, several manuscript copies of the poem are extant. See Edwin Greenlaw et al., eds., *The Works of Edmund Spenser: A Variorum Edition. The Minor Poems*, 2 vols. (Baltimore: Johns Hopkins University Press, 1947), 2:107–40.

[7] Ben Jonson thought the author of the letter (AB) was Essex, and this has been accepted by Blair Worden. However, given that the presentation copy in the Bodleian had 'ex dono Annae Barnes' embossed on the frontispiece, Jonson was probably wrong and AB was Anne Barnes. See Blair Worden, "Historians and Poets," *Huntingdon Library Quarterly* 68 (2005): 71–93, here 84.

[8] Cornelius Tacitus, *The End of Nero and the Beginning of Galba, Fower Books of the Histories [and] The Life of Agricola*, trans. Sir Henry Savile (London, 1591), 263, n. 16.

[9] Worden, "Historians and Poets," 84.

[10] William A. Armstrong, ed., *Elizabethan History Plays* (Oxford: Oxford University Press, 1965), 2.2.934; 2.3.1085–89 (196, 201). The date of *Woodstock* is uncertain, although usually taken to be written about 1591.

became "the Load-starre of his thought" and the object of his lust.[11] Definitely not an allusion to Burghley!

But perhaps no contemporary parallel was intended in these particular historical dramatizations. The favourites in these works displayed such similar characteristics that they may have simply represented the archetypal figure of the favourite: all were low-born, all flatterers, all arrogant; all were accused of lining their pockets with the help of their besotted king; all put their private interests before the public good. Furthermore, as Edward II and Richard II had recently been popularized in both Raphael Holinshed's and John Stow's chronicles, it is possible that late Elizabethan poets and playwrights were seeking to do no more than dramatize the reigns of monarchs whose stories had enlivened the chroniclers' pages.

It is possible, but unlikely. Why else did these writers interject new material that would draw attention to the ruling queen and her court? In Act 4 of *Woodstock*, for example, the moon-goddess Cynthia (by the 1590s a pseudonym for Elizabeth) makes an appearance in the play for no ostensibly good reason; her knights, moreover, turn out to be King Richard and his mignons in disguise ready to pounce on and arrest the hero, Thomas of Woodstock.[12] Marlowe's *Edward II* also alludes to the court of Elizabeth when in Act I Gaveston describes lavish "Italian masques" and "pleasing shows" that recall the entertainments devised at Kenilworth in 1575 and at Cowdray and Elvetham in 1591 (including one idealized pastime that re-enacted the story of Diana and Actaeon).[13] Then later in the act, the king and favourite are shown exchanging miniature portraits, an Elizabethan rather than a medieval practice.[14] A more explicit reference to Elizabeth occurs in the prologue of Drayton's *Peirs Gaveston;* there, the ghost of Gaveston (who acts as narrator) directly compares the present queen with her medieval forebear:

> Such a one he was as Englands Beta is,
> Such as she is, even such a one was he,
> Betwixt her rarest excellence and his
> Was never yet so neare a *Sympathie*.
> To tell your worth, an to give him his due
> I say my soueraigne, he was like to you.[15]

---

[11] Michael Drayton, *Peirs Gaueston Earle of Cornwall His Life, Death, and Fortune* (London, [1594?]), sig. C2r.

[12] *Woodstock*, 4.2.2070–88 (233).

[13] Christopher Marlowe, *The Troublesome Raigne and Lamentable Death of Edward the Second, King of England* (London, 1594), 1.1.50–70.

[14] Marlowe, *Edward the Second*, 1.4.127.

[15] Drayton, *Peirs Gaveston*, sig. B2r.

If these writers did intend their audiences to pick up and play with these coded references to the Elizabethan court, who might then be the contemporary favourite they alluded to? Well, the courtier of the early 1590s who most corresponded to the ambitious upstart whose sexual attractiveness and powers of flattery captivated a monarch was Sir Walter Ralegh. As we shall see later, he was described in very much those terms throughout the 1580s and early 1590s. Admittedly, no explicit references identifying him can be found in any of these literary works, but some suggestive moments and descriptions are present in all of them. Take Drayton's *Peirs Gaveston*. There the narrator comments about the court of Edward I (suggesting a contrast with that of both Elizabeth and Edward II): "Then Machiavels were Loth'd as filthier toades," and "The vilest Atheist as the plague despise." While "Machiavels" could apply to many people at Elizabeth's court and besides was a common epithet for favourites, "Atheist" had by 1593 become peculiarly associated with Ralegh. In 1592, using the pseudonym of Philopater, the Jesuit Robert Persons accused Ralegh of keeping "a School of Atheism," and thereafter Ralegh's unorthodox religious views became so great a subject of gossip that an investigation was instigated in 1594.[16] Then, in the play *Woodstock*, the plain-speaking nobleman, Thomas Woodstock, duke of Gloucester, had much in common with Robert Devereux, second earl of Essex, who was in fact a descendant of the fourteenth-century duke. Consequently Woodstock's enemies, who had won the king's favour and were all upstart knights, could be taken as representations of Essex's known rivals, notably Ralegh.

In Marlowe's *Edward II* the historical coincidence of Gaveston's title of earl of Cornwall—repeatedly mentioned in the play—also serves to evoke the figure of Ralegh, who had been lord lieutenant of that county since 1585. Similarly, Gaveston's actual exile to Ireland where, says Mortimer junior, he will purchase "such friends / as he will front the mightiest of us all" coincidentally mirrors the episode in 1589, when Ralegh was thought to have left court for Ireland in order to escape the hostility of his enemies.[17] Marlowe may have just been following his sources here, but the emphasis on these points in the play is suggestive. Another suggestive moment comes when Mortimer Junior describes Gaveston in Act 1:

---

[16] Drayton, *Peirs Gaveston*, sig B2r. The enquiry into atheistical practices in Dorset in 1594 is thought to have been designed to catch Ralegh. See Walter Oakeshott, *The Queen and the Poet* (London: Faber & Faber, 1960), 51. In his epigram "Against an Atheist" Sir John Harington makes references to the blasphemies of Paulus, his pseudonym for Ralegh. See Harington, *Epigrams*, no. 14 (London, 1618; repr. in facs., Menston: Scolar Press, 1970), sig. E1r.

[17] Letter from Sir Frances Allen to Anthony Bacon, August 1589: "My Lord of Essex hath chased Mr R. from the court, and hath confined him to Ireland." *Memoirs of the Reign of Queen Elizabeth, from the Year 1581 Till Her Death. . .*, ed. Thomas Birch, 2 vols. (London, 1754), 1:57.

> He wears a lord's revenue on his back
> And Midas-like he jets it in the court...
> He wears a short Italian cloak
> Larded with pearl, and in his Tuscan cap
> A jewel of more value than the crown.[18]

I may be reading too much into these lines, but to me they conjure up Ralegh in his short cloak, encrusted in pearls, as depicted in the famous portrait of the late 1580s.

Whether audiences saw any allusions to Ralegh in these literary court favourites is unrecorded; whether authors intended him to be can only be a subject of speculation. It is indisputable, however, that that during the 1580s and '90s Ralegh was described by observers and rivals in terms of the characteristics of the stereotypical court favourite. Although in the main either questionable or inaccurate, these descriptions have been repeated until today and in my view have misrepresented both Ralegh and the queen; for if the Elizabethan Ralegh was the base court-favourite, the queen had to be initially the besotted and foolish monarch responsible for his meteoric rise in the 1580s and then the capricious and cruel mistress whose sexual jealousy ruined his career after his marriage to Bess Throckmorton was revealed in the summer of 1592. Indeed Elizabeth is presented in that way in several historical works as well as the films *The Virgin Queen* (1955), starring Bette Davis, and *Elizabeth: The Golden Age* (2007), starring Cate Blanchett.

Just as in the history plays members of the medieval nobility attacked the figures of Gaveston, Tresilian, Sir Henry Greene, and Sir Edward Bagot for their "base and obscure" birth, so many Elizabethans sneered at Ralegh's lowly origins. The earl of Oxford, for example, was said to have jested that Ralegh was a jack and an upstart, while Essex famously referred to him as a "knave" and a man who deserved his disdain.[19] Indeed Robert Naunton, writing a decade or so after Ralegh's execution, felt compelled to protest against this description on the grounds that "the Queene in her choyce never toke in her favor a meere new'd man, or a Mechanicke."[20] Naunton was right: Ralegh's low birth had certainly been exaggerated; he came from a long established, if minor, gentry family in Devon, and was not without influential family connections: his aunt had been Elizabeth's trusted gentlewoman Kat Ashley till her death in 1565; Arthur Gorges, his cousin, was related to Charles Arundel who probably effected an introduction to the earl of Oxford, while his half-brother Sir Humphrey Gilbert had by the mid-

---

[18] Marlowe, *Edward the Second*, 2.5.11–12, 1.4.404–7, 412–14. Note too that in Woodstock the courtiers are said to "pill the poor, to jet in gold" 2.2.821 (p. 193).

[19] Robert Naunton, *Fragmenta Regalia* (London, 1641), 33; Oxford, Bodleian Library, Tanner MS. 76, fol. 84v and 77, fol. 178.

[20] Naunton, *Fragmenta Regalia*, 33.

1570s made important connections at court, including the earl of Leicester and Sir Francis Walsingham. Another kinsman was Sir John Zouche, a colonel of the army in Munster, who wrote in his favour to Lord Burghley.[21] Although no Dudley or Devereux, Ralegh's family was no more "obscure" than that of, say, Sir Christopher Hatton, Sir Thomas Heneage, or even Sir William Cecil.

Critics also cast Ralegh in the form of the stereotypical favourite when they portrayed him as an individual whose rise was largely undeserved, owing little to merit and everything to his good fortune in attracting royal favour. Essex's poetic jibe, calling Ralegh "Fortunes childe," was shorthand for this point; the anonymous author of the poem "Staye Conick soule thy errante" disparaged Ralegh further when he complained that "Fortune was blyende to rayse" him.[22] Once again Naunton tried to correct the commonly expressed view of Ralegh's unworthiness: according to the *Fragmenta Regalia*, Elizabeth had noticed Ralegh after he had presented her and the council with a carefully argued set of proposals for policy in Ireland. Ralegh, Naunton concluded, did not owe his success to chance but to his own hard work, "a strong naturall wit, and a better Judgment."[23] Although Naunton's appraisals were influential, Thomas Fuller writing in the 1640s put far greater emphasis on Ralegh's wit than on his judgment. Omitting any mention of the young soldier's sound advice on Ireland, Fuller instead relayed two new stories, based on gossip, that highlighted Ralegh's superficial qualities as a courtier and extravagant gestures of self-promotion: he had caught Elizabeth's eye, explained Fuller, by spreading "his new plush cloak" on a "plashy ground" and had charmed her with a witty couplet scratched onto a window.[24]

In truth, the sources written at the time are tantalizingly quiet about Ralegh's early appearance at court and how he came to the notice of the queen, but we can be fairly confident that Elizabeth was not smitten with him at first sight. It is true that as early as February 1580 he was described as "one of the extraordinary Esquires of the Body of the Queen Majesty,"[25] but this position did not save him from spending short spells in prison after involvement in two separate

---

[21] D. C. Peck, "Raleigh, Sidney, Oxford, and the Catholics, 1579," *Notes and Queries* 223 (1978): 427–31; *Calendar of State Papers, Ireland 1574–1585*, ed. Hans C. Hamilton (London: HMSO, 1867), 331.

[22] 'Another answeare thought to bee made' by R. Essex, Oxford, Bodleian Library, Rawlinson MS. Poet. 212, fol. 91r. Bodleian Library, Tanner MS. 306, fol. 188r-v.

[23] Even the *Oxford Dictionary of National Biography* (45:842–59) does not refer to the specific incident reported by Naunton, *Fragmenta Regalia*, 34. The two contributors also emphasize Ralegh's sexual attractiveness.

[24] Thomas Fuller, *The Worthies of England* (London, 1663), 262.

[25] David Beers Quinn, *Set Fair for Roanoke: Voyages and Colonies 1584–1606* (Chapel Hill: America's Four Hundredth Anniversary Committee, University of North Carolina Press, 1985), 6. Ralegh was described as such in a legal case brought to Chancery.

affrays. Nor did Elizabeth then seek to keep him by her side, as she normally did her intimates, for in July 1580 he was sent off to Ireland as captain of a hundred men to help the lord deputy, Lord Grey, quell the Desmond rebellion in Munster.[26] After returning to London at the end of the year with a dispatch from Grey which he discussed with the queen and her councillors, Ralegh was still not detained at court but went back to serve again in the province. By this time, Ralegh feared he was condemned to remain forever in a backwater, and therefore sought out Walsingham and Leicester as patrons. Six months later he was growing desperate, and in August 1581 expressed his anxiety that Leicester had "utterly forgotten me" and assured the earl that "I am and wilbe found as ready, and dare do as miche in your service as any man you may cummande."[27] Rescued by Leicester, Ralegh in early 1582 escorted François, duc d'Anjou, to Brabant as a minor figure in the earl's retinue,[28] and only after his return did the queen begin to notice and favour him. In October 1582 Sir Christopher Hatton told Elizabeth of his concern that Ralegh had displaced him in her affections.[29] In early 1583 came the first reports that Ralegh "hath her majestes favore above all men in the court."[30] Also in that year, he received his first major royal grants: some leases reverting to the crown, possession of Durham House in London, and the right to issue licences to keep taverns and sell wines. These were followed the next year with further grants of land, a lucrative licence to export woollen cloth, and the offices (shared with his brother Carew) of lieutenant of the Isle of Portland in Dorset and captain of the castle there.[31]

From the mid-1580s onwards observers and informants were describing Ralegh as a Gaveston-like figure: one called him Elizabeth's minion;[32] another

---

[26] *Acts of the Privy Council of England*, 1578-80, ed. John Roche Dasent (London: HMSO, 1895), 388–89, 421; 1580–81 (London: HMSO, 1896), 96.

[27] Agnes Latham and Joyce Youings, eds., *The Letters of Sir Walter Ralegh* (Exeter: University of Exeter Press, 1999), 5–7, 10.

[28] Ralegh's presence was not noted in court gossip nor in William Camden's later account.

[29] Sir Harry Nicolas, *Memoirs of the Life and Times of Sir Christopher Hatton* (London: R. Bentley, 1847), 277–78.

[30] Letter from Maurice Browne to John Thynne, transcribed in David B. Quinn and Neil M. Cheshire, eds., *The New Found Land of Stephen Parmenius* (Toronto: University of Toronto Press, 1972), 203–4.

[31] *Calendar Patent Rolls 1582–1583*, List and Index Society 286 (Kew, Surrey: List and Index Society, 2001), no. 863; *1583–1584*, List and Index Society 287 (Kew, Surrey: List and Index Society, 2001), nos. 102, 145, 974.

[32] Thomas Morgan to Mary Queen of Scots, 10 April 1585 and 31 March 1586, *Calendar of Cecil Manuscripts at Hatfield*, 24 vols. (London: Historical Manuscripts Commission, 1889), 3:97.

reported that "They say she now loves him beyond all others."[33] Hints were dropped that he was getting above his station: "He is very soumptous in his Aparell . . . all the vessell with which he is served at his stable [table], is silver with his owne armes on the same." In 1583 he was said to have a retinue of at least thirty men; a year later the number reported had risen to 500.[34] One report in 1586 described him as intolerably proud and arrogant, a man who grew rich on the revenues of the country at the expense of the poor.[35]

It was taken for granted that Ralegh, like the stereotypical court favourite, exercised too great a sway over the queen and used his influence to promote his own sectional interests rather than the common good. In 1583, for example, Maurice Browne warned John Thynne that Ralegh would "ever be practisinge against yow" in a dispute between Thynne and Ralegh's brother Carew over a piece of family property; and that Thynne would lose out "considering the great and especiall favour that Water Rawley is in with her majestie." Significantly Browne did not suggest that Thynne should seek out another patron to counterbalance Ralegh's influence with the queen—presumably because he thought no-one else's voice would carry any weight with her. Instead, he advised Thynne to ask Leicester "to perswade master Rawley to desist from the same," for the earl was "the only man that can command or perswade with master Walter Rawley" to stop him "doinge you that hurt."[36] Browne was not alone in his perceptions of Ralegh's malign influence with the queen. In 1584 Burghley warned Sir John Perrot that he alienated Ralegh at his peril: Ralegh, he explained, "is able to do you more harm in one hour than we are all able to do you good in a year."[37]

Ralegh was also quite regularly accused of carrying out one of the tricks against "great men" that Savile described in his annotations on Tacitus—taking advantage of their absence from court to speak ill of them to the monarch.[38] In 1586 "very pestilent" reports reached Leicester, who was commanding the English army in the Netherlands, that Ralegh had stabbed him in the back by criticizing his service. Although Elizabeth denied that Ralegh had behaved in

---

[33] Victor von Klarwill, ed., *Queen Elizabeth and Some Foreigners* (London: John Lane, 1928), 338. See also "Journey through England and Scotland made by Lupold Von Wedelin in the years 1584 and 1585," trans. Gottfried Von Bülow, *Transactions of the Royal Historical Society*, n.s. 9 (1895): 223–70, here 265.

[34] Quinn and Cheshire, *Parmenius*, 205; Von Klarwill, *Queen Elizabeth*, 339.

[35] *Calendar of State Papers Foreign, Elizabeth 1586–1588*, ed. Sophie Crawford Lomas (London: HMSO, 1927), 655.

[36] Quinn and Cheshire, *Parmenius*, 207. Carew Ralegh had married Thynne's stepmother and they were in dispute over the dower property at Corsley.

[37] Michael MacCarthy-Morroch, *The Munster Plantation: English Migration to Southern Ireland 1583–1641* (Oxford: Clarendon Press, 1986), 52.

[38] Latham and Youings, *Letters*, 32–33.

this underhand way, suspicions continued to be aired "of ill done to the Earl."[39] Unsurprisingly, then, Leicester's stepson, the earl of Essex, could all too easily believe in 1587 that Ralegh had used his power over the queen to do him and his sister harm: "for whose [i.e. Ralegh's] sake, I fare she [the queen] would both grieve me, and my Love and disgrace me in the eye of the World."[40] Four years later Ralegh was again reported as carrying out a trick against Essex; in October 1591, while Essex was serving in Rouen, Robert Cecil told a correspondent that Ralegh had deliberately let Elizabeth know that Essex had created a large number of knights. This was information which Essex's friends were trying to keep quiet and that Ralegh presumably knew would anger the queen.[41]

Ralegh was certainly not beyond trying to score points against his rivals; nor was he the only courtier to behave in this fashion. Furthermore, not only were these tales of his unbecoming conduct not necessarily true, but also they imply that he had a pre-eminence at court and influence over the queen that I now want to demonstrate were clearly exaggerated. In the first place, the rewards Elizabeth gave to Ralegh, though unpopular, were not out of line with those she granted to other courtiers. What is more, the offices Ralegh held were on the whole appropriate for someone who had experience as a soldier, ship owner, and sea captain, while the financial rewards he received were both recompense and necessities for royal service. The land and licences granted in 1583 enabled Ralegh to keep an establishment in London and maintain a position as a courtier with close access to the queen; those of 1584 allowed him to equip an expedition to discover the "heathen and barbarous lands" specified in the queen's letter patent of that year. The English manors granted in Dorset, Cornwall, and Devon provided him with the authority and status to act as lord lieutenant of Cornwall, MP for Devon, lord high Steward of Cornwall, and lord warden of the stannaries, and to carry out the duties associated with the other, more minor, offices he held in the West Country. These offices, moreover, were not simply sinecures. Although he had a deputy to carry out the routine tasks, Ralegh was ultimately responsible for the duties associated with his offices and received orders from the privy council to deal with specific matters, whether enlisting tin-miners for the army, sending out ships from the west to intercept Spanish shipping, or supervising the spoil from privateering voyages. As lord lieutenant of Cornwall and vice-admiral of

---

[39] Robert Dudley, earl of Leicester, *Correspondence of Robert Dudley, Earl of Leycester, during His Government in the Low Countries, in the Years 1585 and 1586*, ed. John Bruce, Camden Society 27 (London: Camden Society, 1844), 207; *Calendar of the Manuscripts of His Grace the Duke of Rutland*. 4 vols. (London: Historical Manuscripts Commission, 1888), 1:234.

[40] He blamed Ralegh for speaking to the queen against his sister with the result that she had been barred from joining the court at Lady Warwick's house. See Oxford, Bodleian Library, Tanner MS. 76, fols. 84v-85r.

[41] University College London, Ogden MS. 7/41, fol. 24r.

the west Ralegh had much work to do during the Spanish war, particularly in the Armada year: in December 1587 he went down to the west to assess the defences of Devon and Cornwall; in August 1588 he was sent to the south coast "to conferre" with Lord Admiral Howard; and the following month he was ordered to supervise the selection of a hundred Cornishmen to be soldiers and to transport them and provisions in three ships to Ireland where the Spaniards had reportedly landed.[42] Ralegh, then, was no mere "toy-boy"; in addition to entertaining the queen at court, he was expected to serve the realm in ways fitting for a man with a track record of success in military and naval affairs.

Second, Ralegh never possessed a monopoly over the queen's affections, favour, or counsel. Certainly during the mid-1580s he was the first of the younger men to join the inner circle at court, but Elizabeth took pains to reassure her older courtiers and ministers that Ralegh's rise in no way compromised the warmth of her feelings towards them. So in October 1582 in response to signs of anxiety from Hatton, Elizabeth undertook never to give him good cause to doubt her favour, and two years later she made good her word: when told that Ralegh had taken over Hatton's lodgings in Croydon, where the court was residing, she "used bitterness of speech against Raleigh" telling Hatton's friend Heneage "that she had rather see him [Ralegh] hanged than equal him with you, or that the world should think she did so."[43] Elizabeth demonstrated her continuing loyalty towards Hatton by elevating him to be lord chancellor in April 1587, at a time when Ralegh had not yet secured a major household office, and the following year it was an older favourite, Sir Thomas Heneage, not Ralegh, who was appointed vice-chamberlain of the household. By then, Ralegh had to share Elizabeth's favour not only with Hatton and Heneage but also with younger, up-and-coming courtiers like the earl of Essex and Sir Charles Blount. Only after Hatton's death in November 1591 did Ralegh obtain a household office that gave him regular access to the queen (the captaincy of the guard), but the importance of the post should not be exaggerated. Some biographers and historians have claimed that Elizabeth made the appointment, so that "he would be near her at all times";[44] yet barely three months afterwards (in March 1592) the queen granted Ralegh permission to sail with the fleet to the coast of Spain, where he would spy out the naval preparations of the enemy and prey on their shipping on his return.[45]

Throughout the 1580s Elizabeth maintained her earlier strategy of keeping open different lines of access to royal patronage, and preventing any one of her courtiers or ministers from securing overweening influence. Wanting harmony

---

[42] *Acts of the Privy Council 1588* (London: HMSO, 1897), 212, 277.

[43] Nicolas, *Hatton*, 277, 415.

[44] Stephen J. Greenblatt, *Sir Walter Ralegh: The Renaissance Man and His Roles* (New Haven: Yale University Press, 1973), 56.

[45] Oxford, Bodleian Library, Ashmole MS. 830, fol. 85r-v. The discovery of the secret marriage prevented him from going.

at court, she did not play off one courtier against another in order to intensify their competitiveness for her favour and enhance her own power.[46] On the contrary, she tried to quash rivalries through maintaining a balance in her patronage and nipping in the bud outward signs of discord amongst her courtiers. In the summer of 1587 she tried her utmost to drive Essex to make friends with Ralegh. After Blount and Essex fought a duel, she reprimanded them both and insisted upon their reconciliation.[47] When Essex challenged Ralegh to mortal combat in 1588, councillors not only calmed down the two men but also worked together to keep knowledge of the quarrel from the queen, who would, they knew, be furious that the two courtiers could not contain their rivalry.[48]

Ralegh, then, had to share royal favour. Furthermore, despite the reputation of his "bould and plausible tongue" and claims that the queen "tooke him for a kind of Oracle,"[49] he seems to have exercised relatively little political power or influence over her. Not only was he never made a councillor, but it was by no means easy for him to persuade Elizabeth to adopt his policy suggestions. So, although she provided him with the authority to seek the new lands in America, he was unable to persuade her to underwrite the 1585 voyage and turn it from a private to a state-sponsored venture, as he wished. When his recommendations for policy were adopted, they had the support of at least one leading councillor—Burghley in the case of the paper Ralegh produced on military tactics in Ireland after the Desmond rebellion and Walsingham in the case of the Virginia voyages.[50]

Unlike Leicester or Essex, Ralegh built up no political following and attracted few clients. It is true that he helped a few family members, men from the southwest, and soldiers he had served with in Ireland climb onto the lower rungs of royal service, though even here Ralegh was not usually their only patron.[51] Occasionally, he also proved able to secure small favours for friends, such as securing for them grants of land in Ireland.[52] However, the extant sources suggest that outside his own household or the world of seamanship and exploration

---

[46] For an alternative view, see Edward Edwards, *The Life of Sir Walter Raleigh*, 2 vols. (London: Macmillan, 1868), 1:62; Christopher Haigh, *Elizabeth I* (London: Longman, 1988), 99–100.

[47] Paul Hammer, *The Polarization of Elizabethan Politics* (Cambridge: Cambridge University Press, 1999), 84–85.

[48] The National Archives, SP12/219, fol. 115r.

[49] Naunton, *Fragmenta Regalia*, 34, 35.

[50] The National Archives, SP 63/96/30 &31 and SP 63/88/40.3.

[51] For instance, George Carew believed he owed his promotion to the council in Ireland as much to Burghley as Ralegh. *Calendar of the Carew Papers Preserved in the Archiepiscopal Library at Lambeth 1589–1600*, ed. J. S. Brewer (London: Longmans, Green, 1869), 40.

[52] *Calendar of the Patent and Close Rolls of Chancery in Ireland 1576–1602*, ed. J. C. Morrin (Dublin: HMSO, 1862), 202.

he was not a very active patron. Book dedications to him were rare even during the years when he thrived at court. As was to be expected, Thomas Hariot and Richard Hakluyt dedicated editions of their works on exploration to Ralegh,[53] and Edmund Spenser addressed the dedicatory letter of *The Faerie Queene* to his friend in 1590.[54] However dedications that suggested Ralegh was considered to be a valuable patron were remarkably few: Thomas Churchyard in 1588 dedicated his poem *A Sparke of Friendship* to Ralegh in thanks for his "good speeches" to the queen on the poet's behalf "by the which I got some comfortable recreation to quicken my spirites and keepe me in breath." In 1586, John Case dedicated *The Praise of Musicke* to Ralegh, hoping it would be read by him when "your worship shall have any respite from your weightier affaires" and claiming it would be better received if published under Ralegh's protection. Generally, however, in the decade after 1582 writers looked to other patrons to promote or protect their compositions.

When it came to seeking political favours from the queen, the evidence, though scant, suggests that suitors seldom looked to Ralegh for assistance, or at least not exclusively. Burghley did ask Ralegh to speak up for his son-in-law the earl of Oxford, who was in trouble with the queen in May 1583, but the lord treasurer also turned to Hatton.[55] Similarly when a certain R. Fynes was suing for a parsonage in 1587, he asked Ralegh together with Leicester and Hatton to promote his cause. Fynes, moreover, protested to Leicester and afterwards to Burghley that he had not actually petitioned Ralegh for help but simply accepted it when offered: "in respect he [i.e. Ralegh] was allied unto my wife, and he had made offer of his best help, I might not but entertain his friendship with thanksgiving."[56] For all his warnings about Ralegh's standing with the queen, Maurice Browne did not really believe that Ralegh was the only man who counted at court. Otherwise why did Browne advise Thynne that Leicester, Walsingham, and Hatton should all be cultivated and "used as occasion shall serve as especial good friends" to advance his interests?[57]

---

[53] Thomas Hariot, *A Briefe and True Report of the New Found Land of Virginia* (Frankfurt am Main, 1590). Richard Hakluyt also dedicated to Ralegh his English translation of René Goulaine de.Laudonniere's *A notable historie containing foure voyages made by certayne French captaynes vnto Florida . . .* (London, 1587).

[54] For Spenser and Ralegh, see Jeffrey B. Morris, "To (Re)fashion a Gentleman: Ralegh's Disgrace in Spenser's *Legend of Courtesy*," *Studies in Philology* 94 (1997): 38–58; David Norbrook, *Poetry and Politics in the English Renaissance* (Oxford: Oxford University Press, 2002), 130.

[55] Latham and Youings, *Letters*, 14.

[56] *Calendar of Cecil Manuscripts at Hatfield*, 3:251. As Leicester had by this time quarreled with Ralegh, Fynes may have made this excuse to protect himself.

[57] Alison Wall, "Maurice Browne and his Patrons in the 1580s," *Parergon* 21 (2004): 47–65, here 59.

Nor was Ralegh thought untouchable because of the queen's favour towards him. In 1584 the vice chancellor and members of the senate of Cambridge University challenged his sole right to license vintners in the city and imprisoned one of his agents and licensees, John Keymer, who had resisted the university's attempts to close down his establishment. Despite Ralegh's protests and pressure, the university, possibly with the support of Leicester and Burghley (high steward and chancellor respectively), won its case; Keymer remained in jail for nearly two years and when released was prohibited from selling wine in Cambridge.[58] The lord deputy of Ireland, Sir William Fitzwilliam, was equally unafraid of offending Ralegh, and in 1589 challenged Ralegh's right to certain lands in Munster, leading Ralegh to complain "in Irlande they thincke that I am not worth the respectinge."[59]

For all these reasons, the hold of Ralegh on Elizabeth's affections seems to me to be neither as strong nor as total as is usually suggested. So why then did Elizabeth react so passionately to Ralegh's marriage when it was revealed in late May 1592? A month under house arrest and four more in the Tower was excessive punishment for a secret marriage even by Elizabeth's standards. Did this, therefore, indicate sexual jealousy on Elizabeth's part? Like Anna Beer, I think not.[60] Then again, I'm not convinced by Beer's argument that Elizabeth was suspicious that the choice of name for Ralegh's newborn son, Damerie, indicated a sinister plot against her. Elizabeth's anger, if extreme, was understandable without explanations of this kind. Quite simply, she felt she had been duped by Ralegh, who had not only failed to ask permission to marry one of her gentlewomen of the privy chamber and kept the birth of their child secret, but had also deliberately told Robert Cecil a barefaced lie, when he protested "before God, ther is none, on the face of the yearth that I would be fastned unto."[61] This betrayal of her trust was particularly galling and hurtful because Elizabeth had consistently defended Ralegh against those who had accused him of deceitfulness. Perhaps Elizabeth hoped to secure an abject apology by putting him under house arrest, but his contrition was unforthcoming, and in these circumstances she decided he and his wife deserved a stretch in the Tower.

Ralegh's disgrace was greeted with ribald glee in some quarters. However, pleasure at his downfall was not universal; Robert Cecil, John Hawkins, and Lord Admiral Howard, in particular, tried to temper the queen's anger, not least because they appreciated that Ralegh's service was valuable. Others found it difficult to believe that the reverse in Ralegh's fortunes would be permanent, and over the next few years court gossip was quick to pick up on every sign (usually

---

[58] Latham and Youings, *Letters*, 20–21, 27.

[59] Latham and Youings, *Letters*, 50–51, 68–69, 71, 379.

[60] Anna Beer, *Bess: The Life of Lady Ralegh, Wife to Sir Walter* (London: Constable and Robinson, 2004), 71.

[61] Latham and Youings, *Letters*, 63.

mistaken) that Ralegh might soon be restored to royal favour.[62] As Fortune's child, dependent on the mutability of royal favour, Ralegh could well rise again after being cast down so dramatically, and the words of Gaveston in Drayton's poem could well have come from the mouth of Ralegh:

> Blind fortune, chance, worlds mutability
> Advancing peasants and debasing Kings
> Raise me up, now casts me down, acts me up again.

Because few men believed his political career was over, Ralegh did not cease to be branded with the characteristics of the court favourite after 1592. Indeed, presentation of him as a liar carried more weight once he had been caught out deceiving the queen. Ralegh was certainly not the most truthful of men,[63] but he suffered probably more than he deserved from a reputation for mendacity. Puns on his surname (Raw Lie) circulated in verse in the later 1590s, and his poem "The Lie," which was widely read from around 1595, did much to associate his name with deceit even though the poem was actually a critique of worldly deceit. It was this reputation as much as the fabulous nature of his descriptions of Guiana that caused Ralegh's account of his voyage to be greeted with incredulity and led to the unfair allegation that he had fabricated the adventures from his home in the West Country.

Both before and after his disgrace, Ralegh was accused of a more insidious form of dishonesty than barefaced lies such as these. Like Gaveston, King Richard II's minions, and Cardinal Wolsey, he was said to use deceitful flattery first to win, then to maintain, and finally to recover royal favour. The most devastating critique came from the pen of a disappointed rival for court favour, Sir John Harington, probably before June 1592. Using, as he often did, the name Paulus as a pseudonym for Ralegh,[64] the disgruntled Harington wrote:

> No man more servile, no man more submisse,
> Then to our Soueraigne Lady Paulus is.
> He doth extoll her speech, admire her feature,
> He calls himselfe her vassall, and her creature
> Thus while he dawbes his speech with flatteries plaster
> And calls himselfe her slave, he growes our Master.[65]

---

[62] Birch, *Memoirs of the Reign of Queen Elizabeth*, 1: 151; *Calendar of the Manuscripts of Lord De L'Isle and Dudley, Preserved at Penshurst Place*, 6 vols. (London: Historical Manuscripts Commission, 1933), 2:182, 198, 200.

[63] MacCarthy-Morroch, *Munster Plantation*, 187. In a note before his execution he withdrew a statement made a year earlier that a lease granted to Henry Pyne had been forged.

[64] By calling him Paulus, Harington was probably alluding to the heretical Paulician sect which denied Christ was the son of God.

[65] Harington, *Epigrams*, sig. M, no 61.

With only one letter written by Ralegh to the queen surviving, it is impossible to assess the truth of Harington's charge or to judge whether or not Ralegh's line of flattery exceeded that of other courtiers, though it is hard to see how his words in prose could be more unctuous than those of Hatton. The only evidence of Ralegh's "flatteries" can be found in his poems and the speeches and behaviour he was recorded as making while incarcerated in 1592. The early poems written in the 1580s, however, seem to be conventional works of a courtier, often employing the Petrarchan tropes and rhetoric that were currently fashionable at court. During his period under arrest in the summer of 1592, Ralegh again used Petrarchan tropes when he acted out the role of the choleric and melancholic lover denied sight of his inaccessible mistress, one time falling into a rage, another time threatening to kill himself. There is no question that Ralegh intended his behaviour to be repeated to the queen.[66] His Cynthia poems written around that time express the same despair at losing his mistress's favour but, with their emphasis on the queen's mutability, they contain as much bitterness at the queen's capriciousness as praise for her divine qualities. So yes, Ralegh was a flatterer, but who wasn't—at least on the surface—during the last decades of Elizabeth's reign?

During his time in the wasteland of royal disapproval, Ralegh used every device in his arsenal to win back royal favour. He offered the queen more than her fair share of his spoils from the privateering venture that captured the huge East Indian carrack, the *Madre de Dios*. He set off for Guiana determined to shower his sovereign with gold, land, and the allegiance of new subjects, while the narrative he wrote on his return was (in the words of Louis Montrose) "fashioned with a view to securing the queen's forgiveness and favour."[67] In 1596 he served his mistress in war, commanding one of the four squadrons in the Cadiz expedition, and so that his bravery, leadership qualities, and personal sacrifice (he was wounded in the leg) would not pass unnoticed, he quickly presented an account for circulation that emphasized his own role in the successful part of the enterprise.[68] However, this work of self-publicity soon backfired. Essex immediately challenged Ralegh's version of events at Cadiz, stressing his own fortitude and virtually accusing Ralegh of cowardice in pushing for a return homewards instead of staying on to secure a base on the mainland.[69] Within Essex's circle,

---

[66] Patrick Fraser Tytler, *Life of Sir Walter Raleigh* (Edinburgh: Oliver & Boyd, 1833), 131–32; Latham and Youings, *Letters*, 53.

[67] Louis Montrose, "The Work of Gender in the Discourse of Discovery," *Representations* 33 (1991): 1–41.

[68] Letter to Arthur [Gorges] from Cadiz, 21 June 1596, Latham and Youings, *Letters*, 145–50.

[69] Walter Bouchier Devereux, *Life and Letters of the Devereux Earls of Essex 1540–1646*, 2 vols. (London: J. Murray, 1853), 1:364, 378, 385–88.

Ralegh was again cast in the role of a master of deceit, which, judging from Lord Admiral Howard's account of the expedition, was unfair.[70]

Thanks to his service at Cadiz as well as the intercession of Cecil, Howard, and Essex, Ralegh was permitted access to the privy chamber in April 1597 and two months later was received "very graciously" by the queen.[71] For the rest of the reign, although not exactly a "court favourite," he was still considered a man who could expect to rise further because of the favour he enjoyed with the queen. His unpopularity correspondingly grew, exacerbated in 1597 by another spat with Essex from which there was to be no reconciliation. When comparing Essex and Ralegh's respective positions in 1597, William Camden commented: "For the Queen's Favour, wherein they both stood very fair, strangely procured contrary Effects, Hatred of the People against Ralegh ... and Love to Essex."[72] Throughout the late 1590s hatred against Ralegh was expressed in libels, gossip, and slanderous words that extended well beyond the confines of the court.[73] During the Essex "rebellion" the earl accused Ralegh of planning his death, and once the earl was executed, he was held to be the instrument of Essex's destruction. Later in the year Ralegh was the target of hatred in parliament where he was accused of using the crown prerogative to milk the poor—a standard charge applied to favourites. By the end of the reign Ralegh was an isolated figure. In mid-1601, Cecil had distanced himself from his one-time ally, possibly because he was fast becoming the new patron of the ex-members of the Essex circle. Consequently, Ralegh was left dangerously exposed, and the poison poured into the ear of James VI by Ralegh's enemy, Lord Henry Howard, found no antidote in friendly words from Cecil.

Scholars have long recognized that Ralegh should not be taken at his own word, as his writings and reported speech were theatrical, dissembling, and the product of "self-fashioning."[74] But historians should further be wary of taking Ralegh at the word of others, for his contemporaries also fashioned him. Their descriptions of him during the late Elizabethan period match far too closely the descriptors of the conventional court favourite for historians to feel comfortable with their accuracy. A two-way process may well have been operating: writers drew on Ralegh's career to bring contemporary significance to their own drama, while their own depictions of the court favourite created a distorting lens though which Ralegh was viewed. Ralegh's unpopularity therefore stemmed as much

---

[70] *Calendar of Marquess of Bath, at Longleat, Wiltshire*, 5 vols. (London: Historical Manuscripts Commission, 1907), 2:44–47.

[71] *Calendar of the Manuscripts of Lord De L'Isle*, 2:258.

[72] William Camden, T*he Historie of . . . Princesse Elizabeth, Late Queene of England*, 3rd ed. (London, 1675), 535.

[73] *Calendar of Cecil Manuscripts at Hatfield*, 9:342, 10:167.

[74] Greenblatt, *Sir Walter Ralegh*, ix, 44. Montrose, "The Work of Gender in the Discourse of Discovery," 1–41.

from contemporary identification of him with a Tresilian or Gaveston as from his own behaviour or attributes. As for Elizabeth, the discourse of the court favourite miscasts her as a monarch who was always capricious, too easily manipulated, and attracted to a man's appearance rather than his worth. This characterisation — still fashionable today — also requires re-examination.

One final point: while the "court favourite" is undoubtedly a literary construct, does the term represent a political reality — is it a meaningful designation for any of Elizabeth's courtiers? I think not. After all, no one man emerged as pre-eminent in Elizabeth's court; and no one enjoyed an exclusive bond of intimacy with the queen. Elizabeth's style of political management discouraged the emergence of one favourite or even a small group of 'mignons'. So let us be bold and banish the term from our political nomenclature. We can then better investigate and appreciate the cultural and political developments (such as the influence of Tacitean history and disaffection with the late Elizabethan regime) that led to the trope of the "court favourite" emerging so prominently in the latter part of the queen's reign.

Elizabeth I and Court Display

Debra Barrett-Graves

E. K. Chambers has observed that "The tradition of pageantry had its roots deep in the Middle Ages."[1] The spectacles associated with Elizabethan military exercises, with their roots grounded in the medieval tournament,[2] represent an important phenomenon — the "imaginative re-feudalization of culture" that occurred in early modern England.[3] Alan Hager shows how "the extreme amount of ceremony and ornament in Elizabeth's court, from the nicknaming, sonnet production, and oral euphuism, to the masques, tilts, and processions, served not only to impress the public and, through report, foreign rulers of a 'woman's rule,' but also tied the hands of an aristocracy now used to thinking of the royal succession, perhaps, as the prize of military conquest, a very male activity."[4] In the early modern period, governing princes on the European continent and in England frequently relied upon court display for political purposes: "Elizabeth made regular public appearances, sponsored official portraits, and engaged in elaborate court rituals that created an interaction between sovereign and subjects."[5] Diane Bornstein, in her introduction to *The Book of Honor and Arms* (1590) and *Honor Military and Civil* (1602), concurs that the use of pageantry constituted a hallmark of Tudor political policy. Not only were these military pageants and exercises important elements of coronation events and wedding festivities,

---

[1] E. K. Chambers, *The Elizabethan Stage*, 4 vols. (Oxford: Clarendon Press, 1967), 1:106.

[2] David Crouch, *Tournament* (London: Hambledon & Continuum, 2005) provides a good overview of the medieval tournament and its development.

[3] Frances A. Yates, "Elizabethan Chivalry: The Romance of the Accession Day Tilts," *Journal of the Warburg and Courtauld Institutes* 20 (1957): 4–25, here 22.

[4] Alan Hager, *Dazzling Images: The Masks of Sir Philip Sidney* (Newark, DE: University of Delaware Press, 1991), 25.

[5] Mary Hill Cole, *The Portable Queen* (Amherst: University of Massachusetts Press, 1999), 145.

but they were also "the basic entertainment at all major political and diplomatic celebrations."[6]

Among other politically significant forms of court display, the formalized military exercises that the Tudor monarchs sanctioned, known generically as "jousts of peace," provided an arena for the monarch to show off his or her magnificence in a microcosmic setting that included spectators from all stations of English society. These organized military displays could also be used to impress foreign ambassadors by demonstrating the martial skills of English fighting men. On a national level, these formalized military exercises allowed Elizabethan courtiers to demonstrate their loyalty, through their staged performances, while concurrently seeking preferment from their sovereign. On a social level, the tilts, tourneys, and barriers, which comprised the jousts of peace, helped to unite all members of Elizabethan society in a festive atmosphere that celebrated the English nation-state while simultaneously maintaining the hierarchical divisions that segregated and shaped society. Owing to varying performances and the disparate natures of audience members, the jousts of peace celebrated throughout Elizabeth's reign yielded for their participants no single, universal meaning. Events might serve the political agendas of aspiring participants or even provide a field upon which to settle jealous rivalries. Just as easily, they could further the political aspirations of the English monarch. By examining representative occasions for these types of court display, one can begin to comprehend the meaning behind the imaginative fabric of Elizabethan military exercises and events, whether inspired by personal, patriotic, political, or religious motives.

Before the regular occurrence of the Accession Day Tilts, Elizabeth understood the political merits of associating military pageantry with her reign. As a female monarch, Elizabeth had to delegate her martial responsibilities to the men who served her, and the military displays fulfilled several important functions. Mary Hill Cole asserts that an early 1559 martial display at Greenwich serves as a case in point:

> The tilt, gunfire, and organized bands marching around the field conveyed the image of strength, victory, and unity. For reasons of gender and precedent, Elizabeth wanted the Greenwich muster to highlight her promise and confidence as a military leader. Because as a woman she would not lead troops into battle, her presence at mock ones suggested, nevertheless, her symbolic participation in them.[7]

---

[6] See the Introduction to Diane Bornstein's facsimile reproduction of William Segar's *The Book of Honor and Armes (1590) and Honor Military and Civil (1602)* (Delmar: Scholar's Facsimiles & Reprints, 1975), i.

[7] Cole, *Portable Queen*, 155–56.

Similarly, when on progress, Elizabeth assumed a martial role by conducting ceremonial inspections, surveying fortifications, and being entertained by mock battles.[8] Elizabeth was not temperamentally inclined to pursue foreign wars; she preferred, instead, to create imaginative "bellicose ceremonies that expressed England's power."[9] John Nichols records an unusual test of military prowess. During her visit to Sandwich in 1573, Elizabeth enjoyed watching a staged naval tilt: two individuals perched on planks in their respective boats were pulled toward each other, with the victor using his lance to strike his opponent's wooden shield and knock him into the water.[10]

At the beginning of the Tudor monarchy, Henry VII had borrowed ceremonial military display from the Burgundian court to validate his own role as an English monarch. Alan Young notes that "Throughout Europe . . . the tournament had become recognized as the public spectacle *par excellence*, which a national leader could use in the profoundly serious political exercise of displaying his or her magnificence."[11] The Tudor monarchs who most emulated Henry VII's use of military display were his son, Henry VIII, and his granddaughter, Elizabeth I. The youthful age of Edward VI, Henry VIII's son and successor, and the uneasy tensions between England and Spain when Mary I wed Philip of Spain, while not completely obviating tournament pageantry and display, did not allow it to flourish to the same degree as it did in the reigns of Henry and Elizabeth.[12] During the periods when military sport was politically advantageous, one must recall that "in terms of propaganda to bolster the status of the monarch, Tudor and Jacobean tournaments were the most frequent and lavishly financed form of spectacle to be used for this purpose. They were never mere entertainment . . . extravagant fantasy, or archaic exercises of obsolete military skill."[13] In fact, the variety of military games had an important agenda—to acquire honor, which ultimately served both prince and courtiers; to express a subject's loyalty to his sovereign; and to facilitate opportunities for the loyal subject to profit from the patronage system.[14]

---

[8] Cole, *Portable Queen*, 163.

[9] Cole, *Portable Queen*, 2.

[10] John Nichols, *The Progresses and Public Processions of Queen Elizabeth*, 3 vols. (London: J. Nichols & Son, 1823; repr. New York: Burt Franklin, 1966), 1:338.

[11] Alan Young, *Tudor and Jacobean Tournaments* (Dobbs Ferry: Sheridan House, 1987), 22.

[12] See Young's discussion, "To Them that Honour Desyreth," *Tudor and Jacobean Tournaments*, 11–42.

[13] Young, *Tudor and Jacobean Tournaments*, 25.

[14] Young, *Tudor and Jacobean Tournaments*, 23.

II

While jousts were also performed to celebrate Elizabeth's birthday on 7 September, Young identifies two specific types of occasions during Elizabeth's rule when jousts of peace occurred. They either marked "special events to honour visiting foreign dignitaries, or they formed part of the regular annual celebration of Elizabeth's accession each 17 November."[15] My initial interest lies with the types of pageantry that generally took place during the first decades of Elizabeth's tenure as queen regnant. For example, Chambers notes and describes the 11 November 1565 wedding military exercises performed to honor the marriage of Ambrose Dudley, the earl of Warwick, and Lady Anne Russell.[16] The brief events that occurred, as sketched by Chambers, indicate the similarities of how martial entertainments would be announced and enacted, whether for a wedding, for the foreign ambassadors, or just for the sheer bravado of youthful gallants who wished to praise and entertain Elizabeth. Typically, an appointed herald would announce the preliminary challenge. On the day of the event, the challenger would face all opponents, who might show up dressed in fanciful costumes. For Warwick's wedding each challenger was "accompanied by a patron and by an Amazon [who led] his spare horse." After circling the tournament field, challengers would either present their impresa shields by proxy or, more simply, hang them up, before demonstrating their military prowess in tilting, tourneying, and fighting at the barriers. A banquet could follow the final round of speeches.[17] Young cites another tourney held in celebration of the marriage of Henry Knollys to Margaret Cave at Durham Place where similar martial exercises honored the nuptial event (1565).[18] It seems reasonable that Elizabeth would have graced other weddings, with similar court displays, to demonstrate her approval of important marriages.

A well-documented account exists of the martial exercises enacted at Whitehall for the Duc de Montmorency, a visiting French ambassador, on 14 June 1572. During this nighttime demonstration, which was lit by blazing torches, Montmorency enjoyed seeing Elizabeth's fighting men engage in skirmishes at the barriers at the palace rather than in its tiltyard.[19] The lavish displays and seating arrangement of the spectators held special political significance, allowing

---

[15] Young, *Tudor and Jacobean Tournaments*, 35.

[16] Chambers, *Elizabethan Stage*, 1:142.

[17] Chambers, *Elizabethan Stage*, 1:142–43.

[18] Young, "Appendix," in *Tudor and Jacobean Tournaments*, 201; Young cites as his source *Calendar of Letters and State Papers relating to English Affairs [of the Reign of Elizabeth], Preserved Principally in the Archives of Simancas*, ed. Martin A. S. Hume, 4 vols. (London: HMSO, 1892–1899), 1:452.

[19] William Segar, *The Book of Honor and Armes*, bk. 4 (London: Richard Jones, 1590), 96–97. See also Young, *Tudor and Jacobean Tournaments*, 202.

participants to gauge their hierarchical roles in the Elizabethan commonweal. With the queen at the center of the court ceremony, "the staging of a tournament was both a calculated display of magnificence and a powerful demonstration, both literally and figuratively, of the hierarchical structure of the body politic, from the single figure of royalty in the most central and most lavishsly-appointed [sic] viewing place, flanked by the ranks of the nobility and civic officials, to the thousands of commoners in their own stands."[20]

The 1581 entertainment known as *The Four Foster Children of Desire*, again presented for visiting French dignitaries, has had some of its pageantry preserved by Henry Goldwell. The detailed description of events affords readers a chance to ponder the message intended for the French ambassadors, to interpret the counsel being offered to Elizabeth by her courtiers, and to comprehend the significance of the tournament for the English viewing audience. Examined in its social and political milieu, *The Four Foster Children of Desire* is replete with complex socio-political connotations and implications that reveal how the unsuccessful love siege proleptically points to the failure of any threatened religious or military attack against England. An effective way of providing the queen with counsel without undermining her authority was by creating "entertainments" that offered advice on the current affairs of state by using allegorical and fictional genres. As one of Desire's four Foster Children, Philip Sidney had the perfect opportunity to offer advice related to the vexed question of the queen's marriage to Anjou.[21]

In this tourney-play, the tiltyard upon which the ritualistic invention takes place symbolizes that the marriage proposal is a battle for power between French and English, Protestants and Catholics. The tourney-play's meanings extend beyond implications about the failure of the proposed marriage to include pointed statements about the strength of the English nation that would be able to withstand the threat to English Protestantism posed by the papacy or the possibility of foreign invasion. The impenetrable fortress of Beauty in which Elizabeth resides corresponds to the unassailable strength and security of the English nation. This ambassadorial tournament balances in equipoise its ritual nature and ludic representations, which appear in its elaborately staged displays, sieges, songs, speeches, and tilts; and, in its complex pageantry, also reflects Sidney's own vexed relationship with the queen. As Louis Adrian Montrose argues, "Sidney's symbolic offering of submission to the great goddess" is necessarily qualified because "it also contained an aristocratic analogue of the Saturnalian rites of misrule."[22]

---

[20] Young, *Tudor and Jacobean Tournaments*, 90.

[21] Jean Wilson, *Entertainments for Queen Elizabeth I* (Woodbridge: Brewer, 1980), 61–62.

[22] See Louis Adrian Montrose, "Celebration and Insinuation: Sir Philip Sidney and the Motives of Elizabethan Courtship," *Renaissance Drama*, n.s. 8 (1977): 3–35, here 28–29.

In the early years of Elizabeth's reign, before the Accession Day Tilts began appearing with the regularity of the later years, Young views participation in the jousts of peace as a prime opportunity for courtiers to vie for royal favor. As Montrose observes, "the grace that the faithful worshiper hopes from his goddess is preferment," although hopefuls such as Sidney and Edmund Spenser never attained the desired advancement.[23] Elizabeth must have found equal profit and satisfaction in having occasions for manipulating court display to her advantage—to showcase "her magnificence, her subjects' loyalty, and her warriors' prowess in feats of arms."[24] Foreign ambassadors would be expected to report the precision with which Elizabeth's warriors practiced their military skills, and, in doing so, they would bolster the validity and vitality of Elizabeth's position as regnant queen. Another benefit from these martial court displays would result from Elizabeth's ability to consolidate "domestic unity and regal authority at home."[25]

Renaissance theorists frequently refer interchangeably to arms, hieroglyphs, devices, and emblems, and it is worth quoting John Guillim's definition of arms in order to understand the manner in which early modern practitioners of these arts would have valued their roles in the military pageantry:

> *Armes* are tokens or resemblances signifying some act or quality of the bearer.... These *Signes* called *Armes* are nothing else but *Demonstrations* and *Testimonies* of Nobility and of *Worthy*... exploits performed in Martiall services.... [they] may be said to be *Hieroglyphicks*, or *Enigmaticall*... as they were hidden from the vulgar sort, and known to the judicious.[26]

Sir Philip "Sidney's interest in these devices was well known in his own day and for long after.... Camden describes many of Sidney's devices as of especial excellence, of which one example may be given. 'Sir Philip Sidney, to note that he persisted always one, depainted out the Caspian sea surrounded with his shoares, which neither ebbeth nor floweth, and over it: '*Sine refluxu*'" [Without flowing back].[27] Elizabethan tournament devices could be viewed on display in

---

[23] Young, *Tudor and Jacobean Tournaments*, 33; Montrose, "Celebration and Insinuation," 4.

[24] Young, *Tudor and Jacobean Tournaments*, 35.

[25] Young, *Tudor and Jacobean Tournaments*, 35.

[26] John Guillim, *A Display of Heraldrie: Manifesting a more easie access to the knowledge thereof then hath hitherto been published by any, through the benefit of Method*, 4th ed. (London: T. R for Jacob Blome, 1660), 3–4.

[27] John Buxton, *Sir Philip Sidney and the English Renaissance* (London: Macmillan, 1965), 148–49. William Camden's *Remains Concerning Britain* (London: Smith, 1870) contains the original reference (374). Samuel Daniel's translation of *The Worthy Tract of Paulus Jovius* gives what is probably the clearest and most concise account in English of the nature of *imprese*, and of the rules for devising *imprese*. See Samuel Daniel's *The Wor-*

the Shield Gallery at Whitehall, where Henry Peacham, the author of *Minerva Britanna* (1612) especially admired the ones created by Sidney.[28]

Sir Henry Lee, an expert on humanist uses of chivalry, the studied enactments of received medieval chivalric traditions, infused elaborately staged tournaments with learned allusions that yielded imaginative constructions of Elizabethan mythology. As Frances A. Yates has argued, "the rise of the national monarchies . . . used the apparatus of chivalry and its religious traditions to focus fervent religious loyalty on the national monarch."[29] As Elizabeth's longtime champion, Lee included a sentimental song—"His golden locks time hath to silver turned"—during his Retirement Tilt that was presented to the Queen in 1590.[30] While most commentators associate the allusion with either "Arthurian romance . . . [or] neo-platonic love . . . [for] which the helmet as a beehive is a motif,"[31] the striking allusion conjures up the emblematic expression, *Ex bello, pax* [From war, peace]. This sentiment is exactly suited to the retirement of the queen's champion, especially when the speaker claims that his "helmet now shall make a hive for bees / . . . / A man-at-arms must now serve on his knees."[32]

Imagery drawn from the Italian cult of the impresa also provided a basis for Lee's spectacles. Recent scholarship has brought to light a body of materials in miscellanies and in decorated armor and painted shields used in tournaments. Sir William Segar, one of the noted author-heralds active during the late sixteenth and early seventeenth centuries, credits Lee with initiating the Accession Day Tilts. Although Segar associates these tilts with the beginning of Elizabeth's reign, Young cites William Camden, who places their occurrence sometime after "the twelfth year of Elizabeth's reign" (c. 1569–1570).[33]

In his *Remains Concerning Britain* (1605), Camden defines the "Impress [as] a correspondency of the picture which is as the body; and the Motto, which as the soul giveth it life. That is, the body must be of fair representation, and the word in some different language, witty, short, and answerable thereunto."[34] Camden lists several impresas devoted exclusively to an affirmation of the subject's loyalty and faith to the queen, such as the one declared by Camden to be "a very good invention [which] was . . . to shew his stay and support by a Virgin Prince, who

---

thy tract of *Paulus Iouius, contayning a Discourse of rare inventions, both Militarie and Amorous called Imprese* (London: Simon Waterson, 1585), sig. B3v and B4r.

[28] See Henry Peacham, *Minerva Britanna* [1612] (Leeds: Scolar, 1966), Emblem 27.

[29] Yates, "Elizabethan Chivalry," 22.

[30] "At Lee's retirement in 1590 Robert Hales sang a lyric set by Dowland" (Wilson, *Entertainments*, 37).

[31] Wilson, *Entertainments*, 37.

[32] Wilson, *Entertainments*, 37, prints Lee's lyrics. See Geoffrey Whitney's *A Choice of Emblems* (Hants: Scolar, 1989), Emblem 138.

[33] Young, *Tudor and Jacobean Tournaments*, 36.

[34] Camden, *Remains*, 366–67.

presented in his shield the Zodiack, with the characters only of Leo and Virgo, and this word, 'His ego praesidiis' [I rely upon these guardians]."[35]

That Elizabeth sought out many ways to initiate direct contact with her subjects in order to establish a climate of viable monarchy is certain. With "a total of 23 progresses in her 44-year reign,"[36] Elizabeth had the opportunity both to wield power and to manipulate the political arena of her court. The appendix to Young's study of *Tudor and Jacobean Tournaments* lists a total of seventy-two tilts, tourneys, and barriers (albeit not always performed simultaneously), which were enacted throughout the same forty-four-year period,[37] affording an equally profitable arena for controlling the court and its subjects through politically charged and aesthetically pleasing ceremonial court displays.

III

Literary examples of jousts and tournaments also recapture the visual displays, the verbal artistry, and sometimes even the inherent tensions in the subject/monarch patronage system associated with the tilts and tournaments. For example, Thomas Nashe's *The Unfortunate Traveler* (c.1594) contains detailed visual descriptions of the pageantry associated with the challenge issued by Lord Henry Howard, the earl of Surrey, in the court of the duke of Florence. The tournament's theme is based on a challenge—the defense of Lady Geraldine's beauty against all takers:

> His [Howard's] armour was ill intermixed with lilies and roses, and the bases thereof bordered with nettles and weeds, signifying stings, crosses, and overgrowing encumberances in his love; his helmet round-proportioned like a gardener's water-pot, from which seemed to issue forth small threads of water, like cittern strings . . . . Whereby he did import thus much, that the tears that issued from his brains . . . gave life as well to his mistress' disdain (resembled to nettles and weeds) as increase of glory to her care-causing beauty (comprehended under the lilies and roses). The symbol thereto annexed was this: *Ex lachrimis lachrimae* [From tears, more tears]. (316–17)[38]

The description of Surrey's tournament trappings might seem outlandish, an obvious literary parody of tournament display. Its richly connotative details do re-

---

[35] Camden, *Remains*, 377. Dr. James Murphy, California State University, East Bay, translated the motto.
[36] Cole, *Portable Queen*, 22.
[37] Young, *Tudor and Jacobean Tournaments*, 201–5
[38] Nashe, *"The Unfortunate Traveler" and Other Works* (London: Penguin, 1987), 251–370.

semble the equally elaborate costumes worn by Sir Thomas Parrat and M. Anthony Cooke during *The Four Foster Children of Desire* tourney-pageant—matching suits of armor covered with apples and fruit to connote the figures of Adam and Eve, with Eve, of course, sporting flowing locks of hair.[39]

The knight's allegiance to and defense of his prince is symbolized by his shield, as Ramon Lull's treatise on chivalry, printed by William Caxton in 1484, describes:

> The shield is given to the knight to signify the office of a knight, for likewise as a knight puts a shield in between himself and his enemy, right so the knight is in the middle between the prince and the people. And as the stroke that falls upon the shield saves the knight, right so the knight ought to call himself out and present his body to his lord when the lord is in peril of being hurt or taken.[40]

According to Lull, equally significant accouterments for aspiring knights are the sword, which symbolizes justice, and the lance, which symbolizes truth.[41]

The shields carried by the major characters in Edmund Spenser's *Faerie Queene* (1590, 1596) evoke imagery associated with Elizabeth; and, in using such artful reminders, Spenser creates a compliment to Elizabeth through the collective presentation of these knightly devices. For example, the bloody cross of the Redcrosse Knight links him with Elizabeth's role as sovereign protector of the Protestant religion; Arthur's shield depicts princely magnificence, which implies grace and Protestant faith when facing threats from Catholic powers. The semblance of Gloriana in Sir Guyon's escutcheon connects the virtue of temperance with Elizabeth, who was called "sweet sister temperance."[42] Britomart and Arthegall, Spenser's literary progenitors of the Tudors, carry shields with (respectively) English lions, symbolizing Britomart's connection to the British monarchy, and a "crowned ermilin," visually echoing Elizabeth's ermine portrait (1585). Scudamor carries a shield with Cupid accompanied by his bow and arrows, along with a mot that reads *"Blessed the man that well can vse his blis: / Whose euer be the shield, faire Amoret be his"* (*FQ* 4.10.8.8–9).[43] During Sir Satyrane's tournament in Book 4, cantos 4 and 5, Satyrane, as the leading representative of the Knights of Maidenhead, gives over his shield with its Satyr's

---

[39] Wilson, *Entertainments*, 74.

[40] Ramon Lull, *Book of Knighthood and Chivalry*, trans. Brian Y. Price (Union City: Chivalry Bookshelf, 2001), 68.

[41] Lull, *Book of Knighthood*, 64.

[42] As A. C. Hamilton points out, "That Elizabeth was known as 'sweet sister *Temperance*', as W. Camden 1630:6 records, makes the address to her esp. fitting." See *The Faerie Queene*, ed. A. C. Hamilton (New York: Pearson, 2001), 158, note on stanza 5.1–2; 289, note on stanza 4.9.

[43] Quotations from *The Faerie Queene* are from Hamilton's text.

head in order to carry yet another shield with Gloriana's likeness. Calidore, as the knight of courtesy, must oppose the vice of malice on his own because he, unlike his counterparts, lacks a companion. By naming Calidore as the most courteous knight in faery land, Spenser, by association, conjures up once again the semblance of Gloriana, and her court:

> Of court it seemes, men Courtesie doe call,
> For that it there most vseth to abound;
> And well beseemeth that in Princes hall
> That vertue should be plentifully found,
> Which of all goodly manners is the ground,
> And roote of ciuill conuersation,
> Right so in Faery court it did redound,
> Where curteous Knights and Ladies most did won
> Of all on earth, and made a matchelesse paragon. (6.1.1.1–9)

Collectively, the shields carried by Gloriana's knights and *The Faerie Queene's* worthy protagonists praise Elizabeth by evoking Tudor monarchic iconography with its emphases on religion, magnificence, temperance, monarchy, chastity, love, friendship, justice, and courtesy, all telling compliments to Elizabeth. Spenser presents these tournament shields to Elizabeth in an engaging, chivalric gesture that invites the queen to reciprocate with a courteous response.

Spenser also questions the effectiveness of patronage for Elizabeth's courtiers and poets in the martial display of Satyrane's failed tournament. Sir Satyrane attempts to ward off envy by holding a tournament for possession of Florimell's golden girdle. Following the military exercises that occurred over a several-day period, the ladies in attendance are then to be judged for their beauty. After Arthegall, who is disguised as a stranger knight bearing a shield with the mot "*Saluagesse sans finesse*, shewing secret wit" (4.4.39.9) [wildness or savagery without refinement or art],[44] has been defeated during the final day of the tournament by Britomart, the knight with the enchanted lance, Arthegall vows to avenge the "foule despight" he believes himself to have unjustly suffered.

The conclusion of the tournament ends in the discord associated with the judging of the ladies. After viewing the ladies and trying to elevate one among them to earn the praise as most beautiful, Arthur finally suggests that the lady be allowed to choose her own knight: Arthegall has left in a pique, and Britomart wisely prefers Amoret. When the false Florimell selects Braggadochio, the remaining knights break into open conflict, deciding to use force to possess for themselves the false Florimell, the tournament's chosen Queen of Beauty. In this presentation, then, Spenser provides a literary "ensample" of the Elizabethan tournament that fails to uphold its proposed courtly ideals.

---

[44] *Faerie Queene*, ed. Hamilton, 442, note on stanza 39.8–9.

When Florimell's golden girdle fails to remain clasped as each lady, in her turn, attempts to encircle her waist with it, the Squire of the Dames laughs loudly and derisively. Much to the ladies' dismay, he mocks then by exclaiming, "Fie on the man, that did it first inuent, / To shame vs all with this, *Vngirt vnblest*" (4.5.18.6–7). Spenser's allegorizing of the unchaste dames proves quite entertaining. Similar amusement occurs when one of Atin's "thrillant darts" leaves its "forckhead keene" in the shield bearing Gloriana's semblance (2.4.46.1, 8). Pyrrhocles' ferocious attack on Guyon in the next canto (2.5.6.2–3) actually shears away "the vpper marge / Of his [Guyon's] seuenfolded shield."[45] Hamilton's gloss on this passage contextualizes these attacks on Guyon's shield, Gloriana's semblance, and what I believe to be Spenser's allegorizing of contemporary historical attacks on Elizabeth's reputation—as defender of the faith, embodiment of temperance, and dispenser of justice. He explains that "for the knight of temperance the number [seven] suggests the protection given by the four cardinal and three theological virtues . . . against the seven deadly sins."[46]

Spenser's allegorizing of Elizabeth continues further when Arthur challenges Pyrrhocles and Cymochles in the process of their despoiling Sir Guyon of his armor. Guyon has fallen into a swoon after leaving Mammon's house (2.8). In his furious charge, Arthur aims his spear at the breast of Pyrrhocles who has taken Guyon's shield bearing Gloriana's semblance. When Pyrrhocles suddenly throws the shield in front of his chest for protection, the lance pierces both the shield and Pyrrhocles's shoulder. Since Pyrrhocles and Cymochles reappear in the guise of Paynim knights in Book 2, canto 8, Spenser may be suggesting a more specific confrontation: between England and Spain, or even between England and Ireland.[47] The image of Gloriana on Guyon's shield actually hinders Arthur's attempt to best Pyrrhocles, as he often holds his hand from striking the eschutcheon that bears the image his heart worships.

During the celebrations of the marriage festivities of Marinell and Florimell, Spenser renders a more positive literary account of a tournament in Book 5, canto 3. Both the feasting and exercising of chivalric deeds that occur over a three-day period and the awarding of the tourney's prize correspond to the jousts of peace practiced in Elizabethan England. The most humorous aspect of this tournament, however, does not occur in flagrant attacks on Elizabeth's position as England's sovereign but rather in the form of blows threatened upon Gloriana's semblance on Sir Guyon's shield. The marriage tournament ends in concord only after Arthur—who had borrowed Braggadochio's shield to disguise himself and, upon returning it, challenged him for attempting to take the credit for

---

[45] *Faerie Queene,* ed. Hamilton, 197, note on stanza 6.1–2.

[46] *Faerie Queene,* ed. Hamilton, 197, note on stanza 6.1–2.

[47] During a private conversation, Thomas Herron of East Carolina University suggested the Irish connection to me.

his (Arthur's) rescue of Marinell—had performed a deed of amazing skill that required the defeat of one hundred knights.

If, as Thomas P. Roche suggests,[48] Braggadochio and Trompart represent Alençon and Simier, then Arthur's baffling of Braggodochio—shaving his beard, and blotting out his arms "Which bore the Sune brode blazed in a golden field" (5.3.14.9), and scourging Trompart—allegorizes the end to Alençon's/Anjou's hopes for a marital alliance with Elizabeth. Impresas often associated Elizabeth with the sun. In Camden's catalogue of impresas, another courtier acknowledges his essence to be in his sovereign when he depicts a sundial and the setting sun with the mot "Occasu desinet esse" [At sunset it ceases to exist].[49] In Satyrane's tournament, the values of chivalry and knighthood are questioned, but in the tournament celebrating the marriage of Marinell and Florimell, Arthur reaffirms the chivalric values of knighthood by castigating the false bravado of the lying Braggadochio.

In *Pericles*, Shakespeare and his collaborator invite audience members and readers to contrast the courtesy and court display that inform Simonides' tournament for the hand of the princess Thaisa with the enigmatical riddle that culminates in premature loss of life at the Syrian court of Anthiochus. In *Pericles*, the martial contest for the hand of Thaisa (2.2) is preceded by the ceremonial display of the knights' shields, with the good king Simonides explicating their veiled meanings. Not having a proper shield, Pericles presents Thaisa with a withered branch sporting a wisp of greenery at its top, which Simonides glosses as meaning that by this the stranger knight hopes to improve his fortunes through winning the princess's hand in marriage.[50] The military prowess of Pericles, as the stranger knight, along with his courteous demeanor, eventually wins him the hand of Thaisa. Aside from dramatic purposes, the socio-political enactments of jousts and tournaments performed in the Elizabethan and Jacobean reigns may have served to inspire a positive display of chivalric ideals at the court of Simonides.

The possibility of personal communication with Elizabeth during tournament rituals combined with the political motivations of aspiring combatants ar-

---

[48] See Thomas P. Roche, ed., *The Faerie Queene* (New York: Penguin, 1987), 1114, note on stanza 10.1. For another reading of Braggadochio, see David Quint, "Archimago and Amoret: The Poem and Its Doubles," in *Worldmaking Spenser: Explorations in the Modern Age*, ed. Patrick Cheney and Lauren Silberman (Lexington: University Press of Kentucky, 2000), 32–42, here 35.

[49] Camden, *Remains*, 375. For the translation of the motto, see Alan R. Young, "English Tournament Imprese," in *The Emblem in Renaissance and Baroque Europe: Tradition and Variety (Selected Papers of the Glasgow International Emblem Conference, 13–17 August 1990)* (Leiden: Brill, 1992), 1–139, here 99, Imprese 308.

[50] William Shakespeare, *Pericles*, ed. F. D. Hoeniger, The Arden Shakespeare (London: Methuen, 1986), 2.2.

guably justified, at least for a time, the substantial financial investment sustained by tournament participants. For Elizabeth's part,

> The physical grandeur of the tiltyards at Westminster, Whitehall, and Greenwich must have been as significant a factor as the actual spectacle of costume, armour, weapons, horses and pageants in expressing royal power, while national unity was perhaps nowhere better in evidence than in the provision of viewing stands for thousands of spectators, arranged so as to express the accepted social hierarchy.[51]

The reasons for and explanations behind the regular enactment of formalized military exercises in the Elizabethan reign are many: youthful bravado, courtly compliment, aspiring ambition, religious defense, national defense, and courteous munificence. As Elizabeth aged, the voices were not always approving. In his recent study of *The Subject of Elizabeth: Authority, Gender, and Representation*, Montrose argues that "Whatever their degree of technical skill or formal innovations, neither image makers nor the images they fashioned were merely transparent images of an omniscient and omnipotent royal will."[52] In the second half of Elizabeth's reign, guided by Sir Henry Lee (among others), the Accession Day Tilts continued to display the sophisticated imagery that served to acclaim Elizabeth Tudor, regnant queen of England, to establish English identity, and, at times, to promote individual political agendas.

---

[51] Young, *Tudor and Jacobean Tournaments*, 122.
[52] Louis Montrose, *The Subject of Elizabeth: Authority, Gender, and Representation* (Chicago: University of Chicago Press, 2006), 13.

Elizabeth I and the Heraldry of the Face

Anna Riehl Bertolet

How does an early modern subject describe the face of a living queen? Classical rhetoric postulates that, as a part of the body, the face may be praised under the rubric of "goods of nature" or omitted altogether, especially if the writer subscribes to Cicero's belief that "true praise . . . should be given to virtue only."[1] Yet, in attempting a description of one's queen, it might not be entirely politic to reduce her to abstractions. As Edmund Spenser has famously expounded in the apparatus of *The Faerie Queene*, the most effective eulogy for Elizabeth I would combine praise to the beautiful woman and tribute to the accomplished queen. A poet has a wide variety of tropes to complete the first task, but giving praise to the monarch without losing sight of her femininity is a trickier business. In tropes drawn from heraldry, Elizabeth's poets found an effective means of conveying both of her essences through a singular fusion of description and symbolism, in Elizabeth's face, of her body politic and her body natural.

The poetic technique of inscribing heraldry onto the monarch's physiognomy was all the more significant because it lent support to Elizabeth's lifelong project of defending her genealogical claim to the throne. The challenge to Elizabeth's legitimacy was one of the most dangerous of the many attempts to undermine her rule, and heraldry was one of the "sovereign arts" that equipped the queen and her supporters with a readily recognized symbolic affirmation of her authority. Therefore, allusions to the Tudor Rose and to Elizabeth's royal coat of arms in poetic descriptions of her face serve predominantly as celebrations of her sovereignty. Although this metaphor comes with its own set of representational complications, it provides a poetic outlet for the male writer's desire to invest his

---

[1] According to Aristotle, the encomium "will usually begin with a favorable notice of his nation, family, comeliness, and education. Such material should be secondary, however, to his noble deeds . . ." (cited in O. B. Hardison, Jr., *The Enduring Monument: A Study of the Idea of Praise in Renaissance Literary Theory and Practice* [Chapel Hill: University of North Carolina Press, 1962], 30). More specifically, "there were the three kinds of praise—goods of nature, fortune, and character—and their 'places'" (205–6). "Goods of nature" would include various praiseworthy qualities pertaining to the body, e.g., beauty.

queen's face with meaning: the metaphorization of her face, seemingly a poetical matter, is in actuality fraught with political undertones. As I will show, this process of investment is complicated by a strong undercurrent of hidden anxiety and metaphoric violence.

Before William Shakespeare penned his famous phrase, the "heraldry in Lucrece' face,"[2] three other Elizabethan poets — Philip Sidney, Edmund Spenser, and Fulke Greville — composed lines of poetry that drew a female face powerfully into the symbolic field of heraldry. In one case, the visage belonged to Stella; in two others, to Queen Elizabeth. In early modern culture, heraldry and facial beauty were readily linked, respectively, to the categories of power and femininity. While many a poet aspired to separate this queen's two major incarnations, formulated in Spenser's *Faerie Queene* as "the one of a most royal Queen or Empress, the other of a most virtuous and beautiful Lady,"[3] others endeavored to embrace both the monarch and the woman. One of the most effective amalgamations of these two personae has been achieved in the metaphoric conflation of Elizabeth's face and the Tudor Rose or her royal coat of arms. The heraldic metaphor is not exclusive to the descriptions of Elizabeth, yet its distinctive use in her case results in an array of meanings specific and unique to this queen.[4]

Edmund Spenser's "Aprill" eclogue from *The Shepheardes Calender* includes Hobbinoll's recitation of Colin's complimentary tribute to "fayre *Elisa*, Queene of shepheardes all" (line 34).[5] Colin announces his intention to "blaze / Her worthy praise" (lines 43–44) and then directs our gaze to Elisa herself:

> See, where she sits upon the grassy green,
>   (O seemly sight)
> Yclad in scarlet like a maiden Queen,
> And Ermines white. . . .

---

[2] *The Rape of Lucrece*, line 64, in *The Norton Shakespeare*, ed. Stephen Greenblatt et al. (New York: Norton, 1997), 643.

[3] Spenser, "A Letter of the Authors…," in *The Faerie Queene*, ed. Thomas P. Roche (London: Penguin, 1987), 16.

[4] Nancy Vickers points out that the body/shield metaphor makes a frequent appearance in the *Blasons anatomiques du corps femenin* (1543). Vickers also notes that, in Sidney's *Astrophil and Stella*, 13, Cupid makes Stella's face his shield. See "'The blazon of sweet beauty's best': Shakespeare's *Lucrece*," in *Shakespeare and the Question of Theory*, ed. Patricia Parker and Geoffrey Hartman (New York and London: Methuen, 1985), 95–116, here 104. These examples, however, do not include a specific figuration of a face as a coat of arms. It may very well be that this metaphor originates in the poetic descriptions of Elizabeth. It is only a few years later (after Spenser and Greville) that Shakespeare extends this metaphor to the "heraldry in Lucrece' face," depicting it as a dynamic interplay between the white (virtue) and red (beauty).

[5] Edmund Spenser, *The Shorter Poems*, ed. Richard A. McCabe (London: Penguin, 1999), 62.

> Tell me, have ye seen her angelic face,
> Like *Phœbe* faire?
> Her Heavenly haviour, her princely grace
> Can you well compare?
> The Red rose meddled with the White yfere,
> In either cheek depeincten lively cheer.
> Her modest eye,
> Her Majesty,
> Where have you seen the like, but there?[6]

E. K., in his "Glosse" on the line "The Redde rose medled with the White yfere," reveals the heraldic intention of this apparently conventional image of Elizabeth's beauty. He provides the following observations:

> By the mingling of the Red rose and the White, it meant the uniting of the two principal houses of Lancaster and of York: by whose long discord and deadly debate, this realm many years was sore travailed, and almost clean decayed. Till the famous Henry the seventh, of the line of Lancaster, taking to wife the most virtuous Princess Elisabeth, daughter to the fourth Edward of the house of York, begat the most royal Henry the eight aforesaid, in whom was the first union of the White Rose and the Red.[7]

Although E. K.'s commentary suggests that Spenser has metaphorically inscribed the Tudor Rose onto Elizabeth's *face*, the preceding stanza of the poem has already used the same heraldic colors, red and white, to picture the queen's robes—and thus has created a larger representational field expressing heraldry that literally covers her body: "Yclad in Scarlot like a mayden Queene, / And Ermines white" (lines 57–58).[8] As Ellen Chirelstein has pointed out, in portraiture, "family colours and symbolic charges were sometimes worked into the

---

[6] Spenser, *Shorter Poems*, 62–63, lines 55–72.
[7] Spenser, *Shorter Poems*, 68.
[8] In recent criticism, there has been a distinct tendency to unfold eroticized subtexts of these descriptions. For example, in her discussion of "Aprill," Philippa Berry compares Spenser's description of Eliza to that of Diana in Ovid's *Metamorphoses*: Berry suggests that "Eliza is naked, clad in the 'Scarlot' and 'Ermines white' of her own skin." See *Of Chastity and Power: Elizabethan Literature and the Unmarried Queen* (London: Routledge, 1989), 80. Similarly, Louis Montrose cites the line depicting Belphoebe's cheeks as "roses in a bed of lillies shed" as an example of a "rhetorical play between the prohibition and provocation of desire": for Montrose, "the internal rhyme on 'bed' and 'shed' imparts to the description of her maidenly modesty a subliminal suggestion of her defloration." See "The Elizabethan Subject and the Spenserian Text," in *Literary Theory / Renaissance Texts*, ed. Patricia Parker and David Quint (Baltimore: Johns Hopkins University Press, 1986), 303–40, here 326–27.

design of the dress or armour of the sitter."[9] In this light, Spenser's treatment of Elizabeth's face as a type of fabric or canvas that may be custom-patterned is emphatic. While the red and white of Elizabeth's face and attire echo and reinforce each other, however, the conceptual difference causes some tensions. For instance, are the colors of the face intrinsic to the skin, or can they be donned and then taken off, like the robes? A question arises about how much of the queen's legitimate heraldry is imprinted onto her face naturally and how much of it is painted onto her skin cosmetically. Spenser's word choice in the following line, "In either cheek depeincten lively cheer," gestures to the art of cosmetics, a site of many polemical battles of the time. As a result of this suggestive line, the image of Elizabeth's cheeks painted like Tudor Roses simultaneously acknowledges and questions her political authority. The image additionally betrays the male poet's suppressed anxiety about praising a female monarch: Spenser imagines that her very face bears the symbolic confirmation of her power, and yet he leaves it up to his reader to contend with the possibility that these roses may be washed off her cheeks.

Although it is difficult to determine the exact chronological relationship of Fulke Greville's Sonnet 81 to Spenser's "Aprill,"[10] the iconographic resemblance between the two depictions (the awe-inspiring sovereign sitting motionlessly on display)[11] allows them to be considered as companion pieces:

> Under a Throne I saw a virgin sit,
> The red, and white Rose quarter'd in her face;
> Star of the North, and for true guards to it,
> Princes, Church, States, all pointing out her Grace.
> The homage done her was not borne of Wit,
> Wisdom admir'd, Zeal took Ambitious place,
> State in her eyes taught Order how to fit,
> And fix Confusions unobserving race.
> *Fortune* can here claim nothing truly great,
> But that this Princely Creature is her seat.[12]

---

[9] E. Chirelstein, "Lady Elizabeth Pope: The Heraldic Body," in *Renaissance Bodies: The Human Figure in English Culture c.1540–1660*, ed. Lucy Gent and Nigel Llewellyn (London: Reaktion, 1990), 36–59, here 48.

[10] Almost all of Greville's works, including the sonnet sequence *Caelica*, were published posthumously.

[11] This iconographic mode is itself heraldic in the sense that, as Chirelstein emphasizes, the essentially heraldic images are "flat, schematised and immobile" ("Lady Elizabeth Pope," 39).

[12] Fulke Greville, *Certaine Learned and Elegant Workes of the Right Honorable Fulke Lord Brooke Written in His Youth, and Familiar Exercise with Sir Philip Sidney* (London, 1633).

The *Coronation* portrait and Elizabeth' armorial bearings, courtesy of the National Portrait Gallery, London, and the Newberry Library.[13]

Helen Hackett rightly sees the second line as "explicitly linking the blazon of a courtly mistress with the heraldic blazon."[14] Indeed, the metaphor of a quartered rose draws on the heraldic practice of dividing the field of a coat of arms into four sections (technical lingo terms it a "quarterly" partition). As explained by Nancy Vickers, the two objects of description—shield and body—are historically connected through the two early modern meanings of the term *blazon*: "first, a codified heraldic description of a shield, and, second, a codified poetic description of an object praised or blamed by a rhetorician-poet."[15] However, scholars have not addressed the significance of the *face* as the site of this linkage.

First of all, the face lends itself to the heraldic metaphor on a purely geometric level: consider, for example, Elizabeth's armorial bearings and the shape of her face in the best-known full-face portrait in coronation robes. The outline of a typical "heater" shield, with its elegant curves swooping from the wide top and meeting at the bottom point, resembles a mask that could be fitted onto a human

---

[13] Robert Cooke, "Armorial bearings of the kings and noble families of Great Britain from the reign of William the Conqueror to that of James I," Newberry Library, Case MS. F 0745, 1915.

[14] Helen Hackett, *Virgin Mother, Maiden Queen: Elizabeth I and the Cult of the Virgin Mary* (New York: St. Martin's Press, 1995), 168.

[15] Nancy J. Vickers, "'This heraldry in Lucrece' face'," *Poetics Today* 6 (1985): 171–84, here 175.

face.[16] Second, both Elizabeth's coat of arms and the Tudor Rose frequently include the royal crown that sits atop the shield or the flower in the same fashion as it appears above the queen's visage, thereby suggesting the treatment of heraldic images as a kind of face. Furthermore, the symmetrical quartering of a coat of arms is also compatible with the partition of the face—both natural, following the line of the nose and the imaginary line connecting the eyes, and artistic, often performed in preparatory sketches for drawing a portrait.[17]

The natural map of the "quartered" face, however, stands in contrast with the traditionally diagonal mirroring of the design of the quartered coat of arms (the imagery and colors of the bottom left segment, for instance, correspond to those in the top right). An imposition of the heraldic pattern onto a face inevitably reorganizes natural facial elements. Even more importantly, it inscribes the face with a new meaning. If a physiognomy serves as a marker of individuality, the metaphoric stamping of a face with a heraldic emblem, itself an important expression of early modern identity, leads either to veiling the natural features (thus closing up their own meaning) or superimposing one pattern upon the other. The naturally and culturally encapsulated identity and meaning of one's face, therefore, are either replaced or conjoined with those recorded in one's coat of arms. In England, a similar replacement was already taking place in the name of Reformation: Elizabeth's arms, for instance, were habitually used to designate her "absent / presence"; her emblem hung in the churches in place of religious imagery washed away by the iconoclastic wave.[18]

Consequently, the imposition of heraldry on the queen's face activates a complex interplay of two kinds of power: that of a shield and that of a face. When Sidney's Cupid wins the competition for the fairest armor because Stella's "face he makes his shield,"[19] he conjoins the two powers by cleverly exploiting Stella's beauty. As a piece of functional armor, however, long before its emblematic and symbolic roles became an end in themselves, a shield was meant both for an easy

---

[16] This particular shape is that of a classic "heater," the basic and most practical shape for a shield in a battle. On the evolution of the shapes of shields, see Rodney Dennys, *The Heraldic Imagination* (New York: Clarkson N. Potter, 1975), 43–44.

[17] Albrecht Dürer (1512), for instance, makes such partitioning in his drawings of human faces in his *'Dresden Sketchbook'*; his sketches were familiar to the Elizabethans from Haydock's translation of Lomazzo's treatise on painting. See *The Human Figure by Albrecht Dürer: The Complete 'Dresden Sketchbook,'* ed. Walter L. Strauss (New York: Dover, 1972), no. 110.

[18] In my use of this concept, I follow Mary Hazard, who adapted a phrase "absented presence" from Philip Sidney's *New Arcadia* to explore the politics and dynamics of presence and absence at Elizabeth's court. 'Present / absence' refers to the "physical presence of one who signals personal separation from foregrounded action," while 'absent / presence' indicates the "felt presence of one physically absent." See *Elizabethan Silent Language* (Lincoln: University of Nebraska Press, 2000), 236.

[19] *Astrophil and Stella* 13, line 10.

identification of the bearer and for protection of his body.[20] In response to the development of full-body armor, the early moderns have substituted the shield's primary protective function with a declarative one, and thus endowed the shield with a purely rhetorical power.[21] The face, however, exerts its own kind of command—and the queen's face, in particular, is immensely powerful, as confirmed by the records of Elizabeth's social interaction.[22] For this reason, the convergence of her shield and face has a potential to increase Elizabeth's power symbolically or alter it. It can combine the expressive and aesthetic power of the face and the inherent protective and rhetorical power of the shield—or replace the former with the latter, thereby deactivating the queen's ability to exercise her authority through the conventional use of her face. And insofar as, for a woman, that use is traditionally predicated on her beauty, while heraldry is predominantly a masculine domain, the superimposition of the two inevitably causes a gender-related shift in meaning. In this sense, the ambivalent potential of the complimentary imagery employed by Spenser and Greville mirrors the instability of numerous rhetorical moves made by Elizabeth herself and those who represented her, aiming to redeem the queen's female gender by either strengthening or replacing it with masculine characteristics.

Although heraldry, like genealogy, is said by some scholars to be gender-biased,[23] that statement is only a partial truth: the practice of quartering the arms often purports to represent heraldic inheritance without making distinction of gender.[24] Elizabeth's royal coat of arms, passed down to her from Edward III,[25] reflected the marital union of Edward II and Isabella of France in the emblematic representation of the two countries, pictured respectively on the four segments of her shield as lions on the red field and fleurs-de-lis on the blue

---

[20] See Vickers' summary of the place accorded to the coats of arms in Tudor England in "'The blazon of sweet beauty's best'," 104–5.

[21] The collateral existence of both the protective and rhetorical functions is evident, for instance, in the description of Sir Gawain's shield that bears imagery on both the inside and outside. The painted shields of the multiple characters of Spenser's pseudo-medieval *Faerie Queene* look back to the same tradition.

[22] For a detailed discussion of the rhetorical effect of Elizabeth's facial expressions during social interactions, see Anna Riehl, *The Face of Queenship: Early Modern Representations of Elizabeth I* (London and New York: Palgrave Macmillan, 2010).

[23] Vickers, for instance, quotes Lawrence Stone's statement about the preference given to the male line in the early modern genealogical and heraldic records ("'The blazon of sweet beauty's best'," 105).

[24] See the sections "Arms of ladies" and "Quarterings and marshaling" in the entry for "Heraldry" in *Encyclopedia Britannica* (*Encyclopædia Britannica Online*, searched 13 October 2006).

[25] Strictly speaking, Elizabeth's coat of arms is that of Henry IV, who modified the French quarters of Edward III's shield from fleur-de-lis semé to France Modern (i.e., reduced the number of fleurs-de-lis to three).

field. This union, however, was about a dozen generations away from that of Elizabeth's natural parents. Much closer to her was the nodal marriage of Henry Tudor and Elizabeth of York—the foundation of the Tudor dynasty that united the houses of Lancaster and York, symbolically represented by the superimposed red and white roses, white petals contained within red ones. While it was not featured on the shield itself, the Tudor Rose badge was a crucial dynastic signifier and was frequently incorporated into Elizabeth's arms. A substantial number of Elizabeth's portraits sport the Tudor roses either as props or as fabric patterns.[26] Variations of this floral symbol move from the corner of the portrait to the queen's person or hand and finally to the pattern on her dress. Spenser's implantation of the rose onto Elizabeth's face and, for instance, William Roger's depiction of the queen as *Rosa Electa*[27] exemplify two metaphoric applications of the Tudor Rose: implicitly, as Elizabeth's entire body, often represented by her red attire trimmed in white fur; and explicitly, as Elizabeth's face. Even though red and white are the traditional colors of ideal Renaissance beauty, visual representations may only hint at the use of heraldic metaphor of the queen's visage; coloring of Elizabeth's face in a precise Tudor-rose-like fashion would appear grotesque.[28] Not only does Spenser use the two hues of the Tudor rose to suggest Elizabeth's beauty, however, but he also makes a point of reminding us about the flower's historic significance. It is this choice that points to the political implications of the heraldic inscription.

The importance of this coexistence of the two roses in the queen's face is thrown into an even greater relief when, in *Henry VI, Part 3* (1595), Shakespeare traces the deathly floral symbolism on a face of a young man mistakenly killed by his own father in one of the hectic battles between the Yorkists and Lancastrians.

> The red rose and the white are on his face,
> The fatal colours of our striving houses;
> The one his purple blood right well resembles,
> The other his pale cheeks, methinks, presenteth.
> Wither one rose, and let the other flourish—
> If you contend, a thousand lives must wither. (2.5. 97–102)

As King Henry's comment links the red and white roses with the morbidity of blood and paleness, it marks both with fatality. Yet Henry sees only one solution

---

[26] For a survey of the imagery of roses (especially eglantine roses) associated with Elizabeth, see Roy Strong, *The Cult of Elizabeth: Elizabethan Portraiture and Pageantry* (London: Pimlico, 1999), 68–73.

[27] Roger's engraving is reproduced in Roy Strong, *Portraits of Queen Elizabeth I* (Oxford: Clarendon Press, 1963), 116, fig. E.29.

[28] For a discussion of a variety issues surrounding representation of Elizabeth's face in portraiture, see Riehl, *The Face of Queenship*.

to the deadly contention: one rose must "wither" so that the remaining one can "flourish." He is blind to the possibility of a "fair conjunction," a floral hybrid effected later by Shakespeare's newly crowned Henry VII (*Richard III*, 5.8.20).

Viewed apart from its dynastic significance, metaphorical treatment of the queen's face as a rose is deeply traditional: as an emblem of virginity in general, and the Virgin Mary in particular, it evokes Elizabeth's sacred virtues; as a flower of Venus,[29] it carries conventional Petrarchan connotations. In fact, Spenser's praise of Elizabeth's cheeks ("The Red rose meddled with the White yfere, / In either cheek depeincten lively cheer") is in itself completely conventional.[30] It is E. K.'s annotation that makes Spenser's metaphor truly heraldic. Greville, however, makes use of heraldic terminology and thus eliminates the need for a gloss: "The red, and white Rose quarter'd in her face." These explicit demarcations of both poets' heraldic intentions, however, are accompanied by a curious choice of verbs loaded with hidden ambivalence. If "meddled" suggests mixing, it also recalls contention, not in the fatal militant sense suggested by King Henry, but perhaps referring to the ongoing turmoil at court generated by and around the queen. If to "quarter" may mean to "station, place, or lodge in a particular place" (*OED*), the application of this verb to the Tudor badge signals a necessarily heraldic signification and thus seems to refer to the partition of a coat of arms. However, this division also evokes the horrendous method of execution by quartering the body, still employed during the Elizabethan age and sanctioned by the queen.[31] Even though the context constrains these disturbing connotations, they cannot be entirely effaced.

Both of these latent meanings echo within early modern mentality. When Shakespeare arrives at the subject, he famously stages a struggle between "beauty's red and virtue's white" in Lucrece's face.[32] Likewise, Greville's allusion to quartering belongs to the genre in which some scholars see an artistic expression of a man's violent impulses in relation to a woman: the aforementioned poetic practice of blazon, a method of description that catalogues the parts of a woman's body. Vickers argues that this approach is rooted in the myth of Diana and Actaeon; the male poet finds himself in the position of a voyeur who stands in danger of punishment by dismembering, and "hence he projects scat-

---

[29] Strong, *The Cult of Elizabeth*, 68.

[30] His friend Sidney, however, while drawing on the same tradition, uses unmistakable heraldic terminology that doubles as a conventional metaphor ('gules,' 'field') when he depicts Stella's rosy cheeks: "roses gules [red] are borne in silver field." See *Astrophil and Stella* 13, line 11.

[31] The above meanings of both verbs are drawn from the *OED*.

[32] *The Rape of Lucrece*, lines 65, 68.

tering onto [the female he attempts to describe] through the process of fetishistic overdetermination."[33]

Enumeration of parts, however, is what emphatically *does not* happen in Spenser's and Greville's descriptions of their female sovereign. The vision of Elizabeth's face is limited, except for a brief reference to her eyes, to naming of the two colors, red and white, and an indication of their—perhaps somewhat uneasy—arrangement on her countenance. We are meant to see a few vibrantly red or pink configurations—scarlet lips and rosy cheeks—on the delicate pale background of Elizabeth's complexion. In other words, unlike a blazon proper, this vision is not created by division. And yet the heraldic metaphor implies certain restrictions: if Elizabeth's face is a shield, as Greville's sonnet suggests, the field must be marked by the lines of partition; if her cheeks are Tudor roses, as in Spenser's eclogue, their shape and distribution of colors must conform to the badge whose iconography is evoked in E. K.'s commentary. Greville, in particular, is eager to allude to the royal coat of arms rather than stop at the floral badge, as Spenser does. In effect, Greville repaints Elizabeth's arms, substituting for the French and English quarters those of the Plantagenet Houses of Lancaster and York. Cultural connotations of quartering and reinscription of the face in these poems imply an intrusion. Admittedly, figurative language makes it seem like a very mild sort of violence, insofar as a prudent reader stops short of literalizing the metaphors. Nonetheless, these tropes convey the poets' desire to inscribe meaning onto the monarch's face, and in their zeal to conflate a compliment to a woman and a tribute to a sovereign, they brand her countenance with imagery that exceeds the bounds of harmless flattery and spills into the dangerous waters of infringement. Greville was hardly evoking the horrific wounds that could be inflicted on the queen's face by quartering, but both he and Spenser could have imagined a milder violation of Elizabeth's visage: repainting it cosmetically or even tattooing it in the fashion of the Picts whose habits of self-decoration fascinated the Elizabethans.[34] However, this codified violence is not only hidden but naturalized because both poets sensibly focus their heraldic allusions on a flower with symbolic meanings pertaining both to power and beauty.

---

[33] Nancy J. Vickers, "Diana Described: Scattered Woman and Scattered Rhyme," in *Writing and Sexual Difference*, ed. Elizabeth Abel (Chicago: University of Chicago Press, 1982), 95–110, here 104.

[34] According to Fenja Gunn, "The Picts covered themselves in coloured images of birds and animals . . . [as] a means of establishing a tribal identity and, within the tribal unit, of distinguishing social rank. . . . During the Roman occupation, when the ancient Britons adopted conventional clothes, they transferred the painted designs of birds and animals from their bodies to their shields, and eventually these images formed the basis for heraldic devices." See *The Artificial Face: A History of Cosmetics* (New York: Hippocrene, 1975), 53–54. In this sense, the Tudor Rose inscribed on the face is a regression to the tribal habits of the Picts.

Furthermore, even as it flatters Elizabeth's complexion, historical and cultural extensions of the image of the Tudor Rose complicate its use as a metaphor for the queen's face. In both texts, besides the poetic convenience, the focus on this flower emphasizes Elizabeth's Englishness. Although she never gave up on her inherited claim to France, including it in her formal title and persistently incorporating fleurs-de-lis in her iconography, it was the Tudor Rose that symbolized her personal genealogical history. Contrasting herself to her predecessor Mary Tudor, whose mother was Spanish, Elizabeth took pride in being "mere English" and derived much of her popularity from such "pure" origins. The iconographic use of bicolor roses, therefore, boosted national pride. At the same time, the enclosure of the white petals by the red ones asserted predominance of the masculine over the feminine, a union realized through containment of a woman's political value as a means of buttressing a man's claim to the throne.

The heraldic stamp itself, therefore, is an encoded statement on the interplay of royal gender and power. As this stamp is imprinted on the queen's face, her visage emerges as a site of ambivalence and contention between her womanhood and authority, between the feeble flattery to her fleeting beauty and the acute awareness of her ever-present political identity. Every transformation of Elizabeth's features into metaphor rewrites their meaning and is thus in some way intrusive. Even more importantly, the laudatory words that mean to put the woman's beauty in service of her dynastic magnificence end up carrying out an implied violence by forcing a symbolic political pattern onto her natural features. The resulting empowerment of the face, however flattering to Elizabeth the queen, divests it of its multiple rhetorical uses. Quartering implies a simplification, a reduction of its inherent potential to mean: her quartered shield, after all, contains only two distinct parts. Rewriting Elizabeth's features in heraldic terms also curbs the queen's personal and symbolic control of her face; it closes up all of its meanings except two: her rose-like beauty and, even more insistently, the dynastic legitimacy of her power. It is heraldic inscription, however, that stands out as the most ingenuous and meaningful image in the host of attempts to describe the queen's face. In its succinct recovery of the blazon's original function, that of recording the demarcations of a shield, the heraldic metaphor charts the symbolic lineaments of monarchy onto the natural face of a woman.

In all its audacity, the heraldic trope cannot be extricated from the ongoing project of legitimizing Elizabeth as a queen. In advancing that project, albeit in contradictory terms, the creators of these intricate poetic figurations contributed to the exercise of one of the most vital of her sovereign arts, that of asserting her royal authority as an authentic member of the Tudor line.

Elizabeth I and State Terror in Sixteenth-Century Ireland

Vincent P. Carey

As Elizabeth Tudor began her state procession from the Tower of London on 14 January 1559 for her coronation the next day at Westminster Abbey, few could have guessed the momentous events that would unfold over her long reign. Between her coronation in 1559 and death on 24 March 1603, this female monarch not only bested Spain, the superpower of the western world, but also supervised the conquest of Ireland—an ambition held by her rather distantly related ancestors, dating back to the twelfth century. There was much uncertainty as to her abilities, legitimacy, and intentions in January 1559. Advanced Protestants hoped she would act as the equivalent of the biblical Deborah and restore the true church, while committed Catholics viewed her as illegitimate, quite literally the bastard child of the scandalous Anne Boleyn. We can be certain that Elizabeth gave little thought and knew next to nothing about the kingdom her ancestors claimed on the other side of the Irish sea. By the time the aged queen "turned her head to the wall and her eyes to God" in March 1603, however, Elizabeth had become quite knowledgeable on the subject and had supervised—admittedly from a distance—the brutal subjugation of its native lords and people.

My central concern in this essay is to examine this process, more specifically the relationship between Elizabeth, the focal point of the policy apparatus, and the unfolding subjugation of Ireland. One central aspect of this operation was the unleashing of an increasingly brutal war that, at its height in the latter half of 1602, had all the characteristics of a genocidal fury. This intense violence, in fact, had a slow but steady evolution from the 1570s onward. As insurgency followed insurgency and religious hatred heightened the stakes, international intrigue and eventual Spanish intervention made desperate the need to crush Irish opposition.

Despite a plethora of studies on sixteenth-century Ireland, starting with Nicholas Canny's 1976 seminal work *The Elizabethan Conquest of Ireland: A Pattern Established*[1] and including studies of the army, constitutional politics,

---

[1] Nicholas Canny, *The Elizabethan Conquest of Ireland: A Pattern Established* (Hassocks, Sussex: Harvester Press, 1976).

and English colonial ideology, few have considered the attitude of the "supposed" prince of the realm to this mounting cycle of insurgency and counter-insurgency violence.[2] This situation is hardly surprising. Irish historians have, to a large extent, been more concerned with the situation in Ireland. Despite the last thirty years of work, there is still so much we do not know and still so much to do. We have not comprehensively dealt with the relationship between the ruler in London and events on the ground in Ireland. More problematically, many Irish historians have, at least until recently, been hesitant to discuss this topic lest they view the horrendous violence unleashed in Ireland in the name of Elizabeth anachronistically. The reasons for this avoidance are complex, and I have alluded to them elsewhere.[3] In so doing, however, Irish historical scholarship runs the risk of misrepresenting the nature of the process by which Ireland was finally conquered, and consequently, leaving less comprehensible the legacy of bitterness inherited by later generations. This is especially problematic when our language is dominated by notions of "reform" government and governors and when the end result of the conquest is described as the political "integration" of Ireland into the Stuart kingdom and the British state by 1603. This is not to say that the language of politics and constitutionalism has no place in our narrative; however, it should not serve to "normalize" a process that was accompanied by unprecedented brutality, which in the last years of the Nine Years War saw scorched-earth tactics, massive population dislocation, and massacre as regular forms of state terror in Ireland.

Was Elizabeth aware of the nature of the brutal war that unfolded in her name? And, if she was, what was her attitude towards it? Did she share her military commanders' attitude towards the Irish? How much of her outlook was expressed in her copious correspondence?

Elizabeth's first notable encounter with Ireland came early in the reign during the lord deputyship of Sir Thomas Radcliff, the earl of Sussex. Though a substantial courtier in his own right, Sussex had committed himself to solving the problem of the "reformation" of Ireland by a three-pronged strategy of colonization in the Gaelic Midlands: secure the borders of the Pale (the area of concentrated English jurisdiction), extend English government by the use of provincial councils, and finally control Ulster through the subjugation of the great Gaelic lord, Shane O'Neill,

---

[2] The one exception to this neglect is the thought-provoking article by Hiram Morgan, "'Never any realm worse governed': Queen Elizabeth and Ireland," *Transactions of the Royal Historical Society*, n.s. 14 (2004): 295–308.

[3] Vincent P. Carey, "'What pen can paint and tears atone?': Mountjoy's Scorched Earth Campaign," in *The Battle of Kinsale*, ed. Hiram Morgan (Bray, Co. Wicklow: Wordwell, 2004), 205–16.

"Sean an Diomas." Sussex's efforts over the period from 1558 to 1564 were to prove not only futile but also counterproductive.[4]

One of the unanticipated consequences of Sussex's military efforts was a trip to court by O'Neill orchestrated by the Old English dynast Gerald Fitzgerald, the eleventh earl of Kildare. The submission of O'Neill was one of the most dramatic face-to-face encounters between Elizabeth and Gaelic Ireland. Contemporary accounts of the event in January 1561 focused on the "exotic" nature of Shane and his followers: "gazed at with no less admiration . . . than nowadays they do them of China or America."[5] Historians commenting on this event have generally focused on O'Neill's political demands and issues.[6] What is often passed over in this incidence is the drama of incommensurability between the two parties. Preceded by the spectacle of a troop of Irish soldiers, or galloglass, Kildare led the entourage into the queen's presence. The earl's kinsman Shane O'Neill followed and performed his abject submission to the astonishment and delight of the assembled court and its distinguished visitors.[7] Yet the court's entertainment derived primarily from the experience of what Camden recorded as O'Neill's bizarre "howling." For Elizabeth and her court, the spectacle of O'Neill and his military entourage represented foreignness, an otherness made worse by her inability to understand a word of the language her supposed Irish subject was speaking.[8]

---

[4] Ciaran Brady, *The Chief Governors: The Rise and Fall of Reform Government in Ireland* (Cambridge: Cambridge University Press, 1994); Steven Ellis, *Ireland in the Age of the Tudors 1447–1603: English Expansion and the End of Gaelic Rule* (London: Longman, 1998); Colm Lennon, *Sixteenth-Century Ireland: The Incomplete Conquest* (Dublin: Gill & Macmillan, 2005).

[5] Camden's *History*, quoted in D.B. Quinn, *The Elizabethans and the Irish* (Ithaca, NY, and Washington, DC: Folger Shakespeare Library, 1966), 152–53.

[6] Ciaran Brady, *Shane O'Neill* (Dundalk: Historical Association of Ireland, Dundalgan Press, 1996), 37–38; Ellis, *Ireland*, 277–81, and Canny, *Elizabethan Conquest*, 40.

[7] William Camden, *Annales Rerum Anglicarum et Hibernicarum Regnante Elizabetha, ad Annum Salutis 1589* (London, 1615), 78–79; also, A.F. Vossen, ed., *Two Bokes of the Histories of Ireland, compiled by Edmunde Campion* (Assen: Van Gorcum, 1963), 139; John Izon, *Sir Thomas Stucley, 1525–78, Traitor Extraordinary* (London: A. Melrose, 1956). See also Vincent Carey, *Surviving the Tudors: The 'Wizard' Earl of Kildare and English Rule in Ireland, 1537–1587* (Dublin: Four Courts Press, 2002), 117–18, and Brady, *Shane O'Neill*, 43–47.

[8] As Valerie McGowan-Doyle notes, this lack of a basic knowledge of Ireland's cultural makeup even extended to the Old English. She relates the episode in 1562 when Elizabeth asked Christopher St. Lawrence, seventh baron of Howth (a leading member of a delegation of colonial magnates to court) if he actually spoke English! McGowan-Doyle's paper "Elizabeth's Role in Elizabethan Imperialism In Ireland," read to the Queen Elizabeth I Society in Houston, March 2006, lays out a clear research agenda for the future study of the topic of Elizabeth and Ireland.

This general lack of commensurability made the resort to violence much more acceptable in the effort to subdue Gaelic Ireland. With the return to Ulster of an emboldened and increasingly reckless O'Neill, Lord Deputy Sussex came to rely on the use of martial law as an economical means of reducing both O'Neill and the Gaelic following his aggressive policies had stirred up. Martial law was cost-effective because the commissioners were licensed to collect the profits of their work. Commissions of martial law "legally" entitled the bearer to a third of the moveable goods and possessions of the dead "traitors." According to David Edwards, "this acted as an incentive to slaughter: the more 'suspected traitors' the commissioners killed, the more traitors' goods they and their followers received."[9] It was unlikely that these military men would make exemplary neighbors or that they could convince the natives of the pacifistic and "reform" intent behind the various colonization schemes to be attempted in Elizabeth's name in the coming decades.

Sir Henry Sidney, the lord deputy who succeeded Sussex in October 1565, shared his predecessor's commitment to colonization as part of a wider project for the self-financing reform of Ireland. Envious of the Spanish example in America and inspired by the works of classical writers, Sidney entertained colonial fantasies that were to be tested in Gaelic Ireland. The deputy envisaged the establishment of colonies of Englishmen throughout the country to serve, as Nicholas Canny puts it, as "oases of civility in a desert of barbarism."[10] Three major colonial initiatives were planned during his administration: Sir Thomas Smith's colony of Ards in County Down, the first earl of Essex's scheme in Clandeboy in the same area, and the settlement of Sir Warham St. Leger in Cork. All three schemes were abysmal failures. The experience of these settlers is significant, however, for the long-term development of English colonization and the story of the escalating violence of the so-called Elizabethan period. In each instance, initial fantasies of Roman-style colonies quickly faded as the settlers struggled to expel a hostile indigenous population. Frustrated by their own inability to do the necessary agricultural work and infuriated by constant resistance, the settlers lashed out at the natives. The result was outbursts of slaughter like the first earl of Essex's extermination in 1575 of six hundred MacDonnells, mostly women and children, on Rathlin Island.[11] The significance of this event and others like it

---

[9] David Edwards, "Beyond Reform: Martial Law and the Tudor Reconquest of Ireland," *History Ireland* 5.2 (Summer 1997): 16–22, here 18. These 'entrepreneurial' tendencies were endorsed as a complement to reform for most of the sixteenth century. See Ciaran Brady, "The Captains' Games: Army and Society in Elizabethan Ireland," in *A Military History of Ireland*, ed. Thomas Bartlett and Keith Jeffrey (Cambridge: Cambridge University Press, 1996), 135–59.

[10] Canny, *Elizabethan Conquest*, 67.

[11] For the failure of these schemes, see Canny, *Elizabethan Conquest*, chap. 4, esp. 120–21, and Lennon, *Sixteenth-Century Ireland*, 278–84.

lay in the fact that, increasingly, some New English officials articulated the view that the Gaelic Irish, and in this instance Mac Donnell Scots, were an unreasonable people and that normal ethical restraints were unnecessary when dealing with them. It needs to be noted here that the Queen herself commended Essex for the Rathlin Island venture.[12] While Essex made clear that his captains Drake and Norris, who had carried out the slaughter in July 1575, were acting against intruding Scots and taking a castle on the island by storm, he also admitted that the troops, in their frenzy, moved on to hunt women and children who had sought refuge in the caves and on the cliffs on the island. Essex's terse comment that "Things do fall out otherwise than was looked for" was an acknowledgment of the incongruity of slaughtering non-combatants in flight. Yet, at the same time, he called for letters of commendation and an invitation from the queen to reward his subordinates for the deed.[13]

As for things falling "out otherwise" than intended, Sidney's "programmatic" policies to extend English rule by curbing the power of the English-Irish or Old-English nobles also had proven disastrous. By encouraging colonizing enterprises in the English-Irish regions through the process of searching out defective titles and by cracking down on the feudal forces and exactions of the feudal lords, he had managed to provoke a rebellion in 1569 in Munster that combined the hitherto inveterate enemies of the Butler and Desmond houses with an extensive array of their Gaelic allies.[14] Luckily for the brothers of "Black Tom," the earl of Ormond, Elizabeth's favorite and distant relation, the Butlers were to be pardoned in the field upon their submission. Elizabeth would repeat this pattern throughout her reign, especially when it involved the English-Irish. If the traditional nobility in her Irish realm could be persuaded to submit, she proved continuously willing, at least until 1580, to pardon their offenses, even including their raising of the banner of rebellion. Elizabeth, a social conservative by nature, had no desire to eliminate the ancient nobility of her putative Irish realm.

Yet at the same time, Elizabeth and her council seemed unperturbed by the lengths Sir Humphrey Gilbert, her military governor in Munster, went in order to defeat the more long-lasting and stubborn Gaelic Irish resistance in the same first Desmond rebellion in Munster. Led by James Fitzmaurice Fitzgerald, a cousin of the earl of Desmond and the captain of his forces, the insurgents adopted the badge of a religious crusade on behalf of the restoration of Catholicism. Gilbert went about the task of suppressing this insurgency with a systematic use of scorched-earth tactics and the adoption of a self-conscious theatre of cruelty

---

[12] "Elizabeth to Essex," 12 Aug. 1575, *Calendar of Carew Manuscripts*, ed. J. S. Brewer and William Bullen, 6 vols. (London: Longmans, Green, 1867–1873), 2:21.

[13] "Essex to Privy Council," 31 July 1575, in *Calendar of State Papers Ireland: Tudor Period, 1571–1575*, rev. ed., ed. Mary O'Dowd (Kew: Public Record Office, Irish Manuscript Commission, 2000), 880–82.

[14] Lennon, *Sixteenth-Century Ireland*, 212–18; Ellis, *Ireland*, 295–98.

in order to leave "nothyng of the enemies in safetie, whiche he could possibilie waste, or consume."[15] He specifically targeted the Gaelic "churls," the subordinate labouring classes, "men and women alike 'so that the killing of theim by the sworde was the waie to kill the menne of warre by famine'."[16] His inventive cruelty, specifically targeting the Gaelic leadership, used terror tactics like the one "infamously" described by his pamphleteer Thomas Churchyard:

> the heddes of all those . . . which were killed in the daie, should be cutte of from their bodies and brought to the place where he [Gilbert] incamped at night, and should there bee laied on the ground by each side of the waie . . . ledying into his owne tente so that none could come into his tente for any cause but commanly he must passe through a lane of heddes . . . and yet did it bring greate *terrour* to the people when thei sawe the heddes of their dede fathers, brothers, children, kinsfolke and friendes, lye on the grounde before their faces, as they came to speake with the said collonell.[17]

Gilbert was obviously conscious of the efficacy of terror and clearly understood its value both as practice and as a form of state "theatre." His results were widely praised by the administration, and Sidney knighted him, claiming that the effectiveness of his tactics allowed for a *tabula rasa* reconstruction of Munster: "the iron is now hot to receive what print shall be stricken on it."[18]

Though clearly an innovator, Gilbert resorted to "Greate terrour,"[19] an approach that would become the norm in the decades following as international intrigue and Irish rebellion combined to create an inflammatory mix, especially after the issuance of the papal bull that excommunicated Elizabeth in 1570. In addition to politico-religious conflict, a new and heightened ferocity in English treatment of the Gaelic Irish emerged with the colonization efforts of the 1570s. Nicholas Canny attributes this departure to the influence of Renaissance civilization theory upon the colonists who believed themselves absolved from ethical reproach when dealing with cultural inferiors. This absolution from the standard codes of military conduct was reinforced by an emerging pamphlet literature that purported to provide the evidence for the barbarism of Irish society

---

[15] Quoted in Rory Rapple, "Justifying Violence in Elizabethan Ireland: The Case of Sir Humphrey Gilbert," a paper read to the Yale Genocide Studies Program Seminar, 30 September 2004.

[16] Rapple, "Justifying Violence."

[17] Thomas Churchyard, *Churchyarde's Choise*, quoted in Canny, *Elizabethan Conquest*, 122 (emphasis added).

[18] Lennon, *Sixteenth-Century Ireland*, 217; Richard Bagwell, the nineteenth-century historian, comments that Sidney "praised him [Gilbert] to the skies, and seems not to have had the slightest misgiving about the wisdom or morality of his conduct." See *Ireland under the Tudors*, 3 vols. (London: Longmans, Green, 1885–1890), 2:168.

[19] Bagwell, *Ireland*, 2:168.

and culture.[20] Confirmation for this view of Gaelic society is evident in one of the period's most significant published works on Ireland, John Derricke's *Image of Irelande*, published in 1581.[21] Dedicated to Philip Sidney, the work was a panegyric for Henry Sidney's Irish campaigns and was more than likely composed during the deputy's last and pointedly unsuccessful tour of duty from 1575 to 1578. Symbolically represented by the "woodkerne," the Irish are cast as, by nature, addicted to rebellion and destruction. As a symbol of anarchy, the kerne, or lightly armed footsoldier, labeled a "pestiferous generation," is dehumanized and demonized. Advancing an argument for severe brutality like the terror tactics of a Gilbert or the savage war ordered by Sidney against the Gaelic lords of the Midlands, Derricke rhetorically asks: "How then may man have company with this hurtful generation? Or sons of men with noisome worms enjoy their consolation?"[22] Significantly, Derricke's assessment of the bestial nature of Irish rebels and his endorsement of the most extreme forms of state terror against them precede by almost twenty years the similarly extreme views of tracts like Edmund Spenser's *View*. Certainly by the mid-1590s, the poet Spenser endorsed the outlook that the Irish were by nature beyond the common law and that only by the extermination of their ruling elites, the starvation of the masses, and the brutality of martial law could they be brought from their "delight of licentious barbarism, unto the love of goodness and civility."[23]

In truth, Spenser's apprenticeship in the process of extending English rule in Ireland was quite bloody. His first service was as secretary to the notorious Lord Grey de Wilton, the lord deputy assigned the task of putting down the second Desmond rebellion. Bursting forth in 1579 with the return of James Fitzmaurice Fitzgerald from exile in Catholic Europe, the insurgency was eventually joined by the English-Irish magnate the earl of Desmond and his Gaelic vassals smarting from years of government harassment and encroaching colonization. The stakes in this struggle were raised even higher when the Geraldines and their allies were aided by the landing of papal forces in the south of Ireland in late 1579. This landing represented a key ideological development in Irish history, symbolized by the raising of the papal banner over the fort at *Dun an Óir* or Smerwick, near Dingle in County Kerry.

Though much ink has been wasted on the fruitless question as to whether Spenser was at Smerwick or not when Grey encircled it in November 1580, it is far more important, as I have argued elsewhere, to consider the ensuing act

---

[20] Quoted in Canny, *Elizabethan Conquest*, 127.
[21] John Derricke, *The Image of Irelande* (London, 1581), repr., ed. D. B. Quinn (Belfast: Blackstaff, 1985).
[22] Derricke, *Image of Irelande*, 185.
[23] Ciaran Brady, "Spenser's Irish Crisis: Humanism and Experience in the 1590s," *Past and Present* 111 (1986): 17–49, here 24–25.

of slaughter and the official and semi-official reactions that it elicited.[24] In early November, with the arrival of a long-awaited English flotilla, Grey's siege and bombardment of the fort began. Negotiations with the garrison began on the evening of the ninth and, according to the English sources, culminated in an unconditional surrender on the tenth.[25] On the morning of 10 November, Grey and his officers watched as the enemy officers marched forward to surrender "trayling theyr ensigns rolled."[26] The lord deputy then sent one of his officers and company into the fort to ensure that the rest of the garrison had laid down their arms. Having ascertained that the weapons of the enemy were taken care of, i.e. by assigning officers to guard both them and the booty, he ordered his bands drawn up and sent them to execute the defenseless prisoners. According to Hooker, "capteine Raleigh together with capteine macworth, who had the ward of that daie, entered into the castell & made a great slaughter, manie or the most part of them being put to the sword."[27] Despite the efforts of the officers, the soldiers, "pumped up" as they would have to have been to kill up to six hundred unarmed individuals, eventually lost control and pillaged the fort and their victims. The intensity of the moment after the surrender and securing of the fort was noted by Grey when he describes how "I sent straight certin gentlemen in to see their weapons and armures layed downe & to gard ye munition & victaile there lefte for spoile. Then putt I in certeyn bandes who straight fell to execution. There were 600 slayne; munition & vittaile great store, though much wasted through the disorder of ye souldier, *w[hi]ch in yt furie could not bee helped*."[28] On the restoration of order, the bodies were disposed of, mostly by being thrown over the cliff.

As indefensible as these actions seem today, viewed in the context of the European wars of the age the killing itself and the numbers involved are unremarkable in terms of contemporary military engagements and religiously inspired outrages. Nor would the treatment of the Irish prisoners collected in the fort strike contemporary commentators as shocking: the prisoners as well as the women

---

[24] This subject is treated at greater length in Vincent P. Carey, "Atrocity and History: Sir Arthur Grey, Edmund Spenser and the Slaughter at Smerwick (1580)," in *Age of Atrocity: Violence and Political Conflict in Early Modern Ireland*, ed. David Edwards, Pádraig Lenihan, and Clodagh Tait (Dublin: Four Courts Press, 2005), 79–94. Unfortunately, the present essay was written and delivered at the annual meeting of the Queen Elizabeth I Society before this volume was available. The introduction by the editors excellently covers similar topics.

[25] "Grey to Elizabeth," 12 Nov. 1580 (P.R.O. S.P. 63/78/29). See also the vivid account in John Pope-Hennessy, *Sir Walter Ralegh in Ireland* (London: K. Paul, Trench, & Co., 1883), 207–11.

[26] "Grey to Elizabeth," 12 Nov. 1580.

[27] John Hooker, "The Supplie of This Irish Chronicle Continued from the Death of King Henrie the Eight, 1546 Untill This Present Yeare 1586," in Raphael Holinshed, *The Second Volume of Chronicles* (London, 1586), 171.

[28] Hooker, "Supplie," 171 (emphasis added).

and children camp followers were simply hanged. The treatment of the Catholic priests who were captured in the fort would not seem notable in the Irish context either. At Smerwick, the Catholic prisoners were kept alive for a day, interrogated, tortured by having their bones broken by a blacksmith's hammer, and finally hanged from the wall of the fort.[29]

For an advanced Protestant like Grey, however, these actions were excusable because he saw himself battling the forces of the Antichrist, and his "success" against the forces of the Pope could be understood only in terms of divine will.[30] Writing days after the event on 28 November, Grey asserted that the English success against the foreign force was not the result of their own efforts "but of the providence and mighty power of god."[31]

This rhetoric of "deliverance" is also evident in Queen Elizabeth's letter of reply and congratulation to Grey written on 12 December 1580:

> As the most happie successe youe have latly had against certaine invad[e]rs sent by the Pope, contayned in yo[u]r l[ette]res brought unto us by our servant [Edward] Denny doth incomparably shew the greatnes of God's love and favor towards us; so your care and paine in following the same and courage in execucon thereof deserveth great thancks and commencions at our hands.[32]

Elizabeth intended, in this letter, no pun with the use of "execucon," and not only approved of the action but in fact demanded to know why the officers had been saved. Understanding full well the message sent by an act of terror, she demanded to know why the entire garrison was not punished or reserved for punishment by the crown:

> ... a principal should receive punishment before an accessory: which would have served for a terror to such as may be hereafter drawn to be executioners of so wicked an enterprise, when they should hear that as well the heads as the inferiors had received punishment according to their demerits.[33]

---

[29] John Copinger, *The Theatre of Catholique and Protestant Religion, ..., Wherein the Zealous Catholic May Plainelie See the Manifest Truth, Perspicuitie, Euident Foundations and Demonstrations of the Catholique Religion: Together with the Motiues and Causes Why He Should Perseuer Therin ... Written by I.C Student in Diuinitie* (Saint-Omer, 1620), 578–79. For the most recent and important study of the construct of martyrdom in this context, see Clodagh Tait, "Adored for Saints: Catholic Martyrdom in Ireland c. 1560–1655," *Journal of Early Modern History* 5 (2001): 128–59.

[30] Carey, "Atrocity and History."

[31] "Grey to the Lord Treasurer," 28 Nov. 1580 (B.L. Add. MS. 3392); on Grey's Puritanism and Smerwick, see Richard McCabe, *Spenser's Monstrous Regiment: Elizabethan Ireland and the Poetics of Difference* (Oxford: Oxford University Press, 2002), 83–89.

[32] "Elizabeth to Grey," 12 Dec. 1580," transcribed in Pope-Hennessy, *Sir Walter Raleigh*, 212–14.

[33] "Elizabeth to Grey," 12 Dec. 1580.

Rather than being unaware of the brutality carried out in her name, Elizabeth not only knew but also approved of the elimination of those she considered rebels and invaders by any means possible and even accepted the utility of acts of extreme "terror"—a word she and her servitors frequently used—to weaken resistance or to prevent a repeat offence. Despite William Camden's later claim in the *Annales* that Elizabeth detested this massacre, he endorsed the official claim that the slaughter was necessary on the grounds of enemy strength. He also wrote that, as a conscious act of terrorization,

> it was concluded against the minde of the lord deputie who shed teares, that the captaines should be saved, and the rest promiscously put to the sword *for a terrour*, and that the Irish should be hanged; which was presently performed: Yet the Queene wished rather it had beene left undone detesting from her heart the cruelty though necessary against those that yeelded themselves, hardly did she allow of the reasons of the slaughter comitted.[34]

Camden's somewhat convoluted and retrospective assessment that Elizabeth detested acts of state cruelty, though recognizing them as necessary, is one that has appealed to historians ever since. Represented as a moderate in matters of religion[35] and variously indifferent, fiscally conservative, and conventional in terms of the Irish situation, Elizabeth is frequently portrayed as functioning as a "brake" on the aggressive policies of her lord deputies and as either opposed or even hostile to the radical military solutions of many of her New English officers on the ground in Ireland.[36] And while it is certain that Elizabeth's fiscal conservatism, traditionalism in terms of the role of the feudal aristocracy, and erratic support for expensive "programmes" of government expansion served to frustrate any effort to effectively conquer Ireland in a timely manner, it seems clear to me that Elizabeth was not adverse to the application of state violence when she deemed that the situation warranted it.

Yet, much to the frustration of the New English soldiers and administrators on the ground, Elizabeth was also willing to "pardon" opponents especially if the immediate danger had passed and the opportunity for cost-cutting presented

---

[34] Quoted in William Camden, *Annales or, the History of the Most Renowned and Victorious Princesse Elizabeth,* trans. R. N. (London: Thomas Harper for Benjamin Fisher, 1635), 215 (emphasis added).

[35] The best syntheses of the vast scholarship on Elizabeth and her reign are David Loades, *Elizabeth I* (London: Hambledon & London, 2003); Carole Levin, *The Reign of Elizabeth I* (New York: Palgrave, 2002); and Wallace MacCaffrey, *Elizabeth I* (London: Edward Arnold, 1993).

[36] The most sustained treatment of Elizabeth's reign that pays extended attention to Ireland is Wallace MacCaffrey, *Elizabeth I: War and Politics, 1588–1603* (Princeton: Princeton University Press, 1992), especially Part V.

itself. As war with Spain turned from cold to hot, especially in the period after the Armada, Elizabeth and her beleaguered isle needed to marshal resources because of commitments in the Low Countries, in France, and on the high seas. Reducing commitments in Ireland meant that often pardons in the field were the cheapest way to temporarily smother the flames.

This approach did not necessarily weaken Elizabeth's authority or diminish her sense of monarchical honor. Viewing both punishment and pardon as the purview of the monarch, Elizabeth wrote to Thomas Butler, the earl of Ormond, in late December 1597 authorizing him to allow the submission of the increasingly dangerous Hugh O'Neill, the earl of Tyrone, who had been goaded into intrigue with Spain and open resistance by the machinations of the New English administration in Dublin. In this letter, Elizabeth reminded Ormond that she was "not so alienated from hearkening to such submissions as may tend to the sparing effusion of Christian blood," yet she warned him that "traitors" were to be submissive and penitent, not coming in to her as if "one prince did treat with another." She cautioned the earl to avoid in the ceremony the language of peace and war and instead to reinforce the rhetoric of "rebellion in them and mercy in us."[37] Alternating between force and mercy, Elizabeth perceived that monarchical honor demanded the humbling of Gaelic ethnic pride. If this contrite groveling was not forthcoming, she warned Ormond: "we will cast off our sense of pity or compassion and upon what price so ever prosecute them to the last hour."[38]

Elizabeth's flexible approach to the infliction of pain on her opponents was based on her perceived financial exigencies and on her sense of a "calculus of honor."[39] If disaster could be averted, money saved, and her honor maintained, the queen was more than willing to put the brakes to the failed programs or the draconian tactics of her senior officials in Ireland. And as England's foreign entanglements mounted and its geopolitical isolation increased due to open war with Spain, Elizabeth's "stop-and-go" tactics might have made sense; however, for many of her male subordinates in Ireland and the "hawks" at court, the monarch's obvious aging and seeming vacillation only reinforced their frustration and disenchantment, a disenchantment that sometimes expressed itself in misogynistic terms.[40] Her failure to follow through with support for outright conquest,

---

[37] "Elizabeth to Thomas Butler, earl of Ormond," 29 Dec. 1597, in *Letters of Queen Elizabeth*, ed. G. B. Harrison (New York: Funk & Wagnalls, 1968), 256–57.

[38] "Elizabeth to Butler," 29 Dec. 1597.

[39] The phrase is used by Margaret King in *Women of the Renaissance* (Chicago: University of Chicago Press, 1991), 29, where it refers to the complex relationship between the sexual honor of a woman and her family and community. The original term is in Guido Ruggiero, "'Più che la vita caro': onore, matrimonio e reputazione femminile nel tardo Rinascimento," *Quaderni Storici*, n.s. 66 (1987): 753–75, here 753–55.

[40] For a variety of misogynistic outbursts against Elizabeth and female rule, see Carole Levin, "'We shall never have a merry world while the Queene lyveth': Gender,

her countermanding and even recall of governors (Grey is a good example here) often elicited a sexist animosity rooted in the contemporary incongruity of martial male prowess in the field being blunted by female indecisiveness and, in their eyes, weakness in the face of rebellion.[41] As Paul Hammer succinctly notes, the conduct and direction of war posed a particular difficulty for the female ruler, eliciting unsympathetic and frequently hostile responses from her leading courtiers and generals:

> Although countless panegyrics publicly praised Elizabeth as a war-leader, both during her lifetime and after her death, the private opinions of her generals and admirals were rather different. They believed that the queen's gender made her indecisive, unable to persist with a course of action, excessively parsimonious and prone to pacifist sentiments . . . In 1598 Essex bluntly told a French envoy that England's government was hampered by "two things . . . delay and inconstancy, which proceeded chiefly from the sex of the Queen."[42]

We can find many allegorical hints of this male frustration and anxiety in New English writing on Ireland. Elizabeth is portrayed as the threatening Diana or as Circe, for example, who treated her male servants as dumb beasts.[43] The clearest expression of male frustration is to be found in the outburst of Sir John Perrot, the lord deputy from 1584 to 1588: "if she use men thus, she will but have cold service . . . Ah now silly woman, now she will now curb me, she shall not rule me now . . . God's hounds, thus is to serve a base bastard piss kitchen woman."[44]

This outburst is interesting from another perspective in that it indicates the level of control the monarch could exert on her personnel in Ireland. While it is true that, when the army was in the field, there was little Elizabeth could do to

---

Monarchy, and the Power of Seditious Words," in *Dissing Elizabeth: Negative Representations of Gloriana*, ed. Julia M. Walker (Durham, NC: Duke University Press, 1998), 77–95.

[41] Louis Montrose discusses this animosity and ambivalence, especially as it related to figures like Walter Raleigh, in "The Work of Gender in the Discourse of Discovery," in *New World Encounters*, ed. Stephen Greenblatt (Berkeley: University of California Press, 1993), 177–217.

[42] Paul E. Hammer, *Elizabeth's Wars* (Basingstoke: Palgrave, 2003), 2.

[43] See the Circe references and the threatening Diana allegory in Richard Beacon, *Solon His Follie, or A Politique Discourse Touching the Reformation of Common-weales Conquered, Declined or Corrupted*, ed. Clare Carroll and Vincent Carey, MRTS 154 (Binghamton: MRTS, 1996). See also Clare Carroll, "Representations of Women in Some Early Modern Tracts on the Colonization of Ireland," in eadem, *Circe's Cup: Cultural Transformations in Early Modern Ireland* (Cork: Cork University Press, 2001), 48–60.

[44] Quoted in Morgan, "Elizabeth and Ireland," 302. As Morgan notes, Elizabeth had the last laugh in that she acquiesced in a trumped-up treason trial against the former deputy which saw his conviction and eventual death in the Tower in 1588.

direct it; the fear of loss of her favor and influence at court, however, determined the officials' actions on the ground.[45] The classic example of this process at work is, of course, the second earl of Essex's disastrous campaign against Tyrone's insurgency in 1599. Nonetheless, the failure of this expedition and the earl's "emasculation" are far less important for understanding Elizabeth's relationship to state violence than the lord deputyship of his successor, Charles Blount, Lord Mountjoy. Essex's failure in Elizabeth's eyes was as much a consequence of the slight to her honor as of his secret conversation with Tyrone, his failure in arms, and the "intolerable charge [expense]" of his mission. Even prior to the certainty of his failure, Elizabeth alerted the earl to the fact that Tyrone's success "hath blemished our honour"[46] and warned him not to fail her. Essex's subsequent ineptitude was a slight to her royal dignity and authority, but this was exacerbated by the fact that he had treated O'Neill, "a bush born kerne" according to the queen, like an equal, as a "prince." In so doing, he had directly challenged her authority, and by engaging in secret conversation, the two elite males had directly challenged her sense of female sovereignty.[47] Worse still, Essex had given this Gaelic lord his trust, as fatal an error in Elizabeth's words "as to trust a devil upon his religion."[48] As well as a severe sense of the "dishonourable" nature of Essex's secret negotiation with O'Neill, we may also detect by 1600 a strain of ethnic animosity in Elizabeth's writing as, for instance, when she notes: "for what pity is there among them that can tie them to the rule of honesty for itself, who are only bound to their own sensualities . . ."[49]

It could be argued that this ethnic disdain was also a factor in Elizabeth's decision to endorse Mountjoy's scorched-earth campaign that followed in the wake of the defeat of the Spanish landing in Kinsale in 1602. Repeated Irish mauling of the English units, the introduction of Spanish forces, personal and ethnic disdain for O'Neill, all coalesced for her to order Mountjoy to a "universal prosecution" of a people she had referred to in an earlier personal letter to him as "Tartaros."[50] As Mountjoy marched north into Ulster, he was given *carte blanche*

---

[45] For a sophisticated analysis of the perilous relationship between the deputy in the field and the politics of court, see the work of Ciaran Brady, especially *The Chief Governors*.

[46] "Elizabeth to Robert Devereux, earl of Essex," 14 Sept. 1599, in *Letters of Queen Elizabeth*, 269–74.

[47] The issue of Elizabeth's sense of majesty as challenged in Ireland is fruitfully explored in Brandie R. Siegfried, "Queen to Queen at Check: Grace O'Malley, Elizabeth Tudor and the Discourse of Majesty in the State Papers of Ireland," in *Elizabeth I: Always Her Own Free Woman*, ed. Carole Levin et al. (Aldershot: Ashgate, 2003), 149–75.

[48] "Elizabeth to Robert Devereux," 17 Sept. 1599, in *Letters of Queen Elizabeth*, 274–76.

[49] "Elizabeth to Robert Devereux," 17 Sept. 1599.

[50] "Elizabeth to Charles Blount, Lord Mountjoy," 15 July 1602, in *Letters of Queen Elizabeth*, 292–94; "Elizabeth to Charles Blount," c. 1601, 289.

by the queen to use whatever means necessary to end the war. The chosen method was to scorch the earth and to burn and kill all that got in the way.

The resort to scorched-earth tactics was not new in the recent Irish wars; it was already in widespread use in Munster under the direction of the then provincial president Sir George Carew.[51] Even in Ulster it was by now commonplace, especially at the hands of Arthur Chichester operating out of Carrickfergus, of which he was governor. What was novel, and perhaps unprecedented even by contemporary European standards, about the particular scorched-earth campaign which began in June 1602 was its unprecedented scale and systematic nature. In a coordinated and methodical fashion, Mountjoy with his reduced but still substantial army moved from the south, Dowcra from the northwest, and Chichester from the north and east in a campaign of systematic destruction of crops, animals, dwellings, and people. Formal government correspondence reveals the coordinated and systematic nature of the proceedings.[52] Chichester, writing to Cecil on 22 June, notes how he and Dowcra "back burn" their way to the town of Dungannon.[53] On the next day, Mountjoy entered the town, Tyrone's main base. The deputy then held a field conference with Dowcra and Chichester, noting how their success in scorching the earth was already leading to the practical problem of sustaining the invading army: "The country is so eaten that I think we can hardly live there with our horse. . . ."[54]

The environmental destruction that Mountjoy worried about was, in fact, so extreme that, in July, Thomas Philips, one of the captains, predicted the impending starvation of O'Neill's cattle by the winter's onset, reporting: "I could see no plain but was eaten as bare as the commons in England where the sheep are fed." This frenzy of destruction included the killing of untold numbers of Gaelic peasants, in fact of anyone encountered who did not, or could not, flee: "We do now continually hunt all their woods, spoil their corn, burn their houses, and kill so many churls, as it grieveth me to think that it is necessary to do this."[55] Mountjoy could report the effectiveness of such brutality by the end of July, after, to use his own words, he had finished "spoiling and ransacking."[56] By early October, all of Ulster west of the Blackwater was devastated except for Tyrone's refuge on the Fermanagh borders, which the English army had as yet failed to devastate. But even here, as Mountjoy confidently noted, the combination of the followers of

---

[51] Carey, "'What Pen Can Paint'," 226.

[52] Explored at greater length in Carey, "'What Pen Can Paint'."

[53] "Chichester to Cecil," 22 June 1602, in *Calendar of State Papers Relating to Ireland, 1601–3 (with Addenda, 1565–1654) and of the Hanmer Papers* (London: H.M. Stationery Office, 1912), 415–16.

[54] "Mountjoy to Cecil," *Calendar of State Papers Ireland 1601–3*, 416–17.

[55] "Mountjoy to Carew," 2 July 1602, in *Calendar of Carew Manuscripts*, 4:263–64.

[56] "Mountjoy to the Privy Council in England," 29 July 1602, in *Calendar of State Papers Ireland 1601–3*, 458–59.

Tyrone meant that they themselves were using up all the scarce resources of an already depleted environment. Mountjoy almost glibly reports to Cecil in London that "there is growing so extreme a famine amongst them that there will be no possibility for them to subsist."[57] In reporting to the privy council in England in early January 1603 of the extremity of O'Neill's position and of his enemy's overtures for surrender, the deputy could not help but note that all his men were "weary of their extreme labours."[58] These labors not only had broken the back of Elizabeth's most serious Irish insurgency but, as Mountjoy observed, when combined with bad harvests in the Pale and Carew's endeavors in Munster, had brought the entire country to the precipice of mass hunger. This "universal prosecution" endorsed, indeed ordered, by Elizabeth was the ultimate in state terror.

There can be little doubt that Elizabeth sought an end to this, the most threatening of insurgencies to confront her regime, and that she accepted the savage means utilized. Ultimately, despite efforts at moderation early in the reign, I would like to suggest that Elizabeth's endorsement of the "festival of cruelty" initiated by men like Sidney and supervised and carried out by men like Gilbert in Munster, Cosby in the Midlands, Bingham in Connacht, and Essex in Ulster prepared the ground for, and inured officialdom to, the outright savagery of the last nine years of the reign. The genocidal fury unleashed by Mountjoy in Ulster in the summer of 1602 must also be laid at Elizabeth's door. As the monarch and CEO of the operation,[59] she must bear primary responsibility for the actions of her subordinates in Ireland. While it is popular and indeed comforting to see Elizabeth as one of the "Unwarlike sex," to use her own words, might we not be more honest if we were also to accept her own willingness, expressed in the famous Armada speech at Tilbury in 1588, to do whatever it took to preserve her honor and to be the "general, judge and rewarder" of her subordinates in the field?[60] Ultimately, as "general," if at times an inconsistent one, Elizabeth must bear responsibility for the devastation wrought in her name, and historians

---

[57] "Mountjoy to Cecil," 12 Oct. 1602, in *Calendar of State Papers Ireland 1601–3*, 496–97.

[58] "Mountjoy to Cecil," 8 Jan. 1603, in *Calendar of State Papers Ireland 1601–3*, 551–52.

[59] See Norman Jones, "Elizabeth, Burghley, and the Pragmatics of Rule: Managing Elizabethan England," in this volume, 143-56.

[60] "Elizabeth's Armada Speech to the Troops at Tilbury," 9 Aug. 1588, in *Elizabeth I: Collected Works*, ed. Leah S. Marcus, Janel Mueller, and Mary Beth Rose (Chicago: University of Chicago Press, 2000), 325–26. Though there is some dispute as to whether she actually made this speech, the editors of the *Collected Works* refer to it as "reputed," while Susan Frye questions the evidence for it in "The Myth of Elizabeth at Tilbury," *Sixteenth Century Journal* 23 (1992): 95–114. Janet M. Green uses paleographic and literary evidence to authenticate the speech. See 'I My Self': Queen Elizabeth I's Oration at Tilbury Camp," *Sixteenth Century Journal* 28 (1997): 421–45; and Steven W. May, "Queen Elizabeth to Her Subjects: The Tilbury and Golden Speeches," in this volume, 125-41.

who seek to reinterpret her as the consummate female ruler must also include the darker side of her reign that unfolded in Ireland and left a legacy of bitterness that still resonates today.[61]

To downplay Elizabeth's role in, to paraphrase Walter Mignolo's book title, "the darker side of the Renaissance"[62] is to do a double disservice to our understanding of the past. In the first instance, it denies agency to Elizabeth the female ruler, and secondly, in accepting Elizabeth's own rhetoric of female weakness, rhetoric she utilized to powerful effect, we absolve her from responsibility for the terrors unleashed in her name—terrors that, by today's standards, could land her, as head of state, in The Hague on charges of (at best) war crimes or (at worst) attempted genocide.[63]

---

[61] Amongst major scholars of Elizabeth, Wallace MacCaffrey is exceptional in his recognition of the utter failure of her policies in Ireland and especially of the ensuing brutal legacy of conquest: "It was achieved in agony and pain through the misery and deaths of countless of the queen's subjects. It was altogether unheroic, the accomplishment of men who were not seeking the glories of imperial conquest or martial fame but struggling against a foe they despised, in a slogging campaign of attrition. It evoked on both sides a venomous outpouring of hatred which would permanently poison relations between the two islands." See *Elizabeth I: War and Politics*, 432.

[62] Walter Mignolo, *The Darker Side of the Renaissance: Literacy, Territoriality and Colonialism* (Ann Arbor: University of Michigan Press, 2003).

[63] I am extremely grateful to Clare Carroll, Hiram Morgan, and Willy Maley for their comments and assistance on this essay. I also would like to thank Mary Burgess and Jim Smyth and the Keough Institute for Irish Studies for the opportunity to visit the University of Notre Dame. Chris Fox and the Institute provided financial support for the preparation and delivery of the original keynote address. Needless the say, the views here expressed are my own.

Elizabeth Through Venetian Eyes

John Watkins

Almost paradoxically, Venice's place in the Elizabethan imagination exceeded its actual place in Elizabethan foreign politics. In *Volpone*, the fast-and-loose dealings of the Rialto provided Ben Jonson a convenient cover for his satire on London's own commercial classes. Shakespeare used the famously cosmopolitan city as the setting for two different plays that place racial and ethnic hatred in the foreground: *Othello* and *The Merchant of Venice*. Padua was a Venetian possession in Shakespeare's day, and its university was under Venetian auspices. Perhaps Kate, in *The Taming of the Shrew*, owes as much as Portia and Desdemona to the Venetian reputation for "super-subtle" women.[1] Given the city's association with women who defied patriarchal convention, it should come as no surprise that common rumor linked Elizabeth herself—the woman whose frail female body belied her kingly heart and stomach—with the City. The great seventeenth-century gossip Francis Osborne reported long-standing speculation that Elizabeth "had a *Son* bred in the State of *Venice*," although Osborne himself argued that such rumors were more suited to a "romance" than to a serious history.[2]

One of the things that made Venice loom so large in the English imagination was its remoteness: England had comparatively few commercial, and even fewer political, contacts with Venice during Elizabeth's reign. The foreign powers that mattered most for England in the sixteenth century were along the North Atlantic: France, Spain, and Spain's rebellious subjects in the Netherlands. The papacy had a huge mythic impact on English thinking, but its diplomatic significance lay in its close relationship with Spain. If Venice did not matter much to Eng-

---

[1] William Shakespeare, *Othello*, in *The Riverside Shakespeare*, ed. G. Blakemore Evans, 2nd ed. (Boston: Houghton Mifflin, 1997), 1.3.356. For further discussion of the status of women in early modern Venice, see Jutta Gisela Sperling, *Convents and the Body Politic in Late Renaissance Venice* (Chicago: University of Chicago Press, 1999); Stanley Chojnacki, *Women and Men in Renaissance Venice: Twelve Essays on Patrician Society* (Baltimore: Johns Hopkins University Press, 2000).

[2] Francis Osborne, *Traditional Memoirs on the Reign of Queen Elizabeth*, in *The Miscellaneous Works of That Eminent Statesman, Francis Osborn, Esq.*, 2 vols. (London, 1722), 2:42. See Carole Levin's discussion of Osborne in this volume, 92.

land, England mattered even less to Venice. As Venice tried to preserve its waning reputation as the mistress of the Adriatic and eastern Mediterranean, it was mostly concerned with the expansionist empires that controlled the Mediterranean's eastern and western ends: Spain and Turkey. It also fretted a lot about Spanish influence in Italy and particularly on the papacy.[3] Until the very end of Elizabeth's reign, when English ships started appearing in the Mediterranean in larger numbers than ever before and interfering with Venetian trade, the Republic did not worry much about England.

One sign of England's relative non-importance to Venice was the Republic's failure to send an ambassador or even an envoy to Elizabeth's court until the last weeks of her life. By the late sixteenth century, exchanging resident ambassadors had become a common feature of diplomatic practice. But the diplomatic culture of early modern Europe was continually evolving, and the terms governing the exchange of ambassadors in one context did not necessarily apply to another.[4] The exchange was not always reciprocal, and not all residents enjoyed the rank and title of "ambassador." Fairly regular diplomatic communication often unfolded between powers who had no official diplomatic relationship with each other. For example, when Elizabeth needed to deal with Venice or vice versa, negotiations typically took place under the auspices of a third national party. The English ambassador to the French court often discussed Anglo-Venetian matters with the Venetian ambassador to France. Almost everything that the ruling Venetian signory knew about English affairs came to them second-, third-, or even fourth-hand, through the reports both of their ambassadors to France, Spain, and the Empire and of their Bailo, or merchant-diplomat, stationed in Turkey.

This diplomatic indirection is where my story begins. Given the evolving nature of sixteenth-century diplomatic practice, Venice's failure to honor Elizabeth with a resident ambassador was not necessarily an expression of hostility or contempt. Nevertheless, Elizabeth took it as one. For four decades, her ambassadors to various European courts expressed her resentment to their Venetian counter-

---

[3] Frederic C. Lane, *Venice: A Maritime Republic* (Baltimore: Johns Hopkins University Press, 1973), 241–49; Robert Finlay, *Politics in Renaissance Venice* (New Brunswick, NJ: Rutgers University Press, 1980); Elizabeth G. Gleason, "Confronting New Realities: Venice and the Peace of Bologna, 1530," in *Venice Reconsidered: The History and Civilization of an Italian City-State, 1297–1797*, ed. John Martin and Dennis Romero (Baltimore: Johns Hopkins University Press, 2000), 168–84.

[4] For the most comprehensive survey of early modern diplomatic culture, see Garrett Mattingly, *Renaissance Diplomacy* (Boston: Houghton Mifflin, 1955). For further discussion of the peculiarities of the Venetian system, see Andrea Zannini, "Economic and Social Aspects of the Crisis of Venetian Diplomacy in the Seventeenth and Eighteenth Centuries," in *Politics and Diplomacy in Early Modern Italy: The Structure of Diplomatic Practice, 1450–1800*, ed. Daniela Frigo, trans. Adrian Belton (Cambridge: Cambridge University Press, 2000), 109–46.

parts on almost every possible occasion. Their persistence raises important questions about the relationships between material interests and more elusive understandings of national and monarchical dignities in the early modern period. Why did Venice hesitate to acknowledge in more formal terms the reality of a relationship that it continued to enjoy with England, and why did that hesitation so annoy Elizabeth, given its relatively insignificant practical consequences? I want to argue that Venice's formal alienation from Elizabeth arose from a diplomatic stance that paradoxically linked the republic directly to her: a commitment to political neutrality in the face of Reformation and Counter-Reformation efforts to divide European diplomatic relationships along sectarian lines. Throughout most of Elizabeth's reign, Venice shied away from her from fear of upsetting its own delicate relationships with Spain and the papacy. Only when those relationships became unsustainable near the turn of the seventeenth century could it finally reach out to Elizabeth as a woman who shared something of its own diplomatic vision.

Elizabeth's relationship with Venice divides more or less conveniently into two phases: before and after the middle of the 1580s. Before the 1580s, Venice maintained a conspicuous distance from the new queen. Diplomatic records suggest that the Venetians spent this time trying to get a sense of where she was taking her realm and of how her Protestantism might alter the European balance of power. By the middle of the 1580s, Venice began responding still cautiously, but in noticeably more positive ways to Elizabeth's overtures. This second period marks a long, often halting prelude to the resumption of formal diplomatic ties in the year of Elizabeth's death. As John Guy and other historians have suggested, this second period of Elizabeth's reign witnessed a series of changes in her domestic and foreign policies as she found herself pursuing a more openly bellicose role in European affairs.[5] England was not the only European power that changed course in the 1580s. Early in that decade, a new generation of Venetian rulers rose to power determined to resist Spanish and papal interference in the republic's foreign and domestic affairs. Eventually, this shift allowed the Venetians to draw closer to England, and the English to draw closer to the Venetians.

The first, more alienated phase of Anglo-Venetian relations dawned with Elizabeth's accession and ended gradually in the 1580s, roughly between the Venetian political crisis of 1582, in which the aggressively anti-Spanish party came to power, and 1588, when England and Spain went to open war. Reformation propagandists like John Foxe may have viewed Elizabeth's re-Protestantization of the English Church as a manifestation of Providence, but many—arguably most—continental Europeans viewed it as a step likely to aggravate an already dangerous polarization of Catholic and Protestant interests. The last thing Venetians and other states who were steering a neutral course in the escalating

---

[5] John Guy, ed., *The Reign of Elizabeth I: Court and Culture in the Last Decade* (Cambridge: Cambridge University Press, 1995), 1–19.

conflict between Reformation and Counter-Reformation hysteria wanted was another extremist state on the diplomatic horizon. The problem was less Elizabeth's religion *per se*, or the religion of her realm, than the fear that her Protestantism would lead to persecutions of English Catholics and resident foreigners, and to a bellicose foreign policy.

After all, Venetians felt that they already had one extremist state in Philip II's Spain, a power that posed almost as serious a threat to Venetian interests in the Mediterranean as Ottoman Turkey, a Muslim empire, despite the fact that Spain and Venice were both Catholic. That threat had become infinitely greater during the first year of Elizabeth's reign when the Treaty of Cateau-Cambresis between Philip and Henri II of France settled for Spain the sixty-year Franco-Spanish conflict over the possession of the Italian peninsula.[6] Habsburg Spain now ruled Naples (meaning virtually all of Italy south of Rome), Sicily, and Milan. The duchy of Tuscany was a Spanish satellite, and so was the papacy. Venice alone remained outside the sphere of Spanish influence, and it had to keep a careful watch not only on Spain and its Italian satellites, but also on the other, imperial branch of the Habsburg family that sat on its northern border.

Habsburg culture threatened Venice not only politically and militarily but also spiritually and ideologically in ways that would have a profound impact on its relationship with England. Philip II's commitment to monarchical centralization and to the Counter-Reformation Church in its most repressive aspects ran counter to three of the most crucial aspects of the Venetian civic myth. In stark contrast to the Spanish monarchy, Venice was first and foremost a republic in which a doge with markedly restricted powers presided over a series of councils and committees that were seen as the actual bearers of sovereignty.[7] Secondly, the city's constitution was fiercely aristocratic, and the ruling elite spent much legislative time and effort trying to ward off any threats to its hegemony. From a Venetian perspective, a defense of aristocratic privilege was inseparable from the defense of republican liberties. Only a distinct ruling caste could possibly have the sophistication necessary for conciliar government, and a strong aristocracy presumably offered the best shield against despotism.[8] Venetians watched with obvious discomfort throughout the sixteenth century as centralizing western monarchs demoted their countries' nobilities and staffed national bureaucracies

---

[6] Angelantonio Spagnoletti, *Principi italiani e Spagna nell'età barocca* (Milan: Mondadori, 1996).

[7] Lane, *Venice*, 87–117, 251–73; Edward Muir, "Was There Republicanism in the Renaissance Republics? Venice after Agnadello," in *Venice Reconsidered*, ed. Martin and Romero, 137–67.

[8] Gerhard Rösch, "The *Serrata* of the Great Council and Venetian Society, 1285–1323," in *Venice Reconsidered*, ed. Martin and Romero, 67–88; also Stanley Chojnacki, "Identity and Ideology in Renaissance Venice: The Third *Serrata*," in *Venice Reconsidered*, ed. Martin and Romero, 263–94.

with men of lower rank. Thirdly, situated at the boundary between Latin and Eastern Christendom, and between the Christian and Islamic worlds, Venice had cultivated a tradition of relative ethnic and religious toleration. We need to be careful about treating this in overly idealistic terms; neither the Venetians nor any other Europeans had anything like the modern notion of liberty of conscience as an inalienable personal right. As a merchant republic, Venice was willing to put up with a certain degree of heterodoxy and even infidelity to foster trade with its Greek, Slavic, and Muslim neighbors.[9] But what began as an economic expedient acquired a greater ideological significance when the Habsburg-dominated papacy tried to impose the Counter-Reformation, complete with Jesuits and unbridled Inquisitors, on the stubbornly independent Venetians.[10]

Venice's long-standing commitment to aristocracy, republicanism, and a pragmatic toleration of religious difference overdetermined its relationship with England throughout Elizabeth's reign and colored the terms in which its citizens portrayed her character and government. The more uncomfortable they became with the Spanish domination of Italy, the more they could see in Elizabeth a potential ally. This was even more true once it became clear around 1568 that Elizabeth herself was not going to fall into the sphere of Spanish influence through marriage either to an Austrian archduke or to Philip II himself. What Elizabeth and Venice most shared during the first half of her reign was a wary neutrality in the face of Philip II's imperial and theocratic vision. On opposite borders of Habsburg-dominated central and southern Europe, one holding on to its rights in the Mediterranean and the other consolidating its claims to the Atlantic, they knew they had a common potential enemy that neither wanted to rouse into open warfare. Venetians clearly admired the slippery foreign policy of this woman who always sought, in the words of one ambassador, "to throw the stone but conceal the arm."[11]

As Europe's greatest connoisseurs of the diplomatic subtleties that preserved peace in the face of international aggression, the Venetians followed Elizabeth's marital negotiations with particular interest. There were, of course, practical grounds for this attention, since a marital alliance between England and any continental prince might shift the always precarious balance between Valois

---

[9] For insight into the complexities of Venetian "toleration" in social practice, see the essays in *The Jews of Early Modern Venice*, ed. Robert C. Davis and Benjamin Ravid (Baltimore: Johns Hopkins University Press, 2001).

[10] William J. Bouwsma, *Venice and the Defense of Republican Liberty: Renaissance Values in the Age of the Counter Reformation* (Berkeley: University of California Press, 1968), 293–338.

[11] *Calendar of State Papers and Manuscripts Relating to English Affairs, Existing in the Archives and Collections of Venice and Other Libraries of Northern Italy*, ed. Rawdon Brown and G. Cavendish Betinck, 38 vols. (London: HMSO, Longman, Green, 1864–1947), 7:427.

and Habsburg power on which Venice's own security rested. But for the professional diplomat, watching Elizabeth orchestrate competing European factions also provided something akin to aesthetic delight. The Alençon negotiations (1572–1581), for example, figured in dozens of letters written to the signory from France and Spain alike as Venetian ambassadors tried to guess Elizabeth's motives in undertaking the negotiations. While some ambassadors passed along an exhaustive list enumerating the advantages and disadvantages that both parties might obtain from the match, others speculated that Elizabeth was simply setting up a smokescreen to conceal some secret purpose: "It is believed the Queen of England has no object in view except giving empty words, in order that she may not be hindered in the matter of affairs in Scotland, where by means of her partisans, she is diligently endeavouring to bring the whole of that kingdom into subjection."[12] Commenting on the rumor that Elizabeth might be trying to arrange a match between the nine-year-old king of Scotland [the future James I] and one of the Infantas, Hieronimo Lippomano, the Venetian resident in Spain, commented that "Princes are wont to avail themselves of matrimonial negotiations in many ways, but the queen of England, who is accustomed to befool the world with negotiations for her own marriage, will have to treat here with [Philip II], a master thoroughly versed in the same art if she designs to do the same thing with respect to the King of Scotland, her successor."[13] For Lippomano and for the dozens of other Venetian diplomats who served the Republic during the second half of the sixteenth century, Elizabeth was a master of the same arts that they aspired to master.

As much as the Venetians welcomed Elizabeth's ability to thwart Philip on one side of his vast holdings, and as much as they admired her ability, so like their own, to keep her country at peace during turbulent times, they also recognized that Elizabeth and Philip had some things in common that ran counter to Venetian traditions of oligarchic republicanism. Like Philip, Elizabeth was a centralizing monarch whose family had risen to power by reining in the native nobility and replacing them with "new men" dependent on monarchical favor for their enhanced social standing. A consciousness of the low birth of many of Elizabeth's most trusted advisors pervades comments on her court by visiting Venetians. A decade after Lippomano commented so admiringly on Elizabeth's diplomatic skills, for example, he complained that she had sent a man of "very unimportant rank" to settle a dispute over import dues in the German Free Maritime ports.[14] According to the Bailo, the Venetians' term for their *de facto* ambassador in Turkey, William Harborne, the first English ambassador to Constantinople, eventually "lodged a vigorous complaint, alleging that other Ambassadors [went] about saying that he [was] a Merchant and not entitled to the rank

---

[12] *Calendar Venice*, 7:601–3, 488.
[13] *Calendar Venice*, 7:539.
[14] *Calendar Venice*, 8:102.

of Ambassador."[15] The Venetian ambassador to Philip II commented sneeringly on Sir Francis Drake's low birth, and the ambassador to the Roman curia noted that even Cardinal Allen was basely born. To the Venetians, social climbing was a characteristically English disease.[16]

In short, the Venetian attitude toward Elizabeth during the first decade or so of her reign was mixed: they admired her diplomatic virtuosity, and they recognized in it something of their own studied attempts to remain neutral in the omnipresent conflict between Habsburg and Valois. But they also saw her as an autocrat who was only too quick to disregard the kind of aristocratic prerogatives on which their own republic rested. For many years, Venice was happy to watch Elizabeth from a distance. But during the 1570s and 80s, political and mercantile circumstances began to change in ways that would demand a more direct diplomatic engagement. In the last year of her life, Elizabeth would finally receive her long-awaited Venetian envoy. But by that point, she had abandoned the neutrality that had once stirred the Venetians' admiration. She was at open war with the Habsburgs, and Venice's renewal of diplomatic relationships with England was an immediate consequence of English aggression in the Mediterranean. It was also a sign that Venice too was also abandoning its decades-long neutrality.

Nothing better typifies the complexity, and I'm tempted to say diplomatic pathos, of unfolding Anglo-Venetian relations than the events surrounding the visit of four Venetian noblemen to Elizabeth's court in 1575.[17] A couple of years earlier, in 1573, Venice had suspended mercantile shipping to England because of the risks posed by English privateers marauding off the coasts of Spain and France. At that time, Valentine Dale, the English ambassador to France, had a candid conversation with his Venetian counterpart about Elizabeth's commitment to maintaining a strong trading relationship with the Republic.[18] As a sign of that continued commitment, Elizabeth welcomed four leading Venetian noblemen to her court. They described their visit in an extended letter to the Senate that reiterated several times the queen's request that Venice formalize their relationship by sending an ambassador. Every detail in the letter works to advance Elizabeth's request by emphasizing her general good will to them and to all Venetians. The particular details that the writers include coalesce in a concerted effort to reassure their senatorial audience of Elizabeth's reliability as a diplomatic partner. The courtly protocols that they describe, for example, appeal to the famous Venetian flair for ceremony and reassure the audience that Elizabeth respects aristocratic prerogatives:

---

[15] *Calendar Venice*, 8:93.
[16] *Calendar Venice*, 8:156, 304.
[17] *Calendar Venice*, 7:524–26.
[18] *Calendar Venice*, 7:486.

The apartment was very crowded, and the nobility assembled there greeted us most cordially with every mark of honour. After a short interval the Queen made her appearance, and on our presenting ourselves her Majesty said, in our own language, "Are you Venetian noblemen?" Falier, as the senior of our party . . . answered, "Yes most Serene Queen; we, your Majesty's servants, came to France with our Ambassador the Lord Zuanne Michiel, and having heard from his Excellency, who was for a long while Ambassador in this kingdom, as also from our citizens, and from men of other nations, of the grandeur and nobility of this realm, and the beauty of the country, and above all the renown of your Majesty, bruited as it is in all quarters, it seemed to us most inexcusable, being so near as France is to these parts, not come to see the country and this Court at the same time."[19]

Elizabeth, according to their account, responded in courtly kind by jokingly referring to herself as the worst of the sights her realm had to offer. Her gracious demeanor; her fluency, and that of many gentlemen of the court, in Italian; and her kind recollections of Michiel as a former ambassador to England during previous reigns suggest her particular eagerness to acknowledge Venice and Venetian decorums. When she directs Burleigh to take her visitors to dinner with other members of her Privy Council, the Venetians note that they are "all most distinguished noblemen," a phrase that deftly glosses over the facts of just how newly arrived some of those gentlemen, including Burleigh himself, actually were. Nothing in this letter hints at the Tudor elevation of "new men," something that figures so prominently in other Venetian accounts of Elizabeth's court. This Elizabeth is almost wholly Venetian in her spirit and in her clearly aristocratic demeanor. In addressing her repeatedly as "Regina Serenissima," Falier and the other nobles also underscore her identity with Venice itself, always referred to as "La Serenissima," "the Most Serene Republic," in diplomatic discourse.[20]

In the Venetian noblemen's account of their visit, even the potentially troubling difference in religion fails to unsettle the atmosphere of mutual respect and admiration between the Most Serene Republic and the Most Serene Queen of England. The Venetians attended her in the presence chamber, "at the hour when her Majesty was to pass through on her way to chapel." She in fact interrupted her conversation with them to hear the service, which the Venetians described in careful and significant detail:

> This service consisted, first of all, of certain Psalms chanted in English by a double chorus of some thirty singers. A single voice next chanted the

---

[19] *Calendar Venice*, 7:524.
[20] *Calendar Venice*, 7:524.

Epistle; after this another voice chanted the Gospel, and then all voices together chanted the Belief.[21]

What first appears as a conspicuously irrelevant program note points in fact to the letter's central diplomatic objective of fostering a closer tie between the two countries. The description reduces the distinction between Catholic and Protestant cultures to a mere difference in language; the familiar morning sequence of psalms, epistle, gospel, and creed is still all there, although chanted in English, rather than in Latin. The letter's repeated emphasis on the linguistic sophistication of Elizabeth and her court dampens the potential divisiveness of even this novelty. The ease with which Elizabeth and her councilors—"almost all of them speaking our Italian tongue, or at least all understanding it"—shift from English into other European languages proves that the vernacularization of the liturgy is hardly a sign of increased xenophobia or cultural isolation. The writers are careful not to editorialize too explicitly, and they never quite say that they *attended* the Protestant service themselves, but the letter itself leaves as open as possible the observation that the Creed that Elizabeth and her courtiers confessed during the service is fundamentally the same one shared by the Venetians.

This remarkable letter, with its account of specific requests by Elizabeth and her leading courtiers for the re-authorization of a Venetian resident in England, was read before the Senate on 25 February 1575. It was then followed up by a motion in Council to grant Elizabeth her long-awaited ambassador. But the vote that followed could not have been more disappointing: "For the original motion, ayes forty-four, and noes one hundred and thirty-one. So the noes had it."[22] Virtually everyone in the Venetian diplomatic community supported giving Elizabeth what she wanted by the establishment of a resident embassy in England. But there is no mystery as to why the Senate refused: they were afraid of the papal response. For many years, every time the subject came up, the papal nuncio chastised the doge for even considering such a measure.

But by the late 1570s, the Venetians were becoming less acquiescent. As William J. Bouwsma has noted in his magisterial account *Venice and the Defense of Republican Liberty*, a new generation was coming to power that took a more aggressive stance against Spain and the papacy that it dominated.[23] When the papal nuncio complained yet again in 1578 about the warming of Anglo-Venetian relations, he met a new doge and heard a significantly new kind of response. Niccoló da Ponte, who was unabashedly anti-Spanish and deeply resented Spanish influence on Rome, assured the nuncio that Venice was not planning to send Elizabeth an ambassador. But he qualified that assurance by pointing out in no uncertain terms that other Catholic powers, including France, Spain, and Portugal,

---

[21] *Calendar Venice*, 7:525.
[22] *Calendar Venice*, 7:26–27.
[23] Bouwsma, *Venice and the Defense of Republican Liberty*, 162–231.

already had residents serving in England.[24] Da Ponte's was not a lone voice. In 1581, Lorenzo Priuli, a leader figure in the rising anti-Spanish, anti-papal party, countered the Roman diabolization of Elizabeth by championing the possibility of her marriage to the duke of Alençon. In dispatches from France, Priuli argued that the pope and his supporters were wrong to characterize the marriage plans as an affront to the Church. According to Priuli, it might even advance the cause of Catholics in England by neutralizing sectarian hostilities.[25]

As Venice grew more defiant of Spanish hegemony, and more resistant to papal interference in both its domestic and foreign affairs, the time seemed ripe at last for a renewal of formal ties with Elizabeth. But almost paradoxically, the same invigorated nationalism that linked England and Venice as allies against Spain also brought them into conflict with each other. Especially during the 1580s and 90s, when English ships appeared in the Mediterranean in greater numbers, first as traders and later as privateers, England seemed to have become more of a threat than an ally. This caught at least one Venetian diplomat off guard. The Bailo at Constantinople was clearly surprised when his government asked him to do everything in his power to thwart Elizabeth's establishment of diplomatic and mercantile ties with the Sultan.[26] His surprise registers the confusion that could arise when economic and political interests ran counter to each other. From a purely political perspective, Venice should have welcomed closer ties between England and Turkey, especially since the English were clearly trying to enlist the Sultan in an anti-Spanish alliance. But the Signory had to weigh this advantage against the arguably greater threat that England posed to their Turkish trade, and for Venetians already concerned about the threat posed to their old markets by the expanding Atlantic trade, an English assault on their own Mediterranean routes was too much to tolerate.[27]

Once England and Spain were openly at war, the Venetians had something else to worry about: the escalation of English piracy.[28] The English hailed privateers who captured Spanish ships as patriots and welcomed the flow of Spanish wealth into English coffers. But the pirates did not restrict themselves to preying solely on Spanish ships. By the end of the sixteenth century, English pirates had so compromised several key Venetian trading routes that the Senate finally voted to send Elizabeth her long-awaited envoy to discuss the matter. Two factors came

---

[24] *Calendar Venice*, 7:589. See also Bouwsma's discussion of Da Ponte, *Venice and the Defense of Republican Liberty*, 229–31.

[25] *Calendar Venice*, 8:3, 15. On Priuli's larger role in the Venetian resistance to Spain, see Bouwsma, *Venice and the Defense of Republican Liberty*, 334–35.

[26] *Calendar Venice*, 8:52–55, 50–51, 58, 67.

[27] For general discussion of the threat posed by the Atlantic trade to Venetian interests, see Lane, *Venice*, 275–334.

[28] Alberto Tenenti, *Piracy and the Decline of Venice, 1580–1615*, trans. Janet and Brian Pullan (Berkeley: University of California Press, 1967), 56–86.

together to overcome the Venetians' forty-year reluctance to honor Elizabeth with an envoy. First of all, there was the scale of the maritime emergency. By the end of 1602, letters poured into the Senate from merchants and diplomats throughout Europe that complained about attacks on Venetian shipping by Englishmen. But as grave as this situation was, it might still have been handled indirectly through conversations between English and Venetian ambassadors serving in third-party European courts. What opened the lines for direct negotiation was Venice's willingness to defy the papacy and its Spanish allies through open conversation with the English queen.

The Venetian diplomat who finally broke the ice, a minor figure named Giovanni Carlo Scaramelli, has achieved lasting fame among students of Elizabeth's life and reign not so much because we have cared about her relationship with Venice but because his arrival coincided with her final illness and death. Because Scaramelli had been trained in the characteristically Venetian art of minutely detailed correspondence, his letters from England to the doge and Senate provide one of the best records that we have of Elizabeth's final days. Elizabeth scholars are all familiar with what they have to say about her sudden decline, gossip about the likelihood of James VI's or Arabella Stuart's succession, and perhaps above all, Robert Cecil's role as the *eminence* not quite *grise* orchestrating the Scottish succession while his mistress lay dying.

Instead of rehashing some of the more familiar and objectively "accurate" passages, I want to focus on some of the letters' odder assertions about Elizabeth, not because I think they are ultimately verifiable, but because some of Scaramelli's most seemingly far-fetched details tell us something about Venice and about Elizabeth's place in the Venetian imagination. The extent to which specifically Venetian concerns overdetermine the shape and character of Scaramelli's narrative, moreover, suggests an evidentiary principle that historians and biographers have ignored in their earlier use of his letters in trying to reconstruct a picture of Elizabeth's last days: all letters, even something as seemingly objective as dispatches, need to be read rhetorically. They were produced not only to tell the Venetians about what was happening in England, but to tell them something about Scaramelli, his powers as an observer, his subtlety as a negotiator, and his commitment to his country and its national myth. Scaramelli was not an Englishman, and he was not writing for future generations of English historians. In several important ways, his letters tell us more about Venetian ideals than they do about English realities.

This is particularly true with respect to Scaramelli's developing sense of Elizabeth's character. His often contradictory portrayal of her owes less to objective observation than to Venice's own ambivalence as a Catholic power at odds with the papacy. It also marks the ambivalence in Venice's relationship with England as a potential political ally against Spain but also as a fierce commercial rival. What appears in the correspondence as an unmediated description of Elizabeth actually arises from the intersection of conflicting diplomatic objectives and anxieties.

The sense of England as economic rival and political ally dominates Scaramelli's account of his one actual meeting with Elizabeth.[29] Opening with an elaborate description of Elizabeth's attire and "hair of a light colour never made by nature," the letter presents her as a hard bargainer who opens her negotiations by exposing her opponent's greatest weakness. In this case, that weakness is what Elizabeth characterizes as Venice's long neglect: "Welcome to England, Mr. Secretary. It is high time that the Republic sent to visit a Queen who has always honoured it on every possible occasion." Scaramelli ought to have had the advantage of the conversation, since English privateers had been ravaging Venetian ships in violation of the republic's neutrality in the war against Spain. But Elizabeth refused to spend much time on the maritime crisis that prompted Scaramelli's visit, which she dismissed as the work of "bad ruffians" whom she would do everything within her power to prosecute. She used the audience instead to press Scaramelli on the issue of Venice's prior diplomatic neglect:

> I cannot help seeing that the Republic of Venice, during the forty-four years of my reign, has never made herself heard by me except to ask for something. Nor am I aware that my sex has brought me this demerit, for my sex cannot diminish my prestige nor offend those who treat me as other Princes are treated, to whom the Signory of Venice sends its Ambassadors. But I am well aware, and so far excuse the Republic, that in the many discussions on this subject she has not been able to obtain leave from certain Sovereigns.[30]

Elizabeth's deft use of rhetorical *occupatio* and *periphrasis* allows her to transform her own potential weakness as a female sovereign into an opportunity to expose the weakest Venetian nerve of all in 1603, its past concessions to a papacy that was soon to place the Republic under interdict for defying its authority. Elizabeth raises the possibility that the Venetians have not wanted to do business with a woman only to dismiss it. After all, the other states to whom Venice has sent its ambassadors—France, Spain, the Empire—have all sent ambassadors to Elizabeth as well. Therefore the real weakness lies with Venice's own subservience to "other princes," a transparent periphrasis for the pope and, perhaps more distantly, the king of Spain. Elizabeth's words effectively unman the Venetians by displacing onto them the suspicion of a kind of womanly subservience to their papal overlord. Elizabeth's pronominal references to Venice as "she"—albeit a diplomatic commonplace—heighten this effect, particularly in contrast to her masculinizing references to herself as a "prince."

By threatening Scaramelli with the effeminizing image of his nation as a papal puppet, Elizabeth established the most favorable terms possible for their subsequent negotiations. Scaramelli got the point and retorted that "the Repub-

---

[29] *Calendar Venice*, 9:531–34.
[30] *Calendar Venice*, 9:533.

lic of Venice, a great Sovereign, and free thanks be to God, . . . has never adopted the principle of consulting any Prince in the world as to her decisions, be he secular or ecclesiastic."[31] Elizabeth's comment provoked Scaramelli to declare the Republic's independence of papal influence, and that confession served to make up in part for her forty-four-year neglect. Although there were still major points of difference between the policies and cultures of the two states, this meeting established a significant point of common understanding. Within a month, Scaramelli could write the signory that he had recovered a large portion of the plundered Venetian merchandise and that Elizabeth was passing a strict order for all her subjects to refrain from privateering within the Mediterranean.

Scaramelli's relationship with Elizabeth was cut short by her illness. He never saw her again, and everything else that he says about her in the letters depends on the mediation of third parties, including recusants and recusant sympathizers. At times, especially in letters complaining about English piracy, Scaramelli stoops to the sectarian language one might expect from an Italian Catholic traveling in England. Arguing that England was dependent on piracy because it could no longer finance its navy, for instance, he observed in a ciphered aside, "To such a state has this unhappy Kingdom come that from a lofty religion has fallen into the abyss of infidelity."[32] But the longer Scaramelli remained in England, the more he learned about English religion, and the more sensitive he became to it in ways that recalled the long-standing Venetian tradition of tolerating, or at least winking at, religious difference.

This more nuanced view of English religion dominates his account of Elizabeth's death and his obituary assessment of her character, the section of his correspondence that is most familiar to modern scholars. But although biographers and historians have treated this as a more or less objective account of her decline, it is characteristically Venetian in what becomes its final emphasis on the insignificance of Elizabeth's Protestantism. What Scaramelli presents as an end-of-life journey of repentance and reconciliation serves on a metanarrative level as a testimony to Scaramelli's own journey from Catholic suspicion and slander to a deeper respect of the religious values that informed Elizabeth's life. As much as his initial assertion that Venice was not subservient to any prince, "secular or ecclesiastic," his account of her death resists the Counter-Reformation imperative to view the world in terms of a sharp opposition between heresy and true religion.

Scaramelli recounts Elizabeth's death as a story of Lenten repentance. According to him, Elizabeth fell sick on Ash Wednesday, "which in the English calendar" coincided with the anniversary of Essex's death:

> So deeply does her Majesty feel this, that on the first day of lent this year . . . she recalled the anniversary of so piteous a spectacle and burst into tears and

---

[31] *Calendar Venice*, 9:553.
[32] *Calendar Venice*, 9:557.

dolorous lamentation, as though for some deadly sin she had committed, and then fell ill of a sickness which the doctors instantly judged to be mortal.[33]

Scaramelli frequently reminds his audience of the liturgical coincidence as he imagines the dying queen regretting her past career, and especially her juridical murders of Essex and Mary Stuart. Before her illness set in, Scaramelli intimates that she was planning a similar fate for Arabella Stuart. But the approach of death cut short her murderous career and gave her time to reflect on her crimes.

At the end of this Lenten narrative, as Easter approaches with its promise of resurrection and capital forgiveness, Scaramelli describes Elizabeth's passing in movingly sympathetic terms:

> That same day she spoke of certain things which weighed upon her conscience, and recalled to mind the death of the Earl of Essex. Then rising to topics of religion, she said that she had been at war with Pontiffs and princes, and touched upon two principal points of variance from the Church of Rome, the use of the vernacular in prayers, and the question of the Sacrament, upon which I will not enlarge; enough that from her remarks and from her prayers that God would not reckon against her in the next life the blood of priests shed by her.[34]

Scaramelli notes that there were even Catholics about court who thought "that in her inner sentiments her Majesty was not far from reconciliation with the true Catholic faith." He finds confirmation for this view in Elizabeth's conservative liturgical preferences: "because it was observed that in her private chapel she preserved the altar with images, the organs, the vestments which belong to the Latin rite, and certain ceremonies which are loathed by other heretics." As if Elizabeth's secret Catholic sympathies are not enough, he concludes his account by noting that Archbishop Whitgift, whose hand Elizabeth held "until she had breathed her last," also "had a disposition towards Catholicism, as he showed by certain external signs, such as his abstention from matrimony, and his use of unleavened bread when administering the sacrament."[35]

For anyone familiar with Elizabeth's religious compromises, nothing that Scaramelli says that is true is particularly new. Everyone knows that she kept a crucifix in her chapel and that her penchant for "vestments which belong to the Latin rite, and certain ceremonies" appalled her more staunchly Protestant subjects. What does sound new in Scaramelli's account—the suggestion that Elizabeth was so Catholic at heart that she came about as close as she could to a deathbed reconciliation with Rome—is patently not true, at least in anything remotely resembling an accurate historical statement. But Scaramelli has devel-

---

[33] *Calendar Venice*, 9:558.
[34] *Calendar Venice*, 9:564–65.
[35] *Calendar Venice*, 9:565.

oped his portrait of her over the course of several letters so that it has a kind of narrative truth and serves as the perfect ending of her life, at least within the conventions of a Lenten *exemplum*. For good reasons, English historians and biographers have dismissed many of his claims as so much recusant rumor or the wishful thinking of an ardent papist. But as we begin to write a new kind of diplomatic history, one that overcomes both the hermeneutic and the nationalistic limitations of an earlier generation, we need to think about the rhetorical context of Scaramelli's writing, his primary audience, and the diplomatic ends of his ecclesiastical mythmaking.

To make the point that English historians have never really considered, Scaramelli wrote as a Venetian at a critical moment in the Republic's history. And as much as he may have distorted the facts of Elizabeth's life and death, he created a powerful story that contributed to Venice's role as a bulwark against the Counter-Reformation. At precisely the point when Venice was provoking papal wrath by turning a blind eye to the sale of heretical books, ignoring Tridentine judicial decrees, taxing the clergy, restricting episcopal freedoms and prerogatives, limiting the influence of the Jesuits, and placing strict controls on the Inquisition, Scaramelli found in Elizabeth I the promise of respect, and possibly even future reconciliation between Protestants and Catholics. His letter suggests to its Venetian audience that the label "Protestant" actually covered a range of beliefs and liturgical practices, a range that complemented what one French ambassador identified as a characteristically Venetian tendency to distinguish between Catholics and Papists.[36] Elizabeth's Protestantism and a patriotic Venetian's Catholicism had a lot in common, including a passionate resistance to the Counter-Reformation. Scaramelli offered in his account of Elizabeth's deathbed piety a witness to Catholic Europeans that Protestantism *per se* was not necessarily as threatening as the Counter-Reformation painted it in justifying its repressive apparatus of interdicts and excommunications.

Within a year of Elizabeth's death, Venice and England had exchanged ambassadors and re-established full diplomatic relations. One might see this as part of what James I's opponents saw as a fundamental sympathy for continental Catholics, and thus a betrayal of Elizabeth's imagined bellicosity. But as in many other ways, James's foreign policy actually fulfilled many of Elizabeth's own dreams. She had kept her realm at peace for three decades precisely by resisting the diplomatic consequences of seeing a world sharply divided into Protestant and Catholic camps. This bias for neutrality, a neutrality that we need to explore further as the diplomatic aspect of an emerging discourse of toleration, linked her not only to her Stuart successors, but also to her Venetian contemporaries. Within two years after her death, Paul V established one final link between them and Elizabeth by placing the Republic under an interdict for its

---

[36] Philippe Canaye, Seigneur de Fresne, *Lettres et ambassade*, 3 vols. (Paris, 1635–1636), 2, part 2:158.

insubordination to Rome. Like Elizabeth's own excommunication three and a half decades earlier, it measured the cost of trying to maintain neutrality in an increasingly polarized world.

Advising the Queen: Good Governance in Elizabeth I's Entries into London, Bristol, and Norwich

Tim Moylan

Critics have long recognized that pageant displays during the reign of Elizabeth Tudor were more than mere entertainments created to gratify a rather too self-possessed queen. Sydney Anglo saw them as a continuation of an earlier Tudor propaganda campaign that had always been calculated to display "the magnificence expected of a potentate" as well as offer "specific comment on an international situation."[1] Roy C. Strong includes them in the range of devices encomiasts used to form and develop the Cult of Elisa. In them, he argues, the "monarchy employed verbal and visual images to hold a divided people together."[2] Malcolm Smuts, Stephen Orgel, Louis Montrose, and others who draw upon the work of Clifford Geertz and Victor Turner interpret these events as channels through which Elizabeth exercised her personal charisma, captivating and "interpellating" her subjects.[3] Germaine Warkentin recognizes that their capacity

---

[1] Sydney Anglo, *Spectacle, Pageantry, and Early Tudor Policy* (Oxford: Clarendon Press, 1969), 2.

[2] Roy C. Strong, *The Cult of Elizabeth: Elizabethan Portraiture and Pageantry* (London: Thames & Hudson, 1977), 114.

[3] Smuts claims Geertz and others under-represent the power of sheer spectacle. He applies Geertz's strategy of "thick description" to argue for the centrality of Elizabeth as an active, physical presence in the spectacles and for her personal charisma working as a tenuous, but sufficient, net around a deeply divided people. See M. Smuts, "Public Ceremony and Royal Charisma: The English Royal Entry in London, 1485–1642," in *The First Modern Society*, ed. A. L. Beier, David Cannadine, and James M. Rosenheim (Cambridge: Cambridge University Press, 1989), 65–94, esp. 67. Stephen Orgel sees them as "consciously designed to validate and legitimate an authority that must have seemed, to what was left of the old aristocracy, dangerously arriviste." For him, as for Anglo, the displays' purpose was directed principally by the crown. See S. Orgel, "Making Greatness Familiar," in *Pageantry in the Shakespearean Theater*, ed. David Bergeron (Athens, GA: University of Georgia Press, 1985), 19–25, here 19. Louis Montrose argues that the

to communicate both a general influence and specific messages was not unidirectional. She points out that civic pageantry not only displayed royal power but also provided a unique opportunity to counsel that power.[4] Recently, William Leahy has challenged New Historicist assumptions about the efficacy of such symbolic display and questioned to what degree the witnesses of these spectacles were in fact passive consumers successfully fashioned into compliant subjects.[5] In fact, the feminist critic Susan Frye sees them as sites in which Elizabeth struggled to maintain her independence and agency as the men around her employed the language of religion, courtly ceremony, and compliment to frame her into more traditional female roles.[6]

It is evident that these interactions between Elizabeth and her subjects defy one-dimensional interpretation. Like Warkentin and Leahy, I suspect that pageant displays were interactive and dynamic encounters rather than straight-forward, top-down propaganda. Like Frye, I believe the encounters involved a certain amount of struggle between Elizabeth and the event sponsors, designers, and performers. Even these critical approaches, however, have not given sufficient attention to the complexity of these relationships and the degree to which these encounters constitute an ongoing "conversation" conducted in the language of ceremony and entertainment. A close reading of the accounts exposes what I suggest is a negotiated performance dialogue, one in which a surprising number of voices can be heard saying remarkable things to a monarch who paid unusually close attention. Listening to those voices opens another window into the period, its people, and its most significant figure.

In this paper, I look specifically at one theme in that dialogue—the theme of good governance—and I postulate that not only did London employ civic ceremony to express its concerns, desires, even directives to the crown but also that

---

pastoral in both literature and performance provided "a means whereby Queen Elizabeth and her subjects could pursue their mutual courtship subtly and gracefully; they could perform a wide range of symbolic operations upon the network of social relationships at whose center was the sovereign." His reading recognizes to a greater degree the possibility that aesthetic creations in multiple genres could serve the purpose of others besides those in authority. See L. Montrose, "'Eliza, Queen of Shepherds All' and the Pastoral of Power," in *The Mysteries of Elizabeth I: Selections from English Literary Renaissance*, ed. Kirby Farrell and Kathleen Swaim (Amherst: University of Massachusetts Press, 2003), 162–91, esp. 163.

[4] G. Warkentin, ed., *The Queen's Majesty's Passage and Related Documents* (Toronto: Centre for Reformation and Renaissance Studies, 2004), 20.

[5] For Leahy's review of recent theoretical approaches to pageant study and his assessment of the New Historicist interpretive approach, see *Elizabethan Triumphal Processions* (Burlington, VT: Ashgate, 2005), 25–51. For his work complicating the uniformity of response in Mulcaster, see 53–100.

[6] See Susan Frye, *Elizabeth I: The Competition for Representation* (New York: Oxford University Press, 1993).

other cities, especially Bristol and Norwich, conveyed similar messages directly related to their local concerns. The London entry has received considerable attention in recent scholarship, but the other two have not. In these latter two entries, the writers balanced immediate, local issues against the larger, national agenda of the crown, all within an elaborate framework of effusive personal compliment. Their pageant displays offer scholars insight into how these growing urban communities conceptualized their relationship to the state, defined both their and the queen's responsibility relative to good governance, and negotiated a relationship that was at once ceremonial, contractual, and personal. London, protective of its liberties, was long accustomed to such negotiations with the crown. Bristol and Norwich, of course, had far fewer direct contacts with royalty, but had no less a sense of autonomy and independence. David Galloway, citing John Evans, notes that "During most of the Tudor period and most of the reign of James I, 'Norwich was a world in itself: urban unrest was limited, the city was capable of handling its own affairs, and communications to and from either Westminster or Whitehall were infrequent.'"[7] Editor Patrick Carter, in the Records of Early English Drama volume on Bristol, traces efforts made by the city to acquire its liberties and to defend them against the encroachment of both local and more distant authorities.[8] A close reading of the accounts of Elizabeth's entries into these cities suggests that London was not the only city exploring the potential inherent in the queen's visit to say something to her about how it expected to be ruled.

This is not necessarily surprising. Many of the civic leaders of these cities had been educated in the humanist tradition, with its emphasis on the obligation of the subject to speak honest counsel to the prince. The practice was pervasive enough to lead historian Patrick Collinson to conceptualize the Elizabethan state as a political hybrid, a "monarchial republic."[9] His suggestive term may overstate somewhat the autonomy of the Elizabethan subject, especially when it came to expressing dissent. Yet the impulse to counsel was common and not restricted only to those close to the center of power. The trick was finding an opportunity, as well as a way of speaking to the powerful, that was diplomatic but compelling. With Elizabeth especially, pageant and entertainment ceremonial provided civic communities what they wanted: both a rare chance at the queen's attention and a flexible medium within which to speak need, fear, desire, and even truth to her.[10]

---

[7] David Galloway, ed., *Norwich: 1540–1642*, REED (Toronto: University of Toronto Press, 1984), xvii.

[8] Patrick Carter, "Historical Background," in *Bristol*, ed. Mark C. Pilkinton, REED (Toronto: University of Toronto Press, 1997), xiv-xx.

[9] P. Collinson, *Elizabethan Essays* (London: Hambledon, 1994), 32.

[10] For another view on the notion of monarchical republic, see Peter Lake, "'The Monarchical Republic of Elizabeth I' Revisited (by its Victims) as a Conspiracy," in *Conspiracies and Conspiracy Theory in Early Modern Europe: From the Waldensians to the French Revolution*, ed. Barry Coward and Julian Swann (Aldershot: Ashgate, 2004), 87–111.

One could expect such an approach in London at Elizabeth's inaugural entry, but the Bristol and Norwich pageants, in 1574 and 1578 respectively, coming as they do near the midpoint of the reign, offer strong evidence that Elizabeth's other cities recognized this opportunity, believed in its efficacy, and persisted in counseling her long after she had matured from a young queen to an established sovereign. They did not appear to miscalculate. Elizabeth, to her credit, usually took the time to both listen and respond.

A discussion of the complex concept of good governance may be given only cursory treatment here, but two overlapping ideas appear to inform the pageant displays. The first is Elizabeth's belief in her right to rule as God's elect, charged alone with the ultimate responsibility for proper management of the state. The second is the developing sense in her civic authorities that management of the "civitas" or commonwealth required the due exercise of authority on all levels of government, including their own decision-making as corporate bodies of aldermen and city officials. Thus, good governance for the people came to signify the proper exercise of collective authority for the good of the community within the bounds of a widely-held national agenda. It is in civic pageantry that those ideals are given their most visible and suggestive form.

The earliest (and now most frequently studied) of Elizabeth's formal entries was her coronation reception into London.[11] My review focuses on how the civic sponsors employed allegory and pageantry to legitimize and reinforce Elizabeth's claim to the throne while at the same time forwarding a set of remarkably assertive expectations, directives, and ideals to her. In effect, they presumed to advise her on what constituted good governance from the city's perspective. In particular, they emphasized that Elizabeth must be, above all, virtuous and solicitous of the welfare of her people, and they strongly suggested that she remain open to counsel, including theirs. In return, they promised to offer sound advice and implied that they would reward her reliance on them with obedience, support, and deference.

London officially received Elizabeth on 14 January en route to her coronation. To welcome her, the city aldermen commissioned pageant displays, speeches, and civic decoration all along the traditional route through the city.[12] Shortly afterwards, Richard Tottel printed an account of her entry entitled *The Qvenes*

---

[11] Besides Leahy and Warkentin, see Frye, *Elizabeth I: The Competition for Representation*; Mary Hill Cole, *The Portable Queen* (Amherst: University of Massachusetts Press, 1999); and David Bergeron, *English Civic Pageantry 1558–1642* (Columbia, SC: University of South Carolina Press, 1971); Anglo, *Spectacle, Pageantry and Early Tudor Policy*; Helen Hackett, *Virgin Mother, Maiden Queen: Elizabeth I and the Cult of the Virgin Mary* (New York: St. Martin's Press, 1995), 41–49.

[12] For a discussion of the symbolic significance of the route itself, see Lawrence Manley, *Literature and Culture in Early Modern London* (Cambridge: Cambridge University Press, 1995), 221–41.

Maiesties Passage. Originally published anonymously, it is now attributed to Richard Mulcaster and provides a detailed account and interpretation of the displays mounted for Elizabeth and of the queen's reactions. In her transit through the city, Elizabeth paused to observe and have explained to her such tableaux as a family tree at Grace Church Street; an allegory of the "Seate of Worthie Governance" at Cornhill; another allegory featuring her as Truth, the Daughter of Time, at Little Conduit; and yet another as Deborah in parliamentary robes consulting with her estates at the Fleet Street Conduit.

In the publication, Mulcaster persistently emphasizes the city's universal acceptance and acclamation of the queen. She was, he declares, "of the people received marvelously entirely . . . so that on either side there was nothing but gladness, nothing but prayer, nothing but comfort" (75).[13] He relates that Elizabeth responded in kind. This relationship, grounded in reciprocity, reflects what Barbara Palmer describes as one of the necessary conditions of kingship from the Tudor perspective—the good will and support of the people.[14] Mulcaster may have been accurate in his description of the popular response, yet both Leahy and Susan Frye point out the over-determined nature of Mulcaster's text, reading it more as hagiography than reportage. Nevertheless, we can accept, I think, that his version reflects, if not reality, then an intense desire for universal accord and support of the new queen, and his idealization constitutes a fervent expression of the belief that good governance begins with the consent and support of the governed.

In the Gracious [Grace Church] Street pageant, Elizabeth encountered the idea that forms the foundation of good governance: the undisputed right to rule. This tableau displayed a selective Tudor genealogy. It consisted of three levels rising one above the other occupied by royal personages. Red and white roses sprang from the joined hands of Henry VII and Elizabeth of York seated on thrones on the first level. These twined together and climbed to a second level shared by Henry VIII and Anne Boleyn, and from their seat rose a single stem to the third level with a single throne "in the which was set one representing the queen's most excellent majesty Elizabeth now our most dread sovereign Lady" (79).[15] The display carefully elides the complicating factors, certainly still alive in the collective memory, of the reigns of Edward and Mary, as well as Henry VIII's marital misadventures. Likewise missing from the family tree is the branch leading to Mary, Queen of Scots. The genealogy has been artfully

---

[13] All citations from *The Queen's Majesty's Passage* are from Warkentin's edition and will appear in-text.

[14] B. Palmer, "'Ciphers to this Great Accompt': Civic Pageantry in the Second Tetralogy," in *Pageantry in the Shakespearean Theater*, ed. Bergeron, 114–29, here 116.

[15] Norwich was in the ancestral territory of the Boleyn family. On the use of Anne's badge of a falcon and other sights that would have reminded the queen of her mother during her visit, see Mary Hill Cole, "Maternal Memory," in this volume, 1–14.

pruned to remove anything that complicates the succession and displays Elizabeth's claim to the throne as beyond dispute. Such elements in the display certainly serve the interests of the crown in effecting a smooth transition. Yet other elements imply messages serving interests in other quarters. Dale Hoak points out Grafton's interpretation of the device in his *Abridgement of the Chronicles of England*. Grafton writes that the display "signified the coniunction and coupling together of our soueraigne Lady with the Gospell and veritie of Goodes holy woorde, for the peaceable gouuernement of all her good subjects."[16] Hoak sees in this and the other displays an emphasis on "imperial religious reform," noting the specific use of the closed, or imperial, crown on the head of the child representing Elizabeth in the next pageant at Cornhill.[17] In the verses spoken by the child, however, the emphasis seems to be on the healing of division. The speaker calls attention to the unifying marriage of Henry VII and Elizabeth of York, stressing that Elizabeth I is the descendent and heir of that union. The final verse implies a parallel between the healing of the earlier dynastic division and the contemporary expectations for Elizabeth.

> Therefore as civil war, and shed of blood did cease,
> When these two houses were united into one
> So now that jar shall stint, and quietness increase,
> We trust, O noble Queen, thou will be cause alone. (80)

In these lines the concern seems less with the confirmation of religious reform than with the cessation of strife and the healing of division, a concern likely shared by moderates in both camps as well as the merchant elite, for whom conflict interfered with business. In the various elements of these complex displays, we can see the effects of interest groups employing elements in the displays to forward specific messages.

The second pageant "in the nether end of Cornhill" identifies qualities thought necessary for "worthie governance" (81). The allegory portrays the queen supported by four virtues: Pure Religion, Love of Subjects, Wisdom, and Justice, and each of these figures treads upon two vices: Superstition and Ignorance, Rebellion and Insolence, Follie and Vain Glorie, and Adulacion and Bribery respectively (82). The allegorists took no chances that the meaning of the allegory should escape the queen or the crowd. A child orator explicated the display telling Elizabeth that "While true religion . . . love of subjects . . . zeal to the prince . . . justice and Wisdom [suppress their contraries] . . . so long shall government not swerve from her right race . . ." (82–83). In addition, "in every void place,"

---

[16] Dale Hoak, "A Tudor Deborah? The Coronation of Elizabeth I, Parliament, and the Problem of Female Rule," in *John Foxe and His World*, ed. Christopher Highley and John N. King (Aldershot: Ashgate, 2002), 73–88, here 82.

[17] Hoak, "A Tudor Deborah?," 82.

Mulcaster observed, "both in English and in Latin [were placed] such sentences as advanced the seat of governance upheld by virtue" (83). Although this unashamedly didactic allegory places Elizabeth in the seat of authority, it also includes struggling vices that reveal a persistent anxiety about their potential to upset the entire structure. More tellingly, Mulcaster comments that, "she [Elizabeth] should sit fast in the same [the seat of government] *so long as* she embraced virtue and held vice underfoot" (83, emphasis added). The consequences for failing to remain virtuous go unvoiced, but the implied caution seems remarkably overt. In this, perhaps, we hear the early stirrings of the many self-appointed moralists who throughout her reign addressed Elizabeth in language and action more forward than they might have dared with her father or grandfather, or indeed with her brother, if he had come fully to manhood.

One of the most interesting of the displays, the device of Truth as the Daughter of Time, compares the previous reign, *Ruinosa Respublica*, with the promise of the future, *Respublica Bene Instituta*.[18] Critics have focused intently on this display since it was in it that Elizabeth famously embraced the English Bible, theatrically declaring her religious allegiance to Protestantism. The representation of Elizabeth as sanctioned by time and circumstance, her symbolic endorsement of Protestantism, and her interjection "Time has brought me hither," deftly recorded by Mulcaster, constitute great state theater. It was not especially original, however, as the city had employed the same device to welcome Mary Tudor with much the same implication, namely to assert that the accession of the monarch was providential, a coming to fruition of God's expressed intention. The irony of the Protestant appropriation of the device was apparently not lost on the Catholic observers. An Italian living in England, Aloisio Schivenoglia, wrote home with a description of the festivities attending Elizabeth's first Christmas, her entry into London, and her coronation. In it he describes the displays and, perhaps drily, observes that its motto was "an allusion to the motto on the money heretofore coined by Queen Mary, her Majesty of holy memory: *Veritas temporis filia*" (108). As with the Grace Church Street display, this pageant seeks to legitimize Elizabeth as well as the shift from a Catholic to a Protestant state and unambiguously associates that shift with a flourishing and prosperous commonwealth. It is generally assumed that this bit of dramatic street theatre was orchestrated by Elizabeth, or at least something she was told to expect. Yet that is not quite the impression one gets from the attendant oration. As with the first two displays, a child explains the allegory and tells her, "We *trust*, oh Queen, thou wilt this truth embrace. / And since thou understandst the good estate and nought / We *trust* wealth thou wilt plant, and barrenness displace" (88, emphasis added). This

---

[18] As Sarah Duncan notes in "The Two Virgin Queens" elsewhere in this volume (29–51, at 47-48), the device of Truth as the Daughter of Time was used in the reign of Elizabeth's sister Mary to celebrate the restoration of Catholicism. Here it is slyly adapted to laud the return of Protestantism [eds.].

central message is reiterated in writing on placards, again in both languages, outlining for her the causes of a ruinous as well as of a flourishing commonweal. As before, the redundancy makes the message almost strident and reveals a considerable anxiety over both the implications of the new faith and the uncertainty of a regime change. This sounds less like a confident public celebrating its new monarch's known religious allegiance than a nervous and decidedly Protestant one asking her to affirm for them what they hoped and expected to see. Mulcaster's enthusiastic spinning belies both the range of religious allegiances in the London audience at the time and Elizabeth's later suspicion of the more forward Protestant reformers.

The allegory of Deborah consulting with her estates reflects the effort to locate a suitable biblical precedent to accommodate the queen's gender. The figure of Deborah has drawn the attention of a number of scholars. For example, Donald Stump examines the repeated association of Elizabeth with such biblical figures in the first half of the reign, and Michele Osherow discusses Elizabeth's representation as Deborah in light of the biblical Deborah's strong presence as a powerful speaker.[19] As Osherow demonstrates, especially conspicuous in this coronation tableau is the presence of the three estates ready to advise the female judge. Tellingly, no mention is made of a cadre of male advisors assisting the biblical Deborah. Indeed, Elizabeth was forthright in seeking the advice and counsel of many as she effected the transition from Mary's to her own reign.[20] In addition, we do not have a clear sense, as in the other displays, of the physical arrangement in this pageant. The effrontery of locating the three estates around Deborah could have been mitigated by visibly staging the councilors on lower levels than Elizabeth, an arrangement used to good effect in the earlier displays. It is also worth noting the absence of any mention of the estates in the child's verse spoken to the queen. Mulcaster, however, carefully points to them and explains that by this pageant Elizabeth "might be put in remembrance to consult for the worthy government of her people . . . [and] . . . that it behooves both men

---

[19] In this volume, see Osherow, "'Give ear, O princes'" and Stump, "Abandoning the Old Testament," esp. 290–91, which argues that Mulcaster and the other designers of the tableau of Deborah were urging submission to counsel as a way of limiting the independence of the young queen, a submission that she never accepted [eds.].

[20] In her first address to the Council members gathered at Hatfield after the death of Mary, Elizabeth told them, "I mean to direct all mine actions by good advice and counsel." See *Elizabeth I: Collected Works*, ed. Leah S. Marcus, Janel Mueller, and Mary Beth Rose (Chicago: University of Chicago Press, 2000), 52. Elizabeth probably did not need to be taught this lesson. She was politic and deliberate in forming her own Council. Early on, she made it a point to develop good working relationships with competent statesmen such as William Cecil and later Francis Walsingham. Though she was always careful to retain control over decision-making, she made "counsel" a regular component of her governance.

and women, so ruling, to use advice of good counsel" (92). Mulcaster articulates here a familiar humanist ideal of good governance, namely that the best originates in a virtuous leader who recognizes the need for, and is amenable to, responsible advice from representative counselors. That the city located all three estates around Elizabeth provides a strong visual declaration that they saw her accession as an opportunity to position themselves where their voices could be heard and carry real political power. Dressing all of the participants, including Deborah, in parliamentary robes went even further to suggest a wider and more equitable distribution of authority. Elizabeth's reaction to this specific display is not recorded, and, of course, she never tolerated anything like the form of government it implied. What is remarkable, however, is that the city risked mounting such a display in the first place.

Elements in the displays and in the account demonstrate that the encounters with the queen during her entry were by no means unambiguously complimentary, and the agenda of the city's aldermen and participating Protestant enthusiasts appears very clear. Elizabeth was certainly aware of their intentions and was very likely to some degree involved in the preparations.[21] Mulcaster's record also reveals her calculated responses to the crowd and the performers[22] so that the entire event appears to have a subtext of negotiation. The model of good governance the coronation pageants hold up to the young queen is striking in the degree to which it suggests a contractual ideal. It emphasizes the queen's personal virtue, but implies consequences for succumbing to vice. It assures her of their acceptance of her right to rule, but is remarkably assertive in urging her consultation with others of all estates. It clearly elevates the queen to almost divine status, but repeatedly emphasizes a mutual commitment of the queen and people to each other and to the collective welfare. Elizabeth's active participation in this symbolic modeling appears to endorse the city's ideal, and Frye notes that, at least in terms of an economic contract, this orientation was, in fact, representative of much of Elizabeth's reign.[23]

The treatment of good governance in the Bristol entertainment is less overt than in either of the other two civic entries. Bristol was not London with its clear

---

[21] Elizabeth directed Thomas Cawarden to release costumes to the city aldermen for use in the pageants. See *The Queen's Majesty's Passage*, ed. Warkentin, appendix II, 121–22.

[22] Upon receiving the city's gift of one thousand gold marks and listening to the Mayor's and the city's request that she "continue their good and gracious Queen," Elizabeth replied, "I thank my lord mayor, his brethren, and you all. And whereas your request is that I should continue your good lady and Queen, be ye ensured that I will be as good unto you as ever Queen was to her people. *No will in me can lack, neither do I trust shall there lack any power.* And persuade yourselves that for the safety and quietness of you all, I will not spare, if need be, to spend my blood. God thank you all" (86–87, emphasis added).

[23] Frye, *Elizabeth I*, 42.

identity as the center of all things English, nor was it Norwich, concerned with the prospect of a French king consort. In 1574, Bristol was, instead, a provincial coastal city animated by the arrival of its monarch on a rare visit. Bristol had been enduring a long trade depression, and its merchants were anxious to discover the root cause(s) of the economic lull.[24] In 1571, they took it upon themselves to end a trade monopoly held by the Merchant Adventurers, but the depression persisted, and they concluded that it must be the "stormy relations between England and the Iberian powers of Spain and Portugal" that were limiting their market prospects.[25] Economic prosperity for Bristol was tied to trade, and trade flourished when international relations were in good order. The efforts to address their economic distress demonstrate how the civic authorities in Bristol understood good governance to work on the local level. Responsibility for international diplomacy, however, lay with the crown. Since the latter had a direct impact upon the former, the city sponsored a three-day allegorical battle to illustrate their conceptualization of the two groups' interdependence. Elizabeth responded in part to these displays by signing the Treaty of Bristol that "secured at least the nominal friendship of Spain."[26]

In addition to trade matters, Elizabeth came to Bristol to address the issue of religious conformity. As Mary Hill Cole points out, she had called a "special commission for ecclesiastical causes within the dioceses of Bristol and Gloucester" that encouraged her trip west and was convened upon her arrival. There she acknowledged that her realm was not yet "a peasable, quiet & well ordered State and Kingdome" but one she hoped the commission, through the exercise of royal authority, could bring about.[27] Bristol's pageants reflect these themes in the allegorical characters Dissension and Persuasion who figure as agents of both religious and international discord as well as challenges to good governance.

We have one account of the Bristol entry, which was written by Thomas Churchyard and printed in 1575 as part of *The Firste Parte of Churchyard's Chippes*. Unlike other writers of more conventional civic entries, Churchyard devised a "conceit" that consisted of an allegorical assault by War on the fort of Peace in a conflict stirred up by Dissension. In the course of a three-day battle conducted on both land and sea, an outpost of the fort, "Feeble Policy," is destroyed, but the main fort, though beleaguered, stands firm. Once something of a stalemate is reached, Churchyard then introduces an ambiguous character, Persuasion, who tries to effect a compromise. Though Persuasion's rhetoric is compelling, he is unsuccessful, and the battle resumes. After three additional assaults and the arrival of fresh forces from the court to assist the fort, War withdraws from the field, and the siege is lifted. The ease by which the charismatic and amoral Dissension

---

[24] Cole, *Portable Queen*, 110.
[25] Cole, *Portable Queen*, 110.
[26] Anne Somerset, *Elizabeth I* (London: Weidenfeld & Nicolson, 1991), 288.
[27] Cole, *Portable Queen*, 141.

inspires violence, the failure of Peace to defend itself through policy alone, and the curious rhetoric of Persuasion all combine to suggest a complex relationship among threat, resistance, and governance. Most significantly, the commitment Peace makes to the queen and this figure's reliance on her "power" acknowledge the state's need for a governor who possesses both the wisdom and power to manage dissent. Churchyard locates the queen squarely in this role.

On her arrival, Elizabeth is greeted by Fame, Salutacion, Gratulacion, and Obedient Good Will who provide her with an overview of the show and its characters. They tell her, "Dissension breeds the Brawll, and that is Pomp and Pried ... The Warrs is wicked world and the Fortress Representeth Peace" (397).[28] The queen plays the part of the "noble judge that shall with speed decied the matter throw" (397). They make it clear that the threat is internal and domestic. Dissension "with drosse and Roemish dregs blind people's humour feeds." He is a "sottell sneak" who with "sopple sugred words, / Haeth sleely crept in brestes of men, and drawn out naked swords" (398). A song "songe [to her] by a very fien Boye" on Sunday refers to "bosom snaeks" and "Hidras heads" and the "troblous time" through which the queen must "traed" (399–400). Although Churchyard has Fame refer to the shows as "sports and mirth, and warlike pastimes playn," the text is informed by a heightened awareness of intrigue, and the queen is represented as the "pillar, prop, and stay" of governance (397, 399).

The central threat to the commonwealth is the persistent fear of Catholic plotting, especially at the instigation of Spain and the pope. The fear is not only the overthrow of Protestantism and reversion to the old faith but more palpably the attendant civic distress. The English were very attentive to the way religious division played out on the continent. Refugee stories of Alva's "Council of Blood" and the St. Bartholomew's Day massacre had driven home how easily religious enthusiasm could degenerate into violent civic disorder. So far, Elizabeth's middle course had prevented such bloodshed in England. She had ended the burnings at Smithfield and had been careful to temper retaliatory Protestant persecution by keeping violence against Catholic recusants in check. She positioned herself as a figure of religious moderation, and her policies had prevented widespread religious unrest. Elizabeth was a figure of civic stability.

Nevertheless, Bristol's officials indicated that they were keenly aware of the lurking threat. Dissension's two appeals are revealing in the way he baits the opposing camps. He first upbraids Peace, the "People Vayne," for their "jewels brave" and attachment to "gay and glyttring gold" (400). A comfortable mercantile sloth has made them soft. They "sleep and snort in sweet perfumed sheets" and "mak . . . no count of faem and publick prayes" (400). He next goads War with the threat of obsolescence. "Peace," he chides, "is bent to truss up soldiers all

---

[28] All references to the Bristol pageants are taken from John Nichols, ed., *The Progresses and Public Processions of Queen Elizabeth*, 3 vols. (London: John Nichols & Son, 1823), 1:396–407. Subsequent citations are provided in-text.

... for wealth will have no warrs" (401). With a bullying taunt, he sneers: "Peace ruells the earth, and wrings thear thumbs ... and saith a fig for war" (401). His words expose deep fears, such as the successful merchant's suspicion that his commitment to "greedy gayen" has led him to neglect the pursuit of larger, more noble ends and the soldier's fear of being made unnecessary by his own prowess. The predictable result is a furious assault by War on the outpost "Feeble Policy" which collapses, leaving the main fort vulnerable to the oncoming siege.

This destruction of "Feeble Policy" and the main fort's later desperation while under assault both illustrate the need for a strong external force to oversee the governance of the city and people. The usual mechanisms—civil laws, tradition, local community values—prove insufficient to contain the seemingly intrinsic urge to transgress. Without a higher authority, the community appears unable to resist the compelling allure in the rhetoric of Dissension. This pull is reiterated when Persuasion conveys War's interests in his parley with the Fort during a momentary cessation of hostilities. In his address, Persuasion seeks to convince Peace of the value of War as a "salve to heale the sinfull soule, and for the state a porge, / That skowrs the body of the Realm" (403). The city, however, is not convinced, claiming "our ruels sutch brawl denies, / Our Traed doth stand on sivill life, and thear our glory lies" (404). Here, the fort's defiance and hope seem to go against reason. Its occupants stand firm only because they are buoyed up by their faith in a "Prince by whom our peace is kept" (405).

This focus on Elizabeth as the city's savior would seem to be the intended climax; however, Churchyard provides one last twist. He records that "Perswasion beiyng dismist, the battry was planted before the Fort, and they within... straitly enclosed" (405). Three successive assaults are repulsed before War again seeks a parley and offers to spare the lives of the people on condition that the "Cortain was beaten down, and the Fort made sawtable" (406). The politically correct response, given as the queen stood watching, was that the fort's defense was not founded on "cortayns nor bulwarks ... but the corrage of good peple, and the force of a mighty Prince" (406). This ending astutely makes the queen the determining factor in the conflict but at the same time carefully includes and validates the power in the "good peple" as well. War flounders ultimately not because of the city's soldiery alone or the overwhelming military assistance from the Prince.[29] War abandons the assault only when it realizes the futility

---

[29] Churchyard records that on the second day "for a better order of warre, and to the ayde of the Fort, cam divers Gentilmen of good callynge from the Court, which maed the shoe very gallant, and set out the matter mutch" (402). Their initial contribution, however, was insufficient to break the siege. Only on the last day, after the third assault "the Enemie ... beholding nue suckors commyng from the Courte to the Forts great comfort, the Enemye agreed on a parley" (406). These new forces apparently tipped the scale, but it should be noted that despite War's concerted efforts, the Fort, almost independent of material help from the Crown, remained unconquered.

of assaulting a *combined* force of people and queen. Churchyard illustrates the commonwealth's need for a monarch to provide both a wider vision and greater resources. At the same time, he tucks inside the elaborate royal compliment a reminder of the power inherent in her subjects. The display implies the concept of shared responsibility in the exercise of good governance and civic authority and in this resembles Collinson's "monarchical republic." Churchyard's deft emphasis on the two groups' obligations to one another, however, also suggests the older, feudal model. In his calculated ambiguity, Churchyard tries to have it both ways. He plays to Elizabeth, who had no republican sympathies whatsoever, and to the Bristol sponsors, who were picking up the tab for his services.

Churchyard also had a hand in the entertainment at Norwich, sharing the creative responsibilities with Bernard Garter and William Goldingham.[30] Like Bristol, Norwich was concerned with mercantile and trade interests, especially the cloth trade with the Netherlands. The city was also a site of considerable religious unrest. As at London, Norwich was overwhelmingly Protestant; the surrounding countryside, however, remained persistently loyal to the old faith. In addition, strains of early Puritanism were evident in the region when iconoclasts waged an assault on the Norwich cathedral in 1570 and when prophesyings became more common, especially under Bishop John Parkhurst.[31] Elizabeth had replaced Parkhurst with Bishop Edward Frerke, directing him to rein in the prophesying. On the progress toward Norwich through East Anglia, the Privy Council interrogated Catholic recusants along the way.[32] The Norwich Elizabeth came to see was bisected by deep religious divisions.

Norwich was also, as David Galloway quotes, "a world in itself . . . capable of handling its own affairs."[33] To a greater degree than either London or Bristol, Norwich used its pageant to emphasize its independent efforts to thrive through industry. In a declamation accompanying the display of the city's fabric trade, Bernard Garter's verse highlights the city's work ethic:

> In this small shewe, our whole estate is seene.
> The welth we haue, we fine proceede from thence,
> The idle hande hath here no lace to feede,
> The painefull wight hath still to serue his neede.

---

[30] For other discussions of the entertainments at Norwich see Hackett, *Virgin Mother, Maiden Queen*, 96–98, and Louis Montrose, *The Subject of Elizabeth: Authority, Gender, and Representation* (Chicago: University of Chicago Press, 2006), 84–87.

[31] Cole, *Portable Queen*, 141.

[32] Some of these had the quality of spectacle; for example, the "discovery" of a statue of Mary at the home of Edward Rookwood and its subsequent public burning. For a detailed account of this progress, including the names of those investigated by the Privy Council, see Zillah Dovey, *An Elizabethan Progress: The Queen's Journey into East Anglia 1578* (Teaneck, NJ: Associated University Presses, 1996).

[33] Evans, quoted in Galloway, ed., *Norwich*, xvii.

The speaker goes on to confess that the city has succeeded not entirely because of its own merits, as he then acknowledges the importance of the queen's good governance:

> So weake we were within this dozen yeare,
> As care did quench the courage of the best:
> But good aduise, hath taught these little handes
> To rende in twayne the force of pining bandes . . .
> . . .Thus through thy helpe and ayde of power deuine,
> Doth NORWICH liue, whose harts and goods are thine!"[34]

The city was independent and competent in its administration. It had absorbed a sizeable immigrant population but set about employing the talents of its refugees, mostly Dutch, Flemish, and Walloon weavers, to "recapture . . . much of the export market."[35] Recognizing earlier than most cities the needs of a growing population of urban poor, the Norwich aldermen were proactive in requiring compulsory contribution for poor relief as early as 1549. Their approach later (1572) served as a model for the central government's policies regarding the same problem.[36] The city's independence is also evident in its displays and effort to convey the sense that all was under control in Norwich, firmly in the hands of the Protestant aldermen whose exercise of their responsibility recapitulated in miniature the model of good governance they claimed to see in the queen and her council.

The authors at Norwich placed the thematic emphasis not on military exercises but on more traditional entry displays, including the mayor's welcome speech, two pageants, and a masque. The theme of good governance became overt again at Norwich, with the authors applying a strategy similar to that of London by focusing specifically on Elizabeth's genealogy, inherent virtues, and affinity with historical models. The mayor welcomed Elizabeth as a "most Royal Prince" possessed of a "chast eye." She was for them the "light of this Realme (as Dauid was of Israell)."[37] She entered through a gate display of the Tudor genealogy and then witnessed a billboard-size display of the city's concept of proper governance entitled the "Causes of this Commonwealth." The next display featured an assortment of illustrious women who represented idealizations both of and for the queen. Later, in the masque, classical gods gave her gifts, many of which represented the qualities expected in a sovereign. The city had definite ideas about the ideal monarch and sought to fashion Elizabeth in accordance with this image. In the process, they

---

[34] Galloway, ed., *Norwich*, 255.
[35] Galloway, ed., *Norwich*, xvii. By 1579, there were about 6,000 aliens in a total population of over 16,000 (xvii).
[36] Galloway, ed., *Norwich*, xvii.
[37] Galloway, ed., *Norwich*, 251.

also sought to assure her of their religious conformity, their capacity for self-governance, and their devotion to her as their independent sovereign.[38]

We have two accounts of the Norwich entertainments, one presumably by Bernard Garter, and the second by Churchyard.[39] Garter was responsible primarily for the official civic presentations. His work emphasizes civic harmony and equates good governance with the proper ordering of the estates, an arrangement that was so successful that "the Prince had hir pleasure, the nobilitie their desire, [and] the whole traine such intertainment . . . [that] there semed but one hart in Queene, Counsaile, and communaltie" (247).[40] As with Mulcaster's publication, Garter's represents the public reception as uniformly positive, harmonious, and self-reinforcing—a situation that was also, most likely, a pleasant fiction.

Such appearance of harmony belied the divisions and unrest that had prompted Elizabeth's specific domestic and international agenda on this visit to East Anglia in 1578. She and the council were concerned not only with matters of religious dissent but also with opening a dialogue with the French about a potential marital alliance. Norwich had trade connections with the Low Countries and had absorbed a sizeable Protestant refugee population. It had suffered under the restrictions imposed by the Spanish embargo earlier in the decade, and it was keenly interested in the queen's policies toward the Netherlands. They were unenthused about the nascent marriage negotiations with the nominally Catholic Francis, duke of Alençon, and especially sensitive to the presence of a French delegation who attended the queen during her visit.[41] In Garter's pamphlet, however, Norwich was a "terrestrial Paradise" (247). He records the town's welcoming procession with the city's bachelors in black with yellow hat bands and all the local dignitaries arranged in "due and comely order" (249). Every detail reinforces the impression of civic harmony—a happy consequence, he implies, of good governance.

---

[38] The mayor emphasizes his role in "order[ing] the gouernance of this citie" in his welcoming oration (Galloway, ed., *Norwich*, 251).

[39] The account is titled *The Ioyfull receiving of the Queenes Most Excellent maiestie into Hir Highnesse Citie of Norvvich* and signed B. G. It was printed by Henry Bynneman in two editions dated 1578 (*STC*, 2nd ed., 11627 and 11628). Churchyard published his own account titled "A Discourse of the Queens Maiesties Entertainement in Suffolk and Norffolk . . ." (*STC* 5226). His was also printed by Bynneman in 1578 and was dedicated to Sir Christopher Hatton. The governance theme is less evident in Churchyard's efforts for the Norwich pageant. It appears he was engaged in negotiating his relationship with the queen and the town, rather than acting transparently in the city's interest.

[40] All references to Garter are to Galloway's edition.

[41] For a succinct review of the political situation that these pageant writers had to negotiate, see Donald Stump and Susan M. Felch, eds., *Elizabeth I and Her Age: A Norton Critical Edition* (New York: W.W. Norton, 2008), 238–40.

In his oration delivered to the queen in Latin, the mayor locates himself in that order and assures the queen both verbally and symbolically of his diligence in office. He acknowledges that he governs by her authority and offers her the emblems of his office as well as the traditional gift of money. He speaks the requisite, polite welcome "on the parte of these my brethren" and all the people (251). He also includes a considerable emphasis on reciprocity: the people pledge their goodwill and desire in order that the queen may be "gracious and favourable vnto [them]" (251). The Mayor appears eager to demonstrate that they have fulfilled their responsibilities. He invites Elizabeth to consider how well the municipal authorities have done their part, "ordering the governance" of the city, having kept it "safe and serviceable," and making its people "studious of God's glory and true religion" (251). This emphasis on the contractual aspect of the relationship is especially striking, though he overtly asks nothing in return but the queen's clemency (251–52). We are fortunate in the Norwich material to have Garter's version of the queen's reply. She is predictably politic, but her response is remarkably similar to the one she gave to the London recorder during the coronation entry. She accepts the gift of money graciously, although she is careful to point out that she does not need it. She has not come for gifts, she says, but simply to claim "that which in right is our owne, the heartes and true allegeaunce of our Subiects" (252). Then, apparently conscious of the Mayor's emphasis on reciprocity, she reminds the city of her own authority saying, "wherof as we assure ourselves in you, so do you assure yourselves in us of a loving and gracious sovereign" (252). Elizabeth was nothing if not deft.

The Mayor's welcome also includes an oddly suggestive metaphor that introduces the notion of reciprocal trust in good governance. The Mayor tells Elizabeth that he desires that her "chaste gaze should penetrate the secret strait corners of our hearts" (251). Instead of granting her the power to be invasive and searching, he expresses the wish that they could lay bare to her vision the contents of their hearts. To risk this openness, he must be convinced of the purity of his city's intent; he must trust that they have nothing to hide. He must also be sure of the queen's clemency; he must trust that they have nothing to fear from her. Governance in this model valorizes genuineness, transparency, vulnerability, and trust. The governance relationship negotiated by this conceit moves beyond the contractual toward the intimate.

After the Mayor's oration, the queen approaches the city gate where a figure from Norwich's mythic past, Gurgunt, awaits her. Unfortunately, a sudden downpour forces her to hurry past him, but, at the city gate, she finds displayed a reprise of the Tudor genealogy from the coronation procession. She next encounters a large display of working looms illustrating the cloth manufacturing trade of the city. Above these is prominently displayed a declaration in English of the "Causes of Our Commonwealth." Garter records them typographically:

>	The causes of this common wealth are,
> God truly preached.
> Iustice duely executed.	The people obedient.
> Idelnesse expelled.	Labour cherished.
> Vniuersall concorde preserued.
>
> (254)

The prominence of the term "commonwealth" again suggests a reciprocal relationship with similar parallels between "Justice duly executed" (respect of the governor) and "People obedient" (response of the well-governed). Significantly, these words appear over the display of working looms, and this juxtaposition not only vividly illustrates the city's industry but also implies that the queen bears some responsibility for the city's continued success through her proper management of trade policy. The city's industry and ingenuity and the queen's responsible policy had to work together to keep "Dame neede in hir caue" (255). Order and peace are presented as essential to commercial success—the object as well as the consequence of good governance.

The second pageant presents a review of illustrious women that in its own way illustrates good governance by figuring models for the queen.[42] Five women address Elizabeth, welcoming and complimenting her. In addition, four assign her a variety of roles: the figure representing the City of Norwich describes her as a loving nurse and mother; Deborah hails her as the Judge; Judith calls her the agent of the Lord; and Hester names her the scourge of the Lord. The fifth, Martia, assigns Elizabeth not a role but the sanction of history, both validating and to some extent normalizing feminine rule. Deborah links personal virtue and proper leadership to the flourishing of the state. She tells Elizabeth, "Where princes sitting in their thrones set god before their sight / and liue according to his lawe, and guide their people right, / There doth his blessed giftes abounde, there kingdoms firmely stand" (257). Judith positions Elizabeth as the Lord's anointed, even as she was, but with considerably more power. If God could see fit to enable her (Judith) to overthrow the tyrant Holofernes, "Then to a Prince of thy surpassing might. / What Tirant liues but thou mayest ouerthrow" (259). Hester cautions Elizabeth to be on her guard against "fraude" as well as force but assures her that those "whiche the Lorde in his defence doth wrap" are proof against the snares of the wicked; Elizabeth, Hester points out, has been shown "proofes" of this defense and "A world of foes of thine hath ouerthrowen" and should continue to be for her "flocke . . . their refuge and their rocke" (259). Good governance, the display implies, follows from the proper fulfillment of all these roles. Elizabeth could hardly have failed to recognize that behind the

---

[42] On the stridently Protestant tenor of the second pageant and its possible connection with the French marriage negotiations then in their preliminary stages, see Stump, "Abandoning the Old Testament," 294–98.

compliment of being associated with these figures was the expectation of living up to the precedents that they set.

The city also hosted a dinner and masque for Elizabeth the night before she departed. The masque, written by William Goldingham, touched on governance in several key ways. It involved a procession of classical gods and goddesses who paraded in pairs around the reception hall multiple times. After each circuit, a pair would give Elizabeth symbolic gifts representative of their particular skill or virtue. After the others had bestowed on Elizabeth tokens representing such traits as power, wisdom, and beauty, the final god, Cupid, handed over his golden arrow, putting into the queen's hand the power to choose her lover herself. Pointedly emphasizing the queen's romantic independence, he says to her, "Though some deserue, yet none deserue like you, / Shoote but this shafte at king or Caesar: He, / and he is thine, and if yout [sic] wilte allowe" (276). This message was likely intended to telegraph to the French ambassadors that the queen was immune from the vagaries of love, but in its expression of faith in her judgment it also resonated with the earlier praises of her virtue and clemency as their governor. In honoring her independence to choose a husband, the pageant effectively reiterated the faith in her articulated in the other displays. The city expected Elizabeth to exercise her authority in a way consistent with the needs of her people. The masque made visible their trust in her to do so in matters of the heart as well as those of policy.

Each of these three entry events invokes the theme of good governance and, in doing so, goes far beyond being simply courteous welcomes or state-sponsored propaganda. They are, I believe, forms of ritual negotiation in which different groups held up to the queen not only complimentary idealizations of her but also models that projected the relationship and type of authority they hoped the queen would demonstrate. In the coronation, Bristol, and Norwich entry pageants, the civic sponsors of the pageants presented concepts of good governance that reflected expectations and desires that often placed specific local or regional concerns in the foreground. For the most part this meant, predictably enough, good social order, the preservation of concord, policies supportive of trade and business, and a genuine desire for a monarchical presence that was competent, responsible, and attentive to the needs of the commonwealth. In addition, they sought to invoke in Elizabeth a prince that recognized their true worth and their commitment to the crown. These sponsors, and by extension most of the people they represented, wanted a governor possessed of a broad social vision and the means and will to counterbalance the tendency of smaller units of government to miss the larger picture. The displays are unfailingly complimentary and routinely emphasize Elizabeth's status and authority, but they also subtly remind her of her responsibility in maintaining a healthy social order. The queen, for her part, generally embraced the roles they gave her. It seems likely she enjoyed how they kept her in the center of attention, but, ever vigilant, she also managed her responses carefully so as to keep uppermost in her subjects' minds just where authority truly lay. One suspects Elizabeth was always well aware of her duties and needed no visual display to remind her of the weight of the crown she wore. Her subjects, however, were taking no chances.

"Give ear, O princes":
Deborah, Elizabeth, and the Right Word

Michele Osherow

"Who hath not heard of Jewish Deborah / Judith, and Jael that slew Sisera?" When "I.G." published these lines in 1605 in his pamphlet *An Apologie for Womenkind* (D3v), he could assume his audience's recognition of these biblical heroines, and particularly the prophetess who makes possible the other characters' tales.[1] Deborah was an especially prominent figure in sermons and pageant displays during the reign of Elizabeth I.[2] The queen was hailed as an English Deborah from the start of her reign until after her death. Her progress through the city of London the day before her coronation included a stop at Fleet Street, where, seated beneath "A Palme Tree," a "seemlie and mete personage richlie apparelled in parliament robes, with a septre in her hand, as a Quene" was presented to the young Elizabeth as "Debora the iudge and restorer of the house of Israel."[3] Though, as was the custom, a child approached the new queen to explain the meaning of the pageant, it was hardly necessary. Elizabeth was identified with the illustrious Deborah, the commander who led her nation into battle against Israel's enemy and restored faith to the chosen people.[4] A judge to whom the

---

[1] Jael appears in the biblical narrative to fulfill Deborah's prophecy that Sisera will be delivered "into the hand of a woman": *The Geneva Bible, a Facsimile of the 1560 Edition*, ed. Lloyd E. Berry (Madison: University of Wisconsin Press, 1969), Judges 4:9. Judith's story is commonly regarded as an embellishment of Jael's historical tale. See Susan Ackerman, *Warrior, Dancer, Seductress, Queen: Women in Judges and Biblical Israel* (New York: Doubleday, 1998), 49–51.

[2] For further discussion and a full list of instances of the use of Deborah as a paradigm for Elizabeth, see Donald Stump, "Abandoning the Old Testament," in this volume, 281–99, esp. 295–97.

[3] *The Quenes Maiesties Passage through the Citie of London to Westminster the Day before her Coronation*, ed. James M. Osborn (New Haven: Yale University Press, 1960), 53–54. On this event, see also the paper by Tim Moylan in this volume, 233–50.

[4] Judges 4:5.

Donald Stump, Linda Shenk, and Carole Levin, eds., *Elizabeth I and the 'Sovereign Arts': Essays in Literature, History, and Culture*. MRTS 407. Tempe: ACMRS, 2011. [ISBN 978-0-86698-455-3]

children of Israel came for guidance, Deborah was divinely raised to save them "Out of the hand of their oppressors."[5]

Though a number of historians note early modern England's regard of Elizabeth as an English Deborah, little study has been made which actively investigates Renaissance perception of this biblical character. Instead, scholars presume an audience familiar with the biblical heroine's history, or provide cursory explanations of it themselves. When discussing Elizabeth as a Deborah, for example, Elkin Calhoun Wilson describes the character as a "Hebrew prophetess" who "brings sweet peace to a troubled land."[6] Although accurate, this description does not convey the complexity of Deborah's position as judge in Israel, nor does it, as Susan Ackerman points out, communicate the "remarkable ways in which Judges' women can be depicted in defiance of traditional gender expectations."[7] One such defiance that would have been apparent to an early modern audience is the way in which speech functions to indicate Deborah's authority. In a time dedicated to keeping women chaste, *silent*, and obedient, Deborah contradicts female silence, and her remarkable use of language was recognized by—and often a source of anxiety for—early modern readers. This paper begins to unpack the characterization of Elizabeth as Deborah by attending to the way speech functions to affirm Deborah's authority and how, in turn, that is reflected or denied in early modern representations of Elizabeth.

To point to Queen Elizabeth's impressive discourse seems unnecessary. Her contemporaries noted it from the outset: Richard Mulcaster the day before her coronation marveled at the "heartiness" of her words and claimed they were "jointly knit."[8] Modern scholars such as Carole Levin and Ilona Bell comment on the elaborate crafting of the queen's rhetoric;[9] Bell calls Elizabeth a "master of intricately enigmatic prose."[10] What has not been observed is how the comparison of Elizabeth to Deborah also attends to Elizabeth's language. Once we examine the intricacies of Deborah's biblical history, we find it a history marked by discursive victories.

---

[5] *Geneva Bible*, Judges 2:16.

[6] Elkin Calhoun Wilson, *England's Eliza* (New York: Octagon, 1939), 64, 88. Wilson dedicates a chapter to Elizabeth as Deborah (61–95), though the biblical story is not told. Instead, Wilson lists references to Elizabeth, which associate her with things divine.

[7] Ackerman, *Warrior*, 5.

[8] *Elizabeth I: Collected Works*, ed. Leah S. Marcus, Janel Mueller, and Mary Beth Rose (Chicago: University of Chicago Press, 2000), 54.

[9] Carole Levin and Patricia A. Sullivan, eds., Introduction, in *Political Rhetoric, Power, and Renaissance Women* (Albany: State University of New York Press, 1995), 7. Also see Bell's essay in this volume, 105–23.

[10] Ilona Bell, "Elizabeth I—Always Her Own Free Woman," in *Political Rhetoric*, ed. Levin and Sullivan, 57–82, here 61.

Deborah's story is found in the Book of Judges, a portion of the Bible that presents a number of unusual female characters, ranging from prophetess to prostitute. These complicated women have been the subject of much critical investigation, most recently by Ackerman in *Warrior, Dancer, Seductress, Queen: Women in Judges and Biblical Israel*. As she observes, Judges' women stand in "striking contrast" to women appearing elsewhere in the Old Testament,[11] particularly owing to their participation in politics and war. Deborah is active in both of these arenas. She is described as "a prophetess, the wife of Lappidoth" who judged Israel.[12] Hers is an image of accord: "And she dwelt under the palm tree of Deborah . . . and the children of Yisra'el came up to her for judgment" (4:5). Israel is a nation divided and a nation oppressed. A twenty-year war with Canaan has worn them down. Canaan's military captain Sisera had nine hundred chariots of iron, and no one would fight him. Deborah's first action in her story is to speak to Barak, a general of the Israeli army, and remind him of his mission: "Go and gather your men to Mount Tavor, and take with thee ten thousand men. . . . I will deliver him into thy hand" (4:6–7). Barak refuses to go to battle against Sisera unless Deborah accompanies him, and she does. But she also warns that because of this cowardice "the Lord shall yield Sisera into the hand of a woman" (4:9).

One might assume that the female hand into which Sisera would be delivered is Deborah's own, but Deborah is more wordsmith than warrior. Instead, the narrative introduces Jael, the wife of Heber the Kenite, to bring about Sisera's demise. Sisera arrives at Jael's tent. She encourages him to trust her, and he enters. Jael covers him with a blanket and gives him milk to drink. Her next move is unexpected: "Then Jael, Heber's wife took a tent peg, and took a hammer in her hand, and went softly to him, and drove the tent peg into his temple and fastened it to the ground for he was fast asleep and weary" (4:21). The prose narrative offers no justification for Jael's deed, nor does it celebrate her success. That is left to Deborah.

Deborah's victory song in Chapter 5 of Judges punctuates her story. In it she celebrates God's deliverance of the enemy into Israel's (and a woman's) hands. Interestingly, Deborah draws attention to her own voice as much as she does the victory: "Hear, O kings; give ear, O princes: *I, even I,* will sing to the Lord" (5:3, emphasis added). She boasts, "The inhabitants of the villages ceased, they ceased in Yisra'el / until I Debora arose, / I arose a mother in Yisra'el . . . / . . . the Lord made me have dominion over the mighty ones" (5:7, 13). In the second half of the psalm, Deborah turns her attention to Jael, describing her as "blessed above women" (5:23). Deborah's song, indeed her biblical history, concludes with the observation that "the land was quiet / for forty years" (5:31).

---

[11] Ackerman, *Warrior*, 6.

[12] Judges 4:4. Unless otherwise indicated, Old Testament translations henceforth are from *The New Jerusalem Bible*, ed. Harold Fisch (Jerusalem: Koren Publishers, 1997). References to the Book of Judges are cited parenthetically by chapter and verse.

This promise of a forty-year peace would have been extremely attractive to Elizabeth's subjects at the start of her reign. Their world was in turmoil from the violent and bloody reign of the late Catholic Queen Mary, and the people turned to the Bible, expecting the sacred text "to supply solutions for pressing problems."[13] In the Bible, Deborah is one such solution. The Fleet Street coronation pageant recognizes this and concludes with these wishes for the new queen:

> A worthie president, O worthie Queene, thou hast,
> A worthie woman iudge, a woman sent for state.
> And that the like to us endure alway thou maist
> Thy loving subjects wil with true hearts and tonges praie.[14]

The comparison of Elizabeth to Deborah is a commendation, but the final lines of the child's speech also reveal an insecurity on the part of the English subjects. They pray that the queen will prove herself worthy of the comparison they make; they do not assert her abilities, but hope for them.

This anxiety extends to Deborah's judicial and discursive functions as well. The prophetess in the pageant is dressed in Elizabeth's parliamentary robes. She is posed with six personages representing the nobility, clergy, and citizenship of England. The description posted above the pageant reads, "Debora with her estates, consulting for the good gouernment of Israel."[15] The recorder of the pageant evaluates the display with the hope that "[Elizabeth] might by this be put in remembrance to consult for the worthie gouernment of . . . her people."[16] This is curious; in the Bible, Deborah never receives advice, she only offers it.[17] This citizen's interpretation of Deborah's story obscures her advisory position. Regardless of the biblical history featuring a woman's wisdom, this author regards the scene as a cue for Elizabeth to seek aid from knowing, male sources. While the representation of Deborah within this pageant associates her with victory and divine appointment, she is removed from the linguistic authority that characterizes her story in other early modern readings.

In Norwich in 1578, England's female monarch again confronts the Bible's female judge. Here, Deborah directly addresses the queen and emphasizes the divinity of her selection:

---

[13] Christopher Hill, *The English Bible and the Seventeenth Century Revolution* (London: Penguin, 1993), 4.

[14] Mulcaster, *Quenes Passage*, 54.

[15] Mulcaster, *Quenes Passage*, 54.

[16] Mulcaster, *Quenes Passage*, 54.

[17] England presents its queen in the image of Deborah, but she appears more restrained and dependent than she who judged Israel. The marginal notes in the Geneva Bible emphasize Deborah's competent judgment defining it as the "Spirit of prophecie, resolving of controversies, & declaring the wil of God" (110).

> But He that neyther sleepes nor slackes such furies to correct,
> Appointed me Debora for the Judge of his elect:
> And did deliver Sisera into a Woman's hande.
> I slewe them all, and so in rest his people helde the lande.[18]

Deborah does speak to the queen in the Norwich pageant, but she also justifies her voice, as if acknowledging the boldness of her act: "Myselfe (oh peerlesse Prince) do speake by proof of matter past."[19] Though the heroine claims her accomplishments give her the right to speak, she does not here identify her accomplishments as speech itself. But the practice Deborah routinely performed was a discursive one; speech is at the heart of her experience.

In her role as prophetess, judge, and poet, Deborah's history is distinguished by her articulate wisdom and the people's reliance upon it. In *Murder and Difference: Gender, Genre and Scholarship on Sisera's Death*, Mieke Bal examines language as the source of Deborah's authority, concluding that the complexity of Deborah's character makes it impossible to distinguish her linguistic performance as poet from her judicial function: "[Deborah] has saved Israel by her faith . . .; by her clairvoyance, her poetry, by her good *judgment*. The power of her song is testimony to this: there is nothing the right word cannot do. Thus she offers, for whoever knows how to listen, an explanation of what it means to *judge*: to pronounce the right word in a given situation."[20]

Surprisingly similar observations about Deborah's language may be found in early modern reflections. In 1601, Richard Vennar recognizes Deborah's song as evidence of superior judgment in his "Prayer for the prosperous Successe of hir Majestie's Forces in Ireland." Using Deborah's history to characterize Elizabeth, Vennar prays that his queen might "circumvent that rebellious Sissera, that [her] judgment (like a naile), may pierce into the braine of his malitious practices."[21] Vennar's prayer that the queen's judgment will prove as effective as Jael's tent peg registers the potency of Jael's deed while privileging Deborah's (and Elizabeth's) skill. Furthermore, the author alleges that this skill is one that will be established in lyric. His hope that "our Soveraigne may sing with Debora after the victorie"[22]

---

[18] *Progresses and Public Processions of Queen Elizabeth*, ed. John Nichols, 3 vols. (London: John Nichols & Son, 1823), 2:147.

[19] *Progresses*, 2:146.

[20] Mieke Bal, *Murder and Difference: Gender, Genre and Scholarship on Sisera's Death* (Bloomington: Indiana University Press, 1988), 56–57. Similarly, Barbara Johnson defines judgment as "nothing less than the wielding of power . . . through language": see *The Critical Difference: Essays in the Contemporary Rhetoric of Reading* (Baltimore: Johns Hopkins University Press, 1980), 102.

[21] *Progresses*, 3:541.

[22] *Progresses*, 3:541.

reiterates a connection between language and female power—Elizabeth's triumph will be indicated by her song.

The power of such a victory song is also emphasized by Thomas Heywood in *The Exemplary Lives and Memorable Acts of Nine The Most Worthie Women of the World: Three Jewes, Three Gentiles, Three Christians*. Heywood depicts Deborah's success as a series of verbal triumphs. She is the first subject in Heywood's volume. He describes her as "our worthy Jewesse . . . . / Rais'd from her sex . . . (by Text allowd)."[23] Deborah is endorsed by God, and more interestingly, by a "Text"—presumably the biblical text. Heywood presents Deborah as one authorized by language; her character exists courtesy of textual authority.

It is not surprising that Heywood should present a character born of language to profoundly engage with it. Immediately, he teaches his readers that Deborah's essence is discursive, and he commends the appropriateness of her name:

> The name *Deborah* in the originall implyeth a *Word*, or a *Bee*, neither was her name any way averse to her nature, for as she was mellifluous in her tongue, when she either pronounced the sacred oracles of God, or sat upon any judicatory causes, amongst his people: so she had also a sting at all times, upon any just occasion to wound and be revenged on his enemies. . . .[24]

Heywood's definition of Deborah's name shows an astute perception of biblical Hebrew. The Hebrew word דבורה (děbôrāh) literally translates to a "bee" or "swarm of bees"; however, the Hebrew root of Deborah, דבר (dābār), means "speech, word," which in the Hebrew Bible is an active agent. When we pair the definitions we find (as Heywood has found) a woman distinguished by potent or "stinging" speech.

Deborah is the first of Heywood's nine worthy women, and Elizabeth is the last. It is clear that his volume is framed to feature Elizabeth, though it was written nearly forty years after her death. Heywood does not explicitly compare Elizabeth to Deborah, but the link between the women is understood; the author opens the chapter on Elizabeth by explaining that the preceding portraitures were necessary for the "accurate expression of this rare heroicke Elizabeth."[25] Those traits conferred upon Elizabeth that are originally attributed to Deborah are her remarkable "Language and learning."[26] Heywood's celebration of Elizabeth's language appears early on in his tract; he describes her as "excellent in

---

[23] Thomas Heywood, *The Exemplary Lives and Memorable Acts of Nine The Most Worthie Women of the World: Three Jewes, Three Gentiles, Three Christians* (London: Thomas Coates, 1640), 2.

[24] Heywood, *Exemplary Lives*, 6.

[25] Heywood, *Exemplary Lives*, 185.

[26] Heywood, *Exemplary Lives*, 185. Traits attributed to Elizabeth in this passage that are first attributed to the other worthy women include piety, virginal purity, beauty and bounty, majesty and magnanimity, goodness, and pity for foreign distressed nations.

Learning" and "exquisite in language . . . who in her tender Infancy was said, almost as soone to speake as to goe, and that her words had sence as soone as found."[27] Of the other women reviewed by Heywood, only Deborah's words receive his admiration. The author adds, Elizabeth "at all . . . times of the day was observed to bee more ready to *pray*, then to *prattle*" (emphasis added).[28]

While Heywood's alliteration is clever, it reminds us that any consideration of a woman's speech is haunted by the image of the prattling female. Elizabeth does not escape it, nor does the biblical prophetess to whom she was often compared. In *The Monument of Matrons*, a text celebrating notable women, Thomas Bentley too clearly displays an anxiety caused by the association of a woman with wise words. He explains the name "Deborah" signifies "a word, a Bee, good utterance, a babler, speech."[29] Like Heywood's, Bentley's definition shows a knowledge of biblical Hebrew, but his definition is curious because nothing in the Hebrew root of the name connotes a particular kind of speech. The divinity inherent in Deborah's words likely prompts Bentley to define her name as a "good utterance."[30] Revealingly, however, he corrupts that definition with the term "babler."[31] The most common definition of "babble" in the sixteenth century was "to talk excessively or inappropriately; to chatter, prate." It also meant "to speak foolishly or incoherently."[32] Though Bentley's entry on Deborah does note the importance of her discourse (primarily in her assurance of Barak and her ability to speak God's words), the author's definition of Deborah's name highlights a difficulty in reckoning the biblical character's history with early modern attitudes towards women's speech. Deborah challenges the Renaissance gender ideology that located women in silent and subservient positions. Though we may observe an early modern discomfort with this challenge, the uneasiness only accentuates the linguistic authority unmistakable in Deborah's tale.

The necessity of such authority was not lost on Elizabeth. In the preface to their recent edition of Elizabeth's *Collected Works*, Leah S. Marcus, Janel Mueller, and Mary Beth Rose write, "Elizabeth's identity as princess and monarch cannot be separated from her identity as author."[33] This fashioning was shaped by the queen herself, "Although my youth and words may seem to some hardly to agree together."[34] Elizabeth seems acutely aware of the pressures placed upon

---

[27] Heywood, *Exemplary Lives*, 187.

[28] Heywood, *Exemplary Lives*, 187.

[29] Thomas Bentley, "Lampe 7," in *The Monument of Matrons* (London: H. Denham, 1582), 137.

[30] Bentley, *Monument*, 137.

[31] Bentley, *Monument*, 137.

[32] *The Oxford English Dictionary*, 2nd ed., ed. J. A. Simpson and E. S. C. Weiner (Oxford: Clarendon Press, 1989), s.v.

[33] *Collected Works*, xiii.

[34] *Collected Works*, 57.

her discourse and the difficulty of directing meaning: "Do I see God's most sacred holy Word . . . drawn to so divers senses, being never so precisely taught, and shall I hope that my speech can pass forth through so many ears without mistaking . . . ?"[35] Though Elizabeth may have felt frustration at the inability to contain her speech, she seemed, too, to recognize her rhetorical skill. Elizabeth's prayers of thanksgiving are littered with thanks for her "knowledge and use of literature and languages."[36] These prayers, or psalms, are a biblical form Elizabeth often imitated, and her verses echo the emphasis on language and performance found in the biblical poems: "I render undying thanks unto Thy divine Majesty with *my mouth*, with my heart, and with all that I am" (emphasis added);[37] "I know that . . . [t]he cup of deliverance should never leave my hands, nor should the new songs ever leave my mouth."[38] Elizabeth's tributes to God are linguistic—further evidence, perhaps, of Bal's claim that "there is nothing the right words cannot do."[39]

The Right Word. The Right Woman. The Right Woman's Words. Though Elizabeth repeatedly refers to David in her thanksgiving prayers, she does not ignore the significance of her biblical foremothers: "Oh my God, my Father, . . . persist . . . in giving me strength so that I, like another Deborah, like another Judith, like another Esther may free Thy people of Israel from the hands of Thy enemies."[40] In this prayer, Elizabeth does not focus on these women's words, but they were women of words; both Deborah and Judith have songs of thanksgiving, and Esther's quiet discourse with her husband saved a nation. Elizabeth refers to these women on the grounds that their histories illustrate that God chooses "the weak things of this world in order to confound and destroy the strong."[41] But if these women are weak, their weakness is not evident in their speech. Deborah's narrative exposes a system of female authority that celebrates and relies upon language. The frequency with which Elizabeth was compared to Deborah suggests it was a convenient way to compliment the queen, and I suggest this

---

[35] *Collected Works*, 168.
[36] *Collected Works*, 141.
[37] *Collected Works*, 156.
[38] *Collected Works*, 145–46.
[39] Bal, *Murder and Difference*, 57.
[40] *Collected Works*, 157.
[41] *Collected Works*, 157, quoting 1 Corinthians 1:27. For all her victory, Deborah cannot elude this early modern presumption of feminine weakness. In his sermon celebrating Deborah and Jael's deed, John Donne concludes that "God by weake means doth mighty workes": see *The Sermons of John Donne*, ed. Evelyn M. Simpson and George R. Potter, 10 vols. (Berkeley: University of California Press, 1953–1962), 4:181. Similarly, John Aylmer summarizes Deborah's history with the observation that "[God] saved his people by the hande of a woman poore . . . God worketh in weakness": see *An Harborowe for Faithfvll and Trewe Subjects agaynst the Late Blowne Blaste, Concerning the Government of Wemen* (London: J. Day, 1559), B3v.

compliment is more complex than has been allowed. Both Deborah and Elizabeth were women who raised their voices "louder than the voice of archers,"[42] a characteristic of all Mothers in Israel.

---

[42] Judges 5:10.

Elizabeth I's Divine Wisdom: St. Paul, Conformity, and John Lyly's *Endymion*

Linda Shenk

In the late 1580s, when religious fervor in England had reached apocalyptic intensity, Queen Elizabeth I attended a performance of John Lyly's *Endymion*—a play that overtly praised her as Cynthia, goddess of the moon. By lauding the queen through this secular figure, Lyly created a world for Elizabeth that, outwardly, seemed far removed from the strident religious discourse of the period. Yet, as David Bevington and Carolyn Ruth Swift Lenz have demonstrated, the play is saturated with religious resonances.[1] Lenz examines the way in which Lyly invokes the context of the play's performance for Elizabeth on Candlemas (most likely in 1588)[2] by echoing the Collect and the day's readings from Solomon's Book of Wisdom. She ends her analysis with a brief suggestion that Lyly uses these parallels to make Elizabeth a figure of divine wisdom. Bevington does not link the play directly with Elizabeth but rather situates it within mounting tensions between England and Spain. Later in 1588, Spain would indeed launch its Armada to attack England from without, even as, I would add, the rollicking voice of the Puritan Martin Marprelate would attack the Elizabethan episcopacy from within.

In this essay, I will reveal an additional set of religious references in *Endymion* that integrates the depiction of Elizabeth directly with religious politics in 1588. Such analysis will shed light on one of the queen's sovereign arts that has received little attention—her authority in ecclesiastical affairs. Lyly's representation of Elizabeth as a figure of divine wisdom is central to understanding the way in which he and other figures of the period, including the queen herself, were creating an expansive, deeply personal, religious persona for Elizabeth associated

---

[1] D. Bevington, "Lyly's *Endymion* and *Midas*: The Catholic Question in England," *Comparative Drama* 32 (1998): 26–46; C. Lenz, "The Allegory of Wisdom in Lyly's *Endimion*," *Comparative Drama* 10 (1976): 235–57.

[2] Theatrical records list a payment to Lyly's company (the Children of Paul's) at Greenwich on 2 February 1588. See E. K. Chambers, *The Elizabethan Stage*, vol. 4 (Oxford: Clarendon Press, 1967), 162.

with unity, order, and love. Lyly creates this image through a series of hitherto unacknowledged references to St. Paul's first letter to the Corinthians. He places the queen at the center of the Pauline rhetoric that dominated discussions of contemporary ecclesiastical controversy and that surfaced repeatedly in rhetoric used to support conformity to England's national church.[3]

When examining England's ecclesiastical polity, scholars have primarily emphasized the efforts of the queen's high-ranking clergy, along with significant apologists such as Richard Bancroft, John Bridges, Richard Hooker, and John Whitgift. Indeed, these figures were the major forces urging conformity, but Elizabeth's own ecclesiastical image also played a substantial role in the discourse of national religious unity. As I have argued elsewhere, Elizabeth and many influential writers in the late 1580s and early 1590s tailored her persona as a national religious leader by associating her with St. Paul's first epistle to the Corinthians. They presented her stance as one of philosophical transcendence rather than narrowly Protestant doctrine. In *Endymion*, Lyly participates in this same approach by depicting Elizabeth as a figure who leads and unifies her nation as a queen of love and divine wisdom. These roles are doctrinally expansive and politically flexible in ways that extend Elizabeth's authority as Supreme Governor of the Church of England into territories that avoid sectarian division. These intertwined royal images make religious conformity a matter of love for the queen and, as a result, are particularly strategic in this period when England and all of Europe were becoming deeply polarized along religious lines. This fracturing was prompting many figures, both in England and abroad, to adopt secular, but religiously-infused, positions to bypass divisions that were causing increased tension in pan-European relations.

Situating Lyly's connection between Elizabeth and divine wisdom in this context provides a window into the way in which Elizabeth's authority in religious politics often manifests itself in guises seemingly unrelated to issues of ecclesiastical polity. To unlock the complexity of Lyly's representation of the queen, I will first demonstrate the extent to which *Endymion* is steeped in 1 Corinthians and then examine his representation of Cynthia alongside concurrent texts that also employ St. Paul relative to Elizabeth and her church. Studying Lyly's play in conjunction with a group of such texts—which will include two of Elizabeth's own articulations—suggests that the queen's ecclesiastical presence is a

---

[3] John S. Coolidge, *The Pauline Renaissance in England: Puritanism and the Bible* (Oxford: Clarendon Press, 1970). A few of the many significant works on ecclesiastical polity and Puritanism include Patrick Collinson, *The Elizabethan Puritan Movement* (Oxford: Clarendon Press, 1967); John Guy, "The Elizabethan Establishment and the Ecclesiastical Polity," in *The Reign of Elizabeth I: Court and Culture in the Last Decade*, ed. idem (Cambridge: Cambridge University Press, 1995), 126–49; and Peter Lake, *Anglicans and Puritans? Presbyterianism and English Conformist Thought from Whitgift to Hooker* (London: Unwin Hyman, 1988).

sovereign art that may arise both in outwardly secular personae and in the seemingly personal rhetoric of love. Lyly's play provides an opportunity to examine ways in which Elizabeth's role as an ecclesiastical figure may be far more pervasive, personal, and even poetic than we have yet imagined.

1 Corinthians and Cynthia's Superior Wisdom

At the heart of Lyly's representation of Elizabeth as Cynthia is his use of 1 Corinthians to place the queen at the philosophical epicenter of the play. Lyly draws especially from the opening chapters of Paul's epistle, where the apostle contrasts the foolishness of earthly wisdom with the joy experienced by those who simply turn to God in love. St. Paul writes: "For the wisedome of this worlde, is foolishnesse with God: for it is written, He compasseth the wise in their owne craftinesse. And againe, The Lord knoweth the thoughts of the wise, that they be vaine" (1 Cor. 3:19–20).[4] Nowhere in his outwardly secular play does Lyly refer to St. Paul outright; it is up to audience members to hear the echoes. These allusions are the most discernable when Cynthia shares the stage with characters explicitly associated with wisdom: the philosophers Pythagoras and Gyptes.

These two figures have come to Cynthia's court in response to her search for the world's greatest sages. She hopes that they can devise a way to counteract the magic that has put the devoted Endymion under a spell of endless sleep. Pythagoras and Gyptes are thus invited to Cynthia's court because of their famed wisdom. With a lovely sense of Pauline inversion, however, it is *Cynthia* who reveals to *them* that their wisdom is foolishness. In fact, Lyly wastes no time getting to this idea; he includes it in Cynthia's opening line to Pythagoras when the philosophers make their first entrance. Cynthia echoes St. Paul's mockery of earthly knowledge (1 Cor. 1:27) when she says, "You see, Pythagoras, what ridiculous opinions you hold, and I doubt not but you are now of another mind."[5] By having Cynthia call Pythagoras by name at the outset, Lyly emphasizes this philosopher's identity and thus makes Cynthia's teasing mockery all the more startling. It is not just any sage who has been convinced that his ideas are "ridiculous" but rather the Greek mathematician and natural philosopher widely esteemed as possessing almost divine knowledge. Pythagoras's great wisdom would have been familiar to many audience members because the poet Ovid gives Pythagoras a lengthy speech at the end of his *Metamorphoses*. Arthur Gold-

---

[4] *The Holy Bible, conteyning the Olde Testament and the Newe* (London, 1588; *STC* 2149). All biblical citations refer to this edition, unless otherwise specified, and subsequent citations appear in-text.

[5] Lyly, *Endymion*, ed. David Bevington (Manchester: Manchester University Press, 1996), 4.3.46–47. All citations are from Bevington's edition, and subsequent citations appear in-text.

ing's well-known translation of this text describes Pythagoras thus: "And though this persone were / Farre distant from the Goddes by site of heauen: yit came he neere / Too them in mynd. And he by syght of soule and reason cheere / Behild the things which nature dooth too fleshly eyes denye."[6] His knowledge, in turn, was of such scope that it comprehended

> The first fonndation of the world: the cause of euery thing:
> What nature was: & what was God: whence snow & lyghtening spring:
> And whither loue or else the wynds in breaking clowdes doo thunder:
> What shakes ye earth: what law ye starres doo keepe theyr courses vnder:
> And what soeuer other thing is hid from common sence.[7]

Pythagoras is a figure who probes wisdom hidden from conventional understanding—a situation that makes the alteration that Lyly's Pythagoras undergoes all the more striking. In fact, Cynthia even expresses confidence ("I doubt not") that his beliefs have been transformed. Her success may be doubly significant because, according to Ovid's description, this famed philosopher, despite all his wisdom and attempts to share it, had "effect but small" on his listeners.[8] Cynthia, by contrast, possesses both powerful wisdom and, as Pythagoras next articulates, the ability to convince others—even him.

Lyly's Pythagoras is quick to confirm that it is Cynthia who has transformed his opinion, and he expresses this change in language associated with religious epiphany. He declares, "Madam, I plainly perceive that the perfection of your brightness hath pierced through the thickness that covered my mind, insomuch that I am no less glad to be reformed than ashamed to remember my grossness" (4.3.48–51). By attributing his mental change to her "brightness," Pythagoras is associating Cynthia with innate virtue. Because she reforms minds through radiance rather than logical argumentation, her wisdom transcends all earthly processes. In addition, Pythagoras's description of his change of perception as light piercing through thickness may even associate Cynthia with specifically divine, Christian virtue because Pythagoras may be invoking 1 Corinthians 13:12. In this famous passage, St. Paul explains, "Nowe we see in a glasse, euen in a darke speaking: but then shall we see face to face. Nowe I knowe vnperfectly: but then shall I know, euen as I am knowen." If such an allusion is present, then

---

[6] Ovid, *The .xv. Bookes of P. Ouidius Naso, entytuled Metamorphosis, translated oute of Latin into English meeter*, trans. Arthur Golding (London, 1567: *STC* 18956), 187r. The idea that Lyly was referring to Ovid's representation of Pythagoras is all the more likely since he had made extensive use of Golding's translations in the *Euphues* texts. See Mike Pincombe, "Lyly and Golding: A New Source for *Euphues and His England*," *Notes and Queries* 51 (2004): 243–44.

[7] Ovid, *Metamorphosis*, 187v.

[8] Ovid, *Metamorphosis*, 187v.

Lyly underscores the fact that Pythagoras possesses an incomplete version of the divine wisdom that Cynthia embodies.

This contrast between divine virtue and earthly knowledge precisely mirrors St. Paul's overall message in 1 Corinthians. The introductory "Argument" to this epistle in the 1560 Geneva Bible (which was dedicated to Elizabeth) demonstrates this antithesis quite succinctly. The Argument describes the false apostles as "being puffed vp with vaine glorie" and then goes on to criticize the "vaine doctrine" and "those vaine glorious braggers." Paul, however, is praised for "setting before their eyes the spiritual vertue, & heauenlie wisdome of the Gospel, which cannot be persuaded by worldlie wit and eloquent reasons but is reueiled by Gods Spirit, and so sealed in mens hearts."[9] To maintain the inexplicable aura that effected the "reformation" of Lyly's Pythagoras, this change occurs offstage just prior to the sage's first scene with Cynthia in 4.3. The workings of Cynthia's radiant virtue remain mystical.

Whereas Pythagoras alludes to Cynthia's virtues through the notion of radiance, it is Gyptes who will make an overt reference to them. He follows Pythagoras's claims of reformation with his own praise, extolling the fortune of those who live in Cynthia's court: "They are thrice fortunate that live in your palace, where truth is not in colours but life, virtues not in imagination but execution" (4.3.52–54). Cynthia will also reinforce this focus on her virtues: "I have always studied to have rather living virtues than painted gods" (4.3.55–56). In order to emphasize that Cynthia's living virtues are intrinsic and real rather than artificially created, Lyly contrasts them to paints and "colours"—terms reminiscent of the traditional metaphor for the rhetorical arts as false, cosmetic paints. In the 1590 edition of the Geneva Bible, for example, the note for 1 Corinthians 1:17 makes this specific connection when it glosses the "wisdome of wordes" as "painted speach."[10] Just as Cynthia is able to transform Pythagoras's mind through radiant virtue rather than logical arguments, so too do these references set Cynthia's powerful virtue apart from the mechanics of earthly wisdom.

Pythagoras and Gyptes eventually make a formal renunciation of their former perspectives when, in the concluding moments, they agree to stay in Cynthia's court. This announcement comes after Cynthia proclaims that she will not protect them if they continue to follow their foolish knowledge. In lines that once again echo St. Paul's condemnation of vain, foolish wisdom, she admonishes them: "You, Gyptes and Pythagoras, if you cannot content yourselves in our court to fall from vain follies of philosophers to such virtues as are here prac-

---

[9] I cite from the Geneva Bible here, even though it is a nonconformist text, because it includes an "Argument" for each book of scripture—a feature that the authorized editions of the Bishops' Bible do not contain. *The Bible and Holy Scriptvre Conteyned in the Olde and New Testament* (Geneva, 1560; *STC* 2093), 76r.

[10] *The Bible, that is, the Holy Scriptvres, conteined in the Olde and Newe Testament* (London, 1590; *STC* 2154), 1 Cor. 1:17, n. 21.

tised, you shall be entertained according to your deserts" (5.4.299–303). Whereas editor R. Warwick Bond emends Q's "cannot" to "can,"[11] Bevington accepts Q's original wording, for, as he notes, "*cannot* has its own more threatening logic, that if the scholars cannot abandon vain learning to practise virtue they deserve what they will get." Bevington describes this instance as the "capitulation of the philosopher into the courtier,"[12] and attention to the Pauline context further supports this notion of the courtier. Cynthia's mandate that the philosophers reject their vain earthly wisdom conjures up the unstated preference for the courtier's traditional pose of love even as this overall scenario emphasizes that Cynthia is essentially demanding intellectual conformity.[13]

Cynthia's right to ask for such conformity is divinely blessed (because of its connection to 1 Corinthians), and the conformity she achieves stems from admiring willingness. Her sheer virtue possesses a radiance that, all on its own, naturally changes and edifies others. This characteristic allows Cynthia to create conformity simply through presence rather than proclamation and, in this power, engender voluntary harmony. As I will discuss in more depth shortly, it is interesting to note that this same sense of a natural attraction to the goodness and truth of the national church was present in much conformist rhetoric of this period and that this language was also grounded in St. Paul's discussion of love and the church in 1 Corinthians.

According to St. Paul, all wisdom is folly unless it is grounded in love. The apostle soon takes this notion and applies it, not to personal relationships, but rather to the church. He writes: "And though I haue prophecie, and vnderstande all secretes, and all knowledge: yea if I haue all faith, so that I can remooue mountaines, & haue not charitie, I am nothing" (1 Cor. 13:2). Taken out of context, this passage sounds as though it is about an individual expressing charity (often worded as "love" in earlier Bishops' Bibles), but St. Paul includes this idea at the culmination of his discussion regarding ecclesiastical polity. He is talking about the edification of the church, and for this reason, this chapter in 1 Corinthians and its focus on love were frequently cited in this period's conformist rhetoric.

---

[11] *The Complete Works of John Lyly*, ed. R. Warwick Bond, vol. 3 (Oxford: Clarendon Press, 1902), 5.3.286.

[12] *Endymion*, ed. Bevington, 195, n. 300.

[13] This image of Cynthia's inflexible monarchic power and the philosophers' willing (and swift) conformity to her will stands in stark contrast to Lyly's depiction of Diogenes in *Campaspe*. As Leah Scragg examines, this Cynic rests outside the harmony between Alexander (as a supposed philosopher-king) and the play's other philosophers. See "*Campaspe* and the Construction of Monarchical Power," *Medieval and Renaissance Drama in England: An Annual Gathering of Research, Criticism and Reviews* 12 (1999): 59–83, esp. 65–66.

Love and the Perfection of the Church in Conformity

Most famously, John Bridges uses 1 Corinthians to urge conformity in *A defence of the government established in the Chvrch of Englande for ecclesiasticall matters* (1587). He first conjures up the notion of the Church as a body (1 Cor. 12:13–31) and then uses St. Paul's discussion of love to explain how these different parts must work together to achieve the perfection of the Church. Bridges writes:

> But of the excellencie of loue or charitie, aboue all the giftes and offices that he had named: and maketh this the waie to tend vnto the perfection of the church, concluding thus: And now abideth faith, hope, and loue, these three: but the cheefest of these is loue. This was the full drift of S. Paule in this place, concerning the mysticall bodie of Christe, which is his church or house, and that the building vp thereof: euen, where he speaketh of Gouernors, and of the waye tending to perfection.[14]

Significantly, the end of this passage shows that Bridges uses the metaphor of the body as support for rulers. Indeed, right before making this comment, he emphasizes that earthly governors are "mentioned in expresse termes" in 1 Corinthians 12:28.[15] Bridges uses love and 1 Corinthians as support for conformity to a church unified under Elizabeth as its governor.

When Lyly uses St. Paul's epistle to praise the divine Cynthia in *Endymion*, he invokes conformist discourse but adopts a slightly different tack in justifying Elizabeth's ecclesiastical authority. Whereas Bridges talks about national unity of the Church under Elizabeth, Lyly ties conformity directly to Elizabeth's person. He uses love, but love as an emotional attachment to his queenly moon. Significantly, this more personal language of love is found in 1 Corinthians, but it is a love devoted solely to God rather than to a human beloved. According to St. Paul's schema, all earthly wisdom is useless and vain, but turning to God in love is an appropriate pursuit. The apostle shifts from disparaging intellectual endeavor to calling for the Corinthian congregation to come together in love for God. He then explains that, "as it is written, The eye hath not seene, and the eare hath not heard, neither haue entred into the hart of man, the things which God hath prepared for them that loue him" (1 Cor. 2:9). Lyly has been building this contrast between love and wisdom in *Endymion* since the opening scene through the character that loves Cynthia with a complete adoration: Endymion himself.

---

[14] J. Bridges, *A defence of the government established in the Chvrch of Englande for ecclesiasticall matters* . . . (London, 1587; *STC* 3734), 62. Peter Lake initially drew my attention to this section in Bridges' text in *Anglicans and Puritans?*, 120.

[15] Bridges, *A defence*, 62.

Approaching the Divine Cynthia-Elizabeth in Love

Throughout the play, Endymion has been expressing his unwavering love for the divine Cynthia, and in fact, devotion is his signature characteristic. In Endymion's first lengthy speech in 1.1, he waxes rhapsodic when expressing his adoration. He declares that Cynthia's superlative beauty and virtues make her one "whom time cannot touch because she is divine." He soon gets a bit overwhelmed with emotion and cries out,

> O Cynthia, if thou shouldst always continue at thy fullness, both gods and men would conspire to ravish thee. But thou, to abate the pride of our affections, dost detract from thy perfections, thinking it sufficient if once in a month we enjoy a glimpse of thy majesty; and then, to increase our griefs, though dost decrease thy gleams, coming out of thy royal robes wherewith thou dazzlest our eyes, down into thy swath clouts, beguiling our eyes. And then— (1.1.68–76)

His friend Eumenides interrupts to cut short Endymion's reverie once it takes a titillating turn with Cynthia suddenly disrobing. Indeed, Endymion is engrossed with love that is not aloof from sexual desire. As Catherine Bates emphasizes, his desire is "embedded in the earthly," at least for the first half of the play.[16] What is significant in this passage is how Lyly juxtaposes Endymion's love (however impure) with Cynthia's divinity. As Endymion frequently exclaims, she is "divine" (for example, 1.1.67; 5.1.50–51, 61), and Cynthia herself hints at her divinity, explaining that she, "being placed for light on earth, is also protected by the powers of heaven" (5.4.10–11).

Not only does Endymion's adoration of the divine Cynthia align him with the love St. Paul discusses in 1 Corinthians, but it also echoes a scriptural text appropriate for the play's performance on Candlemas. Lenz notes that King Solomon's apocryphal Book of Wisdom was alluded to in the Collect for that day, as well as in the lessons at matins and evensong.[17] Significantly, Endymion's love for Cynthia resembles Solomon's expressions of love for the figure of Divine Wisdom. Solomon claims, "I haue loued her, and laboured for her from my youth vp: I did my diligence to marrie my selfe with her, such loue had I vnto her beautie" (Wisdom 8:2). Lyly's allusions to the biblical readings for this holy day are further underscored when Endymion ends the speech of rapture by describing Cynthia coming out of her "swath clouts." This image, as R. Chris Hassel, Jr.

---

[16] C. Bates, *The Rhetoric of Courtship in Elizabethan Language and Literature* (Cambridge: Cambridge University Press, 1992), 87.

[17] Lenz, "The Allegory of Wisdom," 235.

observes, is a reference to the swaddled Christ child.[18] Such an allusion is especially fitting since Candlemas was traditionally the day for celebrating the purification of the Virgin Mary and the subsequent presentation of the infant Christ in the Temple.[19] Perhaps even the play's performance venue at Greenwich would have lightly suggested this image because it was at Greenwich that Elizabeth was born and baptized.

Lyly inserts these nods to Cynthia's divinity but still presents Endymion's love for her under the secular cover of Neoplatonic contemplation. Lyly's specific depiction of Endymion as a Neoplatonic quester is especially fitting because it highlights the character's identity in the traditional myth of Endymion. Robert S. Knapp explains that "[A]ccording to Pliny he [Endymion] was the first to find out the orbit of the moon, and according to Artemidorus, Endymion is a lover of sleep, but in other versions, he is an astronomer." Knapp notes that, in contrast, "Lyly, while insisting on the astronomical character of Cynthia, gives his Endimion no other profession than love."[20] Indeed, the love that Endymion expresses is, in keeping with the Pauline references in this play, directed towards a pointedly divine Cynthia.[21] She points to Elizabeth as God's beloved who, Lyly implies, possesses the special wisdom that allows her to draw her nation together in holy love.

Lyly is not alone in infusing seemingly secular images of Elizabeth with biblical references and Christian wisdom. In fact, numerous writers in the 1580s produced texts that channeled apocalyptic fervor into a millennial support for Elizabeth as the unifier of God's "true" church.[22] In a manner that has affinities with Lyly's techniques, these writers created a religious presence for Elizabeth that centered her authority in her person rather than in her position. They portrayed her as the wise and virtuous Queen of God's Word who could lead her unified Church Triumphant into battle against the papal Antichrist.

---

[18] R. C. Hassel, Jr., *Renaissance Drama and the English Church Year* (Lincoln, NE: University of Nebraska Press, 1979), 104–5.

[19] Lenz, "The Allegory of Wisdom," 235.

[20] R. Knapp, "The Monarchy of Love in Lyly's *Endimion*," *Modern Philology* 73 (1976): 353–67, here 355.

[21] Lyly may also have encountered the idea to infuse the Endymion-Cynthia story with Pauline notions from an emblem produced in 1581. This emblem depicted Cynthia cradling Endymion with the Pauline tag *"Cupio dissolui"* (from Philippians 1:23) underneath. See Knapp, "The Monarchy of Love," 355.

[22] I examine this trend in *Learned Queen: The Image of Elizabeth I in Politics and Poetry* (New York: Palgrave Macmillan, 2010). See Chap. 3, "Queen of the Word: Elizabeth I, Divine Wisdom, and Apocalyptic Discourse in the 1580s."

St. Paul and the Unity of Hearts and Hands Devoted to Elizabeth

Typically, Elizabeth is not associated with such militant and apocalyptic discourse, and with good reason. She loathed this divisive rhetoric and its use in urging (if not outright pressuring) her both to adopt more radical religious reform and to engage in war. What is interesting, however, is that in 1588—perhaps the same year as the performance of *Endymion*—the crown authorized the publication of Maurice Kyffin's expanded edition of *The Blessednes of Brytaine*. This text used 1 Corinthians 2:9 to enfold Elizabeth's wisdom into love and divinity, a combination subsequently used to rally England behind its Protestant queen and, in turn, to take up God's sword. In Kyffin's text, Elizabeth's subjects unify in loving adoration of their queen. A brief discussion of this text and its use of 1 Corinthians will establish not only that these ideas were very much in circulation in 1588 but also that Lyly has added a particularly significant twist in his own use of St. Paul.[23]

In the first edition of *Blessednes*, published in 1587, Kyffin celebrates England's strength by beginning with an extended image of Elizabeth as a traditional learned queen. The second stanza lauds her as "A Monarch Mayden Queene" whose "Vertues of her Minde" make her

> *The* Starre *of VVomen Sex,* Graue Wisedoms store:
> *Sententious, speaking Tongs in filed phraze,*
> *Profoundly learnd, and Perfect in eche Lore,*
> *Her* Fame, *no Rav'ning Time, shall euer Raze:*
> Hater *of* Wrong, high Refuge *eke for* Right,
> Concord, *and* Peace, *continuing by her Might.*[24]

Kyffin portrays Elizabeth as a Christian learned prince who combines book learning with moral rectitude. Part of this traditional image is her extraordinary gift for speaking multiple languages and speaking them with the proficiency of the "filed" tongue of eloquence.

When Kyffin produces the expanded edition in 1588, the crown authorizes the second half or, as its title page says, the "Continvation." In this added text, Kyffin no longer focuses his panegyric on Elizabeth's learning but instead emphasizes how much her subjects love her and love God. He creates this new image of Elizabeth through his submerged allusions to 1 Corinthians 2:9 and thereby acknowledges not only St. Paul's notion that love for God will unify the Corinthian congregation but also the presence of this idea in contemporary

---

[23] I provide an in-depth analysis of Kyffin's text in *Learned Queen*.

[24] M. Kyffin, *The Blessednes of Brytaine, or A Celebration of the Queenes Holyday* . . . (London, 1588; *STC* 15097), A3r-v.

ecclesiastical texts that call for religious conformity. In the second stanza, Kyffin proclaims that she "liues in loue of all" as one *"Who hath the harts, of her leege folk in hold."*[25] Only a few stanzas later, he foregrounds this notion of love through the use of the rhetorical figure *anaphora*:

> *Adore we* God *who lends vs still her lyfe:*
> *Adore we* her, *whom* God *hath plas'd in Powre:*
> *Adore we* him *in* her *that Stints our Strife:*
> *Adore we* Both, *Respectiuelie, eche howre:*
> *The* one *in Heav'n Directs vs by his Grace:*
> *The* other *here on Earth, supplieth his place.*[26]

The repetition of "Adore" emphasizes the idea of intense love even as the parallel construction equates love for God with love for Elizabeth. What is particularly powerful about this technique is how it centers England's religious agenda as God's chosen people in the personal image of Elizabeth herself. She becomes the focal point for religious action and national unity—not through the official and formal language of conformity but rather through the personal language of love.

Kyffin will take this language (which has its roots in conformist discourse) and use it to urge English Protestant unity against Spain's Catholic threat. Kyffin layers in the military aspect by building on the apocalyptic reference already imbedded in 1 Corinthians 2:9. As Richard Bauckham indicates, St. Paul refers to the time of future blessedness that the elect will experience after the warfare of the final days.[27] When St. Paul writes "But as it is written" in 1 Corinthians 2:9, he is acknowledging Isaiah 64:4, which reads "For since the beginning of the world, it hath not bene heard or perceiued, neither hath any eye seene another God beside thee, which doest so much for them that put their trust in thee."[28] Isaiah, like St. Paul, stresses the rewards that God bestows on his chosen people; however, in Isaiah, the focus is not on love but violence. The prophet asks God to "cleaue the heauens in sunder and come downe, that the mountaines might melt away at thy presence, Like as at an hote fire, and [that the malicious might boile away] as the water doeth vpon the fire: whereby thy name might bee knowen among thine enemies, and that the Gentiles might tremble before thee" (64:1–2, brackets in original). Kyffin, in his lengthy description of how God has saved England, invokes similar upheaval:

---

[25] Kyffin, *Blessednes*, C2r.

[26] Kyffin, *Blessednes*, C2v.

[27] R. Bauckham, *Tudor Apocalypse: Sixteenth Century Apocalypticism, Millennarianism and the English Reformation: from John Bale to John Foxe and Thomas Brightman* (Oxford: Sutton Courtenay Press, 1978), 273–74.

[28] For the two biblical passages related to Kyffin's text, I use the 1584 edition of the Bishops' Bible, *The Holy Bible, conteining the Olde Testament and the Newe* (London, 1584: *STC* 2141).

> *A* Miracle of mightie Magnitude,
> *Don by the Dreadfull Powre of* Gods *Right hand:*
> *VVherein our* Might *and Meanes he did exclude,*
> *That so himself* most Gloriously *may stand:*
> *It is beyond the Reache of Humane thought,*
> *To think the* Things *he for our sakes hath wrought.*[29]

Uniting the notions of the unfathomable bounty of God's rewards with the language of violent miracles, Kyffin brings together his use of Corinthians and Isaiah. In fact, even the concept of miracles is part of the exegetical tradition for the Isaiah passage. According to the gloss for the opening verses to this chapter in the 1560 Geneva Bible, for example, Isaiah speaks these words as he "continueth his prayer, desiring God to declare his loue toward his Church by miracles, and mightie power as he did in mount Sinái" (note a). Kyffin's notions of might and miracles resonate with this gloss and, in turn, emphasize how England is God's chosen nation.

Writing in the same apocalyptic moment as Kyffin, Lyly also includes a quasi-apocalyptic vision through Endymion's dream in act 5 when Endymion sees a princely eagle besieged by beetles. Lyly had used the same image in his *Euphues' Glasse for Europe* in 1580 when he praised Elizabeth for defending her Protestant nation from Catholic predators.[30] This vision has been clearly (and rightly) linked to England's tensions regarding Spain.[31] Through this choice, Lyly evokes the apocalyptic anxieties and places their images of destruction within the separateness of a dream. What is more, he provides an antidote to this more pessimistic approach to the eschaton by including echoes of 1 Corinthians (associated with a millennial apocalypse) in the main action of the play. Rather than focus on the swords, Lyly finds a representation for Elizabeth that is more empowering, positive, *and* befitting his queen's priorities. What makes Lyly's work in this area particularly clever is the way in which he surrounds Elizabeth with the joy of divine folly. Unlike Kyffin who uses 1 Corinthians 2:9 to make a transition to the idea of warfare, Lyly uses the rest of the Pauline context to emphasize the restorative and unifying aspects of folly, the theme threaded throughout the entire play.

---

[29] Kyffin, *Blessednes*, C4v.

[30] This passage in "Euphues Glasse for Europe" can be found in *The Complete Works of John Lyly*, vol. 2, ed. R. Warwick Bond (Oxford: Clarendon Press, 1902), 215, lines 19–24.

[31] See Bevington, "Lyly's *Endymion* and *Midas*."

Make Folly, Not War

Lyly's use of folly will bolster Elizabeth's image as a queen of peace who, even in gentleness, is still divinely powerful. As St. Paul writes, "God hath chosen the foolish things of the worlde, to confounde the wise: and God hath chosen the weake things of the worlde, to confound the things which are mightie" (1 Cor. 1:27). Lyly modifies the Endymion-moon myth to imply how Elizabeth redirects foolishness into her own divine, transcendent type of folly.

When Lyly depicts Endymion as the one who longingly adores, he is revising the original myth. Typically, it is Cynthia who longs for Endymion.[32] What is more, this myth has been used as an example of folly in such famous texts as Desiderius Erasmus's *Moriae Encomium* (*Praise of Folly*). Erasmus's speaker, Folly herself, uses the moon's adoration of Endymion to support the notion that even the gods fall prey to foolishness: "[E]ven that chaste Diana who ignored her sex and devoted herself to hunting could still lose her heart to Endymion."[33] Folly uses this illustration, among others, to provide secular instances for a very different and more powerful version of folly. God's choice to become flesh is, Erasmus's Folly reminds us, foolishness (cf. 1 Cor. 1:23, 25). For Christ "was made something of a fool himself in order to help <[the folly of mankind]> when he assumed the nature of man and was seen in man's form."[34] This link to Christ now dovetails with Endymion's reference to the swaddled baby in act 1 as well as the performance venue on Candlemas.

Elizabeth herself, in fact, would later make a connection between God incarnate and folly in the French verses that she produced circa 1590.[35] In these

---

[32] Edward de Vere, earl of Oxford (and Lyly's erstwhile patron), invokes the myth of Endymion in its traditional form. In his poem "If care or skill could conquer vaine desire," de Vere describes that "Yet *Phebe* faire disdainde the heavens above, / To joye on yearth her poore *Endimion's* love" (lines 17–18): *The Elizabethan Courtier Poets: The Poems and Their Contexts*, ed. Steven W. May (Asheville: Pegasus Press, 1999), 274.

[33] Erasmus, *Praise of Folly* and *Letter to Maarten van Dorp*, trans. Betty Radice, ed. A. H. T. Levi (New York: Penguin Press, 1993), 27.

[34] Erasmus, *Praise of Folly*, 126. This edition uses brackets to denote items that Erasmus added in 1514.

[35] Elizabeth's autograph copy of these verses is extant; however, her role in producing these verses is uncertain. Steven W. May and Anne Lake Prescott suggest that Elizabeth was translating when they examine these verses in "The French Verses of Elizabeth I," *English Literary Renaissance* 24 (1994): 9–43. Conversely, editors Leah S. Marcus, Janel Mueller, and Mary Beth Rose leave open the possibility that Elizabeth may be the author. See *Elizabeth I: Collected Works*, ed. Marcus, Mueller, and Rose (Chicago: University of Chicago Press, 2000), 419, n. 1. I am more interested in Elizabeth's association with these verses than in making a claim regarding authorship.

enigmatic verses, which are filled with references to Pauline texts,[36] Elizabeth charts her growth from blind ignorance to spiritual enlightenment. As the queen expresses her dawning perception of her divinity in Christ, she often employs images of folly, as she does here when she opens the stanza with folly and ends it with the patristic remembrance that Christ became flesh so that humankind might become divine:

To increase the grief	*Pour accroistre le douleur*
Of my foolish past,	*de d ma passee follie*
Contemplating my Creator,	*Contemplant mon Creatur*
I remembered the making	*Il me souuena du fabrique*
Of me, a sad sinner;	*De moy triste pecheur*
I saw that God redeemed me,	*Ie Vi que Dieu me rachepta*
Being cruel against Him,	*Contre de Luy estant cruel.*
And considering well who He was	*Et reguardant bien qui iL fust*
I saw how He made Himself me,	*Ie Vi* ᵇⁱᵉⁿ *comme il se fist moy*
So that I would make myself Him.	*A si que Ie me fis Luy.*[37]

Elizabeth's progression from foolish sinner to divine with Christ has—like the folly of God becoming human—its own folly because this quest begins with recognizing one's inherent foolishness. Significantly, when Elizabeth expresses her dawning enlightenment (literally at dawn), she describes herself as a young child just learning to walk while a wise God assists her and teaches her the fundamentals. This reference to Elizabeth as a child alludes to St. Paul's description in 1 Corinthians 3:1–2 of "babes in Christ"—those individuals who are not yet fully ready to comprehend true spiritual wisdom. They have begun the path but are still immature.

Lyly, when he fills *Endymion* with so many references to St. Paul, uses this concept of "babes in Christ" to make his entire play a lighthearted but pointed self-advertisement. He shows Elizabeth how her own "children of Paul's"—the very troupe of boy actors performing *Endymion*—are particularly suited to be her players of folly. They are able to take apocalyptic panic and transform it into queen-centered, silently divine merriment.

---

[36] Marcus, Mueller, and Rose provide citations to many of the scriptural passages; see *Collected Works*, 413–21.

[37] The English translation is from *Collected Works*, 419, lines 201–10, and the original French is from *Elizabeth I: Autograph Compositions and Foreign Language Originals*, ed. Janel Mueller and Leah S. Marcus (Chicago: University of Chicago Press, 2003), 92.

The Foolish Wisdom of Children of Paul's

Lyly layers in references to the wisdom of children when he creates a subscene that repeatedly plays on the notion that, as Erasmus's Folly reminds us, children are often equated with fools. Lyly includes this concept in the scene right before Cynthia shows the superiority of her divine wisdom over the ridiculous knowledge of Pythagoras and Gyptes. Lyly has the clownish Constable observe, "You know, neighbours, 'tis an old said saw, 'Children and fools speak true'" (4.2.108–9) and then repeat the same idea only lines later "because children and fools speak true" (4.2.115). Although Lyly does not overtly associate children with heavenly wisdom, Erasmus's Folly does. She explains that Christ gave "thanks because the mystery of salvation had been hidden from the wise but revealed to little children, that is, to fools. <(The Greek word for a child, νήπιος, means 'foolish' and is the opposite of σοφός 'wise')>.)"[38] Lyly leaves open the possibility of conflating fools and children in act 4; he closely juxtaposes this scenario (with its references to fools and children) with the scene only minutes later when Cynthia first enters with the philosophers and disparages the foolishness of their wisdom. These moments, in addition, echo the opening of the play when Lyly framed the whole tale as "ridiculous" in the Prologue. There he addresses Elizabeth with "Most high and happy princess, we must tell you a tale of the Man in the Moon, which, if it seem ridiculous for the method, or superfluous for the matter, or for the means incredible, for three faults we can make but one excuse: it is a tale of the Man in the Moon" (Prologue, lines 1–5). In the Prologue, the ridiculous, superficial nature of the play might ring with Pauline folly and therefore with divine wisdom; however, Lyly reframes "ridiculous" and distances this term from Pauline folly by having Cynthia use this adjective with the philosophers when her virtuous perspective trumps their earthly wisdom.

Adding to his self-advertisement through scattered references to children, foolishness, and wisdom, Lyly places himself directly in the play through its most foolish character, Sir Tophas—a character that Geoffrey Chaucer made the *topos* for an author's lesser self. As Sir Tophas's servant Epiton quips in true Pauline fashion, "Nothing hath made my master a fool but flat scholarship" (5.2.40–41). Sir Tophas's ties with 1 Corinthians are sufficiently complex to warrant their own article. Rather than delve into this new topic, I simply suggest that Lyly's Pauline self-promotion did not go unnoticed. Elizabeth's ecclesiastical hierarchy recognized Lyly's emphasis on his Pauline gifts of folly as (to use Gabriel Harvey's scoffing words) "a professed iester, a Hick-scorner, a scoff-maister, a playmunger, an Interluder."[39] In 1589, Bancroft would commission Lyly to write comical

---

[38] Erasmus, *Praise of Folly*, 124–25, alluding to Matthew 11:25, Luke 10:21.
[39] *Works of Gabriel Harvey, D.C.L.*, ed. Alexander Bulloch Grosart, 3 vols. (London: privately printed, 1884; repr. New York: AMS Press, 1966), 2:132.

tracts against the deeply Pauline voice of Martin Marprelate.[40] What makes Lyly a particularly apt figure for this kind of work is his ability to use ludic folly to support the state. His choices in *Endymion* suggest that he can stew the acerbic "Martin" in his own Pauline juices through a folly that can remain playful and Elizabeth-centered. This strategy will continue to surface over the next few years as the crown seeks to combat the mounting Puritan unrest that the Marprelate scandal brought center stage. In fact, using unity-in-love-for-Elizabeth is a particularly apt counter to this threat. The fictional Martin Marprelate was so persuasive not only because he was funny but also because he took Puritan criticism and gave it a human voice. Likewise, centering conformity in love for Elizabeth exemplifies a similar approach.

Love and Conformity in the 1589 Parliament

In the aftermath of "Martin's" first attacks on the Elizabethan episcopacy, the use of St. Paul and love to support religious conformity occurred throughout the opening events for the 1589 Parliament. Bancroft ends his sermon on 9 February by urging his Parliamentary audience to beware of crafty men who lie in wait to deceive those who should instead "follow the truth in love."[41] Christopher Hatton, like Lyly's *Endymion* the year before, ties this same notion of love directly to love for Elizabeth's person in his speech to Parliament on 4 February. Hatton describes Elizabeth's subjects as "lovinge," emphasizes the harmony of the English Church with churches going back to "the apostles times," and then urges his fellow members of Parliament to express "your lovinge affeccion towardes hir [Elizabeth]." Hatton's primary emphasis in asking Parliament to rally in this period of religious tension is to call for unity in love for the queen. It is only after he articulates this best practice that he brings in Elizabeth's role as monarch to strong-arm those who do not find love sufficiently motivating. Serving as Elizabeth's mouthpiece, Hatton goes on to relate that, in this latter case, Elizabeth orders them as their prince that they may not "so much as once meddle with anie such matters or causes of religion."[42] When Hatton uses the more commanding language of not meddling in religious affairs, he ties it to Elizabeth's status as sovereign rather than Supreme Governor, saving the softer language of love for discussions relating to ecclesiastical polity. I am arguing here that when Hatton fuses adoration for the queen with a nod to the apostolic church, he is conjuring

---

[40] Lyly will write *Pappe with an Hatchet* in which he will include, once again, the image of the beetles and the eagle that he had used in Endymion's dream (5.1.143–46).

[41] *A Sermon Preached at Paules Crosse the 9. of Februarie* (London, 1588/9), 106.

[42] *Proceedings in the Parliaments of Elizabeth*, Vol. 2, *1584–1589*, ed. T. E. Hartley (London: Leicester University Press, 1995), 419–20.

Pauline theology—a combination frequently evoked to bolster Elizabeth's religious authority.

Appropriately, Lyly was serving as an MP in this same Parliament and therefore would probably have been in attendance at both Bancroft's sermon and Hatton's speech. Neither Hatton in his speech nor Lyly in his play ever openly refers to Elizabeth as Governor of her church. Yet both these men use love inspired by St. Paul as a way of tying Elizabeth's subjects directly and emotionally to her in a manner that tacitly underscores her official ecclesiastical role. It seems fitting that Hatton, who often portrayed himself as a lover to his queen, and Lyly, who had emphasized his loving folly previously, were most likely in the same room at this time, both rallying around their divinely wise queen and both showing that Pauline, loving wisdom can serve the state. Lyly's witty use of St. Paul is exceptional, but he will find his match in his queen when Elizabeth herself integrates love, St. Paul, and conformity a few years later.

Elizabeth's Corinthian Call for Intellectual and Religious Conformity in 1592

In 1592, Elizabeth delivered a Latin oration at the end of her nearly week-long visit to the University of Oxford. She structures the entire oration on 1 Corinthians and centers her final demands for religious conformity in the personal love that her subjects feel towards her.[43] She, too, calls for conformity using love for her person in a way that crystallizes in one brief speech so many of the strands this essay has examined.

Similar to Lyly in his silent use of Pauline theology in *Endymion*, Elizabeth pits earthly wisdom against love for a divine presence. She emphasizes this contrast early in the speech when she gives her most overt echo to 1 Corinthians, specifically to 1 Corinthians 2:9. Addressing an audience that contains top-ranking statesmen, clergy, and university officials, she states that intellectual efforts matter very little to her. What she prizes above all else is love.

> Your merits are not the exceptional and notable praises (unmerited by me) that you have given me; nor declarations, narrations, and explications in many kinds of learning; nor orations of many and various kinds eruditely and notably expressed; *but another thing which is much more precious and more excellent: namely, a love that has never been heard nor written nor known in the*

---

[43] I initially drew attention to Elizabeth's extensive use of Pauline references in L. Shenk, "Turning Learned Authority into Royal Supremacy: Elizabeth I's Learned Persona and Her University Orations," in *Elizabeth I: Always Her Own Free Woman*, ed. Carole Levin, Jo Eldridge Carney, and Debra Barrett-Graves (Burlington, VT: Ashgate, 2003), 78–96, here 87–92.

memory of man. Of this, parents lack any example; neither does it happen among familiar friends; no, nor among lovers, in whose fate faithfulness is not always included, as experience itself teaches. It is such that neither persuasions nor threats nor curses can destroy.[44]

It is important to note that when Elizabeth downplays academic efforts here, she is speaking to an audience that has just witnessed (and, in some cases, has helped organize) an extensive array of intellectual demonstrations—all for her. In the opening sentences of her speech, she does express gratitude for these efforts, but her statement about love invokes St. Paul's dismissal of earthly wisdom. Also in keeping with Pauline notions, Elizabeth distinguishes the love they have for her from two earthly matters: other relationships (parents/friends/lovers) as well as the worldly rhetoric of "persuasions" and even "threats."

Elizabeth claims a truly divine-like adoration. Her key revision of the original Corinthians passage underscores this choice: she makes herself, not God, the object of adoration. Though she does not explicitly liken herself to the figure of Divine Wisdom, she places herself in a position that is allied with such knowledge. She goes on to stress that the university "may long be enduring" by making

> its care be especially to worship God—not in the manner of the opinion of all nor according to over-curious and too-searching wits, but as the divine law commands and our law teaches. For indeed, you do not have a prince who teaches you anything that ought to be contrary to a true Christian conscience. Know that I would be dead before I command you to do anything that is forbidden by the Holy Scriptures.[45]

By structuring her entire oration on 1 Corinthians, Elizabeth demonstrates that her ideas are rooted in scriptural authority, which provides the foundation for as-

---

[44] *Collected Works*, 327; emphasis added. In a version of the original Latin, this passage reads: "Non sunt laudes eximiae et insignes, sed immeritae meae, Non doctrinarum in multis generibus indicationes, narrationes et explicationes, Non orationes multis et varijs modis eruditè et insignitèr expressae, sed aliud quiddam est multo pretiosius atque praestantius, Amor scilicet, qui nec vnquam auditus nec scriptus nec memoria hominum notus fuit, cuius exemplo parentes carent, nec inter familiares cadet, imò nec inter amantes, in quorum sortem non semper fides incidit experientia ipsa docente. Talis est iste vt nec persuasiones nec minae nec execrationes delere poterunt" (*Autograph Compositions*, 164).

[45] *Collected Works*, 328. In a version of the original Latin, this passage reads: "Vt diuturna sit haec Academia, habeatur inprimis cura vt Deus colatur non more omnium opinionum, non secundum ingenia nimis inquisita et exquisita, sed vt lex diuina iubet et nostra praecipit. Non enim talem principem habetis quae vobis quicquam precepit quod contra conscientiam verè Christianam esse deberet. Scitote me prius morituram quam tale aliquid acturam, aut quicquam iubeam quod in sacris literis vetatur" (*Autograph Compositions*, 164).

serting that her teachings are not contrary to a Christian conscience. As John S. Coolidge has noted, the idea of "not contrary to scripture" was "the rallying cry of Conformity."[46] Elizabeth not only uses this politically charged language but also goes one step beyond it to position herself and her laws as educators. Just as Lyly depicts Cynthia schooling the philosophers, Elizabeth asserts her ecclesiastical authority in the role of her nation's religious educator. In this way, she places herself and her laws at the center of establishing England's church doctrine.

The outcome of such schooling is that England will be strong and unified—a unity that Elizabeth continues to color with a distinctly conformist hue:

> [E]ach and every person is to obey his superior in rank, not by prescribing what things ought to be, but by following what has been prescribed, bearing this in mind: that if superiors begin to do that which is unfitting, they will have another superior by whom they are ruled, who both ought and is willing to punish them. Finally, be of one mind, for you know that unity is the stronger, disunity the weaker and quick to fall into ruin.[47]

Even Elizabeth's call to conformity is grounded in St. Paul because the apostle's main hope for the Corinthian congregation was that they come together in love for God, a love that would heal their deep divisions. "Nowe I beseech you, brethren, by the name of our Lord Jesus Christ, that yee all speake one thing, and that there be no dissentions among you: but that ye be perfectly ioyned together in the same mind, and in the same meaning" (1:10). When St. Paul expresses the need for unity, he chastises the Corinthians for claiming that their main allegiance is to certain teachers rather than the more essential focus: God and Christ. In a similar move to a more fundamental and less sectarian church, Elizabeth requires unity by demanding that her subjects follow *her* doctrine rather than any certain sect of Christianity. She is preparing the way for a distinctly Anglican church that does not need Protestant, Catholic, or Puritan affiliations.

Significantly, Elizabeth established the foundation for these articulations by celebrating the transcendent love that her subjects have for her person. In part, her decision to conflate religious unity with love-for-queen allows her to shift the basis for religious practices away from sectarian interests and the exegetical territory that dominated ecclesiastical controversy since the 1570s. Her strategy creates a nationalistic focus through a more emotion-driven approach. In a sense, it is sometimes easier to have England's subjects rally around their divinely wise

---

[46] Coolidge, *Pauline Renaissance*, 7.

[47] *Collected Works*, 328. In a version of the original Latin, this passage reads: "[V]nusquisque in gradu suo superiori obediat, non praescribendo quae esse deberent, sed sequendo quod praescriptum est, hoc cogitantes, Quod si superiores agere coeperint quae non decet alium superiorem habebunt a quo regantur qui illos punire et debeat et velit. Postremò, vt sitis vnanimes, cùm intelligatis vnita robustiora, separata infirmiora, et citò in ruinam casura" (*Autograph Compositions*, 165).

Queen of Love rather than follow the commandments of their Supreme Governor of the Church. In his *Of the Lavves of Ecclesiasticall Politie*, Hooker will emphasize how effective women can be in serving the church because of their emotion and focus on people. "Apter they are through the eagernesse of their affection, that maketh them which way soeuer they take, diligent in drawing their husbands, children, seruants, friends and allies the same waie."[48] Using love to bolster Elizabeth's ecclesiastical authority capitalizes, in a way, on the image of women as successful makers of community. Love can be one of Elizabeth's queenly discourses of conformity.

Attention to how Elizabeth and Lyly, for example, use love to create this kind of personal ecclesiastical presence opens avenues for finding ecclesiastical politics in unexpected places — even royal panegyric with no overt religious references. In the essay that concludes this collection, Donald Stump observes a marked movement away from comparisons between Elizabeth and Old Testament figures, beginning in the early 1580s. He attributes this shift to her growing aversion to the Bible-thumping rhetoric of radical Protestants. My essay suggests an additional layer to his study to reveal that, in some instances, the seemingly secular images of Elizabeth that replaced those from the Old Testament are steeped in Christianity. This move to the secular and away from the Old Testament seeks to allay the divisive and controversial rancor that had gained such a foothold in an England (and a Europe) that was becoming increasingly polarized along religious lines. In fact, I would venture to suggest that the image of Elizabeth as a Queen of Divine Consequence actually intensifies in the last two decades of her reign, as the issue of unity becomes urgent. The queen herself, her conformist bishops, and even her merry playwrights turn to Pauline wisdom as they build the Anglican Church with tomes, with witty literature, and with a divinely wise *and loving* Governor-Queen.

---

[48] Richard Hooker, *Of the Lavves of Ecclesiasticall Politie* (London, 1593; STC 13712), 18.

Abandoning the Old Testament: Protestant Dissent and the Shift in Court Paradigms for Elizabeth

Donald Stump

I

It is a curious fact that so many of the best and most familiar poems written in praise of Queen Elizabeth idealize her as if she were a pagan goddess. Though she is sometimes represented in such figures as a shepherdess, a courtly or Petrarchan mistress, or the queen of the fairies, she is best known in the guise of classical deities, particularly Astraea, Diana, and the moon goddess Cynthia (or Belphoebe). Since Elizabeth was arguably most important to her subjects as a defender of the Protestant Reformation, both in England and on the Continent, it is strange that so little of the best work about her — most of it written in the last two decades of her reign — draws its analogs from biblical, or even distinctly Christian, sources.[1]

This is especially puzzling since, until the early 1580s, she was commonly compared with, or urged to follow the example of, great figures from the Old Testament. In exhorting and representing Elizabeth, writers frequently invoked

---

[1] Studies by Roy C. Strong, John N. King, Helen Hackett, and others who have analyzed images of the queen in relation to specific periods and incidents in her reign have not treated this anomaly in any detail. E. C. Wilson's early discussion treats the imagery involving classical goddesses as a logical extension of the veneration afforded her as the Defender of the Faith, but does not consider the clash with prevailing religious sensibilities that such figures entailed. See Roy C. Strong, *The Cult of Elizabeth: Elizabethan Portraiture and Pageantry* (London: Thames & Hudson, 1977), and idem, *Gloriana: The Portraits of Queen Elizabeth I* (London: Thames & Hudson, 1987); John N. King, "Queen Elizabeth I: Representations of the Virgin Queen," *Renaissance Quarterly* 53 (1990): 30–74; Helen Hackett, *Virgin Mother, Maiden Queen: Elizabeth I and the Cult of the Virgin Mary* (New York: St. Martin's Press, 1995); E. C. Wilson, *England's Eliza* (Cambridge, MA: Harvard University Press, 1939), 57–60.

biblical women such as Eve,[2] Sarah,[3] Dinah,[4] Deborah,[5] Esther,[6] Huldah,[7] Judith,[8] Susannah[9] — and even Jael.[10] They also employed a long list of male figures,

---

[2] John Stubbs, *The Discoverie of a Gaping Gvlf* (London, 1579), A2r. Since the mass of surviving material from Elizabeth's reign is enormous, my citations of scriptural references can be only representative, not exhaustive. The sources that I draw on include E. C. Wilson's *England's Eliza*, John Nichols's *Progresses and Public Processions of Queen Elizabeth*, and E. K. Chambers's *Elizabethan Stage,* as well as the indexes in collected works of prominent Elizabethan literary figures and a good deal of material that Susan Felch and I have reviewed in compiling the anthology *Elizabeth I and Her Age: A Norton Critical Edition* (New York: W. W. Norton, 2009).

[3] Thomas Bentley, *The Monument for Matrones* (London, 1582), 288.

[4] Stubbs, *Gaping Gvlf*, A3v (implicit).

[5] Richard Mulcaster, *The Passage of Our Most Drad Souereigne Lady Quene Elyzabeth Through the Citie of London to Westminster, the Daye before Her Coronacion* (London, 1559), D3r-D4r. Richard Grafton, *Graftons Abridgement of the Chronicles of Englande* (London, 1570), fol. 179r. John Knox, Letter to Elizabeth, 1559: *The Works of John Knox*, ed. David Laing, 6 vols. (Edinburgh: J. Thin, 1854–1895), 6: 50. John Calvin, "Letter XV," to Sir William Cecil, 1559: *The Zurich Letters*, 2nd ser., trans. Hastings Robinson (Cambridge: Cambridge University Press, 1845), 34–35. John Aylmer, *An Harborowe for Faithfvll and Trewe Subjects* (London, 1559), B3v, D2v-D3r, O4r. John Hales, "An Oration . . . to the Queen's Majesty; and delivered to her Majesty by a certain Nobleman, at her first Entrance to her Reign," quoted in John Foxe, *The Acts and Monuments*, ed. George Townsend, 8 vols. (London: Seeley, Burnside, & Seeley, 1843–1849; repr. New York: AMS, 1965), 8:678. Mr. Griffin, "Triste absti letum," 1572, quoted in *The Progresses and Public Processions of Queen Elizabeth*, ed. John Nichols, 3 vols. (London: John Nichols & Son, 1823), 1:316. Lawrence Humphrey, Oration to the Queen at Woodstock, 1575, quoted in Nichols, *Progresses*, 1:597. "A Meditation wherin the godly English geueth thankes to God for the Queenes Maiesties prosperous gouernment hitherto," quoted in Edward Hake, *A Commemoration of the Most Prosperous and Peaceable Raigne of our Gratious and Deere Soueraigne Lady Elizabeth* (London, 1575), C4r. Bernard Garter and William Goldingham, *The Ioyfvll Receyuing of the Queenes most excellent Maiestie into hir Highnesse Citie of Norwich* (London, [1578]), C1v–C2r. John Lyly, *Euphues and His England* (1580), in *The Complete Works of John Lyly*, ed. R. Warwick Bond, 3 vols. (Oxford: Clarendon Press, 1902), 2:209–10. Bentley, *Monument*, 262, 272.

[6] Hake, *Commemoration*, A7r. Garter and Goldingham, *Ioyfvll Receyuing*, C2r–C2v. Bentley, *Monument*, 262.

[7] Calvin, "Letter XV," 34–35.

[8] Aylmer, *Harborowe*, B3v, O4r. Hales, "Oration," quoted in Foxe, *Acts and Monuments*, 8:676 (implicit). Garter and Goldingham, *Ioyfvll Receyuing*, C2r. Bentley, *Monument*, 262, 272.

[9] Hake, *Commemoration*, A8r. Anthony Munday, "A Dialogue betweene a Christian and Consolation" (1582), in *Ballads from Manuscripts*, ed. W.R. Morfill, 2 vols. (Hertford: Ballad Society, Stephen Austin & Sons, 1868–1873), 2:187.

[10] "Meditation," quoted in Hake, *Comemmoration*, C4r. Humphrey, "Oration" quoted in Nichols, *Progresses*, 1:597. Bentley, *Monument*, 262, 272.

including Adam,[11] Abel,[12] Joseph,[13] Moses,[14] Joshua,[15] Gideon,[16] Samuel,[17] David,[18] Solomon,[19] Zerubabel,[20] Elijah,[21] Jonah,[22] Daniel,[23] Nehemiah,[24] and the reformer kings of Judah: Asa, Hezekiah, Josiah, and others.[25]

By the early 1580s, however, the Old Testament heroes and heroines were rapidly going out of fashion at court. In works as various as royal entertainments, welcoming speeches, poems for special occasions, devotional works, and polemical tracts, such figures were rarely held up for comparison to, or emulation by, the queen. Between 1558 and 1582, I have found about twenty such works containing well over a hundred references to exemplary Old Testament figures.

---

[11] Hales, "Oration," quoted in Foxe, *Acts and Monuments*, 8: 675. Stubbs, *Gaping Gvlf,* A2r.

[12] Bentley, *Monument*, 705.

[13] "Oration of the Minister of the Dutch Church," quoted in Garter and Goldingham, *Ioyfvll Receyuing,* D1v–D2r. Bentley, *Monument,* 262, 271, 721.

[14] Aylmer, *Harborowe,* I4v–K1r. Hales, "Oration," quoted in Foxe, *Acts and Monuments,* 8:675–76 (implicit). *Geneva Bible* ***3r. Hake, *Commemoration,* A6r (implicit). "Meditation," quoted in Hake, *Commemoration,* B7r, C1r, C2v, C4r. Bentley, *Monument,* 262, 271, 706, 724.

[15] Aylmer, *Harborowe,* P4r-P4v. "Meditation," quoted in Hake, *Commemoration,* C4r. Stubbs, *Gaping Gvlf,* B1r. Bentley, *Monument,* 262, 271–72.

[16] Aylmer, *Harborowe,* B3r; Stubbs, *Gaping Gvlf,* F1r.

[17] Bentley, *Monument,* 262, 268, 687.

[18] Aylmer, *Harborowe,* B3v, O4r, O4v. Hales, "Oration," quoted in Foxe, *Acts and Monuments,* 8:677–78. Humphrey, "Oration," quoted in Nichols, *Progresses,* 1:597, 598. "Meditation," quoted in Hake, *Commemoration,* B7r, C2r, C4r. Oration of the Mayor of Norwich, quoted in Garter and Goldingham, *Ioyfvll Receyuing,* B1v. Stubbs, *Gaping Gvlf,* A7v. Bentley, *Monument,* 262, 270, 272, 288, 292, 306, 687, 706, 709, 712, 716, 721, 725, 726, 728. Beza, *King's Heast, or Gods familiar speech to the Qveene,* quoted in Bentley, *Monument,* 306, 349, 350.

[19] Hales, "Oration," quoted in Foxe, *Acts,* 8: 678, 679. *Geneva Bible* ***4r. "Meditation," quoted in Hake, *Commemoration,* C2r, C4r–C4v. James Sanford, Preface, *Houres of Recreation, or Afterdinners, Which May Aptly be Called The Garden of Pleasure,* by Ludovico Guicciardini, trans. James Sanford (London, 1576), A3v. Stubbs, *Gaping Gvlf,* B8r. Bentley, *Monument,* 262, 272, 279, 709.

[20] *Geneva Bible* ***2r. Bentley, *Monument,* 298.

[21] "Meditation," quoted in Hake, *Commemoration,* C3r.

[22] Stubbs, *Gaping Gvlf,* C2r. Bentley, *Monument,* 262.

[23] Elizabeth's prayer before coronation, quoted in Mulcaster, *Passage,* E4r–E4v. Munday, "Dialogue," rpt. Morfill, *Ballads,* 2:187.

[24] Stubbs, *Gaping Gvlf,* B1v. Humphrey, "Oration," quoted in Nichols, *Progresses,* 1:597.

[25] Hales, "Oration," quoted in Foxe, *Acts and Monuments,* 8:676 (implicit). *Geneva Bible* ***2r – ***4 r. "Meditation," quoted in Hake, *Commemoration,* C3r. Stubbs, *Gaping Gvlf,* B1r. Bentley, *Monument,* 272, 687.

Between 1583 and 1603, however, I have located only five works containing a total of six references.[26] My scan has not been exhaustive. I have not attempted, for example, to examine parliamentary acts or petitions, government documents, the routine correspondence of officials or churchmen (which are too numerous to survey), or the prescribed liturgies of the English Church or the mass of sermons delivered at court (which, by their very nature, turn to scripture in offering exempla). Alexandra Walsham's recent examination of a number of such works, as well as many more that were not composed for the attention of the queen or the court, suggests that comparisons with the Old Testament heroes and heroines were still fairly common among militant Protestants in the country at large.[27] My rather extensive search of literature connected more directly with the court reveals, however, a dramatic falling-off in their use there. By the mid-1580s, aspiring young writers addressing the queen or seeking to catch her eye in that arena were rarely comparing her with Old Testament figures, and in consequence, her public image was becoming less overtly implicated in the religious turmoils of the day.

All this was happening, moreover, precisely when the Catholic threat to England was greatest and Protestant zeal was at its height. The period saw the harshest anti-Catholic measures of Elizabeth's reign. Following the covert arrival of the Jesuit leaders William Campion and Robert Parsons in 1580, the repression accelerated steadily through the discovery of the Throckmorton and Babington assassination plots against Elizabeth in 1584 and 1586, the execution of Mary Stuart in 1587, and the invasion of the Spanish Armada in 1588. Despite this crescendo in Protestant fervor, however, writing about the queen that was generated at court in the last two decades of the reign is oddly silent on the Old Testament figures that Protestants were once so fond of citing.

This fact is all the more surprising when one considers the affiliations of the poets who set the fashions in poetic representations of the queen during this period. Most of the "new poets" of the generation of Spenser, Sidney, and Ralegh were closely associated with the most aggressively Protestant faction in the

---

[26] Hake, "Oration," quoted in Nichols, *Progresses* 2:465 (Moses implicitly, David), 468 (Moses). John Stockwood, Epistle Dedicatory, *A Right Godly and Learned Discourse upon the Booke of Ester,* by Johannes Brenz, trans. John Stockwood (London, 1584), B3v–B4r. Edmund Spenser, *The Faerie Queene* (London, 1590), 3.4.2. Mary Sidney, Countess of Pembroke, *Collected Works,* ed. Margaret P. Hannay, Noel J. Kinnamon, and Michael G. Brennan, 2 vols. (Oxford: Clarendon Press, 1998), 2:102–4. I do not include elegies or memorials written after the queen's death because such works typically reprise images from throughout the reign and because the political forces at work on royal paradigms end with a monarch's death.

[27] A. Walsham, "'A Very Deborah?' The Myth of Elizabeth I as a Providential Monarch," in *The Myth of Elizabeth,* ed. Susan Doran and Thomas S. Freeman (Houndmills, Eng.: Palgrave Macmillan, 2003), 143–56.

government and might have been expected to draw on a full range of scriptural materials. In fact, they did little to slow the abandonment of Old Testament paradigms and much to hasten it. Two major genres that the so-called "new poets" adapted and pressed into service to the queen—the courtly or Petrarchan love lyric and the pastoral—were by their very nature not well suited to represent Elizabeth as a prophetic figure or as a militant Defender of the Faith against Catholic forces on the Continent. Neither was Sidney's influential pastoral romance, *Arcadia*. Spenser's representations of the queen as Una and Mercilla in *The Faerie Queene* served the purpose better, but they were exceptional by any standard and did not draw on the usual Old Testament paradigms invoked in the first half of the reign. After 1582, one occasionally encounters ballads, poems, sermons, or religious works written for a popular audience in which Elizabeth is figured as Moses, Esther, Judith, or Deborah,[28] but such comparisons rarely appear in the work of writers addressing themselves to the queen or the court.

Elizabeth herself seems to have led the way in the shift against such biblical comparisons. Study of her *Collected Works* reveals that, in the first half of her reign, from 1558 to 1582, she alludes to exemplary Old Testament figures twenty-three times in eleven different pieces of her writing.[29] In the second half of her reign, however, the numbers have dropped to a mere six times in three works. In the later years, in fact, she mentions only three male figures (Solomon, Jacob, and Joseph) and never names the biblical heroines at all.[30] Since the volume of *Collected Works* contains only a fraction of the queen's correspondence, my counts are not, of course, exhaustive, but they are suggestive. Particularly revealing are her prayers, where we might expect such references to abound. In those that she composed between 1558 and 1582, we find eighteen references to fifteen different biblical figures who are treated in a favorable light, including the women Deborah, Judith, Esther, and Susanna. From 1582 to the queen's death, by contrast, not a single biblical figure is mentioned. To be sure, prayers from that period are fewer and occupy only half the space, and as the editors point out, they are more personal. Yet it is still striking that they do not invoke a single Old Testament paradigm.

Nothing shows the trend more clearly than the prologue to Thomas Dekker's *Old Fortunatus*. By 1599, when the play was staged before the queen, it was possible to rattle off her most common literary names without mentioning any that are scriptural, or even distinctively Christian. The queen is celebrated as a goddess enshrined in a pagan temple. As the two old men who speak the prologue

---

[28] Besides the examples cited by Walsham in "'A Very Deborah'?," see Wilson, *England's Eliza*, 36–37, 43–44, and 148, and Nichols, *Progresses*, 3:541.

[29] Elizabeth I, *Collected Works*, ed. Leah S. Marcus, Janel Mueller, and Mary Beth Rose (Chicago: University of Chicago Press, 2000), 55, 142, 145–46, 147, 149, 155, 156, 157, 159 (Daniel implicitly?), and 245.

[30] Elizabeth I, *Collected Works*, 198, 371, 411.

travel toward London to join in her cultic adoration, one asks, "Are you then traveling to the temple of Eliza?" and the other replies, "Euen to her temple are my feeble limmes trauelling. Some cal her Pandora: some Gloriana, some Cynthia: some Delphoebe, some Astraea: all by seuerall names to expresse seuerall loues...."[31]

The question, then, is why the queen and her court should have set aside the Old Testament paradigms in the 1580s and 90s. Part of the explanation is undoubtedly that they were following a larger shift in fashions brought about by the rise of Humanism earlier in the century. The growing influence of classical figures in royal iconography during the sixteenth century is evident not only in England but also on the Continent. In the early 1580s, moreover, the generation of English writers coming into prominence had been educated under the uniform grammar-school curriculum established in the early 1560s. They included such prominent figures as Ralegh, the Sidneys, Spenser, Lyly, and Peele, all heavily steeped in the classics. Since the queen herself was proficient in Latin, wrote personal prayers in Greek, and loved the literature and philosophy of pagan antiquity, works derived from the classics were welcome at court.

Another spur to the proliferation of non-scriptural paradigms was the growing popularity of foundation myths based on chronicle accounts of England as Troynovant and on romance representations of King Arthur as a national hero. Elizabeth, like her father, favored works based on these myths, which conveniently sidestepped questions of Tudor legitimacy by tracing the family's Welsh lineage back through King Arthur to the earliest race of Briton kings. Spenser's *Faerie Queene* provides the most elaborate literary representation of this mythic pedigree.[32] In an age of conflict with the Habsburg Empire and the Roman Catholic Church, it did not hurt that such a lineage was neither Roman nor Anglo-Saxon, having its origins in the ancient Trojan Brutus, grandson of Aeneas. The Tudors were thus said to derive from a mythic line as glorious and ancient as that of the founders of Rome and the Empire. In the troubled decades of the 1580s and 90s, court writers and entertainers buttressed their queen's authority by transforming such foundation myths into elaborate and stylized rituals of tiltyard chivalry and quasi-medieval courtly love.[33] Not only did such works lend a comforting sense of antiquity and legitimacy to the monarchy, but they also introduced a tantalizing element of erotic play, quasi-religious homage, and masculine competition for favor into the life of the aging Virgin Queen. It is no coincidence that the extraordinary elaboration and ritualization of the Accession Day tilts as the preeminent festival of the Elizabethan court took place after the

---

[31] Thomas Dekker, *The Pleasant Comedie of Old Fortunatus* (London, 1600), A1v.

[32] See II.x.5–68, III.iii.22–50, III.ix.38–51.

[33] Hackett, *Virgin Mother, Maiden Queen*, 78–80, 83–87; Strong, *Gloriana*, 91–93; and Strong, *Cult,* 121–62. On tournaments, see the essay by Debra Barrett-Graves in this volume, 175–87.

collapse of the French marriage negotiations in the early 1580s, when foreign suitors no longer courted Elizabeth.[34]

It seems to me, however, that the Protestant fervor of the period was too strong for the triumph of Humanist education or the cultivation of Tudor mythology to have been more than contributing factors in the great paradigm shift at court that I have been describing. Most of the "new poets" were committed to an aggressive Protestant agenda, and their grammar-school curriculum included study of the Bible and the Church Fathers as well as the "ancients." Although their reading in the classics, English chronicle history, and Arthurian romance gave them court-approved alternatives to the conventional Old Testament paradigms of the 1560s and 70s, it offered them no compelling reason to pursue those alternatives as exclusively as they did in the 1580s and 90s. Before the great shift, writers such as Aylmer, Griffin, and the authors of the Norwich pageants had mingled biblical material with classical precedents or the "matter of Britain," and one wonders why the new generation of Protestant writers did not adopt that mixed mode as well. They were not, heaven knows, squeamish about mingling material from more than one culture or epoch. Nothing, moreover, in the nature of these alternative paradigms explains the suddenness with which they supplanted the heroines and heroes of the Old Testament.

I would argue, then, for other, less obvious explanations in addition to the long-term trends favoring classical Humanism and Tudor mythmaking. First there was the loss of favor at court suffered by forward Protestants during the controversies over nonconformity and popular "prophesyings" in the 1570s. Then there was the queen's harsh response to the Protestant outcry over her desire to marry the Catholic duke of Anjou at the end of the decade. And finally, there was her compelling need to inspire awe in both her subjects and her foreign enemies in the perilous decades that followed. It was the excessive rhetoric of Bible-thumping favored by forward Protestants, I believe, and their campaign against the French duke that initially brought the Old Testament paradigms into bad odor at court. Heightened international tensions and the outbreak of war with Spain in the 1580s, however, followed by military, economic, and political malaise in the 1590s, assured the ultimate ascendancy of neoclassical and quasi-medieval figures for the queen.

II

In the 1570s, Elizabeth faced an increasingly disaffected group of radical Protestants clamoring for religious reform and for a crackdown on English Catholics. Roused by the Rebellion of the Northern Earls and the threat of Spanish

---

[34] Strong, *Cult*, 133.

invasion in 1569, by the papal bull excommunicating Elizabeth and inviting her overthrow in 1570, and by the Ridolfi assassination plot against her in 1571, many forward Protestants were scandalized that the queen continued to temporize with her Catholic subjects and refused to turn Westminster into Geneva. She, in turn, was eager to maintain the 1559 settlement establishing the order of the English Church and to avoid turning England into the France of the Civil Wars.[35] By 1576, she was also growing increasingly impatient over her largely unsuccessful attempts to rein in nonconformity, limit the number of preachers stirring up the populace, and crack down effectually on the popular Protestant social and religious gatherings known as "prophesyings," which combined Bible study and doctrinal debate with instruction in the art of preaching. In 1576, when the archbishop of Canterbury, Edmund Grindal, tried to protect such meetings from government interference, the simmering conflict between the queen and her most aggressively Protestant subjects came to a head. Angrily suspending Grindal from all but the most routine administrative functions of his office, the queen set a course of markedly colder and more confrontational relations with the faction that he represented.[36]

In the decade before the shift away from Old Testament paradigms took place, then, a deep rift was opening between militant Protestants and their queen. We see it as early as 1570, when Edward Dering, a fellow of Christ's College Cambridge and a reader at St. Paul's Cathedral in London, set out to lecture her about her responsibilities as a monarch, telling her bluntly that her court was corrupt, that she herself was subject to lingering Catholic influences, and that she would soon feel the wrath of God if she did not change her ways. For our purposes, the point to note is that Dering packed his sermon with examples of kings and godly leaders of Israel who took a hard line against idolatry and corruption. Citing roughly 125 passages from scripture, all noted in the margins of the printed text, he marshaled a veritable army of witnesses against the queen. The main charges were that she had failed to put down Catholic elements in England; had allowed dicing, swearing, pleasure-seeking, and worldliness at her court; and had ignored abuses in the training of ministers and the filling of church benefices. Dering's use of scripture is both patronizing and tedious, taking on at times the irritable tone of an exasperated schoolmaster:

> The Lorde open the Queenes Maiesties eyes, that she may looke to this charge: Otherwise if we liued neuer so peaceably vnder her, yet when the Lorde shall come to aske accompte of her stewardshippe . . . , then shee will be founde eating and drinking with sinners. But because we are so

---

[35] Wallace T. MacCaffrey, *Elizabeth I* (London: Edward Arnold, 1993), 310–23.

[36] MacCaffrey, *Elizabeth I*, 319–22. On the dispute with Grindal, see also Norman Jones, "Elizabeth, Burghley, and the Pragmatics of Rule," in this volume, 143–56, esp. 151–53.

dull of hearing, that a litle teaching of our duetie is not sufficient for vs, I will shewe out of the scriptures somewhat more plainly if ought may bee playner, what is the duetie of a Prince. (sig. A8r)

In one particularly offensive passage, the intrepid preacher warned the queen against popish superstition, remnants of which he saw in the cross and candles on the altar in the royal chapel. Ostentatiously assuming the mantle of Jeremiah, he began by defending "prophets" in the Protestant camp who spoke openly against corruption, then turned to the queen's own failings:

be not cruell vnto Gods anoynted, and doe his Prophetes no harme. I neede not seeke farre for offences, whereat Gods people are greeued, euen round about this Chapell I see a great manye, and God in his good tyme shall roote them out. If you haue said somtyme of yourselfe: *Tamquam ouis,* as a sheepe appointed to be slayne, take hede you heare not now of the Prophet . . . as an vntamed & vnruly Heiffer. (A5r)

Part of the sting in this attack lay in Dering's implicit comparison of the pious young Elizabeth of the 1550s with the monarch seated before him in 1570. The image of the "sheep appointed to be slain" echoes John Foxe's account of the two-word message sent by the queen to her servants as she was being taken to captivity at Woodstock after Wyatt's Rebellion: "Tamquam ovis," which called to mind the unjust condemnation of Christ.[37] That a fellow Protestant like Dering should call Elizabeth to repentance by invoking Jeremiah's characterization of Ephraim as an "unruly heifer," in need of chastisement by the Lord (Jer. 31:18), was a sign of the times. Dering's warning that objects in her chapel were offenses against "Gods people" and that God would "roote them out" came perilously close to accusing the queen of idolatry. Having heard herself thus boldly reproved, she responded by depriving Dering of his license to preach.[38]

Between early signs of trouble such as this and the storm of Protestant opposition that broke over Elizabeth during the French marriage negotiations of 1579, the Old Testament paradigms were increasingly employed in ways that she would have found offensive. Sometimes resistance to her initiatives was explicit, as in John Stubbs's pamphlet *The Discoverie of a Gaping Gvlf whereinto England is Like to Be Swallowed by an Other French Mariage, if the Lord forbid not the banes, by letting her Maiestie See the Sin and Punishment Thereof*. In one memorable passage, Stubbs compared the queen with Eve, England with Eden, Anjou with Satan, and the French with carriers of disease—first the bodily infection of syphilis and now, in Anjou, also the mental disease of "atheism":

---

[37] Foxe, *Acts and Monuments*, 8:615; Acts 8:32. My thanks to Susan Felch for pointing out this connection. There is also an allusion to Isaiah 53:7, "Sicut ovis . . . ."

[38] *Dictionary of National Biography*, ed. Sir Leslie Stephen and Sidney Lee, 63 vols. (London: Smith, Elder, 1885–1901), 5:844.

> Because this infection spreeds it selfe after an other maner from the first, they haue sent us hither not Satan in body of a serpent, but the old serpent in shape of a man, whose sting is in his mouth, and who doth his endeuour to seduce our Eue, that she and we may lose this Englishe Paradise.[39]

The remainder of the pamphlet treated the queen as a naive woman in need of better advisors to govern her, lest "this Englishe Paradise" come to ruin. For passages like this and for attacks on Anjou's character, Elizabeth exacted her famous punishment on Stubbs and his publisher, pursuing legal measures to have their right hands chopped off.

Even when the forward Protestants were not so explicit in their opposition, they often invoked the Old Testament heroes and heroines in ways that the queen would have found offensive. Her prolonged struggle with them turned on a matter more basic than reform of the church or nuptial alliances with the French. The underlying issue was royal authority, which Elizabeth and her ministers were concerned to defend at all costs. Following mainly Calvinist teachings on women's rule, forward Protestants hesitated to concede that her authority stood on as firm a foundation, or might be exercised as independently, as that of English kings.

Consider, for example, Richard Mulcaster's account of the coronation pageants of 1559, which reached their climax in a prolonged comparison between Elizabeth and Deborah. By having the biblical figure appear "apparelled in parliament robes, with a sceptre in her hand, as a Queen crowned with an open crowne,"[40] the authors not only highlighted the limitations that the parliamentary system placed on Elizabeth's power, but they also withheld from her the closed, or imperial, crown that she would claim as rightfully hers in later years. By surrounding the pageant Deborah with six councilors, "two representing the nobilite, two the clergie, and two the comminaltye," the writers also suggested that her rule should be guided by men. Mulcaster records that "before these personages was written in a table *Debora with her estates consulting for the good gouernement of Israel*."[41] Needless to say, no such consultations are found in the original story of Deborah. As Michele Osherow points out, moreover,[42] nothing in the pageant suggests Deborah's extraordinary attainments as a ruler: her successes as judge and prophet to her people, as their supreme leader in war, or as the composer and singer of a great victory song, a role first played by Moses

---

[39] Stubbs, *Gaping Gvlf*, A2r.
[40] Mulcaster, *Passage*, D3v.
[41] Mulcaster, *Passage*, D3v.
[42] See Michele Osherow's essay "'Give Ear, O Princes': Deborah, Elizabeth, and the Right Word," in this volume, 251–59.

and Miriam.[43] Elizabeth, of course, lived to rival Deborah in all these roles, including that of singer, which she fulfilled upon the defeat of the Armada.[44] The forward Protestants who crafted her coronation pageants were not prepared for a queen capable of emulating Deborah in so many ways.

Other ostensibly encomiastic invocations of the Old Testament heroines by forward Protestants show the same tendency to underestimate and constrain Elizabeth. Consider Edward Hake's poem *A Commemoration of the Most Prosperous and Peaceable Reign of our Gracious and Dear Sovereign Lady Elizabeth*, which was written to celebrate the queen's accession day in 1575. The poem begins by exalting Elizabeth, claiming that "of all that ever came / From Englishe loynes to royall Seate: / I say, none worthy more / Amongst the race of Englishe kings."[45] Yet Hake continually circumscribes Elizabeth's role in ways that remind us of the coronation pageants. Among the biblical heroines, it is not the commanding figure of Deborah that he invokes but Susannah, who was saved from unjust condemnation by a wise judge, and Esther, who saved Israel by listening to the advice of an astute uncle and by relying on the authority of her husband, King Ahasuerus. Hake writes of the "virgin Queene" Elizabeth,

> Is hand of fleshe her firmest force? is frowning face her swaye?
> Doth subtile drifts drawe forth her peace, or vaunting glory? Nay:
> Of fleshe, the feeblest sexe by kinde: of face not Iunoes faere,
> But mylde Susanna in her lookes and Hester in her cheere.[46]

From one of "the feeblest sexe by kind," Hake did not expect military might or prophetic speech, or even Juno's regal demeanor. Elizabeth is not a suitable companion or counterpart ("faere") to such a goddess. In his view, Elizabeth's "swaye" depended on "mylde" looks and the sort of "cheere" characteristic of Esther, notable for courage, humility, and obedience rather than for command. That Elizabeth did well to be suspicious of such biblical comparisons was made clear in the rest of the poem. Hake continually suggested an underlying distrust of her abilities by stressing the importance of her council and urging her to heed the wisdom of the Protestant preachers pressing her for religious reform. Hake prays, "let her (Lorde) so loue to heare thy godly Preachers voyce, / That shee reiecte not what they teache, but take the best in choyce. / Let pompous state be unto her no stoppe of dew regarde / Ne let the faults of faythlesse mates, at any time be sparde" (B4v). In urging her to take instruction from the very preachers she was cracking down on, and in warning her against surrounding herself with

---

[43] Judges 4–5, Exodus 15. On Elizabeth's reliance on counselors and efforts to secure their assistance, see Tim Moylan, "Advising the Queen," in this volume, 233–50.
[44] Elizabeth I, *Collected Works*, 410–11.
[45] Hake, *Commemoration*, A7v-A8r.
[46] Hake, *Commemoration*, A8r.

"pompous state," Hake was taking a line very like that of Dering, though sweetened with a syrup of praise.

We see the same constraints on royal authority at work when he writes of his countrymen that "With them doth liue a louing Queene who like a mother raignes, / And like a chosen sacred Imp immortall glory gaines" (A7v). From Elizabeth's perspective, the speech was insidious in two respects. One was that she was being cast as "mother" to her people, a metaphor popular among forward Protestants[47] but not, as Mary Beth Rose has shown, with the queen herself after her early years on the throne.[48] The difficulty with such language was that it limited her role to that of a nurturer. In selecting the four main qualities for which the queen was to be praised, Hake fell back on traditional "feminine" attributes: "Truth, mercy, peace, and loue."[49] The abilities to discern the will of God, to judge the nation, and to command its armies as Deborah had done are not among those that Hake chooses to stress.

The other difficulty with Hake's characterization of the queen was that it treated her as a "chosen sacred Imp." If she was indeed the imp, or offspring, of a royal line and had come to the throne by due succession, why, one wonders, did Hake stress the claim that she was "sacred" and "chosen"? As later passages in the work make clear, his respect for her authority had less to do with her royal lineage than with his belief in her divine election. In Calvinist political theory, God sometimes brings women to rule states, but in doing so, He violates the usual order of nature. Only in exceptional circumstances—generally when the men in a state have failed to uphold their responsibilities—do such aberrations have divine warrant.[50] We find the same emphasis on divine election in works by other forward Protestants of the period, from Knox's early letter to the queen on women's rule to Theodore Beza's *King's Heast, or Gods familiar speech to the Qveene*, written two decades later, to Edmund Spenser's 1596 *Faerie Queene*, where the poet, though far more open to women's participation in public affairs

---

[47] Along with the numerous examples cited in Hackett, *Virgin Mother, Maiden Queen*, 255 n. 33, see Stubbs, *Gaping Gvlf*, C7v; Bentley, *Monument*, 272, 276; Beza, *King's Heast*, quoted in Bentley, *Monument*, 307.

[48] Mary Beth Rose, "The Gendering of Authority in the Public Speeches of Elizabeth I," *PMLA: Publications of the Modern Language Association* 115 (2000): 1077–82. See also Helen Hackett, "The Rhetoric of (In)fertility: Shifting Responses to Elizabeth I's Childlessness," in *Rhetoric, Women and Politics in Early Modern England*, ed. Jennifer Richards and Alison Thorne (New York: Routledge, 2006), 149–71.

[49] Hake, *Commemoration*, A8v-B2r.

[50] Calvin, "Letter XV," 34–35. On Calvin's position, see Donald Stump, "A Slow Return to Eden: Spenser and Women's Rule," *English Literary Renaissance* 29 (1999): 403–15.

than Calvin, nonetheless denies their right to rule "Vnlesse the heauens them lift to lawfull soueraintie."[51]

While the role of divinely-ordained exception was one that Elizabeth sometimes allowed herself to be cast in, it afforded, as she well knew, a precarious form of legitimacy. If her subjects should ever come to doubt that God was with her—as Dering, Stubbs, and many other forward Protestants had begun to do in the 1570s—then the basis for her authority would have evaporated. As a woman, she could count on obedience from her most ardently Calvinist subjects only in so far as she could avoid crossing them in matters of religion, and that was not easy to do. Should she disappoint them, little remained as a firm basis for requiring their allegiance—not English tradition (which had hardly any precedents for women's rule), nor the Act of Succession of 1544, nor even, as Calvin presented the case, the dictates of natural law.

It seems to me, then, that the queen's own tendency to shy away from paradigms such as Deborah and Judith in her later writings is entirely understandable. Such figures were being employed against her, not only by hectoring, self-appointed prophets, but also by more supportive Protestants who insisted on celebrating her reign in ways that undercut the very earthly basis of her authority.[52] And if the insistently scriptural rhetoric of the forward Protestants had gradually become a stench in the nostrils of the queen, it must also have begun to smell worrisome to many of the male writers connected with her court. Reactions to it go a long way toward explaining the paradigm shift that we have been examining.

Yet puzzles remain. Why, for example, was the shift so sudden? And why did it take place right around 1580? Though her quarrel with people like Dering and Archbishop Grindal started well before that time, we still find biblical figures being fairly widely invoked in the late 1570s and early 1580s. Why, moreover, did the declining popularity of Old Testament paradigms extend even to women such as Deborah, Judith, and Esther, who had proved so useful in court literature early in the reign? Such compelling images might, one supposes, still have been employed in royal iconography so long as they were not part of a Protestant tirade. The Bible and its conceptions of public and private virtue were, after all, still the dominant ideals of English society. To understand this last and most surprising stage in the retreat from such figures at court, we must turn our

---

[51] Knox, Letter to Elizabeth, 6:50. Beza, *King's Heast*, quoted in Bentley, *Monument*, 309–11. Spenser, *Faerie Queene*, V.v.25.

[52] Walsham also notes in the works that she has studied the same tendency to praise in order to exhort and to accept Elizabeth's authority only so long as the writers deem her to be a special instrument of divine providence to further the reform of the church ("'A Very Deborah?'," 148–50). See also A. N. McLaren, *Political Culture in the Reign of Elizabeth I: Queen and Commonwealth, 1558–1585* (Cambridge: Cambridge University Press, 1999), 237–38.

attention to a sudden and far-reaching shift in international strategy, namely the queen's decision in 1578 to pursue serious marriage negotiations with that widely hated Frenchman, the duke of Anjou.

III

At a time when Elizabeth was warming to the prospect of a union with the Catholic duke, the biblical paradigms posed rhetorical problems—ones so serious, in fact, that they placed the poets who employed them in personal danger. When Protestant writers of the earlier decades of the reign had compared Elizabeth with the Old Testament heroines, the rhetorical advantages had been obvious. Judith and Esther had used their appeal as women to preserve their people from foreign attack, much as Elizabeth had used her wiles as an attractive candidate for marriage to keep the major Catholic powers on the Continent divided and at bay. Susannah hadn't saved anybody but herself, of course, but she was useful in Protestant propaganda all the same, since she, like the queen, was a godly woman imperiled by cunning and corrupt enemies. Deborah was even more useful to English writers, since she had governed God's Chosen People long and well and defended true religion against an idolatrous foreign enemy.

In the first two decades of Elizabeth's reign, the foreign enemy that had offered the greatest threat to God's Chosen People in England was, of course, France. Made especially dangerous in the 1560s by ties with Mary, Queen of Scots, and in the 1570s by the machinations of the pope, who had excommunicated Elizabeth and was actively encouraging her overthrow, the powerful house of Guise lay somewhere behind many of Elizabeth's most serious problems in this period. England had been at war with France as recently as 1557, and Elizabeth renewed hostilities by sending English expeditionary forces to attack the French in Scotland during the winter of 1559–1560. In the 1560s, she deployed regular troops to France to aid the Huguenots during the First War of Religion and permitted involvement by English volunteers in the Third.[53] In this historical context, the biblical heroines—who had all stood up for godliness and justice against irreligious oppressors—did nicely as literary paradigms for the queen.

Once Elizabeth had successfully thwarted the French threat of the 1560s and early 1570s, however, such comparisons became problematic. As early as the mid-1570s, Spain had replaced France as the primary threat to England and the Reformation, and Elizabeth felt compelled to counter Philip II by aligning England more closely with France. Accordingly, in the period from April to June of 1578, she renewed marriage negotiations with Anjou, subsequently taking strong measures to suppress the rising tide of Protestant reaction against the

---

[53] Jasper Ridley, *Elizabeth I* (London: Constable, 1987), 159–60.

match.[54] As we know from her treatment of Stubbs and his publisher, to criticize the queen on this point was dangerous. Since comparisons between Elizabeth and the Old Testament heroines had been popularized during a time when English polemics were directed primarily against France, it is not surprising that they should have passed so quickly out of use when the winds shifted in France's favor. Protestant poets hoping for favor and advancement at court did well to mind their metaphors, for they were precisely the faction being most closely watched by the queen.

Signs of the impact of the French marriage negotiations are apparent in a number of works. In Lyly's *Euphues and His England*, for example—a work published in 1580—we find mention of Deborah, but only in passing. In an otherwise neoclassical passage on Elizabeth as a proponent of peace and England as "a new Israel, [God's] chosen and peculiar people," the author proclaims that the Temple of Janus "is now removed from Rome to England"; its door has not opened for twenty years, which is "more to be meruayled at, then the regiment of Debora, who ruled twentie yeares with religion, or Semyramis that gouerned long with power, or Zenobia that reigned six yeares in prosperitie."[55] The biblical note is sounded ever so lightly. Similarly, Edmund Spenser mentions Deborah in *The Faerie Queene*, invoking her in a passage celebrating the prowess of his heroine Britomart, a fictive ancestor of Elizabeth who, elsewhere in the romance, sometimes serves as an allegorical analog to her. Here, however, the biblical heroine is tucked in among the Amazons Penthisilea and Camilla in a celebration of women's "warlike feates." No direct connection with Elizabeth is made.[56]

The tendency to soften or deflect reactions to such biblical references is nowhere seen more clearly than in the series of pageants and poems presented during the summer progress of 1578 and printed by the publisher Henry Bynneman as *The Ioyfull Receyving of the Queene's most Excellent Majestie into hir Highnesse Citie of Norwich*.[57] Written just two months after Elizabeth's interest in a French marriage had flared again after several years of dormancy, and just a year before the appearance of Spenser's *Shepheardes Calender*, which was the first major work published by the "new poets," the Norwich poems came at a notable turning point in the political and literary climate of the age. The part of the entertainments that is of most interest for our purposes is the second welcoming pageant,

---

[54] Wallace T. MacCaffrey, *Queen Elizabeth and the Making of Policy, 1572–1588* (Princeton: Princeton University Press, 1981), 243–66.

[55] John Lyly, *Euphues and His England (1580)*, in *The Complete Works of John Lyly*, ed. R. Warwick Bond, 3 vols. (Oxford: Clarendon Press, 1902), 2:205, 209–10.

[56] Spenser, *Faerie Queene*, III.iv.2.

[57] Repr. in Nichols, *Progresses*, 2:136–78. The portion of the entertainments by Thomas Churchyard appeared as *A Discourse of the Queenes . . . Entertainment in Suffolk and Norfolk*, repr. in Nichols, *Progresses*, 2:179–213. For more on Churchyard's work, see also Tim Moylan, "Advising the Queen," in this volume, 242–47.

by Bernard Garter.[58] The printed account mentions in passing what I take to be a central point, namely that Garter's poems were read to the queen in the presence of three ambassadors from France (E1r). Since Norwich was known as a hotbed of Protestant agitation, both the author of the pageant and the town fathers who commissioned it faced an interesting rhetorical dilemma. If, in praising Elizabeth, they employed the usual biblical comparisons found in earlier Protestant works of this sort, they risked offending the French ambassadors and, with them, the queen. If, however, they silenced their objections against the French marriage, they would seem to their fellow townsmen little better than cowards and toadies. As one might expect, they chose a middle ground, invoking the names of Deborah, Judith, and Esther, but doing their level best to deflect the royal anger that their pageant might otherwise provoke.

As the published text remarks, the poems were presented on a "Stage . . . replenished with fiue personages appareled like women. The first was, the City of Norwich: the second Debora: the third Judeth: the fourth Esther: the fifthe Martia, sometime Queene of Englande" (C1r). The sequence of speakers was, I think, carefully planned to lead Elizabeth gently into, then out of, the Protestant polemics that occupied the three central speeches of the entertainment.[59]

The first speaker, the female persona of Norwich itself, flattered Elizabeth, calling her, as Protestants were wont to do, "my louing nurse and mother." Then, as if Garter feared that the queen would dislike the pageant, he asked her not to take offence at what was to follow: "Graunt then (oh gracious soueraigne Queene) this only my request, / That that which shal be done in me, be construed to the best" (C1v). There was reason to worry.

The next speech was delivered by Deborah and drew a series of parallels between her life and that of Elizabeth. After telling of her "appointment" by God as a Judge in Israel and of her defeat of the foreign forces arrayed against her, she asserted that God had called Elizabeth to play a similar role in England: "So mightie prince, that puisaunt Lord, hath plaste thee here to be" (C1v). Details of phrasing point up other similarities between the two rulers. For instance, Deborah had ruled Israel "twenty winters long," just as, in 1578 when the entertainment was performed, Elizabeth had also ruled for twenty years. Deborah heightened the comparison, first by calling the ancient Israelites God's "elect," as if they were good English Protestants, and then by charging their enemies with unjust aggression and treachery. Of her enemy, King Jabin, she remarked, "His force was great, his fraude was more," and the ending of the speech included a direct appeal to Elizabeth to stand firm against her own foreign enemies:

---

[58] C1r–C3v, repr. in Nichols, *Progresses*, 2:145–50. Subsequent references are by page signature in parentheses.

[59] In "Advising the Queen," in this volume, Moylan stresses the advice that the five women offer on good governance (249).

> So mightie prince, that puisaunt Lord, hath plaste thee here to be,
> The rule of this triumphant Realme alone belongeth to thee.
> Continue as thou hast begon, weede out the wicked route,
> Vpholde the simple, meeke, and good, pull downe the proud & stoute.
> Thus shalt thou liue and raigne in rest, and mightie God shalt please.
> (C1v–C2r)

With the French ambassadors in the audience, this was dangerous stuff indeed. Since Elizabeth had only recently embarked on her new policy of concerted opposition to Spain, the war of "twenty winters" waged against a foreign enemy could only be interpreted as her long struggle with France. Similarly, the observation that "rule of his triumphant Realme *alone* belongeth to thee" and the admonition to "Continue *as thou hast begon*" (emphasis added) sound suspiciously like advice not to marry but to remain a virgin and to stand up to the king of France and his warlike brother Anjou, as Deborah had stood up to Jabin and his military commander Sisera. The final set of admonitions, beginning "weede out the wicked route," suggests a vigorous campaign against Catholicism on all fronts, both foreign and domestic.

Unwelcome polemics of a similar sort characterized the speeches of Judith and Esther, with the latter warning the queen against foreign enemies who "haue skill, / As well by fraude as force to finde their pray" and who hide their tyrannical intentions in "smiling lookes" (C2r). For the Protestants of Norwich, the "smiling lookes" may have called to mind the queen's new friends, the French ambassadors, who courted her so assiduously and were entertained so warmly during the summer of 1578.

As if to head off an angry reaction by the queen and her guests, Garter quickly dropped his Protestant polemics after Esther's speech, retreating for the remainder of the pageant into the safer language of pagan myth. The last speech—spoken by the legendary Marcia, one of the only queens regnant popularly thought to have ruled England prior to Mary Tudor and Elizabeth[60]—painted an elaborate word picture of the end of the world, when Apollo would exalt Elizabeth over all other monarchs on the grounds that she combined the virtues of Pallas, the Muses, Venus, Mercury, and Juno. By lapsing into pagan myth and puffs of flattery, the poet was, I suspect, intent on taking some of the edge off his earlier Protestant polemics. Since the subsequent entertainments were largely neoclassical rather than biblical in nature, and were not pointedly hostile to the French,[61] the queen may have been pleased that her Protestant subjects in Norwich had

---

[60] See Geoffrey of Monmouth, *The History of the Kings of England*, trans. Lewis Thorpe (London: Penguin, 1966), 101. To Marcia was attributed the legal code known as the *Lex Martiana*.

[61] Goldingham's "Masque of the Gods" ended with a scene in which Cupid gave the Queen a golden arrow to shoot "at King or Caesar" as she thought fit (E3v).

been as civil in their remonstrances as anyone had a right to expect. It seems unlikely, however, that either she or her foreign guests overlooked the political subtext of the second welcoming pageant.

IV

It would be simplistic, of course, to suppose that the changes I have been examining were the only ones at work in the shift away from the Old Testament paradigms. I suspect, for example, that the Kenilworth pageants of 1575 were an early factor in their decline. Fashioned almost exclusively from neoclassical myth and Arthurian legend, the entertainments were the most dazzling and elaborate of the reign. Since they were commissioned by the earl of Leicester—the queen's favorite, leader of the forward Protestant faction at court, and one of England's most influential literary patrons—their impact on other writers must have been substantial. That Leicester and his principal writer, George Gascoigne, shied away from biblical allusions may be an early indication that the queen was growing impatient with tendentious uses of scriptural figures.[62]

Another phenomenon that deserves fuller scrutiny is the advent of the celebration of Elizabeth as an ever-virgin queen.[63] After the French marriage scheme foundered in the winter of 1580–1581, it became increasingly awkward to praise the aging Elizabeth with comparisons to Judith, the enticing widow who tempted an enemy commander by plying him with wine in his tent; to Esther, the concubine who became the wife of an eastern potentate; to Susannah, the vulnerable young woman falsely accused of adultery; or even to Deborah, the faithful wife of Lappidoth. Writers were happy to ascribe to Elizabeth youthful beauty and allure, even when she was old; but they had good reason to avoid comparing her with feminine analogs who had been married, widowed, or sexually abused.

Of even greater importance during the 1580s and 90s, I suspect, was England's precarious position in the world. The Old Testament heroines and heroes had won temporary victories for their people in a long and ultimately unsuccessful struggle against two deadly perils: religious division at home and hostile force abroad. In the second half of Elizabeth's reign, which was mired in religious strife and war with Spain, England faced just these perils. The queen's response seems to have been to rouse her troops and calm her people by distracting them from their vulnerability. She dazzled them with images of strength. We see this new resolve in her portraits, where she allowed herself to be transformed from the relatively modest and stolid figure of the early years into an icon of serene

---

[62] Those that were abstract and could not be used against her, such as the biblical figure of Wisdom discussed by Linda Shenk in "Elizabeth I's Divine Wisdom," elsewhere in this volume (261–80, at 268–69), did not, of course, raise the same concerns.

[63] King, "Queen Elizabeth I," 58–65; Hackett, *Virgin Mother, Maiden Queen*, 95–127.

opulence and power. In the *Armada Portrait* of 1588, she appeared to her people as a supremely victorious monarch, with her hand resting confidently on the globe and the closed imperial crown placed securely at her side. In the *Ditchley Portrait* of three years later, she hovered as an enormous, almost angelic figure over a map of the British Isles, which rested safely at her feet. In the *Rainbow Portrait* of 1600, painted when she was nearing death, she appeared as a youthful sun goddess, radiating light to the world.

Much had changed from the heady early days of the reign, when a young Elizabeth had rallied her people to defend the English Reformation against their Catholic enemies in France. Her most threatening foreign rival was now Spain, and her most influential domestic opposition the forward Protestants. In such a climate, royal imagery involving classical goddesses and pastoral shepherdesses, Petrarchan mistresses and medieval fairies, had the advantage of transporting Elizabeth to fictive realms far removed from the dangers and entanglements that dogged her in reality. That such chaste and distant figures attracted "new poets" such as Peele, Lyly, Ralegh, and Spenser showed their desire not only for symbols of national independence and imperial might but also for royal paradigms safely removed from threats of assassination, insurrection, and invasion. In the end, younger Protestant writers of the 1580s and 90s may have turned from biblical narrative to classical myth and Arthurian legend for much the same reasons that Bernard Garter did in writing the ending of the second Norwich pageant. To drop the scriptural paradigms offered a welcome relief from unwelcome realities, and to invoke them risked the displeasure of the queen.

Bibliography

Primary Sources

Acts of the Privy Council of England, ed. John Roche Dasent. 32 vols. London: HMSO, 1890–1949.
Ascham, Roger. *The English Works of Roger Ascham*, ed. James Bennet. London: T. Davis and J. Dodsley, 1761.
Aske, James. *Elizabetha Trivmphans*. London: Thomas Orwin, 1588.
Aylmer, John. *An Harborowe for Faithfvll and Trewe Subjects, agaynst the Late Blowne Blaste, Concerninge the Government of Wemen*. London: John Day, 1559.
Bacon, Sir Francis. *Works*, ed. James Spedding. 14 vols. London: Longman & Co., 1858.
Bancroft, Richard. *A Sermon Preached at Paules Crosse the 9. of Februarie*. London, 1588/9.
Barwick, George. "A Side-Light on the Mystery of Mary Stuart: Pietro Bizzari's Contemporary Account of the Murders of Riccio and Darnley." *Scottish Historical Review* 21 (1924): 115–27.
Beacon, Richard. *Solon His Follie, or A Politique Discourse Touching the Reformation of Common-weales Conquered, Declined or Corrupted*, ed. Clare Carroll and Vincent Carey. MRTS 154. Binghamton: Medieval & Renaissance Texts & Studies, 1996.
Bell, Ilona. *Elizabeth I: The Voice of a Monarch*. New York: Palgrave, 2010.
Bentley, Thomas. *The Monument of Matrons*. London: H. Denham, 1582.
Beza, Theodore. *King's Heast, or Gods Familiar Speech to the Qveene*. In Thomas Bentley, *The Monument of Matrons*, 306–19. London: H. Denham, 1582.
Bible. London: Christopher Barker, 1590.
Bible: Geneva Edition. 1560. Columbus: Lazarus Ministry Press, 1998.
Geneva Bible, a Facsimile of the 1560 Edition, ed. Lloyd E. Berry. Madison: University of Wisconsin Press, 1969.
Holy Bible. London, 1584.
New Jerusalem Bible, ed. Harold Fisch. Jerusalem: Koren Publishers, 1997.
Burghley, William Cecil. *A Collection of State Papers . . . 1542 to 1598*, ed. Samuel Haynes. 2 vols. London: W. Bowyer, 1740–1759; repr. Ann Arbor: University of Michigan Press, 1991.

Cabala, sive Scrinia Sacra. Mysteries of State and Government. London: G. Bedel and T. Collins, 1654.

Calendar of Cecil Manuscripts at Hatfield. 24 vols. London: Historical Manuscripts Commission, 1889.

Calendar of Documents Relating to Scotland and Mary Queen of Scots, ed. Joseph Bain et al. 5 vols. Edinburgh: H. M. General Register Office, 1898–1987.

Calendar of Letters and State Papers Relating to English Affairs Preserved Principally in the Archives of Simancas, ed. Martin A. S. Hume. 4 vols. London: HMSO, 1892–1899; repr. Nendeln, Liechtenstein: Kraus, 1971.

Calendar of Letters, Despatches, and State Papers, Relating to the Negotiations between England and Spain, Preserved in the Archives at Simancas and Elsewhere, ed. Royall Tyler. 13 vols. London: Longman, Green, Longman & Roberts [etc.], 1862–1954.

Calendar of Marquess of Bath, at Longleat, Wiltshire. 5 vols. London: Historical Manuscripts Commission, 1907.

Calendar of State Papers and Manuscripts Existing in the Archives and Collections of Milan, Vol. I, *1385–1618,* ed. Allen B. Hinds. London: HMSO, 1912.

Calendar of State Papers and Manuscripts Relating to English Affairs, Existing in the Archives and Collections of Venice and Other Libraries of Northern Italy, ed. Rawdon Brown and G. Cavendish Bentinck. 38 vols. London: HMSO, Longman Green, 1864–1947.

Calendar of State Papers, Domestic Series, of the Reigns of Edward VI, Mary, Elizabeth, 1547–1625, ed. Robert Lemon and Mary Anne Everett Green. 12 vols. London: HMSO, Longman, Brown, Green, Longmans, & Roberts, 1856–1872; repr. Nendeln, Liechtenstein: Kraus, 1967.

Calendar of State Papers, Domestic Series, Addenda, 1566–1579, ed. M. A. E. Green. London: Longmans, 1871.

Calendar of State Papers, Foreign, Elizabeth 1586–1588, ed. Sophie Crawford Lomas. London: HMSO, 1927.

Calendar of State Papers, Foreign, 1558–9, ed. J. Stevenson. London: HMSO, Longman, Green, 1863.

Calendar of State Papers, Ireland: Tudor Period, 1571–1575, rev. ed., ed. Mary O'Dowd. Kew: Public Record Office, Irish Manuscript Commission, 2000.

Calendar of State Papers, Ireland 1574–1585, ed. Hans C. Hamilton. London: HMSO, 1867.

Calendar of the Carew Manuscripts, preserved in the Archi-Episcopal Library at Lambeth 1589–1600, ed. J. S. Brewer and William Bullen. 6 vols. London: Longmans, Green, 1867–1873.

Calendar of the Manuscripts of His Grace the Duke of Rutland. 4 vols. London: Historical Manuscripts Commission, 1888.

Calendar of the Manuscripts of Lord De L'Isle and Dudley, Preserved at Penshurst Place. 6 vols. London: Historical Manuscripts Commission, 1933.

Calendar of the Manuscripts of the . . . Marquis of Salisbury . . . Preserved at Hatfield House, ed. Robert Cecil, Marquis of Salisbury, et al. 15 vols. London: HMSO, 1883–1976.

Calendar of the Patent and Close Rolls of Chancery in Ireland 1576–1602, ed. J. C. Morrin. Dublin: HMSO, 1862.

Calendar of the State Papers Relating to Ireland, 1601–3 (with addenda, 1565–1654,) and of the Hanmer Papers. London: HMSO, 1912.

Calendar Patent Rolls 1582–1583. List and Index Society 286. Kew: List and Index Society, 2001.

Calendar Patent Rolls 1583–1584. List and Index Society 287. Kew: List and Index Society, 2001.

Calvin, John. "Letter XV," to Sir William Cecil, 1559. In *The Zurich Letters*, 34–35. 2nd ser. Trans. Hastings Robinson. Cambridge: Cambridge University Press, 1845.

Camden, William. *Annales or, the History of the Most Renowned and Victorious Princesse Elizabeth*. Trans. R.N. London: Benjamin Fisher, 1635.

———. *Annales Rerum Anglicarum et Hibernicarum Regnante Elizabetha, ad Annum Salutis 1589*. London, 1615.

———. *Historie of the most Renowned and Victorious Princesse Elizabeth, Late Queene of England*. 3rd ed. London, 1675.

———. *Remains Concerning Britain*. London: Smith, 1870.

Canaye, Philippe, Seigneur de Fresne. *Lettres et ambassade*. 3 vols. Paris, 1635–1636.

Carey, Robert. *The Memoirs of Robert Carey*, ed. F. H. Mares. Oxford: Clarendon Press, 1972.

Cecil, William, Lord Burghley. *A Memorial Presented to Queen Elizabeth against Her Majesty's Being Engros'd by an Particular Favourites*. 2nd ed. London, 1708.

Charles de Lorraine. *Lettres du Cardinal Charles de Lorraine (1525–1574)*, ed. Daniel Cuisiat. Geneva: Librarie Droz, 1998.

Christopherson, John. *An Exhortation to Alle Menne to Take Hede and Beware of Rebellion*. London, 1554.

Chronicle of Queen Jane and of Two Years of Queen Mary, ed. John Gough Nichols. London: Camden Society, 1849.

Collection of State Papers, Relating to Affairs in the Reigns of King Henry VIII, King Edward VI, Queen Mary, and Queen Elizabeth, From the Year 1542 to 1570, ed. Samuel Haynes. London: William Bowyer, 1740.

Copinger, John. *The Theatre of Catolike and Protestant Religion, . . ., Wherein the Zealous Catholike May Plainelie See the Manifest Truth, Perspicuitie, Euident Foundations and Demonstrations of the Catholique Religion: Together with the Motiues and Causes Why He Should Perseuer Therin . . . Written by I.C Student in Diuinitie*. Saint-Omer, 1620.

Craig, Thomas. *The Right of Succession to the Kingdom of England*. Trans. J. Gatherer. London: D. Brown, et. al., 1703.
Daniel, Samuel. *The Worthy Tract of Paulus Iouius, Contayning a Discourse of Rare Inventions, Both Militarie and Amorous Called Imprese*. London: Simon Waterson, 1585.
Day, John. *Christian Prayers and Meditations in English[,] French, Italian, Spanish, Greeke, and Latine*. London: John Day, 1569.
Dekker, Thomas. *The Pleasant Comedie of Old Fortunatus*. London, 1600.
Deloney, Thomas. *The Queenes Visiting of the Campe at Tilsburie with Her Entertainment There*. London: John Wolfe, 1588.
Dering, Edward. "A Sermon Preached before the Queenes Maiestie the .25. Daye of Februarie . . ., 1569 [n.s. 1570]." In *Two Godly Sermons*, by Edward Dering. London, 1590.
Derricke, John. *The Image of Irelande*. London, 1581; repr. ed. D.B. Quinn. Belfast: Blackstaff, 1985.
Devereux, Walter Bouchier. *Life and Letters of the Devereux Earls of Essex 1540–1646*. 2 vols. London: J. Murray, 1853.
Donne, John. *The Sermons of John Donne*, ed. Evelyn M. Simpson and George R. Potter. 10 vols. Berkeley: University of California Press, 1953–1962.
Drayton, Michael. *Peirs Gaueston Earle of Cornvvall His Life, Death, and Fortune*. London, [1593?].
Dudley, Robert, earl of Leicester. *Correspondence of Robert Dudley, Earl of Leycester, during His Government in the Low Countries, in the Years 1585 and 1586*, ed. John Bruce. Camden Society 27. London: Camden Society, 1844.
Dürer, Albrecht. *The Human Figure by Albrecht Dürer: The Complete 'Dresden Sketchbook,'* ed. Walter L. Strauss. New York: Dover, 1972.
Elder, John. *The Copie of a Letter Sent in to Scotlande*. London: John Waylande, 1555.
Elizabeth I: Autograph Compositions and Foreign Language Originals, ed. Janel Mueller and Leah S. Marcus. Chicago: University of Chicago Press, 2003.
Elizabeth I: Collected Works, ed. Leah Marcus, Janel Mueller, and Mary Beth Rose. Chicago: University of Chicago Press, 2000.
Elizabeth I: Translations, 1592-1598, ed. Janel Mueller and Joshua Scodel. Chicago: University of Chicago Press, 2009.
Elizabeth I. *Letters of Queen Elizabeth*, ed. G. B. Harrison. New York: Funk & Wagnalls, 1968.
———. *The Poems of Elizabeth I*, ed. Leicester Bradner. Providence: Brown University Press, 1964.
———. *Queen Elizabeth's Englishings of Boethius, Plutarch, and Horace*, ed. Caroline Pemberton. EETS o.s. 113. London: K. Paul, Trench, Trüber, 1899; repr. Millwood, NY: Kraus Reprint, 1981.
———. *The Queen's Translation of Boethius's De Consolatione Philosophiae*, ed. Harold Kaylor, Jr. and Philip Edward Phillips. MRTS 366. Tempe: Arizona

Center for Medieval and Renaissance Studies, Renaissance English Text Society, 2009.
Elizabeth I and James VI of Scotland. *Letters of Queen Elizabeth and King James VI of Scotland,* ed. John Bruce. London: Camden Society, 1849.
Erasmus, Desiderius. *Praise of Folly* and *Letter to Maarten van Dorp,* trans. Betty Radice, ed. A. H. T. Levi. New York: Penguin Press, 1993.
Fénelon, Bertrand. *Correspondance diplomatique,* ed. Charles Purton Cooper. 7 vols. Paris: Panckoucke, 1838–1840.
Foxe, John. *The Acts and Monuments of John Foxe,* ed. George Townsend. 8 vols. London: Seeley, Burnside, and Seeley, 1843–1849; repr. New York: AMS, 1965.
Fuller, Thomas. *The Worthies of England.* London, 1663.
Garter, Bernard, and William Goldingham. *The Ioyfvll Receyuing of the Queenes most excellent Maiestie into hir Highnesse Citie of Norwich.* London, [1578].
Geoffrey of Monmouth. *The History of the Kings of England,* trans. Lewis Thorpe. London: Penguin, 1966.
Glover, Robert. *Nobilitas politica vel ciuilis Personas scilicet distinguendi,* ed. Thomas Milles. London: Gulielmi Iaggard, 1608.
Goodman, Christopher. *How Superior Powers Oght to be Obeyd of their Suiects.* Geneva, 1558.
Goulaine de Laudonniere, René. *A Notable Historie Containing Foure Voyages Made by Certayne French Captaynes vnto Florida,* trans. Richard Hakluyt. London, 1587.
Grafton, Richard. *Graftons Abridgement of the Chronicles of Englande.* London, 1570.
Greville, Fulke, baron Brooke. *Certaine Learned and Elegant Workes of the Right Honorable Fulke Lord Brooke Written in His Youth, and Familiar Exercise with Sir Philip Sidney.* London, 1633.
Griffin, Mr. "Triste absit letum." 1572; repr. in Nichols, *Progresses,* 1:316–17.
Grindal, Edmund. *The Remains of Edmund Grindal,* ed. William Nicholson. Cambridge: Cambridge University Press, 1843; repr. New York: Johnson Reprint, 1968.
Guillim, John. *A Display of Heraldrie: Manifesting a More Easie Access to the Knowledge Thereof Then Hath Hitherto Been Published by Any, through the benefit of Method.* 4th ed. London: Jacob Blome, 1660.
Hake, Edward. "An Oration . . . upon the Queenes . . . Birth-day [Sept. 7, 1586]"; repr. in Nichols, *Progresses,* 2:461–81.
———. *A Commemoration of the Most Prosperous and Peaceable Raigne of our Gratious and Deere Soueraigne Lady Elizabeth.* London, 1575.
Hales, John. "An Oration . . . to the Queen's Majesty; and delivered to her Majesty by a certain Nobleman, at her first Entrance to her Reign." In Foxe, *Acts and Monuments,* 8: 673–79.

Harington, John. *Epigrams.* London, 1618; facs. repr. Menston: Scolar Press, 1970.

Hariot, Thomas. *A Briefe and True Report of the New Found Land of Virginia.* Frankfurt am Main, 1590.

Harleian Miscellany, ed. T. Park and William Oldys. 12 vols. London: White & Cochrane, 1808–1813.

Harvey, Gabriel. *Works of Gabriel Harvey, D.C.L*, ed. Alexander Grosart. 3 vols. London: privately printed, 1884–1885; repr. New York: AMS Press, 1966.

Heywood, John. *Gunaikeion.* London, 1624.

Heywood, Thomas. *The Exemplary Lives and Memorable Acts of Nine The Most Worthie Women of the World: Three Jewes, Three Gentiles, Three Christians.* London: Thomas Coates, 1640.

Holinshed, Raphael. *Chronicles of England, Scotland and Ireland.* 2nd ed. London, 1587.

———. *Chronicles of England, Scotland, and Ireland*, ed. Henry Ellis. 6 vols. London: J. Johnson, 1807.

Hooker, John. "The Supplie of This Irish Chronicle Continued from the Death of King Henrie the Eight, 1546 Untill This Present Yeare 1586." In Raphael Holinshed, *The Second Volume of Chronicles.* London, 1586.

Humphrey, Lawrence. "Oration to the Queen at Woodstock, 1575"; repr. in Nichols, *Progresses,* 1:583–99.

Knox, John. *The Works of John Knox*, ed. David Laing. 6 vols. Edinburgh: J. Thin, 1854–1895.

Laneham, Robert, attrib. *Robert Laneham: A Letter*, ed. R. J. Kuin. Leiden: E.J. Brill, 1983.

Latimer, Hugh. *The Sermons of the Right Reverend Father in God, Master Hugh Latimer, Many of which were preached before King Edward VI.* 2 vols. London, 1758.

Latimer, William. *William Latymer's Chronickille of Anne Bulleyne.* In *Camden Miscellany*, ed. Maria Dowling, 4th ser., 39, 23–65. London: Royal Historical Society, 1990.

Lavater, Lewes. *Of Ghostes and Sprirites Walking By Nyght*, 1572, ed. J. Dover Wilson and May Yardley. Oxford: Oxford University Press, 1929.

Leicester's Commonwealth: The Copy of a Letter Written by a Master of Art Cambridge (1584) and Related Documents, ed. D. C. Peck. Athens, OH: Ohio University Press, 1985.

Lull, Ramon. *Book of Knighthood and Chivalry*, trans. Brian Y. Price. Union City: Chivalry Bookshelf, 2001.

Lyly, John. *The Complete Works of John Lyly*, ed. R. Warwick Bond. 3 vols. Oxford: Clarendon Press, 1902.

Maisse, André Hurault, sieur de. *De Maisse: A Journal of All That Was Accomplished by Monsieur de Maisse, Ambassador in England from King Henry IV to*

Queen Elizabeth, Anno Domini 1597, ed. and trans. G. B. Harrison and R. A. Jones. London: Nonesuch Press, 1931.

Malfatti, C. V., ed. and trans. *The Accession, Coronation and Marriage of Mary Tudor, As Related in Four Manuscripts of the Escorial*. Barcelona: Malfatti, 1956.

Marlowe, Christopher. *The Troublesome Raigne and Lamentable Death of Edward the Second, King of England*. London, 1594.

Marprelate, Martin, pseud. *The Marprelate Tracts (1588–1589)*. Menston: Scolar Press, 1967.

Mary Stuart. *Lettres, Instructions, et Mémoires de Marie Stuart, Reine D'Écosse*, ed. Alexandre Labanoff. 7 vols. London: Dolman, 1844.

———. *Queen Mary's Book: A Collection of Poems and Essays by Mary Queen of Scots*, ed. and trans. P. Stewart-MacKenzie Arbuthnot. London: George Bell & Sons, 1907.

May, Steven W., ed. *The Elizabethan Courtier Poets: The Poems and Their Contexts*. Columbia, MO: University of Missouri Press, 1991.

McClure, Norman Egbert, ed. *Letters of John Chamberlain*. 2 vols. Philadelphia: American Philosophical Society, 1939.

"A Meditation wherin the godly English geueth thankes to God for the Queenes Maiesties prosperous gouernment hitherto." In Hake, *Commemoration*, B6[v]–C4[v].

Melville, Sir James. *Memoirs of Sir James Melville of Halhill*, ed. Gordon Donaldson. London: Folio Society, 1969.

Mulcaster, Richard. *The Passage of Our Most Drad Souereigne Lady Quene Elizabeth Through the Citie of London to Westminster, the Daye before Her Coronacion*. London, 1559.

———. *The Queen's Majesty's Passage and Related Documents*, ed. Germaine Warkentin. Toronto: Centre for Reformation and Renaissance Studies, 2004.

———. *The Quenes Maiesties Passage Through the Citie of London to Westminster the Day before Her Coronacion*, ed. James M. Osborn. New Haven: Yale University Press, 1960.

Munday, Anthony. "A Dialogue betweene a Christian and Consolation" (1582); repr. in *Ballads from Manuscripts*, ed. W. R. Morfill, 2:187–88. 2 vols. Hertford: Ballad Society, Stephen Austin & Sons, 1868–1873.

Nashe, Thomas. "The Unfortunate Traveler." In *"The Unfortunate Traveler" and Other Works*. London: Penguin, 1987.

Naunton, Robert. *Fragmenta Regalia*. London, 1641.

Nichols, John, ed. *The Progresses and Public Processions of Queen Elizabeth*. 3 vols. London: John Nichols & Son, 1823; repr. New York: Burt Franklin, 1966.

Norwich: 1540–1642, ed. David Galloway. Records of Early English Drama. Toronto: University of Toronto Press, 1984.

Nowell, Alexander. *A Catechism Written in Latin by Alexander Nowell, Dean of St. Paul's . . . Together with the Same Catechism Translated into English by Thomas*

Norton. *Appended is a Sermon Preached by Dean Nowell Before Queen Elizabeth . . . January 11, 1563*, ed. G. E. Corrie. Cambridge: Cambridge University Press, Parker Society, 1853.

Osborne, Francis. *Traditional Memoirs on the Reign of Queen Elizabeth*. In *The Miscellaneous Works of that Eminent Statesman, Francis Osborn, Esq*. 2 vols. London, 1722.

———. *Works*. 9th ed. London, 1689.

———. *The Works of Francis Osborne*. Ann Arbor, MI: University Microfilms International, 1977.

Parker, Matthew. *Correspondence of Matthew Parker*, ed. John Bruce and T. T. Perowne. Cambridge: Parker Society, Cambridge University Press, 1813.

———. *Correspondence of Matthew Parker, D.D. Archbishop of Canterbury. Comprising Letters Written by and to Him, from A.D. 1535, to his Death, A.D. 1575*, ed. John Bruce and T. T. Perowne. Cambridge: Parker Society, 1853.

Peacham, Henry. *Minerva Britanna* [1612]. Leeds: Scolar Press, 1969.

Plato. *The Dialogues of Plato*, trans. and ed. B. Jowett. 4th ed. 5 vols. Oxford: Clarendon Press, 1953.

Ponet, John. *A Shorte Treatise of Politike Power*. London, 1556.

Proceedings in the Parliaments of Elizabeth I, 1558–1581, ed. T. E. Hartley. 3 vols. London: Leicester University Press, 1981–1995.

Procter, John. *The Historie of Wyates Rebellion*. London: Robert Caly, 1555. Repr. in *Tudor Tracts*, ed. A. F. Pollard, 199–259. Westminster: A. Constable, 1903.

———. *The Historie of Wyate's Rebellion; with the order and maner of resisting the same* (January 1555), in *The Antiquarian Repertory*. 4 vols. London: E. Jeffery, 1807–1809.

Puttenham, George. *The Arte of English Poesie*. Kent, OH: Kent State University Press, 1970.

Ralegh, Sir Walter. *The Discovery of the Large, Rich, and Beautiful Empire of Guiana* (1596), ed. Sir Robert H. Schomburgk. Hakluyt Society, 1st ser. 3. London: Hakluyt Society, 1848; repr. New York: Burt Franklin, 1970.

———. *The Letters of Sir Walter Ralegh*, ed. Agnes Latham and Joyce Youings. Exeter: University of Exeter Press, 1999.

Reilly, Emily Georgiana Susanna, comp. *Historical Anecdotes of the Families of the Boleynes, Careys, Mordaunts, Hamiltons, and Jocelyns*. Newry: J. Henderson, 1839.

Rimbault, Edward F., ed. *The Old Cheque-Book or Book of Remembrance, of the Chapel Royal from 1561 to 1744*. London: Camden Society, J. B. Nichols & Sons, 1872.

Royal Commission on Historical Manuscripts. *Report on the Manuscripts of Lord Montagu of Beaulieu*, ed. Henry John Douglas Scott-Montagu and Sophia Crawford Lomas. London: HMSO, 1900.

Sanford, James. Preface. *Houres of Recreation, or Afterdinners, Which May Aptly be Called The Garden of Pleasure*, by Ludovico Guicciardini. Trans. idem. London, 1576.

Segar, William. *The Book of Honor and Armes*. London: Richard Jones, 1590.

———. *The Book of Honor and Arms (1590) and Honor Military and Civil (1602)*, ed. Diane Bornstein. Delmar, NY: Scholar's Facsimiles & Reprints, 1975.

Shakespeare, William. *Othello*. In *The Riverside Shakespeare*, ed. G. Blakemore Evans. 2nd ed. Boston: Houghton Mifflin, 1997.

———. *Pericles*, ed. F. D. Hoeniger. The Arden Shakespeare. London: Methuen, 1986.

———. *The Rape of Lucrece*. In *The Norton Shakespeare*, ed. Stephen Greenblatt et al. New York: Norton, 1997.

Shell, Marc. *Elizabeth's Glass*. Lincoln, NE: University of Nebraska Press, 1993.

Sidney, Mary, Countess of Pembroke. *Collected Works*, ed. Margaret P. Hannay, Noel J. Kinnamon, and Michael G. Brennan. 2 vols. Oxford: Clarendon Press, 1998.

———. *The Triumph of Death, and Other Unpublished and Uncollected Poems*, ed. G. F. Waller. Elizabethan and Renaissance Studies 65. Salzburg: Institut für Englische Sprache und Literatur, University of Salzburg, 1977.

Sidney, Sir Henry. *Letters and Memorials of State in the Reigns of Queen Mary, Queen Elizabeth, King James, King Charles the First . . . Written and Collected by Sir Henry Sidney*, ed. Arthur Collins. 2 vols. London: T. Osborne, 1746.

Sidney, Sir Philip. *The Lady of May*. In *Miscellaneous Prose of Sir Philip Sidney*, ed. Katherine Duncan-Jones and Jan van Dorsten, 21–32. Oxford: Clarendon Press, 1973.

Smith, Sir Thomas. "Sir Thomas Smith's Orations for and against the Queen's Marriage." In *The Life of the Learned Sir Thomas Smith*, by John Strype, Appendix III. Oxford: Clarendon Press, 1820.

Smyth, John. *The Berkeley MSS*, ed. John Maclean. Vols. 1–2: *The Lives of the Berkeleys, Lords of the Manor of Berkeley*; Vol. 3: *Description of the Hundred of Berkeley*. Gloucester: Bristol & Gloucestershire Archaeological Society, 1883.

Spenser, Edmund. *The Faerie Queene*. London, 1590.

———. *The Faerie Queene*, ed. A. C. Hamilton. New York: Pearson, 2001.

———. *The Faerie Queene*, ed. Thomas P. Roche. New York: Penguin, 1987.

———. *The Shorter Poems*, ed. Richard A. McCabe. London: Penguin, 1999.

———. *Works of Edmund Spenser: A Variorum Edition*, ed. Edwin Greenlaw et al. *The Minor Poems*. 2 vols. Baltimore: Johns Hopkins University Press, 1947.

State Papers Relating to the Defeat of the Spanish Armada Anno 1588, ed. John Knox Laughton. 2 vols. Bungay, Suffolk: Navy Records Society, 1987.

Statutes of the Realm, ed. Alexander Luders et al. 9 vols. London: Eyre and Strahan, 1810–1822.

Stockwood, John. Epistle Dedicatory. *A Right Godly and Learned Discourse upon the Booke of Ester,* by Johannes Brenz, trans. idem. London, 1584.

Stowe, John. *Chronicle of England.* London, 1580.

Strype, John. *Ecclesiastical Memorials, Relating Chiefly to Religion . . . under King Henry VIII, Edward VI and Queen Mary I.* 6 vols. in 3. Oxford: Clarendon Press, 1822.

Stubbes, John. *John Stubbs's Gaping Gulf with Letters and Other Relevant Documents,* ed Lloyd E. Berry. Charlottesville: University Press of Virginia, 1968.

———. *The Discoverie of a Gaping Gvlf.* London, 1579.

T., J. *A Joyful Song of the Royal Receiving of the Queen's most excellent Majesty . . . at Tilbury.* London: John Wolfe, 1588.

Tacitus, Cornelius. *The End of Nero and the Beginning of Galba, Fower Books of the Histories* [and] *The Life of Agricola,* trans. Sir Henry Savile. London, 1591.

Tudor Royal Proclamations, ed. Paul L. Hughes and James F. Larkin. 3 vols. New Haven: Yale University Press, 1964–1969.

Udall, Nicholas (?). *Respublica: An Interlude for Christmas 1553 attributed to Nicholas Udall,* ed. W. W. Greg. EETS o.s. 226. London: Early English Text Society, 1952.

Vennar, Richard. *The Right Way to Heaven, and the True Testimonie of a Faithfull and Loyall Subiect.* London, 1601. Repr. in Nichols, *Progresses,* 3: 532–43.

Verstegan, Richard. *A Declaration of the True Causes.* London, 1592; facs. ed., Ilkley: Scolar Press, 1977.

von Klarwill, Victor, ed. *Queen Elizabeth and Some Foreigners: Being a Series of Hitherto Unpublished Letters From the Archives of the Habsburg Family,* trans. T. H. Nash. London: John Lane, 1928.

Vossen, A.F., ed. *Two Bokes of the Histories of Ireland, Compiled by Edmunde Campion.* Assen: Van Gorcum, 1963.

Whitney, Geoffrey. *A Choice of Emblems.* Aldershot: Scolar Press, 1989.

Wyatt, George. *Extracts from the Life of the Virtuous, Christian, and Renowned Queen Anne Boleigne.* London: Richard & Arthur Taylor, 1817.

Yorke, Philip, 2nd Earl of Hardwicke, ed. *Miscellaneous State Papers, From 1501 to 1726.* 2 vols. London: W. Strahan and T. Cadel, 1778.

Secondary Sources

ABC News Poll: Who Killed JFK? – 11/9/03. "September 11 Conspiracy Theories". http://www.rotten.com/library/conspiracy/september_11_conspiracy_theories/.

Ackerman, Susan. *Warrior, Dancer, Seductress, Queen: Women in Judges and Biblical Israel.* New York: Doubleday, 1998.

Adams, Simon. "Queen Elizabeth's Eyes at Court: The Earl of Leicester." In *Leicester and the Court: Essays on Elizabethan Politics*, ed. idem, 130–50. Manchester: Manchester University Press, 2002.

Alsop, J. "The Act for the Queen's Regal Power, 1554." *Parliamentary History* 13 (1994): 261–76.

Amtower, Laurel, and Dorothea Kehler, eds. *The Single Woman in Medieval and Early Modern England*. MRTS 263. Tempe: Arizona Center for Medieval & Renaissance Studies, 2003.

Anglo, Sydney. *Images of Tudor Kingship*. London: Seaby, 1992.

———. *Spectacle, Pageantry, and Early Tudor Policy*. Oxford: Clarendon Press, 1969.

Archer, Ian. "Government in Early Modern London : The Challenge of the Suburbs." In *Two Capitals: London and Dublin 1500–1840*, ed. Peter Clark and Raymond Gillespie, 133–47. Proceedings of the British Academy 107. Oxford and London: British Academy, Oxford University Press, 2001.

Armstrong, William A., ed. *Elizabethan History Plays*. Oxford: Oxford University Press, 1965.

Arnold, Janet. "The 'Coronation' Portrait of Queen Elizabeth I." *Burlington Magazine* 120 (November 1978): 727–41.

———. *Queen Elizabeth's Wardrobe Unlock'd*. Leeds: W.S. Maney & Sons, 1988.

Axelrod, Alan. *Elizabeth I, CEO: Strategic Lessons from the Leader Who Built an Empire*. Paramus, NJ: Prentice Hall, 2000.

Bagwell, Richard. *Ireland under the Tudors*. 3 vols. London: Longmans, Green, 1885–1890.

Bal, Mieke. *Murder and Difference: Gender, Genre and Scholarship on Sisera's Death*. Bloomington: Indiana University Press, 1988.

Bartlett, Kenneth R. "Barker, William (*fl*. 1540–1576)." *Oxford Dictionary of National Biography*, 3: 899–900. Oxford: Oxford University Press, 2004.

Bassnett, Susan. *Elizabeth I: A Feminist Perspective*. Oxford: Berg, 1988.

Bates, Catherine. *The Rhetoric of Courtship in Elizabethan Language and Literature*. Cambridge: Cambridge University Press, 1992.

Bateson, Mary. "A Collection of Original Letters from the Bishops to the Privy Council, 1564." In *Camden Society Miscellany* 9 (1893): individually paginated, vi, 83 pp.

Beattie, Cordelia. *Medieval Single Women: The Politics of Social Classification in Late Medieval England*. Oxford: Oxford University Press, 2007.

Beem, Charles. *The Lioness Roared: The Problems of Female Rule in English History*. New York: Palgrave Macmillan, 2006.

Beer, Anna. *Bess: The Life of Lady Ralegh, Wife to Sir Walter*. London: Constable & Robinson, 2004.

Begin, J. "The Decline and Fall of the House of Guise as an Ecclesiastical Dynasty." *Historical Journal* 25 (1982): 781–803.

Bell, Ilona. "Elizabeth I—Always Her Own Free Woman." In *Political Rhetoric, Power, and Renaissance Women*, ed. Carole Levin and Patricia A. Sullivan, 57–82. Albany: State University of New York Press, 1995.

———. *Elizabethan Women and the Poetry of Courtship*. Cambridge: Cambridge University Press, 1998.

Belsey, Andrew, and Catherine Belsey. "Icons of Divinity: Portraits of Elizabeth I." In *Renaissance Bodies: The Human Figure in English Culture c. 1540– 1660*, ed. Lucy Gent and Nigel Llewellyn, 11–35. London: Reaktion Books, 1990.

Bergeron, David M. "Elizabeth I's Coronation Entry (1559): New Manuscript Evidence." In *The Mysteries of Elizabeth I: Selections from English Literary Renaissance*, ed. Kirby Farrell and Kathleen Swaim, 21–26. Amherst: University of Massachusetts Press, 2003.

———. *English Civic Pageantry 1558–1642*. Columbia: University of South Carolina Press, 1971.

———, ed. *Pageantry in the Shakespearean Theater*. Athens: University of Georgia Press, 1985.

Berry, Philippa. *Of Chastity and Power: Elizabethan Literature and the Unmarried Queen*. London: Routledge, 1989.

Bevington, David. "Lyly's *Endymion* and *Midas*: The Catholic Question in England." *Comparative Drama* 32 (1998): 26–46.

———, ed. *Endymion*, by John Lyly. Manchester: Manchester University Press, 1996.

Bingham, Caroline. *Darnley: A Life of Henry Stuart, Lord Darnley, Consort of Mary Queen of Scots*. London: Constable, 1995.

Birch, Thomas. *Memoirs of the Reign of Queen Elizabeth, from the Year 1581 till Her Death*. 2 vols. London, 1754.

Bornstein, Diane, ed. Introduction. *The Booke of Honor and Armes (1590) and Honor Military and Civil (1602)*. Delmar: Scholar's Facsimiles & Reprints, 1975.

Bouwsma, William J. *Venice and the Defense of Republican Liberty: Renaissance Values in the Age of the Counter Reformation*. Berkeley: University of California Press, 1968.

Braddick, Michael, and John Walter, eds. *Negotiating Power in Early Modern Society: Order, Hierarchy, and Subordination in Britain and Ireland*. Cambridge: Cambridge University Press, 2001.

Bradford, Charles. *Helena Marchioness of Northampton*. London: George Allen & Unwin, 1936.

Brady, Ciaran. "Spenser's Irish Crisis: Humanism and Experience in the 1590s." *Past and Present* 111 (1986): 17–49.

———. "The Captains' Games: Army and Society in Elizabethan Ireland." In *A Military History of Ireland*, ed. Thomas Bartlett and Keith Jeffrey, 135–59. Cambridge: Cambridge University Press, 1996.

———. *Shane O'Neill*. Dundalk: Historical Association of Ireland, Dundalgan Press, 1996.

———. *The Chief Governors: The Rise and Fall of Reform Government in Tudor Ireland, 1536–1588*. Cambridge: Cambridge University Press, 1994.

Brook, V. J. K. *A Life of Archbishop Parker*. Oxford: Clarendon Press, 1962.

Brown, Elizabeth A. "'Companion Me With My Mistress': Cleopatra, Elizabeth I, and Their Waiting Women." In *Maids and Mistresses, Cousins and Queens: Women's Alliances in Early Modern England*, ed. Susan Frye and Karen Robertson, 131–45. New York: Oxford University Press, 1999.

Brown, Susan. *Sumptuous and Richly Adorn'd: The Decoration of Salisbury Cathedral*. London: Stationery Office, 1999.

Bush, M. L. "The Tudors and the Royal Race." *History: Journal of the Historical Association* 53 (1970): 37–48.

Buxton, John. *Sir Philip Sidney and the English Renaissance*. London: Macmillan, 1965.

Canny, Nicholas. *The Elizabethan Conquest of Ireland: A Pattern Established*. Hassocks, Sussex: Harvester Press, 1976.

Carey, Vincent P. "'What pen can paint and tears atone?' Mountjoy's Scorched Earth Campaign." In *The Battle of Kinsale*, ed. Hiram Morgan, 205–16. Bray, Co. Wicklow: Wordwell, 2004.

———. "Atrocity and History: Sir Arthur Grey, Edmund Spenser and the Massacre at Smerwick (1580)." In *Age of Atrocity: Violent Death and Political Conflict in Ireland, 1547–1650*, ed. David Edwards, Pádraig Lenihan, and Clodagh Tait, 79–94. Dublin: Four Courts Press, 2005.

———. *Surviving the Tudors: The 'Wizard' Earl of Kildare and English Rule in Ireland, 1537–1587*. Dublin: Four Courts Press, 2002.

Carroll, Clare. "Representations of Women in Some Early Modern Tracts on the Colonization of Ireland." In eadem, *Circe's Cup: Cultural Transformations in Early Modern Ireland*, 48–60. Cork: Cork University Press, 2001.

Carter, Patrick. "Historical Background." In *Bristol*, ed. Mark C. Pilkinton, xiv–xx. REED. Toronto: University of Toronto Press, 1997.

Cavanagh, Sheila. "The Bad Seed: Princess Elizabeth and the Seymour Incident." In *Dissing Elizabeth: Negative Representations of Gloriana*, ed. Julia M. Walker, 9–29. Durham, NC: Duke University Press, 1998.

Chambers, E. K. *The Elizabethan Stage*. 4 vols. Oxford: Clarendon Press, 1923.

Chirelstein, Ellen. "Lady Elizabeth Pope: The Heraldic Body." In *Renaissance Bodies: The Human Figure in English Culture c.1540–1660*, ed. Gent and Llewellyn, 36–59.

Chojnacki, Stanley. "Identity and Ideology in Renaissance Venice: The Third Serrata." In *Venice Reconsidered: The History and Civilization of an Italian City-State, 1297–1797*, ed. John Martin and Dennis Romero, 263–94. Baltimore: Johns Hopkins University Press, 2000.

———. *Women and Men in Renaissance Venice: Twelve Essays on Patrician Society*. Baltimore: Johns Hopkins University Press, 2000.

Christy, Miller. "Queen Elizabeth's Visit to Tilbury in 1588." *English Historical Review* 34 (1919): 43–61.

Coch, Christine. "'Mother of my Contreye': Elizabeth I and Tudor Constructions of Motherhood." *English Literary Renaissance* 26 (1996): 423–50; repr. in *The Mysteries of Elizabeth I*, ed. Farrell and Swaim, 134–61.

Cole, Mary Hill. *The Portable Queen: Elizabeth I and the Politics of Ceremony*. Amherst: University of Massachusetts Press, 1999.

Collinson, Patrick. "Ecclesiastical Vitriol: Religious Satire in the 1590s and the Invention of Puritanism." In *The Reign of Elizabeth I: Court and Culture in the Last Decade*, ed. John Guy, 150–70. Cambridge: Cambridge University Press, 1995.

———. *Elizabethan Essays*. London: Hambledon, 1994.

———. *Archbishop Grindal, 1519–1583: The Struggle for a Reformed Church*. Berkeley: University of California Press, 1979.

———. *The Elizabethan Puritan Movement*. Oxford: Clarendon Press, 1967.

Colvin, H. M. *The History of the King's Works, Vol. III-IV, 1485–1660*. London: HMSO, 1975–1982.

Coolidge, John S. *The Pauline Renaissance in England: Puritanism and the Bible*. Oxford: Clarendon Press, 1970.

Crankshaw, D. J., and A. Gillespie. "Parker, Matthew." In *Oxford Dictionary of National Biography*, 42: 707–28.

Crouch, David. *Tournament*. London: Hambledon & Continuum, 2005.

Curd, M. Bryan, "Constructing Family Memory: Three English Funeral Monuments and Patriarchy in the Early Modern Period." In *Framing the Family: Narrative and Representation in the Medieval and Early Modern Period*, ed. Rosalynn Voaden and Diane Wolfthal, 273–92. MRTS 280. Tempe, AZ: Arizona Center for Medieval & Renaissance Studies, 2005.

Davis, Natalie Zemon. "Gender and Genre: Women as Historical Writers, 1400–1820." In *Beyond Their Sex: Learned Women of the European Past*, 153–82. New York: New York University Press, 1980.

———. "Ghosts, Kin and Progeny: Some Features of Family Life in Early Modern France." *Daedalus* 106 (1977): 87–114.

Davis, Robert C., and Benjamin Ravid, eds. *The Jews of Early Modern Venice*. Baltimore: Johns Hopkins University Press, 2001.

Dennys, Rodney. *The Heraldic Imagination*. New York: Clarkson N. Potter, 1975.

Dictionary of National Biography, ed. Sir Leslie Stephen and Sidney Lee. 63 vols. London: Smith, Elder, & Co., 1885–1901.

Dodd, Alfred. *Francis Bacon's Personal Life-Story*. London, New York: Rider, 1949.

———. *The Marriage of Elizabeth Tudor*. London: Rider & Co., 1940.

Dolan, Frances E. *Marriage and Violence: The Early Modern Legacy*. Philadelphia: University of Pennsylvania Press, 2008.
Doran, Susan. "Elizabeth I's Religion: The Evidence of Her Letters." *Journal of Ecclesiastical History* 51 (2000): 699–720.
———. *Mary Queen of Scots: An Illustrated Life*. London: British Library, 2007.
———. *Monarchy and Matrimony: The Courtships of Elizabeth I*. London: Routledge, 1996.
———. "Religion and Politics at the Court of Elizabeth I: The Habsburg Marriage Negotiations of 1559–1567." *English Historical Review* 104 (1989): 908–26.
———. "Seymour, Edward, first earl of Hertford." *Oxford Dictionary of National Biography*, 49: 870.
Dovey, Zillah. *An Elizabethan Progress: The Queen's Journey into East Anglia, 1578*. Teaneck, NJ: Associated University Presses, 1996.
Dowling, Maria. "Anne Boleyn and Reform." *Journal of Ecclesiastical History* 35 (1984): 30–46.
Duncan, Sarah. "'Most godly heart fraight with al mercie:' Queens' Mercy during the Reigns of Mary I and Elizabeth I." In *Queens and Power in Medieval and Early Modern England*, ed. Carole Levin and Robert Bucholz, 31–50. Lincoln, NE: University of Nebraska Press, 2009.
Dunlop, Ian. *Palaces and Progresses of Elizabeth I*. New Haven: Yale University Press, 1993.
Dunn, Jane. *Elizabeth and Mary: Cousins, Rivals, Queens*. New York: Alfred A. Knopf, 2004.
Edwards, David. "Beyond Reform: Martial Law and the Tudor Reconquest of Ireland." *History Ireland* 5 (1997): 16–22.
Edwards, Edward. *The Life of Sir Walter Raleigh*. 2 vols. London: Macmillan, 1868.
Ellenberger, Henri F. *The Discovery of the Unconscious: The History and Evolution of Dynamics Psychiatry*. New York: Basic Books, 1970.
Ellis, Steven. *Ireland in the Age of the Tudors 1447–1603: English Expansion and the End of Gaelic Rule*. London: Longman, 1998.
Elton, G. R. "*Lex terrae victrix*: The Triumph of Parliamentary Law in the Sixteenth Century." In *The Parliaments of Elizabethan England*, ed. D. M. Dean and N. L. Jones, 15–36. Oxford: Blackwell, 1990.
———. *Reform and Reformation: England, 1509–1558*. Cambridge, MA: Harvard University Press, 1977.
———. *The Parliament of England 1559–1581*. Cambridge: Cambridge University Press, 1986.
Erickson, Carolly. *The First Elizabeth*. New York: Summit, 1983.
Fine, Reuben. *A History of Psychoanalysis*. New York: Columbia University Press, 1979.

Finlay, Robert. *Politics in Renaissance Venice*. New Brunswick: Rutgers University Press, 1980.
Fletcher, J. M. J. *The Gorges Monument in Salisbury Cathedral*; repr. *Wiltshire Archaeological and Natural History Magazine* 50 (1932): 16–43.
———. *The Hertford Monument in Salisbury Cathedral: A Lecture*. Devizes, Eng.: George Simpson & Co, 1927.
Fox, Adam. *Oral and Literate Culture in England, 1500–1700*. Oxford: Clarendon Press, 2000.
Freeman, Thomas. "Research, Rumor, and Propaganda: Anne Boleyn in Foxe's Book of Martyrs." *Historical Journal* 31 (1995): 797–819.
Freud, Sigmund. *Collected Papers*, ed. James Strachey. 5 vols. New York: Basic Books, 1959.
Froide, Amy. *Never Married: Singlewomen in Early Modern England*. Oxford: Oxford University Press, 2005.
Fry, Plantagenet Somerset. *Chequers: The Country Home of Britain's Prime Ministers*. London: HMSO, 1977.
Frye, Susan. "Sewing Connections: Elizabeth Tudor, Mary Stuart, Elizabeth Talbot, and Seventeenth-Century Anonymous Needleworkers." In *Maids and Mistresses, Cousins and Queens: Women's Alliances in Early Modern England*, ed. eadem, 165–82.
———. "The Myth of Elizabeth at Tilbury." *Sixteenth Century Journal* 23 (1992): 95–114.
———. *Elizabeth I: The Competition for Representation*. Oxford: Oxford University Press, 1993.
Galloway, David, ed. *Norwich: 1540–1642*. REED. Toronto: University of Toronto Press, 1984.
Gleason, Elizabeth G. "Confronting New Realities: Venice and the Peace of Bologna, 1530." In *Venice Reconsidered*, ed. Martin and Romero, 168–84.
Gordon, Donald. "'Veritas Filia Temporis:' Hadrianus Junius and Geoffrey Whitney." *Journal of the Warburg and Courtauld Institutes* 3 (1939–1940): 228–40.
Green, Janet M. "'I My Self': Queen Elizabeth I's Oration at Tilbury Camp." *Sixteenth Century Journal* 28 (1997): 421–45.
Greenberg, Janelle. *The Radical Face of the Ancient Constitution: St. Edward's "Laws" in Early Modern Political Thought*. Cambridge: Cambridge University Press, 2001.
Greenblatt, Stephen J. *Sir Walter Ralegh: The Renaissance Man and His Roles*. New Haven: Yale University Press, 1973.
Gristwood, Sarah. *Arbella: England's Lost Queen*. New York: Houghton Mifflin, 2003.
Gunn, Fenja. *The Artificial Face: A History of Cosmetics*. New York: Hippocrene, 1975.

Guy, John. "The Elizabethan Establishment and the Ecclesiastical Polity." In *The Reign of Elizabeth I: Court and Culture in the Last Decade*, ed. idem, 126–49.
———. *Queen of Scots: The True Life of Mary Stuart*. Boston: Houghton Mifflin, 2004.
———. *Tudor England*. Oxford: Oxford University Press, 1990.
———, ed. *The Reign of Elizabeth I: Court and Culture in the Last Decade*. Cambridge: Cambridge University Press, 1995.
Hackett, Helen. "Courtly Writing by Women." In *Women and Literature in Britain 1500–1700*, ed. Helen Wilcox, 169-89. Cambridge: Cambridge University Press, 1996.
———. "The Rhetoric of (In)fertility: Shifting Responses to Elizabeth I's Childlessness." In *Rhetoric, Women and Politics in Early Modern England*, ed. Jennifer Richards and Alison Thorne, 149–71. London: Routledge, 2007.
———. *Virgin Mother, Maiden Queen: Elizabeth I and the Cult of the Virgin Mary*. London: Macmillan; New York: St. Martin's Press, 1995.
Hager, Alan. *Dazzling Images: The Masks of Sir Philip Sidney*. Newark, DE: University of Delaware Press, 1991.
Haigh, Christopher. *Elizabeth I*. London: Longman, 2001.
———. *Elizabeth I: Profile in Power*. London: Longman, 1988.
Haller, William. *Foxe's Book of Martyrs and the Elect Nation*. London: Jonathan Cape, 1963.
Hammer, Paul E. J. *Elizabeth's Wars*. Basingstoke: Palgrave, 2003.
———. *The Polarisation of Elizabethan Politics: The Political Career of Robert Devereux, 2nd Earl of Essex*. Cambridge: Cambridge University Press, 1999.
———. "Sharpe, Leonell." In *Oxford Dictionary of National Biography*, 50: 51–53.
Hardison, Jr., O. B. *The Enduring Monument: A Study of the Idea of Praise in Renaissance Literary Theory and Practice*. Chapel Hill: University of Carolina Press, 1962.
Harrington, Paul. "Gorges [née Snackenborg], Helena, Lady Gorges." In *Oxford Dictionary of National Biography*, 22: 994–95.
Hasler, P. W. *The History of Parliament: The House of Commons, 1558–1603*. 3 vols. London: HMSO, 1981.
Hassel, R. Chris, Jr. *Renaissance Drama and the English Church Year*. Lincoln, NE: University of Nebraska Press, 1979.
Howarth, David. *Images of Rule: Art and Politics in the English Renaissance, 1485–1649*. Los Angeles: University of California Press, 1997.
Hazard, Mary. *Elizabethan Silent Language*. Lincoln, NE: University of Nebraska Press, 2000.
Heal, Felicity. "Giving and Receiving on Royal Progress." In *The Progresses, Pageants, and Entertainments of Queen Elizabeth I*, ed. Jayne Elisabeth Archer, Elizabeth Goldring, and Sarah Knight, 46–61. Oxford: Oxford University Press, 2007.

———, and Clive Holmes. *The Gentry in England and Wales 1500–1700.* Stanford: Stanford University Press, 1994.

Henderson, Judith Rice. "Euphues and His Erasmus." *English Literary Renaissance* 12 (1982): 135–61.

Hibbert, Christopher. *The Virgin Queen.* Cambridge, MA: Perseus, 1991.

Hill, Christopher. *The English Bible and the Seventeenth Century Revolution.* London: Penguin, 1993.

Hindle, Steven. "County Government in England." In *Companion to Tudor Britain*, ed. Robert Tittler and Norman Jones, 98–115. Oxford: Blackwell Publishers, 2004.

Hoak, Dale. "A Tudor Deborah? The Coronation of Elizabeth I, Parliament, and the Problem of Female Rule." In *John Foxe and His World*, ed. Christopher Highley and John N. King, 73–88. Aldershot: Ashgate, 2002.

Howarth, David. *The Voyage of the Armada: The Spanish Story.* London: Collins, 1981.

Hudson, Winthrop. *The Cambridge Connection and the Elizabethan Settlement of 1559.* Durham, NC: Duke University Press, 1980.

Hume, Martin A. S. *The Courtships of Queen Elizabeth.* London: E. Nash & Grayson, 1926.

Hunter, G. K. *John Lyly: The Humanist as Courtier.* Cambridge, MA: Harvard University Press, 1962.

Ives, Eric [William]. *Anne Boleyn.* Oxford: Basil Blackwell, 1986.

———. *The Life and Death of Anne Boleyn: 'The Most Happy.'* Oxford: Blackwell, 2004.

Izon, John. *Sir Thomas Stucley, 1525–78, Traitor Extraordinary.* London: A. Melrose, 1956.

Jenkins, Elizabeth. *Elizabeth the Great.* London: Gollancz, 1958.

Johnson, Barbara. *The Critical Difference: Essays in the Contemporary Rhetoric of Reading.* Baltimore: Johns Hopkins University Press, 1980.

Johnson, Paul. *Elizabeth I.* New York: Holt, Rinehart & Winston, 1974.

Jones, Norman. *Faith by Statute: Parliament and the Settlement of Religion.* London: Royal Historical Society, 1982.

———. *The Birth of the Elizabethan Age.* Cambridge, MA: Blackwell, 1993.

Jordan, Constance. *Renaissance Feminism: Literary Texts and Political Models.* Ithaca: Cornell University Press, 1990.

Kantorowicz, Ernst H. *The King's Two Bodies: A Study in Medieval Political Theology.* Princeton: Princeton University Press, 1957.

King, John N. "Queen Elizabeth I: Representations of the Virgin Queen." *Renaissance Quarterly* 53 (1990): 30–74.

———. *Tudor Royal Iconography: Literature and Art in an Age of Religious Crisis.* Princeton: Princeton University Press, 1989.

King, Margaret. *Women of the Renaissance.* Chicago: University of Chicago Press, 1991.

King, Richard John. *Handbook to the Cathedrals of England, Eastern Division.* London: J. Murray, 1862.
Knapp, Robert S. "The Monarchy of Love in Lyly's *Endimion.*" *Modern Philology* 73 (1976): 353–67.
Kumaran, Arul. "Robert Greene's Martinist Transformation in 1590." *Studies in Philology* 103 (2006): 243–63.
Lake, Peter. "'The Monarchical Republic of Elizabeth I' Revisited (by its Victims) as a Conspiracy." In *Conspiracies and Conspiracy Theory in Early Modern Europe: From the Waldensians to the French Revolution,* ed. Barry Coward and Julian Swann, 87–111. Aldershot: Ashgate, 2004.

———. *Anglicans and Puritans? Presbyterianism and English Conformist Thought from Whitgift to Hooker.* London: Unwin Hyman, 1988.
Lane, Frederic C. *Venice: A Maritime Republic.* Baltimore: Johns Hopkins University Press, 1973.
Leahy, William. *Elizabethan Triumphal Processions.* Burlington, VT: Ashgate, 2005.
Lennon, Colm. *Sixteenth-Century Ireland: The Incomplete Conquest.* Dublin: Gill & Macmillan, 2005.
Lenz, Carolyn Ruth Swift. "The Allegory of Wisdom in Lyly's *Endimion.*" *Comparative Drama* 10 (1976): 235–57.
Levin, Carole. *"The Heart and Stomach of a King": Elizabeth I and the Politics of Sex and Power.* Philadelphia: University of Pennsylvania Press, 1994.

———. "Queens and Claimants: Political Insecurity in Sixteenth-Century England." In *Gender, Ideology, and Action,* ed. Janet Sharistanian, 41–66. New York: Greenwood Press, 1986.

———. *The Reign of Elizabeth I.* New York: Palgrave, 2002.

———. "'We shall never have a merry world while the Queene lyveth': Gender, Monarchy, and the Power of Seditious Words." In *Dissing Elizabeth,* ed. Walker, 77–95.
Levin, Carole, and Patricia A. Sullivan, eds. *Political Rhetoric, Power, and Renaissance Women.* Albany: State University of New York Press, 1995.
Llewellyn, Nigel. *The Art of Death: Visual Culture in The English Death Ritual c.1500–c.1800.* London: Reaktion Books, Victoria and Albert Museum, 1991.

———. *Funeral Monuments in Post-Reformation England.* New York: Cambridge University Press, 1991.
Loades, David. *Elizabeth I.* London: Hambledon & London, 2003.

———. *Mary Tudor: A Life.* Oxford: Basil Blackwell, 1989.

———, ed. *John Foxe: An Historical Perspective.* Aldershot: Ashgate, 1999.
Lynch, Michael, ed. *Mary Stewart in Three Kingdoms.* London: Blackwell, 1988.
MacCaffrey, Wallace T. *Elizabeth I.* London: Edward Arnold, 1993.

———. *Elizabeth I: War and Politics, 1588–1603.* Princeton: Princeton University Press, 1992.

———. *Queen Elizabeth and the Making of Policy, 1572–1588*. Princeton: Princeton University Press, 1981.
MacCarthy-Morroch, Michael. *The Munster Plantation: English Migration to Southern Ireland 1583–1641*. Oxford: Clarendon Press, 1986.
Manley, Lawrence. *Literature and Culture in Early Modern London*. Cambridge: Cambridge University Press, 1995.
Manning, C. R., ed. "State Papers Relating to the Custody of the Princess Elizabeth at Woodstock in 1554." *Norfolk Archaeology* 4 (1855): 133–231.
Marcus, Leah. "Shakespeare's Comic Heroines, Elizabeth I, and the Political Uses of Androgyny." In *Women in the Middle Ages and the Renaissance: Literary and Historical Perspectives*, ed. Mary Beth Rose, 135–53. Syracuse, NY: Syracuse University Press, 1986.
Marotti, Arthur F. *Manuscript, Print, and the English Renaissance Lyric*. Ithaca: Cornell University Press, 1995.
Martin, John, and Dennis Romero, eds. *Venice Reconsidered: The History and Civilization of an Italian City-State, 1297–1797*. Baltimore: Johns Hopkins University Press, 2000.
Mattingly, Garrett. *Renaissance Diplomacy*. Boston: Houghton Mifflin, 1955.
Maxwell, Robin. *The Queen's Bastard*. New York: Scribner, 1999.
May, Steven W., and Anne Lake Prescott. "The French Verses of Elizabeth I." *English Literary Renaissance* 24 (1994): 9–43.
McCabe, Richard. *Spenser's Monstrous Regiment: Elizabethan Ireland and the Poetics of Difference*. Oxford: Oxford University Press, 2002.
McIlwain, Charles, ed. *The Political Works of James I*. New York: Russell & Russell, 1946, repr. 1965.
McLaren, A. N. *Political Culture in the Reign of Elizabeth I: Queen and Commonwealth 1558–1585*. Cambridge: Cambridge University Press, 1999.
———. "The Quest for a King: Gender, Marriage, and Succession in Elizabethan England." *Journal of British Studies* 41 (2002): 259–90.
Mears, Natalie. "Politics in the Elizabethan Privy Chamber: Lady Mary Sidney and Kat Ashley." In *Women and Politics in Early Modern England, 1450–1700*, ed. James Daybell, 67–82. Burlington, VT: Ashgate, 2004.
———. *Queenship and Political Discourse in the Elizabethan Realms*. Cambridge: Cambridge University Press, 2005.
Mendelson, Sara. "Popular Perceptions of Elizabeth." In *Elizabeth I: Always Her Own Free Woman*, ed. Levin, Carney, and Barrett-Graves, 192–214.
Merton, Charlotte. "The Women Who Served Queen Mary and Queen Elizabeth: Ladies, Gentlewomen and Maids of the Privy Chamber, 1553–1603." Ph.D. diss., Cambridge University, 1992.
Montrose, Louis Adrian. "Celebration and Insinuation: Sir Philip Sidney and the Motives of Elizabethan Courtship." *Renaissance Drama* 8 (1977): 3–35.

---. "'Eliza, Queen of Shepherds All' and the Pastoral of Power." In *The Mysteries of Elizabeth I: Selections from English Literary Renaissance*, ed. Farrell and Swaim, 162–91.

---. "The Elizabethan Subject and the Spenserian Text." In *Literary Theory/ Renaissance Texts*, ed. Patricia Parker and David Quint, 303–40. Baltimore: Johns Hopkins University Press, 1986.

---. *The Subject of Elizabeth: Authority, Gender, and Representation*. Chicago: University of Chicago Press, 2006.

---. "The Work of Gender in the Discourse of Discovery." *Representations* 33 (1991): 1–41. Repr. in *New World Encounters*, ed. Stephen Greenblatt, 177–217. Berkeley: University of California Press, 1993.

Morgan, Hiram. "'Never any realm worse governed': Queen Elizabeth and Ireland." *Transactions of the Royal Historical Society* 14 (2004): 295–308.

Morris, Jeffrey B. "To (Re)fashion a Gentleman: Ralegh's Disgrace in Spenser's Legend of Courtesy." *Studies in Philology* 94 (1997): 38–58.

Muir, Edward. "Was There Republicanism in the Renaissance Republics? Venice after Agnadello." In *Venice Reconsidered*, ed. Martin and Romero, 137–67.

Neale, J. E. *Elizabeth I and Her Parliaments 1584–1601*. London: Jonathan Cape, 1957.

---. *Queen Elizabeth*. London: Jonathan Cape, 1934.

---. *Queen Elizabeth I: A Biography*. New York: Doubleday, 1957.

Nicolas, Sir Harry. *Memoirs of the Life and Times of Sir Christopher Hatton*. London: R. Bentley, 1847.

Norbrook, David. *Poetry and Politics in the English Renaissance*. Oxford: Oxford University Press, 2002.

Norrington, Ruth. *In the Shadow of the Throne: The Lady Arabella Stuart*. London: Peter Owen, 2002.

North, Marcy L. "Queen Elizabeth Compiled: Henry Stanford's Private Anthology and the Question of Accountability." In *Dissing Elizabeth*, ed. Walker, 185–208.

Oakeshott, Walter. *The Queen and the Poet*. London: Faber & Faber, 1960.

Orgel, Stephen. "Making Greatness Familiar." *Genre* 15 (1982): 41–48. Repr. in *Pageantry in the Shakespearean Theater*, ed. Bergeron, 19–25.

Orlin, Lena Cowen. "The Fictional Families of Elizabeth I." In *Political Rhetoric*, ed. Levin and Sullivan, 85–110.

Osborne, Francis. *The Works of Francis Osborne*. Ann Arbor, MI: University Microfilms International, 1977.

Oxford Dictionary of National Biography. 60 vols. Oxford: Oxford University Press, 2004.

Oxford English Dictionary. 2nd ed., ed. J. A. Simpson and E. S. C. Weiner. Oxford: Clarendon Press, 1989.

Palmer, Barbara. "'Ciphers to this Great Accompt': Civic Pageantry in the Second Tetralogy." In *Pageantry in the Shakespearean Theater*, ed. Bergeron, 114–29.

Palmer, William. "Scenes from Provincial Life: History, Honor, and Meaning in the Tudor North." *Renaissance Quarterly* 53 (2000): 425–48.

Pearson, Andrew Forest Scott. *Thomas Cartwright and Elizabethan Puritanism*. Cambridge: Cambridge, University Press, 1925.

Peck, D. C. "Raleigh, Sidney, Oxford, and the Catholics, 1579." *Notes and Queries* 223 (1978): 427–31.

Perry, Edith Weir. *Under Four Tudors, Being the Story of Matthew Parker*. London: George Allen & Unwin, 1964.

Perry, Maria. *The Word of a Prince*. Woodbridge: Boydell Press, 1990.

Pollard, A. F. "Queen Elizabeth's Under-Clerks and Their Commons' Journals." *Bulletin of the Institute of Historical Research* 17 (1939–1940): 1–12.

———. *The History of England from the Accession of Edward VI to the Death of Elizabeth (1547–1603)*. New York: Greenwood Press, 1969.

Poole, Kristen. "Facing Puritanism: Falstaff, Martin Marprelate and the Grotesque Puritan." In *Shakespeare and Carnival: After Bakhtin*, ed. Ronald Knowles, 97–122. New York: St. Martin's Press, 1998.

Pope-Hennessy, Sir John. *Sir Walter Raleigh in Ireland*. London: K. Paul, Trench, 1883.

Quinn, David B. *The Elizabethans and the Irish*. Ithaca: Folger Shakespeare Library, 1966.

———. *Set Fair for Roanoke: Voyages and Colonies 1584–1606*. Chapel Hill: America's Four Hundredth Anniversary Committee, University of North Carolina Press, 1985.

Quinn, David B., and Neil M. Cheshire, eds. *The New Found Land of Stephen Parmenius*. Toronto: University of Toronto Press, 1972.

Quint, David. "Archimago and Amoret: The Poem and Its Doubles." In *Worldmaking Spenser: Explorations in the Modern Age*, ed. Patrick Cheney and Lauren Silberman, 32–42. Lexington: University Press of Kentucky, 2000.

Raymond, Joad. *Pamphlets and Pamphleteering in Early Modern Britain*. Cambridge: Cambridge University Press, 2003.

Read, Conyers. *Lord Burghley and Queen Elizabeth*. London: Jonathan Cape; New York: Knopf, 1960.

Richards, Judith. "Mary Tudor As 'Sole Queen'?: Gendering Tudor Monarchy." *Historical Journal* 40 (1997): 895–924.

Ridley, Jasper. *Elizabeth I: The Shrewdness of Virtue*. New York: Fromm International, 1989.

Riehl, Anna. *The Face of Queenship: Early Modern Representations of Elizabeth I*. New York: Palgrave, 2010.

Riordan, Michael. "Carey, William (c. 1496–1528)." In *Oxford Dictionary of National Biography*, 10: 89-90.

Rösch, Gerhard. "The Serrata of the Great Council and Venetian Society, 1285–1323." In *Venice Reconsidered*, ed. Martin and Romero, 67–88.
Rose, Mary Beth. "The Gendering of Authority in the Public Speeches of Elizabeth I." *PMLA: Publications of the Modern Language Association* 115 (2000): 1077–82.
Rozett, Martha Tuck. *Constructing a World: Shakespeare's England and the New Historical Fiction*. Albany: State University of New York Press, 2003.
Ruggiero, Guido. "'Più che la vita caro': onore, matrimonio e reputazione femminile nel tardo Rinascimento." *Quaderni Storici*, n.s. 66 (1987): 753–75.
Sanchez, Magdalena S. *The Empress, the Queen, and the Nun: Women and Power at the Court of Philip III of Spain*. Baltimore: Johns Hopkins University Press, 1998.
Saxl, Fritz. "Veritas Filia Temporis." In *Philosophy and History: Essays Presented to Ernst Cassirer*, ed. Raymond Klibansky and H. J. Paton, 197–222. New York: Harper & Row, 1963.
Scarisbrick, Diana. "Elizabeth's Jewellery." In *Elizabeth: The Exhibition at the National Maritime Museum*, ed. D. Starkey and S. Doran, 183–88. London: Chatto & Windus, 2003.
Scragg, Leah. "*Campaspe* and the Construction of Monarchical Power." *Medieval and Renaissance Drama in England* 12 (1999): 59–83.
———. "The Victim of Fashion? Rereading the Biography of John Lyly." *Medieval and Renaissance Drama in England* 19 (2006): 210–26.
Shenk, Linda. *Learned Queen: The Image of Elizabeth I in Politics and Poetry*. New York: Palgrave, 2010.
———. "Queen Solomon: An International Elizabeth I in 1569." In *Queens and Power in Medieval and Early Modern England*, ed. Robert Bucholz and Carole Levin, 98–125. Lincoln, NE: University of Nebraska Press, 2009.
———. "'To Love and Be Wise': The Earl of Essex, Humanist Court Culture, and England's Learned Queen." *Early Modern Literary Studies* 13.2/ Special issue 16 (2007) 3.1–27. http://purl.oclc.org/emls/si-16/shenwise.htm.
———. "Turning Learned Authority into Royal Supremacy: Elizabeth I's Learned Persona and Her University Orations." In *Elizabeth I: Always Her Own Free Woman*, ed. Levin, Carney, and Barrett-Graves, 78–96.
Shephard, Robert. "Sexual Rumours in English Politics: The Cases of Elizabeth I and James I." In *Desire and Discipline: Sex and Sexuality in the Premodern West*, ed. Jacqueline Murray and Konrad Eisenbechler, 101–22. Toronto: University of Toronto Press, 1996.
Sherlock, Peter. *Monuments and Memory in Early Modern England*. Burlington, VT: Ashgate, 2008.
———. "The Monuments of Elizabeth Tudor and Mary Stuart: King James and the Manipulation of Memory." *Journal of British Studies* 46 (2007): 263–89.

Siegfried, Brandie R. "Queen to Queen at Check: Grace O'Malley, Elizabeth Tudor and the Discourse of Majesty in the State Papers of Ireland." In *Elizabeth I: Always Her Own Free Woman*, ed. Levin, Carney, and Barrett-Graves, 149–75.

Smither, L. J. "Elizabeth I: A Psychological Profile." *Sixteenth Century Journal* 15 (1984): 47–72.

Smuts, R. Malcolm. "Public Ceremony and Royal Charisma: The English Royal Entry in London, 1485–1642." In *The First Modern Society*, ed. A. L. Beier, David Cannadine, and James M. Rosenheim, 65–94. Cambridge: Cambridge University Press, 1989.

Somerset, Anne. *Elizabeth I*. London: Weidenfeld & Nicolson, 1991.

Spagnoletti, Angelantonio. *Principi italiani e Spagna nell'età barocca*. Milan: Mondadori, 1996.

Sperling, Jutta Gisela. *Convents and the Body Politic in Late Renaissance Venice*. Chicago: University of Chicago Press, 1999.

Stallybrass, Peter. "Patriarchal Territories: The Body Enclosed." In *Rewriting the Renaissance: The Discourses of Sexual Difference in Early Modern Europe*, ed. Margaret W. Ferguson, Maureen Quilligan, and Nancy J. Vickers, 123–42. Chicago: University of Chicago Press, 1986.

Starkey, David. *Elizabeth: The Struggle for the Throne*. London: Perennial, 2000; New York: Harper Collins, 2001.

———. "The King's Privy Chamber, 1485–1547." Ph.D. diss., Cambridge University, 1973.

———, ed. *Rivals in Power: Lives and Letters of the Great Tudor Dynasties*. London: Macmillan, 1990.

———, and Susan Doran, eds. *Elizabeth: The Exhibition at the National Maritime Museum*. London: Chatto & Windus, National Maritime Museum, 2003.

Stephanson, Raymond. "John Lyly's Prose Fiction: Irony, Humor, and Anti-Humanism." *English Literary Renaissance* 11 (1981): 3–21.

Stone, Lawrence. *The Family, Sex and Marriage in England 1500–1800*. Abr. ed. New York: Harper, 1979.

Streitz, Paul. *Oxford: Son of Queen Elizabeth I*. Darien, CT: Oxford Institute Press, 2001.

Strong, Roy C. *Artists of the Tudor Court: The Portrait Miniature Rediscovered, 1520–1620*. London: Victoria and Albert Museum, 1983.

———. *Gloriana: The Portraits of Queen Elizabeth I*. London: Thames & Hudson, 1987.

———. *The Cult of Elizabeth: Elizabethan Portraiture and Pageantry*. London: Thames & Hudson, 1977; repr. London: Pimlico, 1999.

Stump, Donald. "A Slow Return to Eden: Spenser and Women's Rule." *English Literary Renaissance* 29 (1999): 401–21.

———, and Susan Felch, eds. *Elizabeth I and Her Age: A Norton Critical Edition*. New York: W.W. Norton, 2009.

———, and Carole Levin, eds. *Images of Elizabeth I: A Quadricentennial Celebration*. Special issue, *Explorations in Renaissance Culture* 30 (Summer 2004).
Summit, Jennifer. "'The Arte of a Ladies Penne': Elizabeth I and the Poetics of Queenship." In *The Mysteries of Elizabeth*, ed. Farrell and Swaim, 67–96.
Tait, Clodagh. "Adored for Saints: Catholic Martyrdom in Ireland c. 1560–1655." *Journal of Early Modern History* 5 (2001): 128–59.
Teague, Frances. "Provenance and Propaganda as Editorial Stumbling Blocks." In *New Ways of Looking at Old Texts II*, ed. W. Speed Hill, 119–23. MRTS 188. Tempe, AZ: Medieval & Renaissance Texts & Studies, Renaissance English Text Society, 1998.
———. "Queen Elizabeth in Her Speeches." In *Gloriana's Face*, ed. S. P. Cerasano and Marion Wynne-Davies, 63–78. Detroit: Wayne State University Press, 1992.
Tenenti, Alberto. *Piracy and the Decline of Venice, 1580–1615*, trans. Janet and Brian Pullan. Berkeley: University of California Press, 1967.
Tennenhouse, Leonard. "Sir Walter Ralegh and the Literature of Clientage." In *Patronage in the Renaissance*, ed. Guy Fitch Lytle and Stephen Orgel, 235–58. Princeton: Princeton University Press, 1981.
Thurley, Simon. *The Royal Palaces of Tudor England*. New Haven: Yale University Press, 1993.
Tytler, Patrick Fraser. *Life of Sir Walter Raleigh*. Edinburgh: Oliver & Boyd, 1833.
Usher, Brett. "Backing Protestantism." In *John Foxe*, ed. Loades, 105–34.
———. *William Cecil and Episcopacy, 1559–1577*. Aldershot: Ashgate, 2003.
Vanhoutte, Jacqueline. "Queen and Country?: Female Monarchs and Feminized Nations in Elizabethan Political Pamphlets." In *Elizabeth I: Always Her Own Free Woman*, ed. Levin, Carney, and Barrett-Graves, 7–19.
Veech, Thomas M. *Dr. Nicholas Sanders and the English Reformation, 1530–1581*. Louvain: Bureaux du Recueil, Bibliothèque de l'Université, 1935.
Vickers, Nancy. "'The blazon of sweet beauty's best': Shakespeare's *Lucrece*." In *Shakespeare and the Question of Theory*, ed. Patricia Parker and Geoffrey Hartman, 95–116. New York: Methuen, 1985.
———. "'This heraldry in Lucrece' face'." *Poetics Today* 6 (1985): 171–84.
———. "Diana Described: Scattered Woman and Scattered Rhyme." In *Writing and Sexual Difference*, ed. Elizabeth Abel, 95–110. Chicago: University of Chicago Press, 1982.
von Bülow, Gottfried, trans. "Journey through England and Scotland made by Lupold von Wedelin in the Years 1584 and 1585." *Transactions of the Royal Historical Society*, n.s. 9 (1895): 223–70.
Walker, Julia M. *The Elizabeth Icon 1603–2003*. New York: Palgrave Macmillan, 2003.
———. "Bones of Contention: Posthumous Images of Elizabeth and Stuart Politics." In *Dissing Elizabeth*, ed. eadem, 252–76.

———. "Reading the Tombs of Elizabeth I." *English Literary Renaissance* 26 (1996): 510–30.

———, ed. *Dissing Elizabeth: Negative Representations of Gloriana*. Durham, NC: Duke University Press, 1998.

Wall, Alison. "Maurice Browne and his Patrons in the 1580s." *Parergon* 21 (2004): 47–65.

———. *Power and Protest in England 1525–1640*. London: Arnold, 2000.

Walsham, Alexandra. "'A Very Deborah?' The Myth of Elizabeth I as a Providential Monarch." In *The Myth of Elizabeth*, ed. Susan Doran and Thomas S. Freeman, 143–68. Houndmills: Palgrave Macmillan, 2003.

Warkentin, Germaine, ed. *The Queen's Majesty's Passage and Related Documents*. Toronto: Centre for Reformation and Renaissance Studies, 2004.

Warnicke, Retha M. "Conflicting Rhetoric about Tudor Women: The Example of Queen Anne Boleyn." In *Political Rhetoric*, ed. Levin and Sullivan, 39–54.

———. *Mary Queen of Scots*. London: Routledge, 2006.

———. *The Rise and Fall of Anne Boleyn*. Cambridge: Cambridge University Press, 1989.

Watkins, John. *Representing Elizabeth in Stuart England: Literature, History, Sovereignty*. Cambridge: Cambridge University Press, 2002.

Weinreb, Ben, and Christopher Hibbert, eds. *The London Encyclopedia*. London: Macmillan, 1983.

Weissberger, Barbara F. *Isabel Rules: Constructing Queenship, Wielding Power*. Minneapolis: University of Minnesota Press, 2004.

Wiesner, Merry E. *Women and Gender in Early Modern Europe*. 2nd ed. New York: Cambridge University Press, 2000.

Wilson, Elkin Calhoun. *England's Eliza*. New York: Octagon, 1939.

Wilson, Jean. *Entertainments for Queen Elizabeth I*. Woodbridge: Brewer, 1980.

Wilson, Violet. *Queen Elizabeth's Maids of Honour and Ladies of the Privy Chamber*. London: John Lane, Bodley Head, 1923.

Woolf, Daniel. *The Social Circulation of the Past: English Historical Culture 1500–1730*. New York: Oxford University Press, 2003.

Worden, Blair. "Favourites on the English Stage." In *The World of the Favourite, c.1550–c.1675*, ed. John Elliott and Laurence Brockliss, 160–83. New Haven: Yale University Press, 1999.

———. "Historians and Poets." *Huntingdon Library Quarterly* 68 (2005): 71–93.

Wormald, Jenny. *Mary, Queen of Scots: Politics, Passion, and a Kingdom Lost*. New York: Tauris Park, 2001.

Wright, Pam. "A Change in Direction: The Ramifications of a Female Household, 1558–1603." In *The English Court: From the Wars of the Roses to the Civil War*, ed. David Starkey, 147–72. New York: Longman, 1987.

Yates, Frances A. "Elizabethan Chivalry: The Romance of the Accession Day Tilts." *Journal of the Warburg and Courtauld Institutes* 20 (1957): 4–25.

Young, Alan R. "English Tournament Imprese." In *The Emblem in Renaissance and Baroque Europe: Tradition and Variety (Selected Papers of the Glasgow International Emblem Conference 13–17 August 1990)*, 1–139. Leiden: Brill, 1992.
———. *Tudor and Jacobean Tournaments*. Dobbs Ferry: Sheridan House, 1987.
Zannini, Andrea. "Economic and Social Aspects of the Crisis of Venetian Diplomacy in the Seventeenth and Eighteenth Centuries." In *Politics and Diplomacy in Early Modern Italy: The Structure of Diplomatic Practice, 1450–1800*, ed. Daniela Frigo, 109–46. Trans. Adrian Belton. Cambridge: Cambridge University Press, 2000.
Ziegler, Georgianna, comp. and ed. *Elizabeth I: Then and Now*. Seattle and Washington, DC: University of Washington Press, Folger Shakespeare Library, 2003.

Index

A

Abridgement of the Chronicles of England (Grafton), 238
Accession Day Tilts, 176, 180, 181, 187, 286
Ackerman, Susan, 253
Act of Succession (1544), 293
Adams, Simon, xvi
Agricola, 159
Alençon and Anjou, Francis, duke of, 43–44, 65, 86, 159n6, 164, 179, 186, 222, 226, 247, 287, 289–90, 294, 297
Alexander, 266n13
Alford, Stephen, xvi
Allen, Cardinal William, 5, 223
Alva, Fernando Alvarez de Toledo, duke of, 243
Anglican Church, *see* Church of England
Anglo, Sydney, 233
Anne of Cleves, 57
Apologie for Womenkind, An (I.G.), 251
Arcadia (Sidney), 194n18, 285
Archer, Ian, 147
Aristotle, 42, 189n1
Armada, 5, 46, 47, 94, 126, 131, 132, 167, 211, 215, 261, 284, 291
Armada Portrait, 299
Arnold, Janet, 10
Art of English Poesie, The (Puttenham), 105, 106, 112n18, 122
Artemidorus, 269
Arthur, King, 286, 298, 299
Arthur, Prince, 3, 99
Articles of Religion, 151
Arundel, Charles, 162
Arundel, Henry FitzAlan, earl of, 31

Ascham, Roger, 58
Ashley, Katherine, 16, 18, 19n4, 20, 21, 24, 90, 94, 162
Aske, James, 129–31
Astrophil and Stella (Sidney), 190n4
Axelrod, Alan, 143, 156
Aylmer, John, xvi, 5, 40, 45, 46, 49, 287

B

Babington, Anthony, 284
Bacon, Francis, xv, 1, 97, 102
Bacon, Nicholas, 8, 98, 149–50, 152
Bagot, Edward, 162
Bagwell, Richard, 206n18
Bal, Mieke, 255, 258
Bancroft, Richard, 262, 275–76
Barker, William, 7
Barrett-Graves, Debra, xxi
Bates, Catherine, 268
Bauckham, Richard, 271
Baxter, Edmund, 90
Beauchamp, Edward Seymour, Lord, 69, 71
Beaufort, Mary, 83
Bedford, Francis Russell, earl of, 63, 115
Bedford, John Russell, earl of, 58n16
Bedford, Lucy Russell, countess of, 78n16
Bedingfield, Henry, 107, 108
Beer, Anna, 170
Bell, Ilona, xix
Bentley, Thomas, xxii, 257
Bernhardt, Sarah, 93
Berry, Philippa, 191n8
Bertolet, Anna Riehl, xvii, xxi
Bevington, David, 261, 266
Beza, Theodore, 292
Bible, xxii, 239, 254, 256, 280, 287

Judges, xxii, 253
Psalms, 224
Isaiah, 271, 272
Wisdom, 261, 268
Luke, 148–49
1 Corinthians, xxii, 258n41, 262–72, 274, 275, 277–79
Philippians, 269n21
See also Bishops' Bible, Geneva Bible, Hebrew Bible
Biblical figures associated with Elizabeth
  David, xix, 258, 283
  Deborah, xviii, xix, 201, 237, 240, 241, 249, 251–59, 282, 285, 290–98
  Esther (Hester), 249, 258, 282, 285, 291, 293–94, 296–98
  Jael, 251, 253, 255, 258, 282
  Judith, xix, 249, 251, 282, 285, 293–94, 296, 298
  Moses, 283, 284n26, 285, 290
  Solomon, xix, 261, 268, 283, 285
  Susannah, 282, 291, 294, 298
  Other, 251, 282–83, 285, 291
Bingham, Richard, 215
Bishops' Bible, 265n9, 266
Bizarri, Pietro, 56
Blanchett, Cate, 93, 162
Blessednes of Brytaine, The (Kyffin), 270–72
Blosse, Robert, 90
Blount, Charles, 167, 168
Blount, Christopher, 63
Boethius, 60
Boleyn, Anne, 1–15, 57, 87, 94–95, 198, 237
Boleyn, George, 7, 14
Boleyn, Mary, 5, 6
Boleyn family, 1, 2, 6, 10–12, 14, 237n15
Bond, R. Warwick, 266
Book of Homilies, 153
Book of Honor and Arms, The, 175
Bornstein, Diane, 175
Bothwell, James Hepburn, earl of, 54–55, 64, 87
Bouwsma, William J., 225
Bracton, Henry de, 144
Bridges, John, 262, 267
Bradner, Leicester, 105–6
Bristol, Treaty of, 242

British Library, 55, 134
Broughton, Hugh, 90
Browne, Maurice, 165, 169
Bryan, Lady, 2
Buchanan, George, 60
Buckingham, George Villiers, duke of, 127, 132
Burghley, William Cecil, Lord, xx, 5, 8, 62, 66–68, 94, 99–100, 113, 114, 116, 118, 126, 128, 145, 148–58, 160, 163, 165, 168–70, 173, 224, 240n20
Burley, Simon, 159
Bynneman, Henry, 295

C

Cabala, sive Scrinia sacra. Mysteries of state & government (Bedel and Collins), 127, 130, 132, 140
Caecilia, Lady, 74
Caelica (Greville), 192n10
Calvinism, 290, 292–93
Cambridge University, 7, 11, 125n1, 144, 149–50, 170, 288
Camden, William, 130, 164n28, 173, 180, 181, 183n42, 210
Campaspe (Lyly), 266n13
Campion, William, 284
Canny, Nicholas, 201, 204, 206
Carew, George, 214, 215
Carey, Vincent P., xxi
Carey family, 1, 6, 14
Carlos, Prince of Asturias (Don Carlos), 66n46
Carter, Patrick, 235
Cartwright, Thomas, 92
Cartwright, William, 92
Case, John, 169
Catalogue of Honor (Milles), 137
Cateau-Cambresis, Treaty of, 220
Catherine of Aragon, 2, 4, 9, 99
Catholics, xv, xxi, xxii, 4–6, 8, 36, 43, 45, 47, 49, 65, 66, 89, 95, 97, 100, 115, 122, 132, 148, 155, 158, 179, 183, 201, 205, 207–8, 220, 225–27, 229–31, 239, 243, 247, 254, 271, 272, 279, 284–88, 294, 297, 299
Cave, Margaret, 178

Cawarden, Thomas, 241
Caxton, William, 183
Cecil, Robert, 100, 114n23, 149, 166, 170, 227
Cecil, William, *see* Burghley, William Cecil, Lord
Chamberlain, John, 125n1
Chambers, E. K., 175, 178, 191, 197, 198
Charles, archduke of Austria, 40, 114–15
Charles, archduke of Styria, 56
Charles, cardinal of Lorraine, 59, 67
Charles V, Holy Roman Emperor, 33–34, 37
Charles IX, king of France, 114
Chaseabout Raid, 63
Chaucer, Geoffrey, 275
Cheke, John, 149
Chichester, Arthur, 214
Children of Paul's, 261n2
Chirelstein, Ellen, 191–92
Christianity, 58, 59, 139, 150, 221, 264, 270, 278, 280, 281, 285
  See also Catholics; Protestants
Christopherson, John, 35n28, 41–42, 45, 46, 48
Christy, Miller, 128n12
Church of England, xxii, 144, 148–49, 219, 262, 269, 272, 276, 280, 284, 288
Churchyard, Thomas, 169, 206, 242–45, 247
Cicero, 189
Claude, duke of Guise, 58
Clere, Edward, 12
Clerk, Bartholomew, 6
Clifford, Rosamond, 110
Coch, Christine, 85
Cole, Mary Hill, xviii, 30n2, 176, 242
Collinson, Patrick, xvi, 235, 245
Commemoration of the Most Prosperous and Peaceable Reign of our Gracious and Dear Sovereign Lady Elizabeth, A (Hake), 291–92
Commission of the Peace, 155
Commons, House of, 49, 86, 125, 132–34, 136n34, 136n37
Cooke, Anthony, 183
Coolidge, John S., 279
Cornwallis, Charles, 125n1
Coronation Portrait, 193

Cosby, Alexander, 215
Counter-Reformation, xxi, 219–21, 229, 231
Craig, Thomas, 56
Cranmer, Thomas, 99
Croke, John, 133
Curled Up With a Good Book (Warren), 100

D

Dale, Valentine, 223
Daniel, Samuel, 180
Darnley, Henry Stewart, Lord, 54, 55, 63–64, 66–67, 87, 114
Davis, Bette, 162
Davis, Natalie Zemon, 73n9, 78
Dawtrey, Captain Nicholas, 129, 130
De Bello ac Pace (Bizarri), 56
Defence of the government established in the Church of Englande for ecclesiasticall matters, A (Bridges), 267
Dekker, Thomas, 285
Deloney, Thomas, 128, 130, 131
Demosthenes, 144
Denny, Anthony, 19, 20
Denny, Edward, 209
Dering, Edward, 288–89, 292, 293
Derricke, John, 207
Deryck, Dionisia, 90
Desmond rebellion, xxi, 164, 168, 205, 207
de Vere, John, 99
Devereux, Robert, *see* Essex, Robert Devereux, earl of
de Wilton, Lord Grey, xxi
Diogenes, 266n13
"Discourse of the Queens Maiesties Entertainement in Suffulk and Norffolk" (Churchyard), 247n39
Discoverie of a Gaping Gulf whereinto England is Like to Be Swallowed by an Other French Marriage, if the Lord forbid not the banes, by letting her Maiestie See the Sin and Punishment Thereof, The (Stubbs), 43–44, 158, 289
Discoverie of Guiana (Ralegh), 44
Displaying of the Protestants, The (Huggarde), 45n72
Ditchley Portrait, 299
Dodd, Alfred, 97–98, 102

Donne, John, 105, 123, 258n41
Doran, Susan, xvi, xx, 54, 55, 62, 65, 113n19
Dorset, Thomas Grey, marquis of, 18
Douglas-Home, Alec, 13n60
Dovey, Zillah, 12
Dowcra, Henry, 214
Dowe, Mother Amy, 90
Drake, Sir Francis, 205, 223
Drayton, Michael, 159–61, 171
Dresden Sketchbook (Dürer), 194n17
Dudley, Arthur, 85–86, 90–97
Dudley, Robert, *see* Leicester, Robert Dudley, earl of
Duncan, Sarah L., xvii, xviii, 239n18
Dunlop, Ian, 109n13
Dunn, Jane, 55–56
Dürer, Albrecht, 194n17
Dyer, Edward, 56

E

Ecclesiastical High Commission, 71
Edward, St., crown of, 9, 10n40
Edward I, king of England, 161
Edward II, king of England, 159–61, 195
Edward II (Marlowe), 159–61
Edward III, king of England, 195
Edward IV, king of England, 11n49, 191
Edward VI, king of England, xviii, 9, 10, 16–18, 25, 26, 43, 57, 58n16, 69n1, 79, 87, 177, 237
Edwards, David, 204
Elisa, Cult of, 233
Elizabeth: The Golden Age (film), 162
Elizabetha Trivmphans (Aske), 129
Elizabeth of York, 9, 196, 237, 238
Elton, G. R., 133
Endymion (Lyly), xxii, 261, 262, 267, 269, 270, 274, 276
Englefield, Francis, 90–91, 95
"Epitaph on Elizabeth, L.H" (Jonson), 108
Erasmus, Desiderius, 58, 59, 273, 275
Erik XIV, King of Sweden, 25, 74, 114
"Essay on Adversity, An" (Mary, Queen of Scots), 60

Essex, Robert Devereux, earl of, 56, 61, 63, 98, 100, 119, 159, 161–63, 166, 168, 172–73, 205, 212, 213, 229
Essex, Walter Devereux, earl of, 56, 100–1
Eumenides, 268
Euphues' Glasse for Europe (Lyly), 272
Euphues and His England (Lyly), 264n6, 295
Evans, John, 235
Exemplary Lives and Memorable Acts of Nine The Most Worthie Women of the World (Heywood), 256–57
Exhortation to all menne to take hede and beware of rebellion (Christopherson), 35n28, 41–42, 45

F

Faerie Queene, The (Spenser), 169, 183–85, 189, 190, 195n21, 285, 286, 292, 295
Fénélon, Bertrand, 88
Fire Over England (film), 93
Firste Parte of Churchyard's Chippes, The (Churchyard), 242
Fitzgerald, Gerald, 203
Fitzgerald, James Fitzmaurice, 205, 207
Fitzroy, Henry, 99
Fitzwilliam, William, 170
Florence, Cosimo de' Medici, duke of, 182
Forrest, William, 36
Fortescue, Lady, 20n6
Four Foster Children of Desire, The, 179, 183
Fowler, Robert, 90
Fox, Adam, 89
Foxe, John, 5, 8, 57, 219, 289
Fragmenta Regalia (Naunton), 163
Francis I, King of France, 12
Francis II, King of France, 59, 63, 66
Fraunces, Edward, 90
Frederick II, Holy Roman Emperor, 60
Frerke, Bishop Edward, 245
Freud, Sigmund, 92
Froide, Amy, 65–66
Frost, Robert, 120
Fry, Somerset, 13n60
Frye, Susan, 127, 130, 234, 237
Fynes, R., 169

G

Galen, 42
Galloway, David, 235, 245
Gardiner, Stephen, 99
Gardner, Robert, 90
Gargrave, Thomas, 86
Garter, Bernard, 245, 247–49, 296–97, 299
Gascoigne, George, 298
Gaveston, Piers, 159–62, 164, 171, 174
Geertz, Clifford, 233
Geneva Bible, 254n17, 265, 272
Gilbert, Humphrey, 162–63, 205–7, 215
Glasse of the Synnful Soule, The (Marguerite de Navarre), 12
Glover, Robert, 137
Golden Speech (Elizabeth I), 125, 132–37, 139–41
Golding, Arthur, 263–64
Goldingham, William, 245, 250, 297n61
Goodman, Christopher, 43
Gorges, Arthur, 162
Gorges, Edward, 74
Gorges, Thomas, 72–74, 76–79, 81, 82, 84
  tomb of, 75, 77
Goulaine de Laudonnière, René, 169n53
Grafton, Richard, 238
Green, Janet M., 127, 132
Greenberg, Janelle, 10n40
Greenblatt, Stephen, 120
Greene, Henry, 162
Gregory XIII, Pope, 209, 226
Greville, Fulke, 190, 192, 195, 197, 198
Grey, Arthur Lord, 164
Grey, Catherine, xviii, xix, 1, 3, 69, 71–73, 76, 79–81
  tomb of, 70, 79
Grey, Jane, xix, 1, 3, 11n49, 18, 81n23, 115
Grey, Mary, 115
Grey de Wilton, Arthur Grey, baron, 207–8, 212
Griffin, Mr., 287
Grindal, Archbishop Edmund, 150–53, 288, 293
Guillim, John, 180
Guise family, 58–59
Gunaikeion (Heywood), 105
Gunn, Fenja, 198n34
Guy, John, xvi, 29n1, 54–55, 219
Guzman de Silva, Diego, 91, 114–17
Gyptes, 263, 265

H

Habsburgs, 220–23, 286
Hackett, Helen, 193, 281n1
Hager, Alan, 175
Hake, Edward, 291–92
Hakluyt, Richard, 169
Hamilton, A. C., 183n42, 185
Hamilton family, 64
Hammer, Paul, 212
Harborne, William, 222
Harborowe for Faithfull Subjects, The (Aylmer), 5, 40, 45
Harington, John, 26, 161n16, 171–72
Hariot, Thomas, 169
Hartley, T. E., 125, 134, 136
Harvey, Gabriel, 275
Hassel, R. Chris, Jr., 268–69
Hatton, Christopher, 61, 163, 164, 167, 169, 247n39, 276, 277
Hawkins, Henry, 90
Hawkins, John, 170
Hay, John, 67
Haydock, Richard, 194n17
Hazard, Mary, 194n18
Hebrew Bible, 256
Heneage, Thomas, 115–17, 163, 167
Henry II, King of England, 110
Henry II, King of France, 34, 59, 62, 220
Henry IV, King of France, 85, 195n25, 196
Henry IV (Shakespeare), 196–97
Henry VI, King of England, 11n49
Henry VII, King of England, 9, 69, 80, 81, 83, 84, 177, 191, 197, 237, 238
Henry VIII, King of England, 1, 3–5, 6n23, 9–11, 14–17, 39, 41, 57, 59, 69n1, 80, 87, 99, 158, 177, 191, 237
Hereford, Lettice Knollys, viscountess of, 13, 56, 63, 94, 98, 100, 116
Herod, King, 60

Hertford, Edward Seymour, earl of, xix,
    69, 71–73, 76, 79–82, 84
  tomb of, 70, 79
Heywood, John, 105, 106
Heywood, Thomas, xxii, 256–57
Hilliard, Nicholas, 10n41
Hindle, Steven, 145
Historical Collections (Townshend), 134, 137
*History of the most Renowned and Victorious
    Princess Elizabeth* (Camden), 130
Hoak, Dale, 238
Holinshed, Raphael, 8, 160
Honor Military and Civil (Segar), 175
Hooker, John, 208
Hooker, Richard, 262, 280
Hopton, Owen, 71n5
Horace, 60
Hoskins, John, 125n1
Howard, Charles, Lord Admiral, 131, 167,
    170, 173
Howard, Elizabeth, 5
Howard, Frances, 81
Howard, Katherine, 11n49, 57
Howarth, David, 96
*How Superior Powers oght to be obeyd of
    their subicts* (Goodman), 43
Hudson, Winthrop, 150
Huggarde, Miles, 45n72
Huguenots, 294
Humanism, 58, 59, 286, 287
Hume, Martin, 91
Hunsdon, George Carey, Lord, 6
Hunsdon, Henry Carey, Lord, 6

I

Image of Irelande (Derricke), 207
Inquisition, 221, 231
*Iofull Receyving of the Queene's most Excel-
    lent Majestie into hir Highnesse Citie
    of Norwich, The* (Garter), 237n39,
    295
Isabella of France, 195
Islam, 220, 221
Ives, Eric, 10n40, 13n60

J

James, duke of Châtelherault, 64
James, Mervyn, 146
James I, king of England, xix, 64, 71n3,
    72, 77, 81–84, 222, 231, 235
James II, king of England, 132
James V, king of Scotland, 58
James VI, king of Scotland, 6–7, 12,
    13n60, 88, 173, 227; *see also* James I
Jesuits, 5, 161, 221, 231, 284
Johnson, Barbara, 255
Johnson, Thomas, 129–30
Jones, Norman, xvi, xx
Jonson, Ben, 108, 112, 159n7, 217
*Joyful Song of the Royal Receiving of the
    Queen's most excellent Majesty . . . at
    Tilbury* (T.I./J.), 129–30
Juana, Princess of Spain, 32n14

K

Kenilworth pageants, 298
Kennedy, John F., 101
Keymer, John, 170
King, John N., 281n1
King, Margaret, 211n39
*King's Heast, or Gods familiar speech to the
    Qveene* (Beza), 292
Knapp, Robert S., 269
Knollys, Henry, 178
Knollys, Lettice, *see* Hereford, Lettice
    Knollys, viscountess of
Knollys family, 1, 6
Knox, John, 43
Kyffin, Maurice, 270–72

L

Lancaster, house of, 191, 196, 198
Latymer, William, 7–8
Leahy, William, 234
Lee, Henry, 181, 187
Leicester, Robert Dudley, earl of, 12–13,
    55, 56, 61–63, 66, 67, 85, 89–100,
    113, 114n24, 115–18, 125, 127,
    128, 130, 131, 148, 152, 153, 156,
    163–66, 168–70, 298

Leigh, Thomas, 127, 128, 130–32, 140
Leigh, William, 127n10
Leighton, Elizabeth, 100
Lennox, Margaret, countess of, 83
Lennox, Matthew Stewart, earl of, 63, 66
Lenz, Carolyn Ruth Swift, 261, 268
Leslie, John, bishop of Ross, 61–62
Levin, Carole, xix, 113, 252
Lex Martiana, 297n60
"Lie, The" (Ralegh), 171
Lincoln, Abraham, 106
Lippomano, Hieronimo, 222
Llewellyn, Nigel, 73n8
Loades, David, 43n63, 54
Lomazzo, Gian Paolo, 194n17
Lords of the Congregation, 63
Lull, Ramon, 183
Lyly, John, xxii, 261–65, 266n13, 267–69, 273–77, 280, 286, 295, 299

M

MacCaffrey, Wallace, 54, 216n61
MacDonnell Scots, 205
Madre de Dios (ship), 172
Maitland, William, 38n42, 66, 67
Malpezzi, Francis, xvii
Marcus, Leah S., 31n10, 89, 106n5, 113n19, 257, 273n35
Marguerite de Navarre, 12
Marlowe, Christopher, 159–61
Marprelate, Martin, 261, 276
Mary, queen of Scots, xviii, xix, xxiii, 3, 6, 53–68, 83, 87–88, 97, 114, 115, 199, 230, 237, 284, 294
Mary I, queen of England, xviii, 2, 4, 9, 10, 15, 26, 29–51, 53, 62, 63, 65, 81n23, 83, 87, 107, 108n11, 109, 110n14, 177, 237, 239, 240n20, 254, 297
Mary II, queen of England, 132
Mary of Guise, 58, 63
"Masque of the Gods" (Goldingham), 297n61
Maximilian II, Holy Roman Emperor, 114
Maxwell, Robin, 93–97

May, Steven W., xx, 106n5, 113n19, 120n41, 273n35
McGowan-Doyle, Valerie, 203
McLaren, Anne, xvi, 29n1, 65
Mears, Natalie, 53–54, 114n23
Medici, Catherine de, xv, 59
Medici, Cosimo de, 182
Melville, James, 53, 55–56, 64
Merchant Adventurers, 242
Merchant of Venice, The (Shakespeare), 217
Metamorphoses (Ovid), 191n8, 263
Michiel, Lord Zuanne, 224
Mignolo, Walter, 216
Mildmay Charter, 10n41
Milles, Thomas, 137
Minerva Britanna (Peacham), 181
Mirror for Magistrates, A, 158n2
Mitterburg, Adam von Swetkowich, Baron von, 114
Montmorency, Francis, duke of, 178
Montrose, Louis Adrian, 50, 172, 179, 180, 187, 191n8, 233
Monument of Matrons, The (Bentley), 257
Moray, James Stewart, earl of, 64, 65
Morgan, Hiram, 212n44
Morgan, Thomas, 131
Mother Hubberds Tale (Spenser), 158–59
Mountjoy, Charles Blount, Lord, 213–15
Moylan, Tim, xvii, xxii, 296n59
Mueller, Janel, xviii, 89, 106n5, 113n19, 257, 273n35
Mulcaster, Richard, xxii, 49, 237, 239, 240, 247, 252, 290
Murad III, Sultan, 226
Muslims, *see* Islam
Mythological and legendary figures associated with Elizabeth
   Amazons, 102, 178, 295
   Astraea, 281, 286
   Diana (Cynthia), 160, 172, 191n8, 197, 211, 261–69, 273, 275, 279, 281, 286
   Gloriana (Fairy Queen), xix, 139, 183–85, 286
   Juno, 291, 297

Marcia (Martia), queen of England, 249, 296–97
Mercury, 297
Pallas Athena, 297
Venus, 197, 297

N

Nashe, Thomas, 182
National Maritime Museum (Greenwich), 72
National Portrait Gallery (London), 26, 77n16
Naunton, Robert, 58, 162, 163
Neale, J. E., 54, 136
Neoplatonism, 146, 269
New Arcadia (Sidney), 194n18
New Historicism, 234
Nichols, John, 177
Nine Years War, 202
Nobilitas politica et civilis (Glover), 137
Norfolk, Thomas Howard, duke of, 61
Norman Conquest, 53, 68
Norrington, Ruth, 82n25
Norris, Captain, 205
Northampton, Helena, marchioness of, xix, 72–74, 76–79
    tomb of, 75, 77
Northampton, William Lord Parr of Kendal, marquess of, 76, 146
Northern Earls, Rebellion of, 287
Northumberland, John Dudley, duke of, 11n49, 81n23
Notable historie containing foure voyages made by certayne French captaynes vnto Florida, A (Goulaine de Laudonnière), 169n53
Nottingham, Catherine Carey, countess of Nottingham, 6
Nowell, Alexander, 65

O

Of Ghostes and Spirits Walking by Nyght (Lavater), 92
Of the Lawes of Ecclesiasticall Politie (Hooker), 280
Oglander, John, 60
Old Fortunatus (Dekker), 285
O'Neill, Shane, xxi, 202–4

Orgel, Stephen, 233
Orlin, Lena Cowen, 87
Ormond, Thomas Butler "Black Tom," earl of, 205, 211
Ormonde, earls of, 10
Osborne, Francis, 60, 92, 217
Osherow, Michele, xvii, xxii, 240, 290
Othello (Shakespeare), 217
Ottoman Turks, 220
"Oven Bird, The" (Frost), 120
Ovid, 191n8, 263, 264
Owen, Orville Ward, 97
Oxford, Edward de Vere, earl of, 162, 169, 273n32
Oxford Institute, 99
Oxford University, 125n1, 277

P

Palmer, Barbara, 237
Palmer, William, 146
Pappe with an Hatchet (Lyly), 276n40
Parker, Matthew, archbishop of Canterbury, 7, 8, 149–51, 155
Parkhurst, Bishop John, 245
Parliament, 26, 33, 37, 42, 47n77, 49, 63, 65, 86, 125, 133, 136, 137, 144–48, 151, 276, 277
    Elizabeth in, 138
Parma, Alexander Farnese, duke of, 47, 131, 132
Parma, duchess of, 91
Parr, Katherine, 12n58, 15–22, 57, 76
Parrat, Thomas, 183
Parry, Thomas, 16, 18, 19n4, 20–22, 109
Parsons, Robert, 284
Paul, St., xxii, 262–80
Paul V, Pope, 231
Peacham, Henry, 181
Peake, Robert, 77n16
Peele, George, 286, 299
Pembroke, Lord, 98
Pericles (Shakespeare), 186
Perrot, John, 165, 212
Persons, Robert, 161
Petrarchan poetry, 106, 120, 172, 197, 281, 285, 299

Index

Philip II, king of Spain, xviii, 15, 32n14, 33, 34, 38–41, 43–45, 62, 63, 66n46, 90, 91, 177, 220–23, 294
Philips, Thomas, 214
Pick, Mrs. J. H., 101
Picts, 198
Piers Gaveston (Drayton), 160–61
Plantagenets, 198
Pliny, 269
Plutarch, 60
"Poem on Resignation" (Mary, queen of Scots), 62
Poitiers, Diane de, 59
Pole, Michael de la, 159
Pole, Cardinal Reginald, 37n39, 39n48, 46n76
Pollard, John, 31, 34, 39
Ponet, John, 42, 43
Ponte, Niccoló da, 225–26
Pope, Thomas, 25–26
Praise of Folly (Moriae Encomium) (Erasmus), 273, 275
Praise of Musicke, The (Case), 169
"Prayer for the prosperous Successe of hir majestie's Forces in Ireland" (Vennar), 255
Presbyterians, 153
Prescott, Anne Lake, 273n35
Priuli, Lorenzo, 226
Privy Chamber, 72n7, 74
Privy Council, 16–19, 65, 91, 107, 108, 126, 131, 145, 146, 148, 155, 224, 240n20, 245
Proctor, John, 46n74, 48–49
"Prosopey of Englande unto the Degenerat Englishe, A" (Proctor), 48–49
Protestants, xxii, 2, 5–6, 44, 45, 48, 56, 63, 65, 67, 98, 110n14, 132, 148, 149, 153, 158, 179, 183, 198, 209, 219, 220, 225, 229–31, 239–41, 243, 246, 247, 262, 271, 272, 279, 280, 281, 284, 287–99
  See also Church of England; Puritans
Public Records Office (London), 132
Puritans, xxii, 153, 155, 245, 261, 276, 279

Puttenham, George, 105, 106, 112n18, 122
Pyne, Henry, 171n63
Pythagoras, 263–65

Q

Quadra, Bishop Alvaro de la, 56, 98
Queen Elizabeth I Society, xvii
Queenes visiting of the Campe at Tilsburie with Her Entertainment There, The (Deloney), 128, 131
Queen's Guard, 128
Quenes Maiesties Passage Through the Citie of London to Westminster, The (Mulcaster), 236–37

R

Rainbow Portrait, 299
Ralegh, Carew, 164, 165
Ralegh, Damerie, 170
Ralegh, Sir Walter, xx, 44, 56, 61, 119–22, 161–73, 208, 284–86, 299, 305
Randolph, Thomas, 66, 67
Ratcliffe, Edward, 131
Reformation, 4, 63, 150, 151, 194, 219, 220, 281, 294, 299
Remains Concerning Britain (Camden), 181
Renard, Simon, 33, 36, 38
Respublica (Udall), 47–48
Retirement Tilt, 181
Riccio, David, 64
Rich, Thomas, 126
Richard II, king of England, 159, 160, 171
Richard III (Shakespeare), 197
Ridolfi Plot, 61, 288
Robsart, Amy, 55, 89, 97–100, 116
Roche, Thomas P., 186
Rockwood, Edward, 245n32
Roger, William, 196
Ronsard, Pierre de, 62
Rosa Electa (Roger), 196
Rose, Mary Beth, 89, 106n6, 113n19, 257, 273n35, 292
Ruggiero, Guido, 211n39
Russell, Anne, 178

S

Sackville family, 1
St. Bartholomew's Day Massacre, xv, 243
St. Lawrence, Christopher, 203n8
Sanchez, Magdalena S., 34n21
Sander, Nicholas, 5
Savile, Henry, 135, 159, 165
Savoy, Emmanuel Philibert, duke of, 25
Scambler, Bishop Edmund, 155
Scaramelli, Giovanni Carlo, xii–xxii, 227–31
Scarisbrick, Diana, 13n60
Schivenoglia, Aloisio, 239
Schoolmaster, The (Ascham), 58
Scragg, Leah, 266n13
Segar, William, 181
Sejanus, 158
September 11 terrorist attacks, 101
Seymour, Edward, *see* Somerset, Edward Seymour, duke of
Seymour, Jane, 11n46, 69
Seymour, Mary, 18
Seymour, Thomas, xviii, 16–27, 57–58, 71, 69, 88, 99
Shakespeare, William, xix, 86, 93, 97, 100–2, 105, 123, 186, 190, 196–97, 217; *see also* individual plays
Shakespeare in Love (film), 93
Sharington, William, 18
Sharpe, Leonell, 125–30, 132, 140
Shell, Marc, 12, 13n58
Shenk, Linda, xxii, 60, 298n62
Shepheardes Calender, The (Spenser), 190, 295
"Aprill" (Spenser), 190–92
Sherlock, Peter, 82n27, 83n28, 84n29
Shield Gallery (Whitehall), 181
Shorte Treatise of Politike Power, A (Ponet), 42, 43
Shrewsbury, Francis Talbot, earl of, 31
Shrewsbury, Grace, countess of, 32
Sidney, Henry, 94, 204–7, 215, 286
Sidney, Mary, Countess of Pembroke, 94, 100, 123, 286
Sidney, Sir Philip, 105, 123, 179, 180, 190, 194, 197n30, 207, 284–86; *see also* individual works
Smith, Thomas, 147–48, 204

Smuts, Malcolm, 233
Socrates, 60
Somerset, Ann, duchess of, 80
Somerset, Edward Seymour, duke of, 11n49, 16–17, 20, 22–25, 57–58, 79–80, 88–89; *see also* individual works
Southern, Robert, 90–91, 94
Spanish Armada, *see* Armada
Sparke of Friendship, A (Churchyard), 169
Spenser, Edmund, 100, 105, 123, 158–59, 169, 180, 183–85, 189–92, 195–98, 207, 284–87, 292, 295, 299; *see also* individual works
Stallybrass, Peter, 50n93
Stanford, Henry, 90
Stannaries Parliament, 147
Starkey, R. David, 72, 113n19
Stationers' Register, 129
Stearn, Catherine Howey, xviii, xix
Stewart, Mary, *see* Mary, Queen of Scots
Stone, Lawrence, 35n27
Stow, John, 160
Streitz, Paul, 97–102
Strickland, Agnes, xvii
Strickland Prize, xvii
Strong, Roy C., 233, 281n1
Stuart, Arabella, 82, 227
Stuart, Mary, *see* Mary, queen of Scots
Stubbs, John, 43–44, 65, 158, 289–90, 293, 295
Stump, Donald, xxiii, 206n5, 240
Suffolk, Charles Brandon, duke of, 80
Suffolk, Frances Grey, duchess of, 80, 81
Suffolk, Henry Grey, duke of, 80
Surrey, Henry Howard, earl of, 11n49, 182
Sussex, Thomas Radclyffe, earl of, 116, 144, 202–4

T

Tacitus, 165, 174
Taming of the Shrew, The (Shakespeare), 217
Tennenhouse, Leonard, 119n39
Throckmorton, Bess, 162
Throckmorton, Nicholas, 115–16, 284
Thynne, John, 165, 169
Tilbury speech (Elizabeth I), xviii, 46, 125–32, 140–41, 215

Index

Tottle, Richard, 236–37
Townshend, Hayward, 133–37, 140
Tresilian, Robert, 162, 174
Tudor, Margaret, 64
Tudor, Mary, *see* Mary I, Queen of England
Tudor and Jacobean Tournaments (Young), 182
Tudor Roses, 190, 192, 194, 198, 199
Turner, Victor, 233
Tyrone, Hugh O'Neill, earl of, 132, 211, 213–15
Tyrwhitt, Lady, 24–25
Tyrwhitt, Robert, 18, 23–25, 88–89

U
Udall, Nicholas, 47
Unfortunate Traveler, The (Nashe), 182
Usher, Brett, 156n33

V
Valois, house of, 223
Vanhoutte, Jacqueline, 44
Vennar, Richard, xxii, 255
Vickers, Nancy, 190n4, 193, 197
View of the Present State of Ireland, A (Spenser), 207
Virgin Mary, 36, 48, 50, 86, 197, 269
Virgin Queen, The (film), 162
Volpone (Jonson), 217
von Kunow, Deventer, 98

W
Walker, Julia M., 82
Walsham, Alexandra, 284, 293n52
Walsingham, Francis, 91, 131, 163, 164, 168, 169, 240n20

Warkentin, Germaine, 233–34
Warnicke, Retha, xix, 94–95
Warren, Dean, 100
Wars of Religion, 294
Wars of the Roses, 3
Warwick, Ambrose Dudley, earl of, 56, 178
Warwick, Lady, 166n40
Watkins, John, xxi–xxii
"When I was fair and young" (Elizabeth I), 105–6
White, Bishop John, 40, 49n86
Whitgift, John, archbishop of Canterbury, 154, 230, 262
Wiesner, Merry E., 42n60
William III, King of England, 132
Wilson, Elkin Calhoun, 252, 281n1
Wilson, Thomas, 152
Wolfe, John, 129
Wolsey, Cardinal Thomas, 158, 171
Woodstock (anonymous play), 159–61
Worden, Blair, 159
Worthy Tract of Paulus Jovius (Daniel), *The*, 180
Wotton, Nicholas, 34
Wright, William, 70
Wriothesley, Henry, earl of Southampton, 100
Wyatt's rebellion, 11, 31, 35, 36, 44, 46, 47, 62, 89, 107, 110, 289

Y
Yates, Frances A., 181
York, house of, 3, 191, 196
Young, Alan, 177, 178, 181, 182